ESSENTIAL COGNITIVE PSYCHOLOGY

Essential Cognitive Psychology

Alan J. Parkin
University of Sussex, UK

Psychology Press
a member of the Taylor & Francis group

First published 2000 by Psychology Press Ltd
27 Church Road, Hove, East Sussex, BN3 2FA

http://www.psypress.co.uk

Simultaneously published in the USA and Canada
by Taylor & Francis Inc
325 Chestnut Street, Suite 800, Philadelphia, PA 19106

Psychology Press is part of the Taylor & Francis Group

British Library Cataloguing in Publication Data
A catalogue record for this book is available from the British Library

ISBN 0-86377-672-8 (hbk)
ISBN 0-86377-673-6 (pbk)

Typeset in Palatino by Facing Pages, Southwick, West Sussex
Printed and bound in the UK by TJ International Ltd, Padstow, Cornwall, UK

For Verity Isidora

Alan J. Parkin

30.9.50–12.11.99

Shortly after Alan gave this manuscript to the publishers he died, at the tragically young age of forty-nine. Psychology Press asked me, as Alan's partner and a fellow research psychologist, for help in completing the book—dealing with a number of minor text queries, checking figure captions, writing the glossary and deciding on the cover design. In turn, I called upon a number of Alan's colleagues for their specialist input. I would like to take this opportunity to acknowledge their contribution and to thank them most sincerely for responding swiftly, enabling publication to go ahead according to the schedule Alan had been aiming for.

Drs Nikki Hunkin and Jim Stone helped coordinate the division of labour and handled queries concerning the chapters on memory and visual perception, respectively. Dr Alan Garnham took care of the chapters on knowledge, imagery, language, reasoning and problem solving, as well as making a substantial contribution to the glossary and finding better copies of certain illustrations. Prof. Chris Darwin dealt with queries concerning speech perception and also defined a number of related glossary terms; Dr Claudia Metzler helped with the chapter on attention and handled queries on the reference section; and Dr Ella Squires spent time locating better originals for some of the illustrations. Finally, Dr Ashok Jansari wrote most of the glossary, calling upon Dr George Mather for help with vision topics, Dr Zoltan Dienes for help with memory and connectionism, and some of the people mentioned above for help with their various specialist topics.

I hope you enjoy this book and find it useful. Alan had a talent for presenting ideas clearly and conveying his own genuine enthusiasm and interest. I like to think that he will have a lasting influence, not only through those students with the good fortune to have been taught by him in person, but also through readers of this and his other books and, in turn, through their own students.

Finally, I would like to say how glad I am that Alan thought to dedicate this book to our daughter Verity, who was only 20 months old when he died. His dedication will always stand as a great token of the great love he had for her.

Frances Aldrich
Brighton, February 2000

Contents

Preface

This book arose from the comments of various commissioning editors that there was a gap in the provision for cognitive psychology. Essentially, cognitive psychology is represented either at a very low level in standard introductory texts, or at a level beyond what is really necessary for the bulk of undergraduates in this area—many of whom need a solid grounding in the subject but do not wish to pursue the subject at a higher level. As someone who had to fill this void to carry out my own teaching, I decided to produce a book that met my own needs—more than introductory, less than specialised.

For the above reason the specialist will not find cutting edge stuff here—although I hope that the book is as up to date as possible given my brief. Nor, I hope, will the reader encounter superficial explanations. As the title suggests, I have tried to create a book which contains what I think anyone who calls themselves a psychologist should know about cognitive psychology.

This book deviates somewhat from the norm that has been developing in textbooks recently. I do not have dialogue boxes or example experiments you can do at home—my experience is that students rarely, if ever, make use of these parts of a text. What students want is a clear explanation and that is what I try to provide. However, the end of each chapter contains a list of key terms used and revision questions. The former is really aimed at the revision process—the student who knows what all the key terms mean is halfway to a full understanding. The revision questions highlight key questions addressed in the topic—these can be used as revision questions themselves or as the basis for seminar-based discussion of the topic. There are also suggestions for further reading.

The book is organised around 15 chapters. The first of these concerns the origins of cognitive psychology. Some may think I have overplayed the issue of origins but, in my experience, many students fail from the outset to see what cognitive psychology is all about and why it was intellectually necessary—understanding this, in my view, generally facilitates understanding of the topic as a whole. Next there is a chapter on visual perception. This was difficult to devise because perception is usually taught as a separate course so I had to restrict myself to just some basic ideas. Next comes attention, followed by four chapters on memory, a chapter on knowledge and one on imagery, four chapters on language and final chapters on reasoning and problem solving.

In this book I have concentrated on cognitive psychology and resisted the temptation to treat every topic in terms of cognitive neuropsychology and cognitive neuroscience. The reasons for this are two-fold. First there is simply the limitation of space but, perhaps more importantly, I believe that cognitive neuropsychology and cognitive neuroscience are not, as yet, "core disciplines" of psychology; they are exciting theoretical developments which need, as a prerequisite, a thorough grounding in the basics before their impact can be fully appreciated. For this reason I have introduced these higher level topics only where it seemed essential to advancing a satisfactory account of a topic.

I would like to thank Alan Garnham for pointing me in the right direction concerning various aspects of psycholinguistics. I would also like to thank Sarah Dunworth and Sarah McCallum for their editorial assistance.

Alan Parkin
Brighton, July 1999

The origins of cognitive psychology 1

> *The ancient theory of eidola, which supposed that faint copies of objects can enter the mind directly, must be rejected. Whatever we know about reality has been mediated, not only by the organs of sense but by complex systems that interpret and reinterpret sensory information.*

Ulric Neisser, *Cognitive Psychology*, 1967

My first aim is to explain why cognitive psychology came about and how it arose from earlier attempts to explain the human mind. In taking this perspective one could go back a long way. Ancient Greek philosophers, for example, had many ideas about the workings of the mind and throughout the history of philosophy there have been concerns about issues that we would now see as the domain of cognitive psychology. However, an account of this nature would be a book in itself and I will confine myself to the last 100 years or so.

Towards the end of the 19th century psychology was dominated by an approach known as **introspectionism**. The basis of introspectionism was to study mental processes via a method of subjective self-examination. In a typical experiment subjects would carry out a mental act and then report on their inner experiences. A common topic was the nature of **mental images**; this refers to pictures we all experience in our mind's eye when we are told to imagine something. Images were thought to be the basis of memory so there was great interest in trying to elucidate the properties of images more clearly. Experiments were therefore conducted in which "observers" formed mental images and then answered a series of questions about what they held in their mind. One question, for example, might concern the clarity of the image at different points and another might concern the intensity of colour. By collecting a sufficient number of these observations it was hoped that some consensus could be reached about the structural properties of mental images (e.g. Armstrong, 1894).

From a scientific point of view introspectionism was doomed to failure because its database was totally subjective. Consider the imagery experiment above: how can we be sure that different people use the same scale to describe their subjective impressions? Thus, what is very clear or highly intense for one person might not be for another person. There is also the problem of observer bias in that questions might be structured so as to elicit particular types of answer.

Therefore, introspectionism was easy to criticise as a scientific approach to understanding the mind. However, although their methods were poor, this does not mean that what the introspectionists chose to study was unimportant. Indeed it is often stated that the most famous of the introspectionists, William James, posed many of the central questions which psychology has to answer (James, 1890). However, these insights were swept aside by the arrival of a new and radically different approach to psychological investigation—**behaviourism**.

Behaviourism

Although he was not the originator, the birth of behaviourism is most commonly associated with John B. Watson. John Watson was a colourful character who argued the behaviourist viewpoint from an extremist position. Essentially, he proposed that psychology should not be based on the accumulation of subjective impressions about mental concepts. Watson's view was that psychology should be based solely on observable events and that it should divorce itself from mentalistic concepts such as imagery and consciousness because these were unobservable (Watson, 1913). In developing behaviourism, Watson was undoubtedly influenced by two major scientific figures, Pavlov and Darwin.

Pavlov had worked extensively on understanding the **conditioned reflex** and had shown in a variety of experiments that naturally-occurring responses such as salivation in the presence of food could become associated with previously neutral stimuli such as a bell—a process known as **classical conditioning**. For Watson this was an ideal situation: here was a learning mechanism which apparently could be fully understood simply in terms of the external events experienced by the animal. Pavlov worked on basic reflexes in animals and it might be argued that there are fundamental differences between these phenomena and those that a student of human psychology must study to account for all human behaviour. At this point Watson turned to Darwin and his theory of evolution. In his writings, Darwin had stressed the continuity of species including the then controversial idea that

humans evolved from apes. Crucial to Darwin's thinking was that the continuity between species was not only biological but also behavioural. Thus, in a memorable quote Darwin asserted that: "Psychology will be based on a new foundation, that of the .... acquirement of each mental power and capacity by *gradation*. Light will be thrown on the origin of man and his history."

This illustration shows the stages in human evolution that have occurred over the last 35 million years. As the physical form changed, the mind also developed.

Watson used Darwin's evolutionary theory to argue that psychology could be studied meaningfully by systematic investigation of how simpler animals learned, that all animals, including humans, learned in the same way and that humans were quantitatively, not qualitatively, different from other animals. In his writings, Watson not only sought to dismiss mental concepts from the realm of scientific psychology, he also argued that they could never play any causative role in the explanation of behaviour; they were **epiphenomena**. An epiphenomenon is something that happens as the end result of a process—rather like the exhaust fumes of an engine. Consciousness, for example, was attributed to feedback when the throat muscles initiated speech responses. As for images, Watson denied that they existed at all and challenged anyone to prove him wrong (Bolles, 1979).

Watson's account of learning was, in essence, extremely simple. All behaviour arose as a result of conditioned relationships between stimuli and responses. In order to understand why an individual behaved in a certain way, one need look no further than the observable events surrounding the development of that individual. To make this point forcibly, Watson carried out the now famous experiment on "Little Albert" in which a previously neutral stimulus, a white rat, was paired with a noxious stimulus, a loud bang, until a point was reached where Little Albert cried at the appearance of the rat on its own. Later, Watson suggested that Albert might seek psychoanalytic help to understand his

fear of rats when all that was needed was knowledge about how he had been conditioned.

Early doubts about behaviourism

From the outset, not everyone shared Watson's view that behaviour could be explained fully without the help of unobservable constructs. This was true even for those who worked on learning in animals. Edward C. Tolman was strongly opposed to the idea that all behaviour could be understood solely in terms of the relationship between stimulus and response and, along with his students, he designed ingenious experiments which challenged the extreme behaviourist view. Tolman argued that most behaviour was determined by a general goal rather than a set of inflexible links between stimuli and responses. For example, a bird has the goal of building a nest but the resultant behaviour is flexible, taking account of variations in the availability of nest building material and other events that might intervene during the process.

Linked to this idea of a goal, Tolman argued that when animals were learning they developed an internal representation of the problem they were trying to deal with—something he termed a **cognitive map**. In one experiment, rats were taught to swim through a maze to obtain food from a goal box. The water was then drained from the maze and the rats placed in the maze again. Almost immediately they were able to run through the maze to obtain more food (MacFarlane, 1930).

According to strict behaviourist ideas this transfer of learning should have been a very slow process because of the massive change in responses required (swimming to walking) and stimuli (wet to dry). Tolman argued instead that the rats had developed some internal representation of the maze so that they "knew" where the food was independently of the specific physical conditions under which they had learnt about the maze.

Perhaps Tolman's most famous experiment is one in which rats were first trained to run through a runway to obtain food from a goal box (Tolman et al., 1946, and Figure 1.2a). Once this response was established, the apparatus was changed by the addition of 18 new pathways and the blocking of the pathway the rats had learned to run down (see Figure 1.2b). The interesting question was, where would the rats go now? According to a simple stimulus–response account, the rats would either have no idea where to go or, if some degree of **generalisation** had occurred, they might preferentially choose paths 9 or 10 because these are most similar in position to the trained pathway. In fact, the rats greatly preferred pathway 5—a finding Tolman attributed to the rats having a map of where the food was.

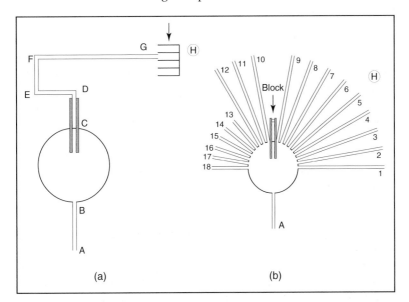

(a)   (b)

FIG. 1.2. (a) Initial training arrangements used by Tolman. The animal learns to run the route indicated by letters A–G to obtain food. H represents a permanently lit light bulb. (b) Learned path is blocked at point D. Stimulus generalisation would predict that pathways 9 and 10 would be most preferred but it was 5 and 6. This indicated to Tolman that the animals must have a map of the training area enabling the most direct route to be taken.

Gestalt psychology

At the same time as Tolman was working on cognitive maps, a group of German psychologists left Nazi Germany and set up a new school of psychology in the USA. This group of psychologists, which included Koffka, Kohler and Wertheimer, became known as the **Gestalt psychologists** (Koffka, 1935). Gestalt means "shape", "form" or "figure" and the basic tenet of these psychologists was that groups of stimuli can have **emergent properties**, or put another way, "the whole can be more than a sum of its parts". Gestalt psychologists developed their arguments largely on the basis of two-dimensional figures that revealed organisational principles which were not inherent in the components of these figures. The most fundamental of the Gestalt "laws" was the law of Pragnanz, or "good form". This stated that if a number of different organisations (gestalts) of stimuli are possible, it is the most stable or "best" that will be preferred. This concept is best understood by looking at Fig. 1.3 which shows four "laws", each of which can be considered as a variant of the law of good form.

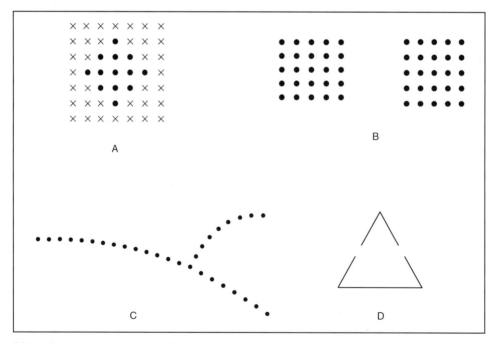

FIG. 1.3. Stimulus arrays illustrating four different Gestalt "laws": (A) law of similarity (similar items grouped together), (B) law of proximity (items closer together form groups), (C) law of good continuation (line of dots follows smooth continuation rather than sudden change of direction), (D) law of closure (gaps are "filled" to indicate a form).

While the Gestalt demonstrations are very powerful, the theory that went along with them was rather weak. The Gestalt psychologists argued that because more than one organisation of a configuration was possible, there must be some internal structure that mediates perception and determines that a particular configuration is preferred. This in itself was a straightforward conclusion, and one that was diametrically opposed to behaviourism, but their ideas as to what the internal representation was were never properly developed. Their principle idea was that of **isomorphism,** in which a particular gestalt was thought to set up a corresponding electrical force in the brain which served as the basis of perception. The Gestalt psychologists were also **nativists**, believing that the mechanisms of perceptual organisation were inherited. We now know that nativist assumptions are not always correct and that experience can determine how we see the world.

Skinner and language

Watson bowed out of academic life prematurely as a result of a domestic scandal, but by then the behaviourist movement had an enormous momentum with new figures adopting the same stimulus response framework. These figures included Edwin Guthrie and Clark Hull but the most famous was B.F. Skinner. The major achievement of Skinner was to establish that conditioning took two forms. We have already considered classical conditioning in which a pre-existing, innate response comes to be associated with a new stimulus. Skinner pointed out that there was another form of learning which he termed **operant conditioning**. According to this idea, an animal may produce a response and, depending on the outcome, that response may or may not be repeated when the same situation is encountered again.

The most famous operant conditioning situation is a rat confronted with a bar. At some point the stimulus of the bar is sufficient to arouse the rat's interest and the animal presses it with one of its paws. In this instance the bar press is met with food. This **positive reinforcement** ensures that this response will happen again. In contrast, delivery of a mild electric shock might serve as **punishment** and make bar pressing less likely. This basic learning situation can be developed by, for example, arranging it so the rat learns that a bar press means food only when a red light is on, or that the bar will deliver food only after a certain amount of time has elapsed.

Skinner shared Watson's mechanistic view of human existence and likewise was not concerned with any notion of internal representations governing behaviour. For Skinner, the development of an individual was entirely determined by the individual's **reinforcement history**. Thus any individual would develop response patterns that were positively reinforced and usually suppress those that received negative reinforcement. Taking it to its extreme, Skinner believed that reinforcement could account for the nature of human society and, in his book *Walden Two* (Skinner, 1948), he envisaged a utopia created by the positive reinforcement of desirable behaviour.

If Skinner had limited himself to the explanation of animal behaviour then it is arguable that the whole course of psychology might have been different. However, Skinner was an extremist and sought to apply his approach as widely as possible, and this took him to the difficult issue of human language. In his book *Verbal Behaviour* (Skinner, 1957) Skinner argued that speech was not the expression of ideas—rather it was the emission of "verbal responses". According to Skinner, all language is somehow under the control of some stimulus so that any utterance is considered to have an identifiable external cause.

Skinner's ideas about language came under attack from the linguist Noam Chomsky who, in a famous book review (Chomsky, 1959), showed just how inadequate a behaviourist account of language was. At one point Chomsky examines the notion of stimulus control of language when considering someone looking at a painting. A person might say: "Dutch" or instead say "Clashes with the wallpaper", "I thought you liked abstract work?", "Never saw it before", "Tilted", "Hanging too low", "Beautiful", "Hideous", "Remember our camping trip last summer?" To account for this variety of responses, Skinner is forced to argue that the picture itself comprises many smaller scale stimuli and that each can evoke a different response. As there is no way of restricting the number of stimuli that might potentially constitute a complex stimulus, Skinner's concept of stimulus control became valueless.

A picture says more than a thousand words, but how many stimuli does it comprise?

Another problem for Skinner is that much of what we hear and say is novel. According to Skinner, our ability to respond to a sentence we have never heard before arises because there is some similarity between that sentence and one we have heard before. Chomsky viewed this idea as "pointless and empty" and that it was much easier to explain our comprehension of novel sentences by asserting that we have internalised the grammar of our language. The need for this idea is neatly illustrated by the phenomenon of over-generalisation which can be observed in children's linguistic development. An example of this concerns irregular plurals, e.g. mouse–mice (see Marcu et al., 1992). At an early stage of development children might use the correct plural but, later on, they start to use an over-regularised form (e.g. "mouses"). How could reinforcement explain this? The child has never heard it before so it could not have met with reinforcement. The only way to explain this is to assert that the child has acquired a rule which it is misapplying—in other words it has formed an internal representation.

Linguistic development of a child involves learning many complex rules regarding words, pronunciation, grammar and meaning.

The birth of modern cognitive psychology

Chomsky's review of Skinner's book had a far reaching impact on the development of scientific psychology. In many ways what happened can be seen as what Kuhn (1970) has termed a **paradigm shift**. According to Kuhn, science exists in two forms, **normal science** and **revolutionary science**. A paradigm describes the general views held by a group of scientists and what they accept to be a range of possible solutions. For behaviourists, learning was seen as the central problem that psychological science had to explain and analysis within a stimulus–response framework defined the form of solution that was acceptable. As normal science progresses it is held to build up anomalies, either data that cannot be explained or experiments whose results cannot be replicated. At some point a consensus arises within the group of scientists that the paradigm is no longer viable and a shift to another paradigm occurs; the birth of cognitive psychology represents just such a shift.

The essence of Chomsky's critique of Skinner was that language could not be explained without recourse to mental constructs. In Chomsky's case, these constructs involved the rules of grammar but psychologists were also quick to realise that the constraints imposed by the behaviourist paradigm prevented the study of other problems which were essential to a full understanding of human behaviour. Foremost among these topics were the mechanism of selective attention, mental imagery, and the nature of human memory. Consciousness, the ultimate bête noire of the behaviourists, also became a respectable term to use, although the attempts to study consciousness objectively were delayed for at least 30 years.

The need to specify mental constructs to explain behaviour immediately caused a problem; how could these constructs be described and specified? The human brain is not like other organs of the body in that looking at its structure does not reveal anything about how it functions. We can see that the wall of the small intestine acts as an absorptive surface, the heart as a pump, and the kidney as a filter. The brain, however, is a large mass of cells and fibres which, no matter how closely we look at it, gives no indication of how we think, speak, and remember. For these reasons cognitive psychologists are forced to seek **analogy** or **metaphor** when attempting to describe a construct within the brain, that is, the workings of the brain are likened to the operation of something that we do understand.

Many different forms of analogy have been employed in cognitive psychology. By far the most dominant of these analogies has been to conceive internal mental abilities as **information processing systems**. The idea of the mind as an information processor reflects the way that early cognitive psychologists drew on ideas from telecommunications and computing. Most fundamental, perhaps, was the idea of **coding**. Every telecommunication system uses some form of coding. At the simplest level Morse Code translates letter information into electrical pulses (short or long) and pauses which are then transmitted along a wire or via radio. At the other end this code is translated back into letters. Similarly, a telephone receiver translates our voice into an electromagnetic code which is then decoded back into our voice at the other end. Cognitive psychologists realised that the concept of coding was central to understanding the representations used by the brain. When we see a picture it is not the case, as the Ancient Greeks believed, that some literal copy of the picture enters our head directly. Rather we extract information from that picture which forms a code. This code is therefore a **symbol** of the original stimulus.

Another important concept was **channel capacity**—the idea that any transmission system has finite limit to the amount of information it can hold. Nowadays, with the advent of optic fibres, the capacity of channels can be huge but, nonetheless, it is still limited. The same is true of humans in that most of our activities are capacity constrained. Our attentional processes, for example, only seem able to attend fully to one message at a time. However, the problem of capacity limitations in humans is not as simple as it is in physical communication devices (see Lachman et al., 1979 for a more extensive discussion of these issues).

One of the oldest problems in experimental psychology has been to establish how much information a human can take in at once—the so-called **span of apprehension**. One measure of this was to show people a card with dots on for one tenth of a second and ask them to say how many dots there were. The brief duration was insufficient to allow counting so this measure was thought to reflect how much information could be directly perceived. Experiments initially showed that about eight dots could be perceived accurately. However to conclude that the capacity of apprehension was "eight dots" was misleading because, in a further experiment, it was found that the similar exposure of five groups of five dots resulted in people accurately reporting the presence of 25 dots. The explanation of this is fairly obvious: people were simply grouping the dots into higher order units of five, thus reducing the information that needed to be remembered, i.e. "five groups of five".

The above experiment shows that human coding is flexible and can take account of the form of the input in order to reduce the amount and nature of information that is actually formed into a code. This is not true of physical systems because these reduce all information to fundamental units known usually as "bits" which in turn allows the absolute capacity of a system to be defined. For a physical system, therefore, 25 dots require far more storage than eight dots. In contrast, human information processing does not reduce information into fundamental units, thus preventing the measure of absolute capacity. Thus, in a human information processing system, we accept the notion of limited capacity but also that this capacity varies according to the nature of the information being dealt with.

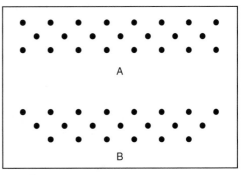

FIG. 1.4.
Span of apprehension varies according to the organisation one can impose on the stimuli. A is easier to remember than B despite the same amount of basic information.

The idea of humans as information processing systems brought with it additional concepts such as the distinction between **serial** and **parallel** processing. Communications engineers had long realised that a channel could be more effective if it were able to transmit more than one message at a time. Indeed Edison, the inventor of the light bulb, showed how telegraph wires could transmit messages in parallel as early as 1874. Psychologists too realised that human information processing systems might be divisible into serial and parallel forms and this issue has occupied a lot of research time.

In essence, therefore, a human information processing system is one which turns an initial input into a set of symbols via the process of coding. These symbols can be stored or manipulated and then retrieved to make a response. To reuse our picture example, we might be asked whether the picture contains someone we know. A code is first extracted from the picture and then matched with stored symbolic information about the physical appearance of people we know. Additional processes establish that a match has been established and the system is able to respond "yes". This is a simple example but it is not difficult to envisage how the idea of information processing systems could be expanded to deal with even the most complex aspects of human behaviour. Solving a problem, for example, can be seen as the coding of the external presentation of the problem into symbolic form, followed by complex manipulation of that representation by other internal symbolic systems representing the knowledge we bring to bear to achieve the solution.

The computer analogy

The concept of human mental life in terms of information processing systems arose quite early. However, there can be no doubt that the idea gained considerable impetus once computers and their capabilities became widely known. The parallels with humans were compelling. As stated by Lachman et al. (1979, p.99):

> Computers take a symbolic input, recode it, make decisions about the recoded input, make new expressions from it, store some or all of the input, and give back a symbolic input. By analogy that is what most cognitive psychology is about. It is about how people take in information, how they recode and remember it, how they make decisions, how they transform their internal knowledge states, and how they translate these states into behavioural outputs.

However, one must be careful about how far this analogy can be taken.

At the organisational level there are some attractive parallels. Computers operate in terms of information streams which flow between different components of the system. This is conceptually similar to the way in which we assume symbolic information flows through human information channels. Also, the various components of a computer system have been used in the construction of hypothetical cognitive systems. All computers have, for example, a **central processing unit** which is the part of the system that undertakes the manipulation of information. At the simplest level, a central processor might take a sequence of numbers and combine them using a particular rule in order to compute an average. This was seen by many as analogous to the mechanism that would be responsible for the same type of mental operation.

Computers also have data bases or **information stores**. These are permanent representations of knowledge the computer has acquired and in many ways these stores are analogous to our own permanent memory. Another feature of computers is the **information buffer**. In computing systems, it is sometimes the case that information has to be held for a period of time while something else occurs. An obvious example is the printing buffer which may hold several pages of text while other, earlier, specified pages are being printed out. The idea that human information processing systems might also have buffers proved attractive, particularly in the area of attention. An example of an information processing system is shown in Fig. 1.5.

For many, the value of the computer analogy went beyond organisational principles and attempts were made to argue that the format used by computers to store and manipulate information shed light on the way this was achieved in the human brain. It should be made clear that no one seriously believed that the human brain used a binary code to represent information. However, it was thought that certain principles used in the organisation of computer-based knowledge might also be present in the human brain. Computers, for example, use various languages to compile programs and it was thought that natural language might be compiled in a similar way. Computer scientists have also devised various ways of storing data and these have frequently been employed as analogies for how the brain stores information. One concept, for example, is the push down stack in which a subset of information is arranged in a "stack" with the most frequently-used information at the top and less frequently-used information at the bottom. This idea was borrowed to account for, among other things, category frequency effects: the fact

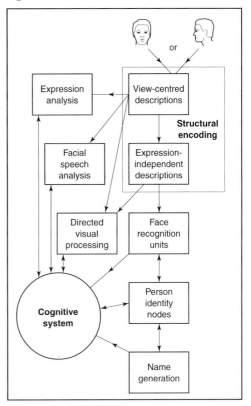

FIG. 1.5. An illustrative information processing system. The system is that proposed by Bruce and Young (1982) to account for face recognition. See text for further discussion.

that we can identify a common member of a category faster than an uncommon one. Other ideas about data structuring include lists, trees and networks and these have also been evoked to explain the organisation of human knowledge.

Using human information processing as a scientific theory

Our position so far is that we can use the idea of information processing to characterise the nature of human mental processes: those processes that intervene between the presentation of stimuli and the production of a response. We have seen that a system of this kind can have various components which may have different properties. It should also be stressed that information processing accounts almost invariably address some specific aspect of mental processing rather than being an all-embracing account of cognition. It is also typical to refer to these proposed information processing systems as **models.** A model is often more than an analogy in that it is specified in sufficient detail to make clear predictions about how humans would behave in certain situations.

Once we have a model, how do we set about using it as the basis of a theory? This brings us to the core assumptions of cognitive psychology. The first rather obvious point is that cognitive psychologists believe that mental processes actually exist even though they are unobservable. Moreover, it is also assumed that humans deal actively with the world in which they live. Put another way, humans can manipulate information they are exposed to internally in order to moderate their responses in particular situations. Thus humans can solve problems, make decisions, and alter the nature of their knowledge. Later, when we study phenomena such as insight, we will see that these changes can occur suddenly without reference to external events— phenomena that do not square with the behaviourist view that responses patterns change by a gradual process of conditioned modification.

While I have gone to some length to emphasise the shortcomings of behaviourism in developing a full understanding of human mental ability, it should also be stressed that the behaviourists did leave an important legacy to the new generation of researchers: the view that any explanation of human mental processes should be rigorous. Thus for cognitive psychologists, initially at least, there was no return to the subjective chaos of introspectionism. Instead cognitive psychologists based their science on observable responses just as the behaviourists did. The only difference was that the measurements they took were more wide ranging.

One of the key measures used by cognitive psychologists is **reaction time**. A reaction time is defined as the time elapsing between the presentation of something to an individual and the production of a response. A very simple reaction time, for example, might be the time taken to press a button when a light came on. The assumption about reaction times is that variations in their length can allow various inferences about how mental operations are taking place. Consider the example of a task in which a person has to look at an array of numbers and decide whether a target number is present. This process might be serial, in that each number in the array is examined sequentially, or parallel with all the array being examined simultaneously for the presence of the target. These two proposals make very different predictions about how reaction time would be affected by varying the size of the array. If the detection process is serial then reaction time would increase systematically with array size but, if search is a parallel process, array size would not affect reaction time.

Cognitive psychologists also examine the nature of responses made by subjects in their experiments and the conditions under which those responses are made. Behaviourist studies of human memory had been concerned almost entirely with **paired associate learning** in which subjects had to learn associations between unrelated pairs of words (e.g. "nail"—"map") and would then be tested for the response ("map") in the presence of the stimulus ("nail"). Cognitive psychologists realised that there was far more variety in memory than that. Initially they extended memory experiments to explore what people did when asked to recall information without a stimulus being present, so-called **free recall**. This approach enabled two new sources of information about the processes underlying memory performance. First, the pattern of recall might indicate what factors were important to the subject. Consider an experiment in which a word list is apparently a random collection of words but does in fact contain potential organising factors such as the presence of items from several categories. An experimenter may wish to know whether the subject uses this category information to promote recall and, to test for this, examines whether the subject's recall is organised around category themes with items from each category being recalled sequentially.

Errors are also a common phenomenon in recall and are known as **intrusions**. The nature of intrusion errors can be an important clue to what is going on in recall. If, for example, a person is asked to remember "bat" but recalls "cat" it suggests that part of the code the person is using to remember is based on the sound of the word. Errors have been a particularly productive source of data elsewhere in cognitive psychology. Theories of speech production, for example, have leaned heavily on error data to propose different stages of production. Spoonerisms such as "you have hissed my mystery lesson" indicate that the component sounds of words, **phonemes**, exist independently at some point and thus can be wrongly combined. Furthermore, the fact that virtually all Spoonerisms occur within phrases indicates that the sounds of words are only assembled once the content of a phrase has been determined.

While the above are observable responses it must be said that cognitive psychology has not remained wholly objective in this respect. Initially it was thought that subjects' own comments about what they were doing in experiments were not valid and should not be used as evidence. This undoubtedly reflected the new cognitive psychologists' behaviourist upbringing which had stressed that subjective statements about mental states were valueless. However, as cognitive psychology progressed, it became increasingly obvious that one could not ignore what people said they were doing—at least in certain experimental situations. Memory is a very good example because it became clear that people were often able to devise their own **strategies** when carrying out an experiment and the extent to which they did or did not do that could dramatically alter the amount and nature of what they remembered. Even more extreme was the development of certain research areas, such as problem solving, in which people's subjective reports of what they were doing (**verbal protocols**) were essential sources of data; in some ways a return to introspectionism also reflected in some recent studies of mental imagery.

Nativism and nomotheism

An important aspect of the behaviourist viewpoint was that all humans were identical in terms of the learning mechanisms that resulted in an individual's accumulation of stimulus response relationships—a concept that is known as **nomotheism**. Thus it was assumed that all individuals learned in the same way just as it was assumed that organs such as the heart, liver and lungs operated in the same fundamental way across individuals. The behaviourists were not **nativists** in the sense that they did not believe that humans had innate dispositions to develop in a particular way. The behaviourists believed that the human was essentially a "blank table" or **tabula rasa** upon which any given set of associations could be registered depending on the experiences of the individual. Thus, in an almost infamous quote, Watson claimed: "Give me a dozen healthy infants... and I'll guarantee to take any one at random and train him to become any type of specialist... regardless of talent" (Watson, 1924, p.104).

Cognitive psychologists implicitly adopted, at least at the outset, a strong nomothetic view of human mental processes in that they presumed that any information processing model they devised was applicable to all. However, this strong assumption soon became problematic as the influence of **individual differences** became increasingly apparent. Humans vary on a wide variety of psychological dimensions; they can be happy or sad, extrovert or introvert, be culturally distinct and so on. Many studies have shown that various sources of individual differences can influence many types of mental operation, so undermining the idea cognitive processes occur in a uniform manner across all individuals. Although demonstrations of individual differences are many and varied the general rule is that the more complex a cognitive process is, the more likely it is to be prone to individual differences.

As to nativism it is true to say that cognitive psychologists have not shown any great concern with this issue. However, there have been some notable exceptions, one of which concerns the remarkable process of **language acquisition**. Anyone acquainted with young children cannot help being impressed by the speed at which they acquire language. This rapidity has led some to suggest that there is an **innate language mechanism**—an inherited predisposition to recognise and process the constituents of language. Because a child will learn any language it is assumed that this mechanism is sensitive to more abstract aspects of language rather than the specific sounds of any particular linguistic form.

Generally, the position of cognitive psychology appears to be one of compromise, accepting that some abilities are innate but that various factors can shape the way that processes actually develop. Assessing the balance of these two things is what lies at the basis of the **nature–nurture debate**. As with individual differences, the nature–nurture issue is

Cultural and individual variations help to show that a nomothetic view of human mental processes is over-simplistic. For example, in Arabic countries it is normal to barter when purchasing goods, but such behaviour in Western societies may be seen as obsessive and unacceptable.

more prominent when higher order mental abilities are considered. Thus, with visual processes, it is generally considered that these are principally, if not exclusively, determined by innate mechanisms. At the other end of the scale, factors influencing an individual's level of intelligence are the substance of considerable debate in which extremist positions of both kinds have been adopted.

Good and bad cognitive psychology

So far, cognitive psychology has been presented in a very positive light as an approach which gets to the heart of explaining human mental processes. Therefore it is time to take stock and become aware of the potential limitations and pitfalls of this approach. Fig. 1.6 shows a somewhat cynical view of an information processing model in which an input undergoes successive stages of processing until an output is achieved. The essential message of this diagram is that the depiction of mental processes in terms of information flow between components is almost pointless if one cannot state what the components are, how they operate, and what the nature of the information flowing between them is.

Good cognitive psychology involves the depiction of mental processes in an explanatory form, i.e. the manner in which a given component operates is explained as fully as possible. Essential to this explanation is the requirement that the description of a component is sufficiently detailed to allow predictions about how it works to be tested via experimentation. If a component is specified in such a vague way that it could explain any pattern of observed behaviour it is scientifically valueless. Current cognitive psychology is very much a mixture of good and bad and throughout this book we will encounter theories ranging from the very precise to the totally vague. With something as complex as the human mind to understand we should, perhaps, be unsurprised that much of what it does can be explained only in vague inadequate terms. Equally, however, we should not be content with this vagueness. If cognitive psychology is to be judged as a proper science it is better to identify inadequate aspects of a particular

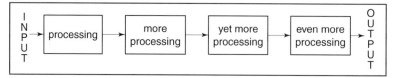

FIG. 1.6. An example of a bad information processing model.

model rather than allow these to undermine those aspects of the model that achieve scientific respectability.

Connectionism

Since the beginning of the 1980s cognitive psychology has been increasingly influenced by the concept of **parallel distributed processing (PDP)** or, as it is more often known, **connectionism** (Rumelhart and McClelland, 1986). PDP models are implemented as computer programs known as **networks**. Unlike the information processing models, connectionist models do not comprise separate components. Instead they are specified as a network of nodes or units linked to each other by connections which can be either inhibitory or excitatory in nature. In addition, the strength of any connection can be modified by assigning a particular weight. It is an important feature of these models that information about any concept is distributed across many nodes and is not the property of a single node. Different pieces of information thus correspond to different patterns of activity within the same network (see Fig. 1.7).

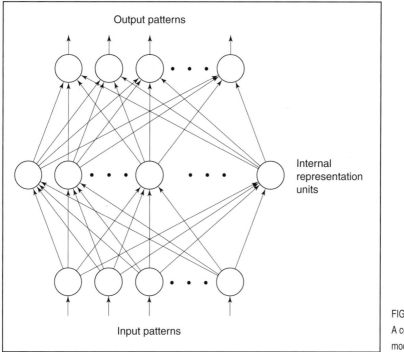

FIG. 1.7.
A connectionist model.

Unlike information processing models, which are static representations of how we think a particular cognitive operation occurs, PDP networks are able to learn by using rules or **algorithms** to change interconnections between the nodes of the network. One method of learning is the back-propagation algorithm which is a means of making an output conform to a desired state. For any input, the system is informed about what the resulting output should be. This information is compared with the actual state of the network when the stimulus is present and an adjustment is made. This process is incremental and networks need many exposures to a stimulus before it learns the correct output. Methods like back propagation allow a network to represent information. Because human learning is not characterised by having pre-existing knowledge of the desired outcome, algorithms like back-propagation have obvious limitations. However, proponents of PDP models argue that it is the properties of the established network that are of interest to psychologists rather than the manner in which they become established. In this way PDP networks form an alternative to information processing models as a way of thinking about how a given cognitive system operates.

In this book we will not be greatly concerned with connectionist models as my aim is to familiarise students with the basic issues of cognitive psychology and the kinds of phenomena that occur. However, the reader should be aware that connectionist modelling has become an essential aspect of more advanced theory development in cognitive psychology and that awareness of its relevance is an important further step in understanding current approaches to the explanation of cognition. Thus it is increasingly the case that part of the evidence used to evaluate a model of a mental process is whether or not a connectionist model based on the assumptions of the model will actually mimic the performance of a human.

Cognitive neuropsychology

Until about 15 years ago, mainstream cognitive psychologists took little interest in human neuropsychology, i.e. the study of how damage to the brain affects subsequent behaviour including cognitive function. However, neuropsychology underwent a minor "revolution" as cognitive psychologists began to realise that people with acquired cognitive deficits could provide important information about the nature and organisation of cognitive function in normal people. At the heart of this enterprise was the belief that brain-damaged subjects could reveal insights into the **cognitive architecture** of mental processes. The idea of cognitive architecture is linked very closely to the conception of cognitive mechanisms in terms of information processing systems. Thus the model depicted in Fig. 1.5 can be considered as a model of the cognitive architecture of facial recognition.

Cognitive neuropsychology embraced two more important concepts. First it made the assumption that any cognitive system is modular. The idea of **modularity** in relation to cognitive function was first introduced by David Marr (Marr, 1982) in his pioneering studies of vision (see Chapter 2), but its major impact on cognitive neuropsychology is most commonly attributed to Fodor and his seminal book *Modularity of Mind* (Fodor, 1983). The essential point about modularity is that any aspect of the cognitive system is organised as a series of modules, each of which has a distinct function and that, together, these modules carry out some larger scale function. Modules are seen to act in an **encapsulated** manner in that they only perform one function. Fodor defined modules in a highly specific manner but recent theorists have used the term more flexibly (e.g. Coltheart, 1999).

Both the idea and advantage of a modular cognitive system can be illustrated by an analogy with an audio system. This will have various modules, e.g. amplifier, CD player, speakers, tuner and so on. With a system like this it is possible to change various components without affecting the others, such as upgrading the CD player, and it is also possible to add new modules, e.g. the addition of a graphic equaliser. It is thought the same applies to cognitive processes; each one is separate and thus can change independently of other modules in the system.

The second assumption is **neurological specificity** which assumes that different modules are located in anatomically distinct parts of the brain (Shallice, 1988). Armed with this assumption, one can make the further prediction that brain damage will produce, in at least some cases, specific disruption of a particular module within a system and that the person's behaviour as a result of that damage will be consistent with that state of affairs. Crucial to this form of investigation is the concept of **double dissociation**. Neurological damage can result in damage that affects different modules selectively. If patients are found who are impaired on task A but normal on task B, it could be stated that tasks A and B dissociate from one another. An example of this would be language and memory; it is perfectly possible for someone with amnesia to have no language problems. More important to the neuro-psychologist, however, is a dissociation that happens within a particular system since this can give insights into processing within that system. If within a system such as object-recognition, a patient is impaired on task A but normal on task B, it could be stated that task A is more difficult than task B and therefore brain-damage is more likely to affect processing on this task. However, if another patient was found who was normal on task A but impaired on task B (i.e. the converse of the first patient), then this argument could no longer be valid. This state of affairs is known as double dissociation. An example is that it is possible to find patients who have a problem in recognising objects (known as **agnosia**) but have no problems with recognising faces, whilst there are selective patients who have a problem in recognising faces (known as **prosopagnosia**) but have no problems in object-recognition. This double dissociation therefore can lead to neuropsychologists treating the two tasks as separable tasks rather than one simple task.

We can make this idea more concrete by referring back to the model of facial memory. Although results from normal subjects played some part in the generation of this model it is fair to say that the major evidential basis for it was studies of people who had developed facial processing problems as a consequence of acquired brain injury. Thus the separation of four distinct modules each dealing with the extraction of different kinds of information arose principally from the observation of people who had selective difficulty dealing with one specific characteristic of a face such as identity or expression (e.g. Young et al., 1993). It should also be borne in mind that modules may themselves be comprised of smaller modules. Recently, for example, the "expression analysis" module has been decomposed into modules dealing with the separable processing of fear and disgust (Young, 1997).

In this book I will make considerable reference to data from cognitive neuropsychology but I have not made the inclusion of neuro-psychological data compulsory for every topic. Rather I have only included it where discussion of neuropsychological findings provides a key element in the explanation of a particular cognitive function. For broader coverage of neuropsychology the reader is referred to my own recent book (Parkin, 1996), together with the wide range of other books listed under the general heading of neuropsychology.

Cognitive neuroscience

Cognitive neuroscience is a term that has come into use only recently and there is still confusion as to what it actually means. At one end it has undoubtedly been hijacked by cognitive neuropsychologists as an alternative label which enables them to use a more scientifically respectable label for what they are doing; thus much cognitive neuropsychology has suddenly become cognitive neuroscience. In my view, cognitive neuroscience is much less re-stricted and involves any research which attempts to integrate issues regarding cognitive function with direct assessments of brain function. The earliest form of cognitive neuroscience was the attempt to relate cognitive functions to brain struc-tures via post mortem studies of the brains of people who had interesting acquired cognitive deficits. Unfortunately this approach is limited because it is retrospective—if one discovers something interest-ing about the relation between brain and cognitive function it cannot be followed up.

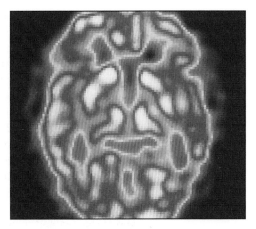

Positron emission tomography (PET) scan of a normal human brain, showing brain activity. PET scans are useful in pinpointing specific brain areas that are metabolically affected by disease.

More recently, the advent of detailed **structural neuroimaging** techniques (e.g. **magnetic resonance imaging**) has allowed detailed anatomical information about the locus of brain damage to be revealed in a living person, thus removing the retrospective problem of post mortem data. However, the information is purely structural and tells you simply that damage to part X of the brain affects this function but not that one. Much more useful are so-called **functional neuroimaging techniques**, the most prominent of which are **positron emission tomo-graphy** (PET) and **functional magnetic resonance imaging** (fMRI). Both these techniques allow researchers to map changes in blood flow

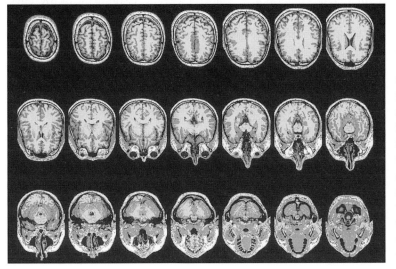

Magnetic resonance image (MRI) scans of a normal human brain. The middle images clearly show the rounded eyeballs and nasal cavity. MRI scanning creates "slice" images through the body that are useful in detecting tumours.

across different parts of the brain while a normal person is carrying out a cognitive task. In this way tasks can, for example, be characterised as similar or different depending on which areas of the brain are particularly activated during task performance.

At the time of writing, functional neuroimaging is proving an extremely popular (although very expensive) means of investigation. As is typical of psychology there has been a vast rush to collect functional neuroimaging data in a fairly uncritical fashion. However, cracks are beginning to appear in that initial findings thought to be clear cut are now proving over-simplistic or difficult to replicate. In addition, others are drawing attention to fundamental shortcomings of neuroimaging data (Weldon, 1998). One particular problem is that neuroimaging data are the result of a subtraction method. Subjects perform a task which is then compared with neuroimaging data from another task. The data correspond to the brain area that is differentially active in the two tasks. Therefore if a brain region is equally involved in two cognitive abilities, it will not be revealed by the neuroimaging data. Another criticism is that functional neuroimaging is simply an advanced form of **localisationalism**. In the early days of cognitive neuropsychology, the location of a person's brain damage was considered irrelevant to the goal of understanding their cognitive deficit—what mattered was the psychological theory one could fit to their pattern of disturbed performance. Now, however, a considerable number of cognitive neuropsychologists, including many who took the former stance, now consider functional neuroimaging data as essential to theory development. In my view this apparent importance has yet to impact itself on mainstream cognitive psychology, and functional neuroimaging data seems content to confine itself to specialist journals.

Overview

- Introspectionism sought to explain mental processes by subjective observation.
- The behaviourists argued that introspectionism was unscientific and that psychology should not concern itself with unobservable internal constructs such as imagery and consciousness.
- Behaviourists argued that psychology should be based on the study of learning and that psychological issues could be studied entirely in terms of the relationship between stimuli and responses.
- The behaviourist position came under attack on the grounds that there were many aspects of human and animal behaviour that could

not be accounted for without recourse to the idea of mental processes.

- Cognitive psychology was the response to the failure of behaviourism. Cognitive psychologists accepted that mental processes existed and that the operation of these processes could be measured scientifically.
- Cognitive psychologists used analogies to describe the nature of mental processes and foremost among these analogies was the idea that human mental processes were a reflection of internal information processing systems.
- The information processing approach was used to devise models of how different cognitive processes operated. These models served to make predictions about how people would respond in experimental situations.
- Learning was no longer the central issue for psychology. Cognitive psychologists tackled a wide range of human mental abilities including those which the behaviourists viewed as unscientific. Reaction time, error production and response patterning became the basic measurements of the new science.
- Cognitive psychology initially assumed that mental processes occur in the same way across all people but this was modified with the discovery of marked individual differences on many cognitive tasks.
- Cognitive psychology tends to take a balanced view of the relation between nature and nurture in the determination of mental processes.
- Cognitive psychology needs to guard against poor specification in the modelling of mental processes.

Suggested further reading

Lachman, R., Lachman, J.L., & Butterfield E.C. (1979). *Cognitive psychology and information processing*. Hillsdale, NJ: Lawrence Erlbaum Associates Inc.

Although pitched at quite a high level, this book provides a very thorough account of the development and assumptions underlying cognitive psychology.

Parkin, A.J. (1996). *Explorations in cognitive neuropsychology*. Hove, UK: Psychology Press.

Provides comprehensive coverage of the rationale underlying cognitive neuropsychology and gives an account of its major research areas.

Revision questions

1 What were the limitations of introspectionism as an approach to understanding mental processes?
2 What was the basic idea of behaviourism and how did it account for subjective experiences such as consciousness?
3 How did Tolman's view differ from Watson's account of behaviourism?
4 What was Gestalt Psychology, what did it achieve, and what were its shortcomings?
5 What is operant conditioning and how did Skinner attempt to extend the idea to account for language?
6 What were Chomsky's arguments against behaviourism as an explanation framework for understanding human language?
7 What are the essential characteristics of the "cognitive approach" to the explanation of mental processes?
8 How far can we take the computer analogy in our attempts to understand human information processing?
9 What did the new generation of psychologists carry over from the behaviourist era?
10 What does cognitive psychology have to say about nativism and nomotheism?
11 What, briefly, is connectionism and why should cognitive psychologists be interested in it?
12 How is cognitive psychology used to construct the cognitive architecture of the brain?
13 What is meant by modularity and why does it confer an advantage on a cognitive system?

Visual perception 2

When I was a student I remember attending a lecture about the human visual system. Midway through the lecture a visiting professor stood and walked to the podium. Addressing the speaker he said, "Look, I can see, I've walked up here, what more is there to know?" This was a profoundly ignorant statement which totally failed to appreciate the scientific challenge posed by the study of perception—in this case the visual system. The things around us do not automatically indicate to us what they are; our perception of the world is built up by internal processes which operate on an initial input that is far removed from what our sense organs initially register. Vision, for example, begins with a two-dimensional image on the retina but ends up as a three-dimensional scene in which there is depth, colour, movement, and so on. Similarly, hearing begins with the mechanical stimulation of cochlea hair cells by sound waves but what we hear is sufficient to allow us to appreciate the complex sounds of continuous speech.

How then do we perceive the world? The prevailing view is to consider the various forms of perception as instances of an information processing system. It is proposed that perception begins with various analyses of the initial sensation which become progressively more complex until a **percept** is formed. A percept is the internal representation derived from the initial pattern of stimulation and it is this that serves as the basis for subsequent identification processes, i.e. determining what an object looks like, sounds like, smells like, and so on.

Forms of perceptual process

We have, as you all know, five senses—vision, hearing, touch, smell and taste. Cognitive psychologists have been very uneven in the time they have devoted to the study of our senses. Most work has been carried out on our visual system because of the dominant role it plays in communication. Next comes hearing, followed by touch, smell and taste. Research into hearing has been quite substantial owing to the need to understand speech perception but the other three senses have received relatively little attention. However, research into touch (often known as **haptic perception**) has received considerable impetus from its relevance to communication aids for the blind. Smell and taste, although subject to some investigation within cognitive psychology, have been of more interest to physiologists. In this book we will be primarily concerned with visual perception (this chapter) and with hearing in relation to speech perception (Chapter 10).

Visual perception is more than a "cognitive photograph"

The first thing to learn about visual perception, and indeed all other forms of perception, is that it is **reconstructive.** The visual percept which we experience as reality does not come about in a manner analogous to the way in which a visual image develops passively in the emulsion of a film. Rather, a visual percept is built up by a wide range of inferential processes which use cues provided by the basic two-dimensional input on the retina. This creates a perceptual reality of three dimensions in which, as we shall see, a constant world is maintained despite considerable distortions in what projects on to the retina.

FIG. 2.1.
What do you see here? (answer on next page).

The reconstructivist view of perception introduces us to a crucial distinction which runs right through a wide range of explanations in cognitive psychology. This is the distinction between **bottom-up** and **top-down processing** (note that the terms **data-driven** and **conceptually-driven** are often used as alternatives). A bottom-up process is one which proceeds from lower levels of analysis to higher levels. In contrast, a top-down process feeds down a system using higher level knowledge to facilitate lower level processes. In normal vision we are not aware of the many complex interactions between bottom-up and top-down processes that occur during visual perception. So, in order to dissociate them, we need "trick" stimuli to demonstrate. Indeed, as you will see, many aspects of visual perception rely on the use of unusual stimuli to illustrate them.

Figure 2.1 may seem meaningless initially, but as you stare at it an organisation will suddenly emerge. This realisation represents the influence of top-down processes which have superimposed pre-existing knowledge on to the input to achieve

a meaningful percept. In this case, top-down information has operated to allow an object to be identified but we must be aware that top-down processing is evident at many different lower levels as well. We will see, for example, that certain theories of visual perception assume that **top-down inferences** are made when particular configurations are encountered—a shape such as >, for example, might be considered as part of a corner. Figure 2.1 depicts a man playing a saxophone and a woman's face.

Marr's theory

Although there have been many theories of visual perception, the most influential has been that proposed by David Marr (Marr, 1982). Although Marr's theory is now quite old, I believe it still provides a good basic framework for studying vision. Marr envisaged three stages in visual perception:

Primal sketch: A visual scene is represented in terms of its fundamental perceptual elements such as edges and bars whose attributes such as

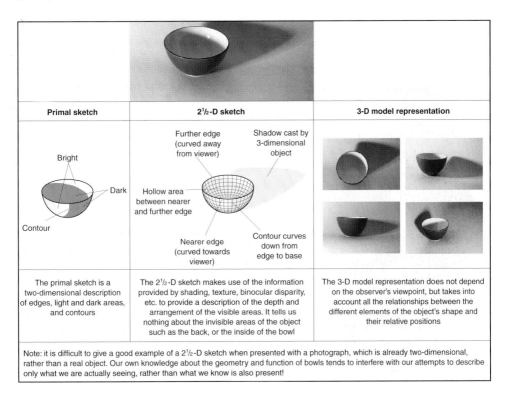

Primal sketch	2½-D sketch	3-D model representation
The primal sketch is a two-dimensional description of edges, light and dark areas, and contours	The 2½-D sketch makes use of the information provided by shading, texture, binocular disparity, etc. to provide a description of the depth and arrangement of the visible areas. It tells us nothing about the invisible areas of the object such as the back, or the inside of the bowl	The 3-D model representation does not depend on the observer's viewpoint, but takes into account all the relationships between the different elements of the object's shape and their relative positions

Note: it is difficult to give a good example of a 2½-D sketch when presented with a photograph, which is already two-dimensional, rather than a real object. Our own knowledge about the geometry and function of bowls tends to interfere with our attempts to describe only what we are actually seeing, rather than what we know is also present!

length, contrast and orientation are also represented. These elements may also be grouped into features such as a conjunction between two lines of differing orientation.

2½D sketch: Information such as depth cues, figure ground discrimination, and surface texture are added. At this point the representation of the stimulus is still **viewer centred** in that the nature of the internal representation is still determined by the observer's viewpoint.

3D sketch: An **object-centred** representation of the object is established. This can be defined as a representation of the object that is independent of the specific viewpoint. At this stage, a full **structural description** of the object becomes available. Thus, even though many important features of an object might be obscured in the current viewpoint (e.g. by the interposition of another object), achievement of the 3D sketch means that our full knowledge about the visual characteristics of the object becomes available.

In the following sections I will describe in more detail the types of processes that go on in each of these stages and, at all points, you will notice how the interaction between top-down and bottom-up knowledge sits at the heart of visual perception.

Primal sketch processes

The formation of the primal sketch is quite a complex process and there are a number of different theories about how it is achieved. The basis of the primal sketch is to convert the basic **intensity map** into the beginnings of a visual image. The intensity map simply conveys the pattern of light and dark across the image and the role of the primal sketch processes is to use this variation in light and dark to construct the position of edges. Edge detection works on the assumption that an edge is present when there is a transition from light to dark or vice versa. However, natural images have numerous transitions between light and dark and most of these are not edges. As a result it is necessary to use an algorithm—a problem solving device—to determine which changes in intensity should be regarded as edges.

Within the theory of Marr and Hildreth (1980) the image (Fig. 2.2, top left) is first processed with a **filter** which highlights areas of intensity change that are "steep" enough to be likely edges. The result of this first filtering operation is an image (Figure 2.2, top right), which is the second spatial derivative of the original image and, as can be seen, it does not

FIG. 2.2.
Primal sketch
processes. Figure on
top right shows the
effect of applying a
filter that finds
intensity gradients in
the raw image (top
left). Figure on bottom
left shows the results
of an algorithm that
identifies zero-
crossings. A zero-
crossing is identified
at each point where
the intensity gradient
(top right) passes
from black to white
(i.e. from positive to
negative) or vice
versa. Figure on
bottom right shows
the pattern of zero-
crossings
superimposed on an
original image.

provide all the edge information needed for a clear image; in particular it does not pick up sufficient information about horizontal edges. To achieve this, a second filter is applied which computes **zero-crossings** (Fig. 2.2, bottom left). Crudely these can be defined as areas of the image where the transition between intensity is most marked. Figure 2.2 (bottom right) shows the result of imposing the zero-crossing algorithm. In addition to edge detection, per se, the formation of the primal sketch is also aided by other cues such as **collinearity** in which edges with similar orientation are judged to be part of the same shape. At this point in the process no object has been identified—the areas defined by different combinations of edges are thus described simply as blobs.

2½D sketch processes

A number of more complex processes are involved in the development of the 2½D sketch. Most fundamental, perhaps, is **figure–ground segregation**, which involves deciding which shapes constitute objects in the foreground and what constitutes background—the aim of

camouflage is thus to reduce figure ground segregation The principle of figure–ground segregation is invariably illustrated by Rubin's famous reversible figure (Rubin, 1958) and I will make no exception to this. As Fig. 2.3a shows this figure can be seen as either a white vase on a black background or two black faces facing each other on a white background. Fortunately for us we are rarely confronted with ambiguous figure–ground problems because we appear to make use of various organising principles, although you may have more difficulty with Fig. 2.3b.

A principle cue to figure–ground is symmetry. If a figure is symmetrical we infer that it is an object: this is why the Rubin figure is a problem because both organisations of the figure lead to symmetrical shapes. Figure 2.4 illustrates this point further. If you look to the left of the figure you perceive black shapes on a white background, but looking at the right,

FIG. 2.3a. Rubin's vase–face illusion indicating alternating figure–ground arrangements.

Fig. 2.3b. A more difficult figure–ground discrimination.

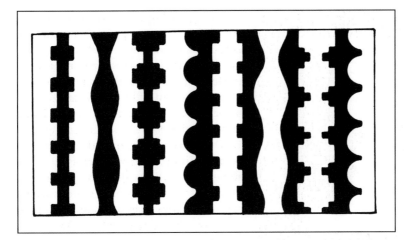

FIG. 2.4.
The principle of
symmetry in
determining
figure–ground
segmentation.

you see white shapes on a black background. **Convexity**, bulging outwards, also suggests a figure even if there are symmetrical cues indicating differently (see also Fig. 2.5). The area occupied by a stimulus is also a cue with smaller areas tending to be perceived as figures. Stimuli with vertical or horizontal orientation are more likely to be perceived as figures and the ability to attribute meaning to a particular segregation also determines figure–ground relations.

Another fundamental component of the 2½D sketch involves **depth perception**, i.e. the translation of the two-dimensional image into three

FIG. 2.5.
The principle of
convexity in
determining
figure–ground
segmentation.

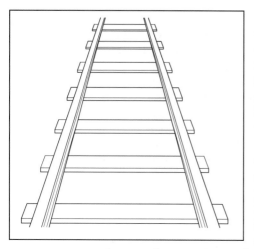

FIG. 2.6.
The railway line: a
classic linear
perspective cue.

dimensions. The perception of depth is the combined product of a number of different cues that divide into those which are **monocular** and those that are **binocular**. A monocular cue is one that can be derived from the vision of a single eye whereas binocular cues derive from the combined vision of two eyes.

One of the most powerful monocular cues is **linear perspective**. Figure 2.6 shows how a railway line provides a very powerful impression of depth. Other monocular cues include **texture gradients** in which depth is indicated by the elements of a texture becoming more dense as they recede into the distance (see Fig. 2.7). The visual system also uses the **contrast** between an object and its background as a cue to depth; as objects gradually merge with the background they are known to become less distinct, so poor definition indicates further distance. Interposition is a depth cue based on the assumption that an object that partly obscures another object must be nearer the viewer. A final binocular cue is **motion parallax** in which depth is indicated by the speed at which things appear to move past you. Consider looking at a forest from a railway carriage; those trees nearest to you will appear to move past very quickly whereas those in the distance will appear to move much more slowly (see Bruce, Green, & Georgeson, 1996; Goldstein, 1989 for reviews).

Binocular cues exploit the fact that we have two eyes and that this can add specific kinds of information to the visual process. We look at an object that is gradually moving closer to us, our eyes converge, and it has been thought that feedback indicating the extent of this **convergence** could provide a cue to depth. However, experiments have

FIG. 2.7.
Texture gradients are
powerful indicators
of depth.

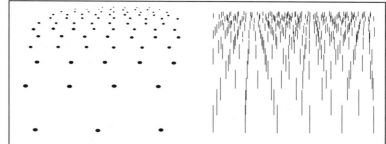

cast doubt on the value of this cue. A second process is **stereopsis**: this refers to the fact that each eye has a different view of an object and the information from this discrepancy can be used to compute depth. The fact that depth perception is impaired if we use only one eye suggests that stereopsis is important but the explanation of how this process operates is far from clear. A particular difficulty is known as the **correspondence problem**, i.e. how does the system establish that part of the image from one eye should be combined with that obtained by the other eye to produce a single percept? Goldstein (1989) provides an account of the problem and Porrill et al. (1999) provides a recent explanation of how correspondence is achieved.

Pattern recognition

Part of the processing contributing to the 2½D sketch involves the identification of two-dimensional patterns, and two types of theory have evolved to explain how this is achieved. The first of these are **template theories** which propose that we store away the specific features of each pattern we know. The inherent problem with this type of theory is the wide variations that can occur in even the simplest stimulus. It is implausible that we should store away a specific representation of every version of a stimulus we might see so template theorists were forced to suggest that **normalisation** processes existed. Essentially, these operated to extract common features from variations in a stimulus that would enable identification of different versions of the same thing. However, even for relatively simple stimuli (such as the number of different ways a single letter might be written), the number of normalisation rules would soon become unwieldy.

The implausibility of the template theory served to focus minds and resulted in **feature comparison models** of pattern perception. These models assume that recognition of patterns occurs via the identification of the individual features that comprise that pattern. These features can be defined at a relatively abstract level. An 'X', for example, can be defined as "two opposing diagonal lines that bisect each other". A description of this kind would then allow X, **X**, x, *X*, and so on to be identified from one basic description.

Support for feature comparison models has been obtained from visual search experiments which require subjects to search an array for a given target. Two forms of array are used. In one the target, e.g. 'Z', shares features in common with other, 'distractor', stimuli in the array, e.g. straight lines, 'X', 'V'. In the second, the array items do not share similar shapes, e.g. 'O' and 'S'. Comparison of search times showed that it took longer to find the targets when the distractors shared visual features, thus suggesting that the stimuli were being analysed at the featural level during the search process (Treisman and Gelade, 1980).

A number of information processing models of feature comparison appeared, the most famous of which was the Pandemonium model (Selfridge, 1959). The principal feature is that processing of the stimulus is divided up into a series of stages, each known as a type of demon. The image demons first form an image of the stimulus which then passes to the feature demons. According to the model there is a feature demon for each different feature in the visual world. Next come the cognitive demons that contain information about the combined featural characteristics of particular stimuli. The cognitive demons are thought to operate in an incremental way, becoming increasingly active as the features extracted from the input come to share more features in common with their own representation. Finally the decision demon assesses the activity of the cognitive demons and, when one has reached a critical level of activation, a response is made according to that demon.

Featural models such as Pandemonium have a certain plausibility but they have a number of difficulties. If they were a true account of events we would, for example, be unable to tell the difference between / \ and X because the degree of feature demon overlap would be similar. This point is illustrated in relation to more complex objects in Fig. 2.8. This difficulty has led to the view that the output of any featural processing could not itself be the basis of perception. Instead, it is argued that perception processes must reach a higher and more abstract level before object recognition can be achieved.

Object recognition

Within Marr's theory of perception, **object-recognition** involves the transition from a **viewer-centred** to an **object-centred** representation of an object. A viewer-centred representation is one that is dependent on the actual view an individual has of an object. To understand this, consider looking directly at the jug depicted in Fig. 2.9. The handle of the jug is on the right side. From this perspective, viewer-centred and object-centred representations of the jug yield the same information: the handle is on the left of the jug. Now examine the situation if the jug is tilted 90 degrees. From a viewer-centred perspective, the handle of the jug now falls on the right side of visual space but from an object-centred perspective the handle is still on the right. Therefore the object-centred description of the object is independent of viewpoint, so allowing the object's features to remain constant irrespective of how you look at it.

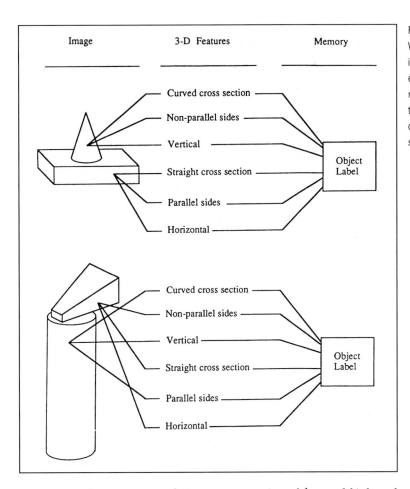

FIG. 2.8.
Why feature extraction
is not a feasible
explanation of object
recognition. Although
these stimuli are
different they have the
same features.

From a subjective point of view our perception of the world is based on object-centred information. We are thus unaware that our exact view of objects is continually changing. This process is known as **object constancy** and it is the outcome of establishing a 3D sketch of the world. As we saw earlier, it has been proposed that the object-centred representation is based on a **structural description** in which the relationships between the various parts of an object are specified (Sutherland, 1973; Bruce et al., 1996). These descriptions are based on the idea that information about the visual properties of objects can be represented as **propositions** (the idea of propositions will be introduced in more detail later but for now it is sufficient to note that a proposition is any statement about which we can answer "yes" or "no"). A table, for example, could be described as having four vertical legs, one in each

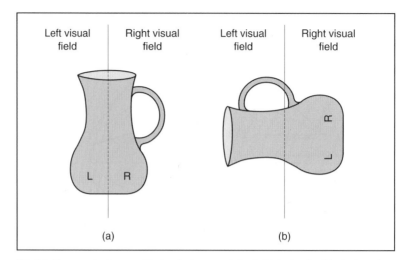

FIG. 2.9. Viewer-centred versus object-centred representation. In (a) the handle of the jug is on the right-hand side of the jug and the right side of our visual field. In (b) tilting the jug results in the handle moving into the left visual field—thus, from a viewer-centred position it is now on the left. However, that is not how you see things: the handle is still on the right side of the jug—this is because your representation of the jug is not view-dependent, it is object-centred.

corner, supporting a flat surface and so on. Any item that met that classification would then meet the basic criterion for a table. Figure 2.10 would therefore be described as "vertical cone on top of horizontal brick".

While structural descriptions overcome many of the difficulties encountered when attempting to specify an object-centred representation, there are still problems. One difficulty is known as the binding problem. If we look at the structural description for Fig. 2.10 "vertical cone on top of horizontal brick", it is necessary to specify that the terms "vertical" and "on top of" relate to the cone-shaped component, whereas "horizontal" and "below" are associated with the brick shape. One solution to this is to have **conjunctive codes** which specify the exact relationship of specific parts (e.g. "vertical cone on top of"; "vertical cone below" etc.). However, it has been argued that the addition of conjunctive coding results in an enormous increase in the amount of information that must be stored away to enable an object to be identified unambiguously. This arises because the number of possible conjunctions in a complex object is so large. There is the added problem that a system of this kind would also have to store away conjunction codes for objects that never occur. Using our example, it might be that cones never occur below bricks but, because we do not know this in advance, we would nonetheless have a code for this possibility. Despite this, most researchers accept the idea of structural descriptions even though the binding problem is difficult to solve at present.

How is object constancy achieved?

One of the most difficult problems is to explain what information is extracted from different views of an object so as to enable a common structural description to be realised. In developing his theory,

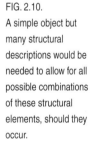

Marr proposed that objects could be thought of essentially as cylinders, each of which possessed a **principal axis**. This point was famously illustrated in the account (Marr and Nishihara, 1978) of how the perceptual system might identify a human being. They proposed that the human body was essentially a group of cylinders, each of which had a vertical principal axis (see Fig. 2.11). In order to divide the shape into segments, the perceptual system made use of **concavity** information, i.e. any concave contour, such as that separating the head from the torso, was regarded as a segment boundary. According to Marr and Nishihara, the principal axis of an object serves as the basis around which other features of an object are organised. It was also argued that the principal axis has the property of **invariance** in that it will remain available as an organising principle regardless of viewpoint, and thus serve as a basis for establishing object constancy across differing views of the same thing.

FIG. 2.10.
A simple object but many structural descriptions would be needed to allow for all possible combinations of these structural elements, should they occur.

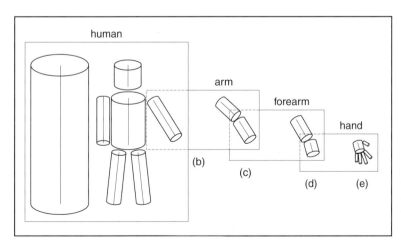

FIG. 2.11.
Marr and Nishihara's concept of the human body as a series of cylinders defined by concavity, each of which has a vertical principal axis.

Biederman's Recognition by Components

The Recognition by Components Model (RBC) (Biederman, 1987; Biederman, 1995) does, like Marr's account, propose that objects are identified on the basis of object-centred structural descriptions. However, the basis by which this representation is achieved is very different. According to the RBC theory, all known objects can be decomposed into a relatively small set of basic components which can be derived from fundamental aspects of the visual input. Crucial to this theory is Biederman's idea of **non-accidental properties**, which refers to patterns of lines or edges whose co-occurrence in the retinal array is thought rarely to occur by chance. Biederman proposed five non-accidental properties and these are shown in Fig. 2.12. According to the theory, each object we know can be represented by some combination of representations known as **geons**. Each geon represents a fundamental shape, such as a cone or cylinder, which is itself specified by some combination of the non-accidental properties of the visual input in combination with the assumption that concave contours in a figure indicate segment boundaries. In turn, each object that we can identify corresponds to a specific structural description of these geons. Each geon is therefore involved in the identification of a large number of objects (see Fig. 2.13).

To support his model, Biederman carried out an experiment in which subjects were briefly presented with different depictions of an object and asked to identify what the object was. These different forms are shown in Fig. 2.14. Along with a normal line drawing there were two degraded forms of the object. In the "recoverable" version the non-

FIG. 2.12.
Biederman's non-accidental properties of the visual image. The figure shows, for example, the two parallel edges are characteristic of a cylinder-like object whereas three parallel edges indicate a brick-like object.

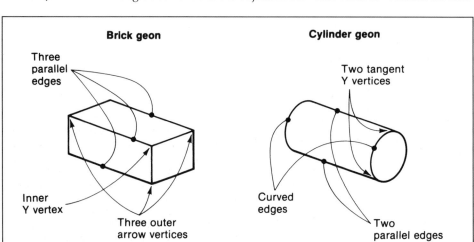

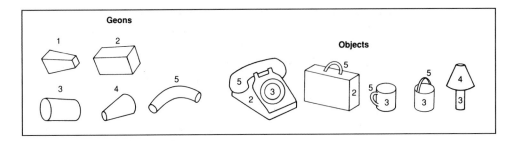

accidental components had been preserved but all other information removed. The "non-recoverable" version represented the reverse. Biederman's hypothesis was that if non-accidental properties of objects were essential to recognition then subjects should be able to identify "recoverable" versions of pictures more accurately than "non-recoverable" versions. The data strongly supported the predictions.

FIG. 2.13. How objects can be constructed from different combinations of geons.

How does RBC explain object constancy? Once again we come across the idea of invariance—the assumption that some aspects of the visual scene remain essentially unchanged irrespective of viewpoint. In the case of RBC theory it was proposed that the five basic non-accidental features could be derived even when most of the retinal information regarding one of those properties was not available. As a result the basic geon structure of an object could be computed from any viewpoint.

Although RBC is centred on our ability to recognise known objects, it has the advantage of explaining how we are capable of seeing objects that we have never seen before. Figure 2.15 shows two pictures. The one on the right is an imaginary object that you would never have seen before yet, despite this, you can see it easily—because it contains various features that are interpretable within the geon framework. Next to it is a picture whose features clearly indicate that it is a box but, despite this, it is impossible to see the whole configuration—the figure has been designed deliberately so that figure–ground cannot be established. What we see here is a figure in which

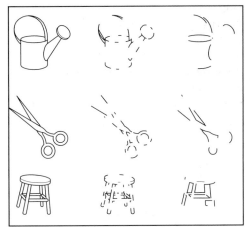

FIG. 2.14. Three types of stimuli used by Biederman. The left column shows the original versions. The middle column shows the recoverable versions. The contours have been deleted in regions where they can be replaced through collinearity or smooth curvature. The right column shows the nonrecoverable versions. The contours have been deleted at regions of concavity so that collinearity or smooth curvature of the segments bridges the concavity. In addition, vertices have been altered, for example, from Ys to Ls and misleading symmetry and parallelism have been introduced.

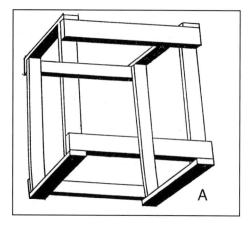 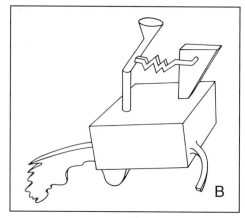

geon-based information cannot be extracted to produce an unambiguous form.

Overview of theories of perception

Perception begins with elementary analyses of the kind Marr envisaged in his notion of a primal sketch. Following on from this is a range of processes such as figure–ground segmentation, processing of depth cues, and pattern recognition which determine a viewer-centred representation of an object (2½D sketch). The next stage involves the transition from a viewer-centred to an object-centred representation. This latter process, equivalent to the 3D sketch of Marr's account, involves the process of object constancy in which any given view of an object makes contact with a higher-level, viewpoint-independent, representation of that object. Theories of object recognition hold that the object-centred representation of an object is based on a structural description of the features comprising an object and their spatial relation. Marr's theory has emphasised the principal axis as central to the determination of a structural description whereas Biederman's theory is based on the extraction of geon-based information.

Perceptual constancy

As we move around, our visual world is constantly changing. Lighting conditions change, the angle from which we view things changes, the distance between us and any given object varies and so on. Despite these continual variations, our visual world has a high degree of **constancy**; somehow our visual system takes account of various fluctuations and provides us with a constant visual world. Just how is this achieved?

Constancy mechanisms appear to occur at all levels of perceptual analysis rather than influence one specific stage.

Colour constancy refers to the phenomenon that our perception of colour does not change greatly with variations in illumination. The mechanisms of colour constancy are not fully understood but one important mechanism is **chromatic adaptation**. Most of our common environments (e.g. home, the office), we experience under varying conditions of illumination: daylight, artificial light, or any combination of both. Subjectively we do not think that things are coloured differently depending on what light is being used yet, objectively, natural and artificial light differ in that the latter has more red in it. If we did not have colour constancy we would tend to see objects illuminated with artificial light as being bathed in red—the fact that we do not reflects a constancy process linked directly to properties of the retina.

Although colour constancy occurs, the fashion conscious should beware. Colours do vary a small amount between fluorescent and daylight illumination. If you are fussy about matching colours to your complexion, it is always better to try on new clothes in daylight. Higher order factors can also influence colour constancy. In one experiment, various shapes were cut from the same sheet of orange-red cardboard. Some of the shapes were associated with red (e.g. tomato) whereas others were not (e.g. mushroom). Subjects tended to see the red-related shapes as more red, thus suggesting that knowledge about objects can help to maintain an object's characteristic colour (Delk and Fillenbaum, 1965). However, despite top-down influences of this kind, the primary basis of colour constancy appears to be physiological (Bruce et al., 1996).

Size constancy describes our ability to see things as roughly the same size despite variations in their distance from us. Consider a person who is six feet away from us and then moves three feet away from us. In purely visual terms this means that the image of that person on our retina has doubled in size. However, our perception of that person does not reflect this and we perceive little change in their size. This process of constancy seems to be achieved by taking into account depth cues. Thus as the person moves nearer, the depth cues indicate that this has occurred and the constancy system scales the percept accordingly.

The use of depth cues to maintain constancy is usually illustrated by the **Ponzo Illusion** (see Fig. 2.16a) in which it is widely assumed that misplaced size constancy information interferes with accurate perception. The figure comprises two long lines tilted towards one another and two shorter lines inside the long lines. Which of these shorter lines is the longest? Unless there is something strange about you,

you will judge the top lines to be longest. Now take a ruler and measure them. You will find that they are exactly the same length. However is this illusion really due to misplaced size constancy? Take a look at Fig. 2.16b. This is a reversible figure which can be seen either as a pyramid with the top squared off or as a square tunnel disappearing into the distance. As the figure reverses the depth cues change: in the pyramid form, line Y is the nearest, so line Z should be perceived as longer and for the tunnel vice versa. Experiments show that this is not the case and that line Y is perceived as longer regardless of which depth interpretation is placed. Nonetheless as Fig. 2.16c shows, depth cues can provide illusory differences in size.

The Ponzo illusion is thus thought to be explicable in terms of lower level visual processes rather than misplaced depth cues (see Robinson, 1972). However, note that 2.16c does produce illusory differences in size due to depth cues. This suggests that depth illusions may be more apparent when actual objects are involved. This appears true for another famous illusion, the **Ames Room**. In this case a room was carefully constructed so that when viewed through the peephole (Fig. 2.17) the room appeared to have a normal rectangular shape. However, the floor plan of the room shows that this is not the case and that one end of the back wall is much nearer the peephole than the other end of the back wall. When two people are placed in the room, the subject perceives a giant on one side of the room and a midget on the other side of the room (it has been claimed that this does work even if you know the people, but from personal experience I dispute this). The illusion arises because

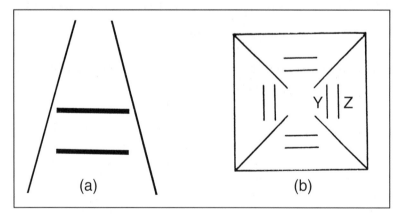

FIG. 2.16. (a) The original Ponzo illusion. (b) A stimulus which can, overall, be seen as either a square tunnel disappearing into the distance or a pyramid-like structure with the top shaved off. As you look at this picture the depth cues will reverse spontaneously. This should affect which line you perceive as the longest if perceived depth is the cause of the Ponzo Illusion—it does not.

FIG. 2.16. (c) Both these mythical creatures are the same size but here the depth cues really do distort picture perceived size.

the visual system assumes the two people are equidistant on the basis of misperceiving room shape. However, the retinal image associated with the person standing at the highest point of the floor is much bigger than the image associated with the person standing at the lowest point of the floor, so, given their equal distance away from the viewing point, the person standing at the highest point of the floor must be a lot bigger. Interestingly, this is a "hard wired effect" in that it does not diminish when the illusion is explained by allowing an aerial view of the room to take place.

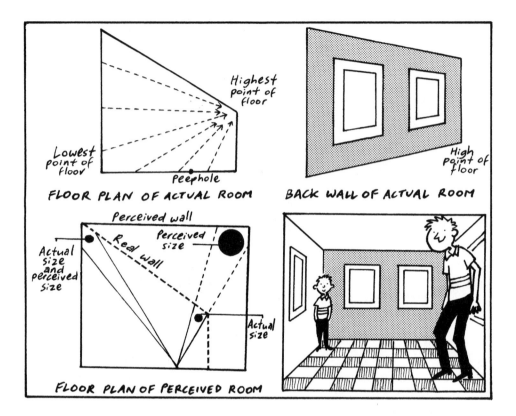

FLOOR PLAN OF ACTUAL ROOM

BACK WALL OF ACTUAL ROOM

FLOOR PLAN OF PERCEIVED ROOM

FIG. 2.17.
Left: drawing of the real dimensions and angles used in the Ames room. Right: The Ames room as seen through the peephole.

Another famous illusion is the the **Müller–Lyer Illusion** which also involves illusory differences in line length. The original illusion (Fig. 2.18a) was constructed using arrows and it was attributed to a high level inference that inward pointing arrows indicated an edge that was close (e.g. a corner) whereas edges facing outward indicated a corner in the distance (Gregory, 1998). Unfortunately, the same illusion can be created using terminal variations that have no obvious link with environmentally-familiar configurations (Fig. 2.18b–e). Once again a lower level explanation is required (Greene and Nelson, 1997). One idea, for example, is that people automatically compute the length between the tip of the fins (or any other object at the end of the lines) and that this interferes with line length estimation.

Shape constancy describes a process in which we tend to perceive an object in its typical shape even though this shape may be greatly distorted by the angle at which we are viewing it. Early experiments showed that shape constancy depended critically on our ability to use contextual information. Thus, when you look at your dinner plate on

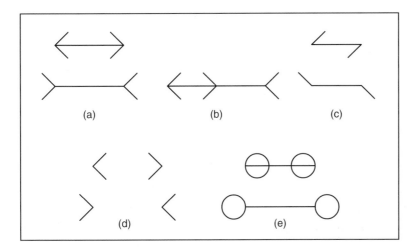

FIG. 2.18.
Variations of the
Müller-Lyer Illusion.

(a)   (b)   (c)

(d)   (e)

the table, you do not perceive an elliptical object, which is what the projection on the retina shows. Rather, the presence of a knife and fork and other paraphernalia indicates the presence of a table and this cues the visual system to perceive the ellipse as a circle.

Gibson and the idea of ecological perception

The account of perception developed so far has been based on the constructivist information-processing approach to cognition with its emphasis on the interaction between bottom-up and top-down information. The **direct perception** approach is non-constructivist and takes the view that visual perception can be explained without any recourse to internal representations or processes, i.e. perception is an entirely bottom-up process. The concept of direct perception was developed by James Gibson (Gibson, 1950; 1994) and based on the idea that the **optic array**—the patterns of light reaching the retina—provided all the information needed to see the world. Gibson formulated his views from work he carried out on trying to improve the landing ability of aeroplane pilots. Crucial to a pilot's landing ability is judging the distance between the aeroplane and the runway. This judgement therefore depends on good depth cues and Gibson proposed that existing ideas about depth cues (e.g. inter-position, relative contrast,

Pilots have to be extremely skilled at judging the distance between the aeroplane and the runway.

motion parallax) could not explain the accuracy with which pilots landed.

Gibson proposed that information about depth was inherent in the optic array itself. A primary example of this idea was the role that texture gradients can play in depth perception (see Fig. 2.7). These gradients are also considered important in constructivist accounts of depth perception but here the idea is that the converging linear perspectives offered by the gradients are used to calculate depth. Gibson's account was different in one major respect. He argued that no calculation was necessary and that the depth represented by the texture gradient was available directly from the optic array itself.

According to Gibson, direct perception was possible because the optic array contained invariant information, a concept we have already encountered. To understand invariance in Gibson's theory, look at Fig. 2.19 which shows three cylinders imposed on a texture gradient. In

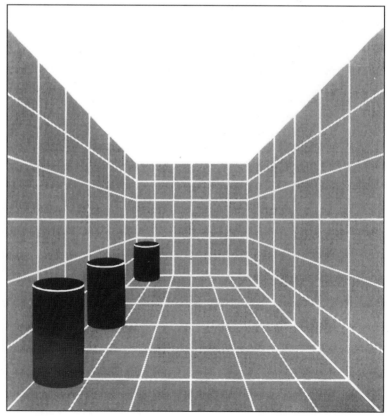

FIG. 2.19.
According to direct perception, this figure automatically suggests, via perspective cues, the relation between size and distance and that no computation is necessary.

constructivist terms it would be argued that information concerning the retinal images of the three cylinders would be compared with the distance information provided by the texture gradient so as to calculate that the cylinders are all the same size and an equal distance apart. According to Gibson, these calculations are unnecessary; equal size of the cylinders is directly available because each cylinder overlaps with an equivalent amount of textural information and each cylinder is separated by equal amounts of texture. Furthermore, the information provided by the texture gradient would not change if you altered the viewing angle as more closely spaced parts of the gradient will always indicate greater distance.

Gibson's theory was all embracing and he made very bold claims about the potential of direct perception. One idea was that of **affordances** which argued that there were invariants in the optic array which suggested that objects had specific properties, such as being a suitable surface to walk on, something to shelter under, something graspable, nutritious and so on. Perhaps most well known was the idea of **optic flow**. As an individual moves through the environment, elements of that environment close to the individual move faster and are more blurred than elements that are farther away. Gibson believed that information from the optic flow patterns was a crucial determinant of movement accuracy.

Gibson attracted many followers but also many critics (see Ullman, 1980, but see subsequent commentaries on Gibson's 1994 article, e.g. Greeno, 1994). One major objection was that Gibson was often rather vague about the nature of invariants in the optic array and others argued that even relatively straightforward proposals such as invariance in texture gradients were not as easy to derive as he proposed. Others struggled with the fundamental idea of "direct perception"—how could a three-dimensional image be derived from a two-dimensional one without some intervening process being involved? Problems of this kind were undoubtedly exacerbated by Gibson's own reluctance to be clear about what he meant by "direct perception".

In retrospect it is probably best to view Gibson as someone who drew attention to the potential richness of information available in the optic array. Optic flow, for example, is a respectable idea with various demonstrations that it can be used as a source of information to calculate such things as collision times. The important point, however, is that there is nothing "direct" about this; optic flow is one aspect of the information that can be extracted from the retina and then internally processed to guide responding.

Overview

- Perception is a deceptively simple but very complex process.
- Most theories of perception are constructivist in that they involve an interaction between top-down and bottom-up processes.
- One of the most influential theories of visual perception is that of Marr. He envisaged perception involving a series of stages moving from the primal sketch, to the 2½D sketch, through to the 3D sketch and the establishment of meaning.
- The primal sketch involves the extraction of basic perceptual elements such as elements and bars by the use of low-level organising principles.
- The 2½D sketch extracts information about features such as depth and figure–ground discrimination. At this point the percept is still viewer-centred.
- In the 3D Sketch an object-centred representation of the object is established. This can be defined as a representation of the object that is independent of the specific viewpoint.
- Various cues such as symmetry, convexity and nature of orientation contribute to figure–ground discrimination.
- Cues to depth can be both monocular, e.g. linear perspective, texture gradient, relative contrast, interposition and motion parallax; or binocular, e.g. stereopsis.
- Template theory has been rejected as a basis for pattern recognition.
- Feature models propose that objects are recognised as clusters of features. The most well-known of these is pandemonium.
- The transition from viewer-centred to object-centred representation involves the act of object constancy. Both template theories and feature theories have difficulty explaining how object constancy is achieved.
- It has been proposed that each object corresponds to a structural description which describes both the constituent elements of an object and the relations between those parts. However, there are difficulties with this view as noted by the binding problem.
- Marr proposed that constancy is achieved by looking for invariance in the images of the same object presented from different view points. One principal source of invariance was the principal axis of an object.
- Biederman proposed that objects comprise sub-units known as geons and that each object is a unique combination of these geons. Object constancy was explained by arguing that geon-based representations contain certain non-accidental features which remain invariant across viewpoint.

- Constancy is the ability to perceive an object as the same despite variations in the actual visual input.
- Colour constancy appears to involve a combination of physiological and psychological processes.
- Size constancy is maintained by invoking depth cues whereas shape constancy seems more determined by our knowledge of the object we are looking at.
- Gibson criticised the constructivist position and argued that the optic array provided all the information needed to see the world.
- Gibson also argued that visual percepts had affordances—perceptual characteristics which suggested their use.
- Gibson's view is largely rejected because it is unable to provide a precise account of how a percept is established.

Suggested further reading

Bruce, V., Green, P.R., & Georgeson, M.A. (1996). *Visual perception: Physiology, psychology, and ecology.* (3rd ed.). Hove, UK: Psychology Press.

This provides a thorough and broad ranging account of all aspects of visual perception.

Goldstein, E.B. (1989). *Sensation and perception.* Pacific Grove, CA: Brooks Cole.

As well as providing an up-to-date and well illustrated-account of visual perception, it also contains sections on the other senses. Access to web sites associated with the book also available.

Gregory, R.L. (1998). *Eye and brain.* (5th ed.). Oxford: Oxford University Press.

A more low level book covering certain issues in this chapter. Not everyone would agree with Gregory's account of certain illusions.

Revision questions

1 What do we mean by a percept?
2 Why do we think of perception as a reconstructive process?
3 Outline Marr's basic concept of how perception occurs.
4 What factors determine figure–ground segregation?
5 Outline the various cues we use to perceive depth.
6 Why are template and feature models of pattern recognition inadequate?

7 What is meant by object constancy and how does it relate to the idea of structural descriptions?
8 What is the "binding problem"?
9 What is the basis of Biederman's RBC theory and what kinds of evidence support it.
10 Explain the role of invariances in the determination of object constancy.
11 Describe the constancies and the mechanisms proposed to account for them.
12 Why are some illusions assumed to involve more top-down inference than is necessary to explain what occurs?
13 What is "direct perception" and should explanations of visual perception take any notice of it?

Attention 3

"You can't do two things at once" is a familiar piece of advice but is it really true? The answer would appear to be "sometimes". We cannot have two conversations at once or watch two TV programmes simultaneously. But we can talk while we drive and listen to music while we exercise. Also we can be distracted by things we are not currently listening to if they are relevant. These examples show us that the idea of **attention** is not a simple matter of "concentration". Rather, attention is a multi-dimensional concept used to describe different features and ways of responding in the human cognitive system.

Sometimes we can divide our attention between simultaneous tasks, but when we are behind the wheel of a car it can be dangerous.

Selective attention

Within cognitive psychology, most research has been aimed at understanding the process of **selective attention**. The modern origins of this research enterprise go back to the early 1950s and the work of a British engineer called Colin Cherry (Cherry, 1953). The motivation for Cherry's work was something he termed the **cocktail party problem**— the fact that humans can attend to one conversation selectively even though there may be many others going on around them.

To examine this problem Cherry devised the **dichotic listening task**. This involved the presentation of two messages, one to each ear, using headphones. Participants in the experiment were instructed to **shadow** one message by repeating it out aloud. The demand for shadowing was assumed to prevent participants paying any attention to information presented on the unattended ear. As part of his investigation, Cherry set out to discover what sorts of data were available about information that was not being attended to.

In the experiments, participants shadowed a verbal message on the right ear while simultaneously being presented with different types of information to the left ear. The principal interest concerned what people noticed about the information presented on the unattended channel. An initial manipulation was presenting the unattended message in either English or German. When asked afterwards in what language the unattended message had been spoken the participants all thought or presumed it was English. Follow-up experiments involved using a male voice, a female voice, a reversed male voice, and a buzzing sound on the unattended channel. All subjects accurately identified speech when it was presented on the unattended channel and they also correctly identified the presence of the buzzing sound. They could also say whether the voice was male or female but only a few listeners thought there was something odd about the reversed speech. Most importantly, no subject could identify any word or phrase that had been presented to the unattended ear. This led Cherry to conclude that certain aspects of the unattended channel were recognised, e.g. pitch, but that "detailed aspects, such as the language, individual words, or semantic content were unnoticed" (p.19).

Cherry's results led to the conclusion that we do identify certain forms of information presented on the unattended channel but that these sources of information are very low level and that no information about meaning is extracted. The problem with Cherry's account is that it does not square with human experience. Returning to our hypothetical cocktail party, you may be having a conversation with one group of people but suddenly find yourself listening to another conversation because something of relevance, such as your name or a related theme, has cropped up. This is a common human experience but it is not predicted by Cherry's conclusions. In order to start listening suddenly to a different but relevant conversation we must have some information about the meaningful content of that conversation yet, according to Cherry's findings we do not extract the meaning from any source of information we are not consciously attending to. Obviously there is something wrong here and we will return to this point later.

Broadbent's filter model

Cherry's view was that we are able to attend selectively because we take in so little about other sources of information we are not attending to. Put another way, attention is so selective that there is nothing much to distract us. This was essentially the view put forward by Broadbent (Broadbent, 1958) who can be credited with the first information processing model of attention or, indeed, any other psychological process. Broadbent's model was known as a **filter model** in which the cognitive system is seen as a series of information processing channels (see Fig. 3.1). Each of these channels is seen as dealing with information from a specific aspect of the environment, such as a particular spatial location. These channels are held to operate in parallel and feed their information to a **buffer store**. Here the information is held for a few seconds while a decision is made concerning which of the channels will be identified for further processing by a **selective filter**. Information from the chosen information source then passes into a **limited capacity channel** at which point it can be said to be the focus of attention. From this point the attended information can then be processed further and used to guide the responses of the individual.

From an experimental point of view the most important issue was how the filter mechanism operated. Broadbent proposed three crucial properties:

- Selection of the chosen channel was based solely on the physical information it contained.
- Information on channels that are not selected undergoes no further processing and is completely disregarded.
- The filter is consciously controlled and switching from one channel to another is an effortful and thus relatively slow process.

Broadbent's concept of the filter was consistent with Cherry's finding that participants only appeared to notice the physical characteristics (e.g. pitch variation) of information channels they were not attending to. Broadbent proposed that only the physical features of channels were monitored to determine selection so it was not surprising that subjects only noticed physical information in shadowing experiments.

Further evidence for Broadbent's model came from experiments involving the **split-span task**. This task involves the presentation of digits simultaneously to both ears via headphones. The digits occur in pairs, one per ear, at the rate of half a second per pair. The participants' task is to report the digits they hear in any order they like. Almost

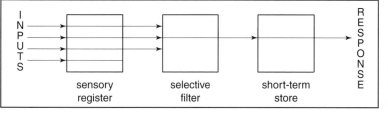

FIG. 3.1.
Broadbent's filter
model of attention.

invariably participants in this task prefer to report the digits on an ear-by-ear basis rather than on the basis of pairs. According to Broadbent's filter model, ear-by-ear reporting is preferred because this requires only one attention switch (e.g. left → right), whereas pair-by-pair reporting would require five attention switches of the same kind. Indeed, when participants are forced to report on a pair-by-pair basis, they make many errors. This was assumed to arise because the attention mechanism was too slow on many occasions and that the second member of a pair had been lost from the buffer before the mechanism attempted to locate it.

Problems with "early selection"

Broadbent's model constitutes an **early selection** model of attention because it proposes that the selection of the attended channel happens at an early stage in stimulus processing. Most importantly, this selection is held to occur prior to the extraction of any meaning. Earlier we noted that the idea of selective attention based solely on the parallel processing of physical attributes seemed at odds with real experience, in that our attention is most frequently drawn to unattended messages that have some meaningful link to what we are consciously doing.

Concerns of this kind led Gray and Wedderburn (1960) to provide a direct test of Broadbent's physical filter theory. They used the same split-span procedure but this time the messages were modified. On one ear the participants heard the sequence 6 AUNT 3 and on the other DEAR 8 JANE. Once again the participants were required to report the information in any order they liked. According to the physical filter theory, participants should still show a strong preference for ear-by-ear reporting. This follows because, with only physical information available (in this case left vs right), the participant has no way of knowing that information in the buffer store (e.g. AUNT, JANE) is meaningfully related to information that is currently being attended to (e.g. DEAR). However, contrary to predictions, participants showed a strong preference to report the phrase DEAR AUNT JANE followed by the digit sequence or vice versa. This result could only be explained by assuming that the filter mechanism was able to process information about the meaning of items in the store and thus acknowledge the link between the three words.

Treisman's attenuation model

In the light of experiments such as Gray and Wedderburn's, Treisman (Treisman, 1960) proposed a revised model of selective attention which is generally known as the **attenuator model**. Among the many experiments conducted was one in which Treisman used a dichotic listening task. Participants were required to shadow a verbal message on one ear while on the unattended ear participants were exposed to a string of words which were not sentences but, in places, contained meaningful phrases. At various points in the procedure there was a switch, with the sense of the attended message continuing on the unattended channel. Treisman found that subjects often changed to shadowing the unattended message when this switch occurred. For example:

Shadowed message: I SAW THE GIRL/song was WISHING
Unattended message: me that bird/JUMPING in the street

(Words in upper case represent shadowing response.)

Treisman's result and others like it could only be explained by concluding that there is some meaningful analysis of unattended information. To account for this, Treisman proposed that all channels entering the buffer store received a degree of semantic analysis. This analysis was described as attenuated to emphasise that unattended information did not undergo full meaningful analysis. However, the analysis that was undertaken was sufficient to detect that an unattended channel had information that was relevant to the attended message. Overall, this attenuated filter process was flexible depending on the meaning of the information being attended to, but it was also thought that some information sources like your own name or "help" might be permanently facilitated (see Fig. 3.2).

At this point you may be wondering about the discrepancy between Treisman's work and Cherry's earlier and emphatic conclusion that unattended channels receive no meaningful processing. The reason for this is straightforward. In Cherry's experiments participants were asked about information on the unattended channel only after they had completed the shadowing phase. In Treisman's experiments, evidence of semantic processing was obtained **on-line**, or at the moment the information was presented. There is additional evidence that the kinds

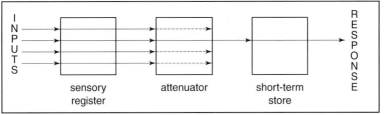

FIG. 3.2.
Treisman's attenuator model of selective attention.

of effects that Treisman obtained do not occur if more than a few seconds is allowed to elapse between the occurrence of semantically-related information on the two channels. Thus, in relation to the above example, "JUMPING" would not be noticed if it occurred a few seconds after GIRL. What this indicates is that meaningful information about the unattended channel is only available for a few seconds after which it is lost if not attended to. On this basis it is no surprise that Cherry's participants knew so little about what happened on the unattended channel because this was measured **off-line**.

Late selection theories

The problem with Treisman's theory is that the concept of attenuation is poorly specified. Just what is an attenuated processing of meaning? What features of a word's meaning are made available by this mechanism? An answer to this difficulty was to propose that all unattended inputs undergo a full analysis of meaning prior to one channel being selected for processing (see Fig. 3.3). A number of these **late selection theories** were put forward, notably Deutsch and Deutsch (1963).

A feature of late selection models was that they were put forward largely as theoretical possibilities as opposed to theories supported by existing experimental evidence. Subsequent to this, various experimental data did appear to support the idea of late selection by apparently showing a degree of sophisticated semantic analysis occurring on unattended channels. An often cited experiment is MacKay's (1973) experiment in which participants first shadowed sentences which were lexically ambiguous. Thus in the sentence "They threw stones toward the *bank* yesterday", the word "bank" can be interpreted in relation to either the sense of "river" or "money". At the same time as these sentences were being presented, a disambiguating word, e.g. "money" or "river" was presented on the unattended channel. Following presentation of these sentences participants were given pairs of sentences, one biased to each meaning of "bank", and asked which of the sentences most closely corresponded to the sentence

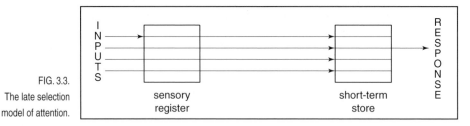

FIG. 3.3.
The late selection
model of attention.

they had heard. MacKay obtained a reliable biasing effect in that recognition favoured the interpretation of the sentence suggested by the unattended word.

While MacKay's experiment suggests a substantial amount of meaningful processing of unattended information, the data do not readily allow us to conclude that the analysis is "full" because it is not clear what evidence would indicate that a meaningful analysis had been "fully" carried out. Indeed additional data from MacKay's study suggested that analysis of unattended information was not complete. He carried out a similar experiment to the above except that this time the sentences involved syntactic ambiguity, i.e. the sentence meant different things depending on how it was grammatically analysed. Thus the sentence "They knew that *flying planes* could be dangerous", either refers to an occupation or a set of objects. MacKay attempted to disambiguate these sentences by presenting phrases such as "growling lions" on the unattended channel but was not able to bias the grammatic interpretation participants placed on these sentences.

There was also evidence that even much simpler information did not undergo full analysis. Treisman and Riley (1969) asked participants to shadow strings of digits presented to one ear whilst ignoring strings of digits presented to the other ear. In addition they were told that a letter would occur on either channel from time to time and, when this happened, they should stop shadowing and indicate that the letter had occurred. Treisman and Riley reasoned that if analysis of unattended information occurred in full, then detection of letters should be equally accurate on both attended and unattended channels. However, they found that detection was twice as likely when the letter occurred in the shadowed message and thus argued against the idea of late selection.

Subliminal perception and late selection

Evidence relating to the late selection model is somewhat confusing. On the one hand, MacKay's results suggest quite a substantial amount of semantic processing of unattended information which is sufficient to allow the disambiguation of a sentence. In contrast, Treisman and Riley's results indicate that analysis of basic letter identity information is not comparable across attended and unattended channels. There is no easy way to resolve this but one possibility may be the shadowing task itself. To be an effective tool the shadowing task must prevent participants listening actively to the unattended channel. However, one cannot be sure that participants do this all the time and variations into the effectiveness of shadowing may complicate interpretation of the findings.

A more convincing case for late selection might be a situation in which meaning is shown to be processed even though there is no direct evidence that the participant was aware of perceiving anything. Such a situation might be provided in experiments purporting to show **subliminal perception**.

Before discussing the evidence, it is important to qualify the term subliminal perception because it can refer to two very different sets of conditions. Subliminal perception can be said to occur when:

- A subject is fully aware of a stimulus but fails to detect some aspect of that stimulus which has subsequent motivating qualities.
- A subject is presented with a stimulus under such degraded conditions that he or she is unable to state accurately whether or not anything was presented at all. Nonetheless, it can be shown that the presented stimulus has a subsequent effect on the behaviour of the individual.

FIG. 3.4.
An apparently harmless advert for gin (from Key, 1972). Can you see the subliminal signal? Answer at end of chapter.

The first type of subliminal perception has been used to varying degrees throughout advertising. The designers of adverts often go to great lengths to build various forms of symbolism into their adverts in the hope that it will motivate individuals to buy the product (Key, 1973). One of these adverts is shown in Fig. 3.4 and it seems a harmless enough advert for gin. However, if you look at it longer you may well notice that there is more to it than meets the eye. Unfortunately, despite numerous claims, there is no reliable evidence that this type of subliminal stimulation can work (Pratkanis, 1992; Pratkanis et al., 1994; Trappey, 1996). However, one should not dismiss entirely the idea that unnoticed aspects of a visual display can have some motivating effect. In a classic experiment by Hess (1975), male subjects viewed pairs of female faces such as those shown in Fig. 3.5. Various decisions were required such as which woman looks more angry or which woman looks more attractive. Negative decisions were consistently biased towards women with small pupils and positive decisions given most often to

Break out the frosty bottle

GILBEYS
LONDON DRY
GIN

and keep your tonics dry!

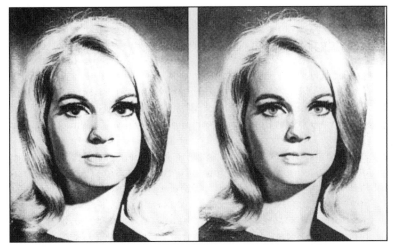

FIG. 3.5.
Two similar faces
except for pupil
dilation. Men preferred
the dilated pupils but
did not give that as
the reason for their
choice. From Hess
(1975).

women with dilated pupils. In most instances, however, the men had no conscious awareness of the basis of their decisions.

The second form of subliminal perception relates directly to our concerns about late selection. If it can be shown that stimuli we do not see or hear can nonetheless influence our subsequent behaviour in a meaningful way then this would be, depending on the nature of the effects, good evidence that semantic processing occurred without attentional involvement.

Once again commercial advertising has been involved via the use of so-called subliminal cuts. These involve the very brief presentation of a motivating stimulus during a film sequence. Presentation is so brief that the subject notices nothing but it is hoped that the information in the cut will increase the probability that the person takes a particular kind of action. As we will see, the evidence that this type of manipulation actually works is non-existent. Nevertheless, subliminal stimulation of this type is banned in the UK and in most states of the US.

The belief in subliminal cuts is often related back to a Canadian experiment in which cinema goers were flashed subliminal messages "Eat Popcorn", "Drink Coca-Cola" during the film. It was claimed that these messages dramatically increased sales but the whole phenomenon was later revealed as a fraudulent publicity stunt. Subsequent work has shown quite conclusively that people cannot be persuaded by subliminal messages even though they think they might have been. Shortly after the "Eat Popcorn" experiment, a second study was carried out in which participants were aware that a subliminal message might be screened during a film. After watching the film participants dutifully reported feeling more thirsty and wanting to eat popcorn. The only problem with the result was that the subliminal message had actually stated "Phone Now"! (Pratkanis, 1992; Pratkanis et al., 1994).

There has also been a widespread belief that subliminal audio messages can influence behaviour. The most dramatic claim involved the rock group Judas Priest who included the subliminal message "Do it" on one of their records. The band were subsequently and unsuccessfully prosecuted for inciting two teenage boys to commit suicide. Subsequent investigations showed that the subliminal influences proposed in these trials were simply not possible (e.g. Hollan, 1975). There has also been a large market in subliminal audiotapes which purport to help you give up smoking, relax more, and so on. Again there is no concrete evidence that these tapes actually work. In one experiment volunteers spent five weeks listening to a subliminal tape which purported either to improve memory or enhance self-esteem (Pratkanis et al., 1994). About half the subjects thought the tape had helped them but this was not revealed by objective tests of improvement. Moreover, around 50% of those who thought their memory had improved actually listened to a "self-esteem" tape and vice versa.

A less dramatic claim is that the meaning of something we do not consciously see might nonetheless "get through" to some extent—not enough to motivate our behaviour but nonetheless have some impact on our cognitive processes. One phenomenon that attracted a considerable degree of investigation was **subliminal priming**. A **priming effect** occurs when prior presentation of a stimulus makes the processing of a subsequent stimulus easier. A **semantic priming effect** occurs when the presentation of a meaningfully-related item, e.g. TABLE, leads to faster identification of a related word, e.g. CHAIR. In a number of experiments Marcel (1983) claimed that semantic priming could occur when the priming stimulus was presented so briefly that it was not consciously detectable. At face value this suggests that meaningful information is available before we attend to a word. However, there were considerable difficulties in replicating this result and, in an overview of the topic, Holender (1986) concluded that subliminal priming effects only occurred when participants in the experiments were able to detect the priming stimulus. Most commonly, this detection might arise because subjects get more "tuned in" to the experiment and thus more able to discern something from the brief subliminal displays.

Resource models of attention

So far our approach to attention has been a structural one in which various components of the system have been specified and their properties investigated, a particular focus being the mechanism employed in the selective filter. A different approach has been to view attention from the perspective of **resource limitations**. Within attention research, the concept of resource refers to the fundamental energy available to initiate and sustain attentional mechanisms. It is assumed that resources are limited but that, within these limitations, there may be considerable variability owing to factors such as tiredness, age, medication effects and so on.

A central issue for resource-based accounts of attention has been the distinction between general and task-specific resources. A general resource is one that can be allocated to any mental task whereas a task-specific research is restricted to a particular type of mental operation. This distinction has been investigated by means of the **dual task** or **divided attention** method in which participants are required to perform two competing tasks simultaneously. The logic of these experiments is that competing demands stretch the resources of the attentional system and, as a result, performance deteriorates. If it is found that competition between any two tasks has the same detrimental effect, then it is assumed that a general attentional resource underlies performance. Alternatively, if the degree of impairment on one task is dependent on the nature of the competing task, it is assumed that task-specific resources are involved.

A well-known experiment supporting the task-specific idea was reported by Allport et al., (1972). Participants were required to shadow an essay by George Orwell presented aurally to one ear while attempting to memorise either an aurally-presented word list, a visually-presented word list, or a picture sequence. Following presentation, memory was tested using a recognition procedure. Striking results were obtained showing that recognition was least affected in the visual memory condition and poorest in the aurally-presented condition (see Fig. 3.6). A further experiment showed that people were able to sight read piano music equally well while shadowing speech as compared to the undivided attention condition (see also Allport, 1993).

FIG. 3.6.

Results obtained by Allport et al. (1972). The dark bars refer to errors in a baseline condition with undivided attention and the lighter bars refer to the concurrent shadowing condition.

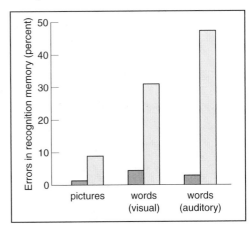

Evidence for task-specific attentional resources was also found in a classic study by Brooks (1968). He asked participants to imagine an "F" in outline (𝔽) and to think of an asterisk moving around its edge. At each change of direction participants had to indicate whether the asterisk had reached an extreme or intermediate point in the outline. Brooks compared three modes of responding: verbal yes/no; tapping— one for "yes", two for "no"; and a pointing response in which subjects had a visual array of "Ys" and "Ns". As participants envisaged the asterisk moving they indicated their response by pointing to the next N or Y location as they moved down the page. There was also a verbal condition in which participants worked their way through a proverb and indicated whether each successive word was a noun or not. Mode of response had little effect on the verbal conditioning although there was a tendency for participants to be slower in the verbal response condition. For the 𝔽 condition, tapping and vocal responding produced comparable response times but the pointing task produced much longer times. This latter result indicated selective interference between the visual response mode and the imaging task and supports the idea of a specific attentional mechanism for visual processing.

The general resource theory has tended to be accepted by default, i.e. a failure to find evidence supporting the task-specific account of attention. However, there is evidence appearing to support the general position. Barsolou (1985) presented participants with ambiguous figures including the well-known rat/man figure (see Fig. 3.7). If you look at this figure you will note that it reverses spontaneously but that this may take a little time. Reisberg (1983) measured time to reverse under normal conditions and with the imposition of various secondary tasks including counting and doing mental arithmetic. Despite the considerable difference between the task demands, reversal of the figures was markedly slowed by the secondary tasks.

FIG. 3.7.
Rat-man figure used by Reisberg (1983).

The above evidence suggests that both general and task-specific resource accounts of attention are correct depending on the experiment in question. There are, however, a number of problems with the theory. One major difficulty is the relationship between task characteristics and the resources assumed to underlie them. While it makes sense to think that two visual tasks share resources it does not follow that a verbal task and a visual task share no resources. Two tasks may, for example, share higher order conceptual operations even though their overt demands are very different. It thus becomes difficult to assert, beyond any question, that two tasks have no attentional demands in common. Thus even in the case of Reisberg's disparate tasks one could envisage common attentional elements leading to interference.

A different problem arises when we consider situations in which a secondary task has no effect on how well people perform the primary task. Consider Allport et al.'s demonstration that people could sight read piano music equally well while shadowing verbal information. The problem here relates to the issue of **automaticity**—the idea that many of our mental capabilities do not require attentional involvement in order to proceed. As a result, no competing task interference is observed because no attention is required. We will consider automaticity in a later section but first we must return briefly to the issue of early and late selection.

Selection and resources in attention

Johnston and Heinz (1978) proposed a "hybrid" model that envisages selective attention as a flexible process influenced by available resources and the demands that different forms of information monitoring place on those resources. Their theory is that early filtering of information, i.e. acceptance or rejection on the basis of physical cues such as spatial position or sound, requires less resources than later filtering based on the meaningful characteristics of different information channels. To evaluate this theory they devised a dual-task experiment in which participants listened to either one, two or three spoken word lists at the same time. One of the lists, e.g. the one in the left ear, was designated the target, thus requiring any other lists being presented to be ignored. At the same time as carrying out this task, participants also watched a screen and had to indicate each time a beam of light appeared.

The logic of the experiment was that the greater the participants' efficiency on the visual detection task, the more capacity they must have available. Thus, if learning condition A allows better visual detection than condition B, it follows that condition A is placing less demands on resources than condition B. The most illustrative comparison in the study involves two conditions, each involving the simultaneous presentation of two lists. In the "different voice" condition, participants had to ignore the list spoken in a different sex voice to the target list but was similar in meaning. In the "different meaning" condition, the same voice was used for both lists but the meaning was different. It was reasoned that the "different voice" condition allowed early selection based on pitch whereas the "different meaning" condition required selection at a later, meaningful, stage. It was therefore predicted that the "different voice" condition would allow greater efficiency on the visual detection task and this was what they found.

The Johnston and Heinz model therefore indicates that the selective filter operates flexibly depending on the demands of the situation and that the demands on resources vary depending on what the filtering mechanism is required to do.

Automaticity

An automatic process can be defined as one that requires no attention for it to occur. All of us possess abilities that meet this definition. A very good example is driving. How often have you got into your car and arrived home unable to remember anything about the journey home? This is a common experience and reflects the fact that mental operations can be executed without attentional involvement. In this section we will explore more about the nature of automatic or, as they are sometimes known, preattentive processes.

One of the best demonstrations of automaticity involves the **Stroop Effect** (Stroop, 1935). In its classic form the Stroop test involves the presentation of a series of colour words each written in one of four colours. In the **congruent** condition each word is written in the appropriate colour, e.g. RED is written in red ink. In the **incongruent** condition each word is written in a conflicting colour, e.g. RED is written in blue ink. In both conditions, the participant's task is to name the ink colour of each word as quickly as possible and this is compared with a baseline condition usually involving colour patches. (It is a curious fact that Stroop's original paper involved a baseline condition in which participants named the colours of swastikas—it is therefore unsurprising that writers rarely refer to Stroop's original work!) The Stroop Effect is the conclusion that participants find the task much harder in the incongruent condition. The Stroop Effect has been investigated intensively and many detailed explanations have been put forward. Nonetheless, there seems little debate that the task is difficult because, fundamentally, the word response is activated automatically and interferes with generating the ink colour response.

Our recent understanding of automaticity begins with the well-known studies carried out by Posner and Snyder (1975). They used a very simple task now known as the **Posner Matching Task**. Basically this task measures the speed at which participants can decide whether two letters are the same (e.g. A A) or different (A B). The critical aspect of these studies concerns the information subjects were given in advance of each of these decisions. Essentially, there were three conditions:

"Same": subjects see a priming letter appearing in the decision pair
$$A \rightarrow A A$$

"Different": subjects see a priming letter not in the decision pair
$$C \rightarrow A A$$

"Neutral": a + appears prior to the decision pair
$$+ \rightarrow A A$$

There was also an additional manipulation known as **cue validity** describing the probability that the preceding information was either a good or bad predictor of what appeared on the decision trial. In the high validity condition, there was an 80% probability that the priming letter would be in the decision array, i.e. shown "A", an "A" would appear in the decision array four out of every five times. In the low validity condition, there was only a 20% chance that the preceding letter would appear in the array. The assumption behind the experiment was that the preceding letter would increase the speed at which participants made their same/different decision because information about one or both of the letters in the array had just received prior activation. The more interesting question was whether the validity of the priming letter would have any influence.

The results of the experiment are shown in Fig. 3.8. Looking first at the high validity condition, we can see that there was a substantial priming effect in the "same" condition relative to the neutral baseline condition: thus, prior presentation of a letter led to **facilitation** in decisions about arrays containing that letter. In contrast, the "different" condition resulted in slower decision times relative to baseline: here, prior presentation of a letter that did not then appear in the array resulted in the **inhibition** of response time. These results can be explained on the basis that the high validity condition allows subjects to generate reliable expectancies about what might appear because it is only on 20% of occasions that these expectancies are not confirmed. The cost, however, is slower responding on the 20% of occasions when the prime is misleading.

When we turn to the low validity condition, there is a rather different result. The "same" condition still produces facilitation but there is no inhibition in the "different" condition. Posner and Snyder argued that the differing patterns in high and low validity conditions were

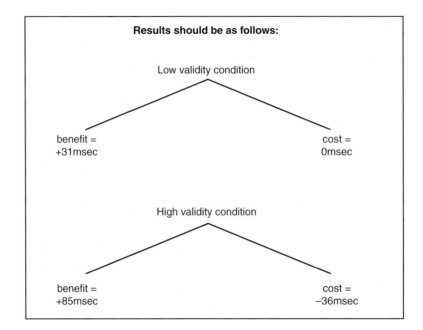

Results should be as follows:

Low validity condition

benefit =
+31msec

cost =
0msec

High validity condition

benefit =
+85msec

cost =
−36msec

FIG. 3.8. Results obtained by Posner and Snyder (1975).
As one way of assessing the Posner and Snyder (1975) results, we can subtract the response times for the neutral condition from those for the same condition; in this way we measure the *benefits* of priming. Likewise, we can subtract the response times for the neutral condition from those for the *different* condition; in this way, we measure the *costs* of being misled. In these terms, the low-validity condition shows a small benefit (from repetition priming) but zero cost from being misled. The high-validity condition, in contrast, shows a larger benefit, but also a substantial cost. The results shown here reflect trials with a 300msec interval between the warning signal and the test stimuli; the results were somewhat different at other intervals.

indicative of different mechanisms operating. In the high validity condition they proposed that the priming letter generated an expectancy that a particular letter would appear. They likened this mechanism to a "spotlight" focusing on a specific part of space. When the expectancy was confirmed, processing was speeded because the spotlight was already in the correct place. However, on the few occasions when expectancies were not confirmed, responding was slowed because the spotlight had to be moved to a different region.

In the case of low validity, they proposed that subjects did not generate expectancies, i.e. the "spotlight" was not focused on a particular location because the probability of this being correct was too low. For this reason, responding was no slower in the different condition compared with the neutral baseline. However, why was there still facilitation? To account for this, they suggested that a fast-acting preattentive priming process was responsible so, even though no expectancies were being generated, facilitation still occurred. These experiments led to the **dual process** theory of attention. According to this theory, presentation of a stimulus automatically activates its representation and information that may be associated with that stimulus. This activation is short-lived and will be superseded, if required, by conscious, effortful processes. Within this theory, automatic activation can lead to facilitation but not inhibition because the latter can only be observed if expectancies are not fulfilled. Returning to the experiment, high and low validity conditions both cause facilitation because, in the former, an expectancy for a particular letter is generated and confirmed whereas, in the latter, automatic activation of the letter representation is available to speed processing. In contrast, only the high validity condition can cause inhibition because it is only here that an expectancy is disconfirmed. Thus in the low validity condition, a mismatch between the priming letter and the array simply means the absence of relevant activation and response speeds comparable to the neutral condition.

Further evidence for dual process theory

Neely (1977) carried out an influential experiment extending the findings and theory of Posner and Snyder. Although the experiment is quite complicated in design the basic idea is quite straightforward. In the experiment, participants were required to make **lexical decisions** about strings of visually-presented letters. Thus, shown GRUTE they would have to decide whether or not it was a word. Our concern is only for two types of trials on which real words were presented for lexical decision. These two types were:

> "Expected–Unrelated": Subjects were told that a particular category word, e.g. BIRD, would, on most occasions, predict word targets from an unrelated category, e.g. ARM, HEAD.

> "Unexpected–Related": On these trials, participants saw the Expected–Unrelated prime, i.e. BIRD, but then saw a word target from that category, e.g. ROBIN.

The other manipulation in this task was the **stimulus onset asynchrony** (SOA) which is simply the time elapsing between the presentation of the prime and the letter string. The shortest SOA was 250msec which increased in intervals up to 700msec.

In this experiment we are concerned with the pattern of facilitation and inhibition obtained in the two different conditions as a function of SOA. As in Posner and Snyder's experiment, facilitation and inhibition are measured relative to a neutral baseline (see Fig. 3.9). If we look at the "Expected–Unrelated" condition we can see that the degree of facilitation builds up as SOA increases. This can be interpreted as reflecting the development of consciously-generated expectancies derived from the task instructions. In the Unexpected–Related condition, we first see a facilitation effect at the shortest SOA but, as SOA increases, this facilitation effect disappears and an inhibition effect develops. What this reflects is an initial automatic activation of the prime word BIRD and its corresponding associate, ROBIN, which provides the basis for facilitation. However, this is short-lived and, once conscious attention is engaged, there is an expectancy for unrelated category words. Thus when ROBIN appears at longer SOAs, inhibition occurs.

The development of automaticity

In the examples used above, the responses manipulated were already considered to have an automatically accessed representation. Thus we do not have to consciously identify letters or activate the meaningful

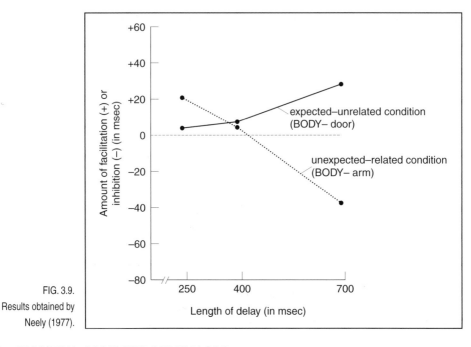

FIG. 3.9.
Results obtained by
Neely (1977).

link between BIRD and ROBIN. Similarly, unless we try and defocus our eyes there is nothing we can do to stop the Stroop effect. However, not all automatic responses are of this type—they have to become automatic. Again, anyone who has learnt to drive will be well aware of this. In the initial stages of learning there can be no question of talking or listening to the radio because conscious effort is needed to remember how the gears work, where the indicators are and so on. It is only through **practice** that responses become automatic.

"Practice makes perfect", but why? In a well-known series of experiments Schneider and Shiffrin (1977; Shiffrin and Schneider, 1977) uncovered some important insights into the development of automaticity. They made use of a **visual search** task in which participants first saw a memory set comprising either one, two, or four single letters. This was followed by a central fixation point, after which a test frame comprising one, two or four target letters appeared. The task was to search the array and decide as rapidly as possible whether a target letter was present. There were long sequences of trials involving either consistent or varied mapping. In the consistent mapping condition, the targets were always selected from the same pool of letters and, in addition, these letters were never used as distractors, i.e. letters not in the target set. Thus if E and Q were used as targets they would never be used as distractors. In the varied mapping condition, targets and distractors were selected from the same pool, i.e. no letter appeared exclusively as a target or distractor (see Fig. 3.10). Importantly,

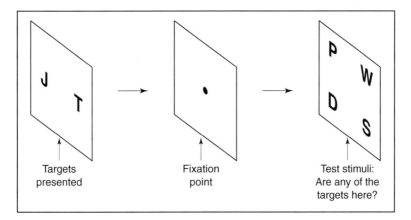

Targets presented   Fixation point   Test stimuli: Are any of the targets here?

FIG. 3.10. Experimental setup used by Schneider and Shiffrin (1977). Participants are first shown a group of "targets"; the number of targets varies from trial to trial. Then participants are shown a fixation point, to ensure that their eyes are pointed in the right direction. Finally, they are shown a group of test letters, and they must respond to "yes" if *any* of the targets are present in this group.

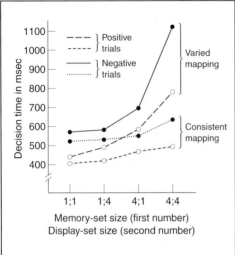

Decision time in msec

1100 — Positive trials
1000 — Varied mapping
900 — Negative trials
800
700
600 — Consistent mapping
500
400

1;1   1;4   4;1   4;4

Memory-set size (first number)
Display-set size (second number)

FIG. 3.11.
Results obtained by
Schneider and
Schiffrin (1977).

participants were given a large amount of practice before the experimental results were obtained.

Figure 3.11 shows the results from trials in which participants correctly identified the presence of a target. If we look first at the consistent mapping condition we can see that response times were very similar across all conditions indicating that neither frame size or memory set size had any effect on participants' response times. Things are very different when we turn to the varied mapping condition. First, search times increase overall as the frame size increases and, second, search times markedly increase as the memory set size increases.

According to Schneider and Shiffrin, these results can be explained in terms of differing demands on attention. In the varied mapping condition it is proposed that subjects have to keep the memory set "in mind" and then compare the letters in the set with those in the frame. This is held to be a sequential process in which each letter in the set is compared with each item in the frame. Accordingly, response times slow down as both the memory set size and the frame size increase. In the consistent mapping condition it was proposed that the repeated association of particular letters with the "yes" response led to the development of a specific link, i.e. E → "target", which did not require conscious effort to implement. This proposal explains why memory set size did not influence performance, but why did frame size exert no effect? The answer here is that automatic processes have an additional property that draws attention to the information they represent in what might be termed a "reflexive way", i.e. one that does not require any intention. The lack of a frame size effect is thus analogous to the more everyday phenomenon of having your attention drawn to a familiar face embedded in a sea of unusual faces.

Norman and Shallice's model

An alternative approach to attention has been proposed by Norman and Shallice (1986) in which they propose that an individual's responses can be controlled in two fundamentally different ways. The majority of responses are under fairly automatic control. They are triggered by environmental cues which in turn contact specific schema, each of which has many subcomponents. A familiar example is driving: some of us may have experienced arriving home having driven several miles but with no recollection of the journey. Yet to have achieved this we would have changed gear many times, operated the indicators, turned left or right and so on. The fact that all this happens without recollection suggests that the various programs used to execute the different component actions are automatic. At some point there may be a clash between two routine activities. To deal with this, Norman and Shallice propose a **contention scheduling** operation in which the relative importance of different actions is assessed and routine behaviour adjusted accordingly.

Because our behaviour is not simply a set of routine automatic operations, there are many occasions when we deliberate and consciously impose a specific action. Consider driving again. If a British person drives in France, many of the routine driving actions are now inappropriate because the traffic drives on the right and not the left. Thus on encountering a roundabout our routine tendency to look right must be inhibited and a look to the left made instead. To explain willed actions, Norman and Shallice propose an additional **Supervisory Activating System** (SAS) which becomes active whenever the routine selection of operations is inappropriate. Thus the SAS will become active when an individual encounters danger, novelty, temptation, and where response options arise that require a decision. Norman and Shallice's SAS concept provides a useful way of understanding slips of action. When I drive home from the University, I always take the same route. This is useful in one sense because it has become highly routine and requires little thought. Problems arise, however, when I have to go somewhere else because frequently I set off on my homeward route. Within Norman and Shallice's model this failure can be attributed to some failure of the SAS to maintain the novel goal.

Unlike other models of attention, the SAS theory leans quite heavily on neuropsychological evidence to support it. Shallice (1988) outlines two types of impaired behaviour that would be consistent with the idea of an SAS-based mechanism controlling attention:

- Because responses controlled by contention scheduling alone have arisen through habit they will change only slowly. Thus, in circumstances where they are strongly triggered, they will persist until inhibited by the SAS. With damage to the SAS, a situation of this kind would give rise to rigid inflexible behaviour.
- If an environment contains no particularly salient information, the SAS would function so as to inhibit responding. However, a deficient

SAS operating in these circumstances might allow inappropriate responses to occur.

On this basis, damage to the SAS might be associated with two types of behavioural difficulty: behavioural rigidity (known as **perseveration)**, and a tendency towards distraction. Evidence for these kinds of deficits has been obtained from patients who have suffered frontal lobe damage, thus leading to the view that attentional mechanisms reside in the frontal cortex. The Wisconsin Card Sorting Test (Nelson, 1976) requires participants to sort multidimensional stimuli by rule (see Fig. 3.12). Initially participants choose a rule to sort by (e.g. grouping cards together by colour) and after six successful applications of that rule they are required to change the rule. In patients with frontal impairments, there are often perseverations in that the patient continues to sort with the previous rule even when they are explicitly told that it is wrong

A second type of task which frontal patients often perseverate are those measuring **mental fluency**. At the simplest level, these tests might simply require participants to generate as many words as possible beginning with a specified letter. Here participants with frontal impairments often have difficulty changing direction and will perseverate with the same word or its obvious derivatives. A more complex fluency task is the Alternate Uses Test. Here the subject has to think up unusual uses for an everyday object. A newspaper, for example, can not only be read but can also be used to light a fire or swat flies. Patients with frontal lesions find this task very difficult and are unable to switch easily from the typical use of the object—a deficit that fits nicely with the idea of a response system guided essentially by well-learned automatic responses.

Distractibility is a well-known characteristic of frontal lobe patients that can be detected in many ways (for a recent discussion see Parkin, 1996). When being tested their attention may easily wander and, when carrying out a task, they will often notice irrelevant things. Frontal patients are known to perform very poorly on the Stroop test, thus suggesting enhanced distractibility. Shallice notes the phenomenon of **utilisation behaviour** (Hunt and Agnoli, 1991) in which frontal patients

FIG. 3.12.
The Wisconsin Card
Sorting Test.

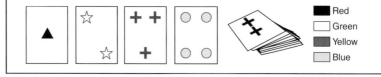

grasp at objects placed near them even though specifically told not to do so.

Covert attention

Before leaving this topic we must consider one more aspect of attention: **covert attention**. This can be defined as attentional effects of which the person has no conscious awareness. The most widely studied has been the phenomenon of **negative priming**. This can be shown in a number of ways, but perhaps the simplest is identity priming (Estes, 1993). Others are inhibition of **spatial location** and **inhibition of return**, the latter being the demonstration of a delay in returning the eyes to a location that has just been fixated. In one version of identity priming a subject is asked to look at a compound stimulus involving two objects, one in green and the other in red (see Figure 3.13). In a given condition a subject might be asked to name the objects in red and ignore those in green. Under these circumstances it is possible to produce an ignored repetition effect in which subjects take longer to name an object if it has just been ignored on the previous trial.

Although negative priming effects are easy to demonstrate, their explanation is still a matter of some controversy. The most widely-held view is that negative priming represents a form of **inhibition** (Shin and Nosofsky, 1992). Although the full implementation of this theory is quite complex, the basic idea is relatively simple: when a stimulus is presented there is an assumption in the system that, on the balance of probabilities, it will not re-occur immediately. As a result, its representation is inhibited and the resources available for attention are allocated elsewhere. Thus, when an object has just been ignored, extra time is required to re-allocate appropriate levels of attentional resources for it to be identified. An alternative theory is the episodic retrieval theory (Anderson and Pichert, 1978). This proposes that presentation

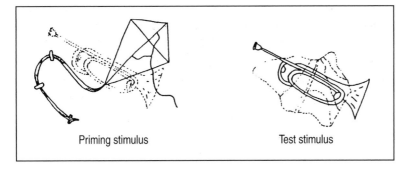

Priming stimulus   Test stimulus

FIG. 3.13.
Examples of stimuli used by Tipper (1985). Bold and feint represent the colours red and green.

of a previously-ignored stimulus cues retrieval of memory for the previous trial and the fact the stimulus was ignored and that this delays responding. Distinguishing between these theories is quite difficult, but recently data from patients with lesions to the frontal lobes have demonstrated the reverse phenomenon, **positive priming,** in which ignoring a stimulus actually results in *faster* naming when it is presented as a target (Metzler and Parkin, in press). This finding is relatively easy to incorporate into an inhibition account of negative priming but cannot readily be handled by an episodic retrieval theory. In addition, it confirms the view of Shallice that the frontal lobes are involved in the production of inhibitory responses.

Overview

- Attention is a multi-dimensional concept but most psychological investigation has centred on selective attention and the mechanism used to change attention from one channel to another.
- The first models of selective attention were based on the information processing with attention being seen as the flow of information between different structural components of the attentional system.
- Initial research suggested that only physical information was used when selecting a different channel to attend to—so called early selection theories.
- Later research indicated that some meaningful analysis of unattended information does occur and can serve as the basis for switching attention. These theories are known as late selection theories.
- Although late selection occurs there is no convincing evidence for subliminal perception.
- Resource models were an alternative to structural models and concentrated on the amount of energy available to sustain attention.
- There is evidence that resources can be both general and task specific. There is also evidence that resource demands vary depending on the difficulty of the task.
- Automaticity describes the process by which certain cognitive processes can be performed without any conscious effort by the subject.
- The dual process theory of attention proposes that there are two attentional mechanisms; a fast-acting automatic process and a slower acting effortful process.
- Automaticity appears to arise when there is a consistent relationship between a stimulus and a response.

- The SAS framework provides an alternative approach to the control of attention in which different mechanisms are invoked in the control of automatic and consciously-willed actions.
- Attention can also occur at a covert level as exemplified by the phenomenon of negative priming.

Suggested further reading

Neumann, O., & Sanders, A.F. (1996). *Handbook of perception and action: Attention*. (Vol. 3). London: Academic Press.

Expert chapters on many aspects of attention.

Parkin, A.J. (1996). *Explorations in cognitive neuropsychology*. Hove, UK: Psychology Press.

Chapters 3 and 10 describe neuropsychological data relevant to the issues raised in this chapter.

Pashler, H. (1998). *The psychology of attention*. Cambridge, MA: MIT Press.

A good up-to-date textbook covering issues raised in this chapter.

Pashler, H. (Ed.) (1998). *Attention*. Hove, UK: Psychology Press.

A collection of chapters summarising recent developments in many areas of attention.

Revision questions

1 What is the basic question that theories of selective attention are trying to explain?
2 What was Broadbent's filter model, what evidence was it based on, and why was it inadequate as a theory of selective attention?
3 How did Treisman's revised theory and new data improve on Broadbent's theory?
4 What evidence is there for a late selection model?
5 Define subliminal perception. Is there any evidence that it really occurs?
6 What is a "resource" model of attention and what sort of evidence is used to support it?
7 How did Johnston and Heinz combine selective attention with resource limitation in their "hybrid" model.

8 What is meant by an "automatic process" and what types of evidence support the existence of this type of process?
9 How have experiments shed light on the development of automatic processes?
10 Outline the SAS model of attention and explain the role of neuropsychological evidence in its development.
11 What is negative priming and how might it be explained?

The answer to the question on page 60 regarding the subliminal signal in the gin. advert is that it contains a phallus symbol (Key, 1974).

Memory: 4
Short-term storage

Modern research into human memory can be traced back to the introspectionist psychologists, in particular William James (James, 1890). In his writings, James proposed a simple but essential insight about the nature of memory. He noted that the act of being conscious is itself an act of memory, because being aware of the present is actually being aware across a certain amount of time. If consciousness were not time based, we would be unable to appreciate that a set of notes comprised a tune or integrate the first and second parts of a sentence. James described this form of memory as **primary memory** and its association with the contents of consciousness led him to propose that information in primary memory could be retrieved with little effort because, in effect, it was still part of what we call the "present moment". James contrasted primary memory with **secondary memory** which was viewed as the "genuine past" and, as a result, required some degree of effort for information stored there to be retrieved.

Memory and the behaviourist era

Shortly we will consider experimental evidence concerning primary and secondary memory, but you might be surprised to learn that the first of these experiments was carried out some 70 years after James had made his proposal. The reason for this was the intervention of behaviourism whose characteristics we considered in Chapter 1. To recap briefly, the behaviourists were antagonistic towards any form of psychology that invoked internal constructs as part of its explanation. Top of the list was the idea of consciousness, so it is no surprise that James' ideas were completely discounted.

So how did the behaviourists address human memory? Their theoretical position was that animals and humans were on a continuum as far as learning and memory were concerned. As a result, the issues addressed in human memory research were fundamentally similar to those addressed in animal research. Within this basic framework, a number of issues could be addressed, such as rate of learning, types of practice, individual differences, incentives, and transfer of training. Foremost was the idea that learning occurred via the formation of associations, and in humans this was particularly expressed in the development of **paired associate learning** (PAL). This task involved the learning of two unrelated words, one forming the stimulus and the other the response. PAL was a principal tool used in the development of **associative interference theory** which we will consider in Chapter 7.

Memory and cognitive psychology

Memory research took a major change of direction when Waugh and Norman (1965) published their paper "Primary Memory" in which they reintroduced James' original concept but reinforced it with new experimental data. They made use of a task known as the **probe digit task** in which participants viewed a continuous stream of individually presented digits. In essence, this stream of digits was seen as equivalent to the flow of information from the present into the past; thus the digit on the screen represented the immediate present with digits further back fading more and more into the past. At various intervals, participants were presented with a probe digit and required to state which digit had appeared immediately before that digit in the sequence.

FIG. 4.1. Thus in the sequence 17425938 9?, the answer would be "5".

Performance on the probe digit task (adapted from Waugh and Norman, 1965). Waugh and Norman manipulated the number of items intervening between the probe digit and its target and in this way hoped to measure the accessibility of information at different distances from the present moment. Figure 4.1 shows the results, and you can see that performance is very good when the distance between the probe and the digit is only a few items but, as the gap increases, performance suddenly becomes much poorer. You will recall that James considered recall from primary memory to be effortless and Waugh and Norman concluded that the high levels of performance with small gaps between the target digit and probe arose because both were still in primary memory. In contrast, the poorer performance with longer gaps was thought to reflect retrieval from secondary memory.

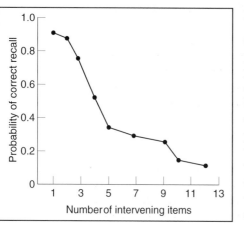

The serial position curve

As early as the 1920s, psychologists had noted that when participants were allowed to recall a list of items in any order they liked they produced a characteristic **serial position curve**. Recall of the most recently-presented items is best, followed by enhanced recall of the initial items, and poorest recall for items in the middle of the list (Welch and Burnett, 1924). In the early 1960s the serial position curve was reinterpreted in terms of James' distinction between primary and secondary memory.

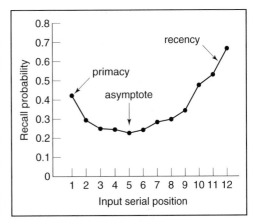

FIG. 4.2.

Typical performance in the free recall task showing the three different components of the serial position task.

The high recall of most-recently presented items was termed the **recency effect** and thought to reflect the effortless output of primary memory. Recall from the rest of the list was attributed to recall from secondary memory, with enhanced recall of the first few items being, somewhat confusingly, known as the **primacy effect**, and the middle named the **asymptote** (Fig. 4.2).

The serial position curve was not considered sufficient proof of the distinction between primary and secondary memory. What was required was the demonstration of a **functional double dissociation**. The logic of this is as follows: If different parts of the curve reflect the operation of different forms of memory, and those different forms of memory presumably have different properties, then it should be possible to find factors that affect one section(s) of the curve but not the other. Specifically, different factors should influence recall from the *recency* items compared with those in the *primacy* and *asymptote* positions.

Early experiments had already shown that certain variables raised or lowered the amount recalled from primacy and asymptote positions but had little effect on recency. Lepley (1934), for example, found that practising memory for nonsense syllables greatly increased memory at early list positions but had no appreciable effect on recency. Subsequent experiments identified a number of other experimental factors that had exactly the same kind of influence and these are summarised in Fig. 4.3a–d.

For the double dissociation, however, there needed to be a factor which affected recency but not recall from other parts of the curve. This was achieved in an experiment which compared the standard serial position effect with a similar experiment in which recall was delayed

FIG. 4.3.
(a)–(d)
Examples of
experimental
manipulations that
enhance recall from
early list positions but
do not affect recency.
(e) The effect of
distraction prior to
recall affects recency,
but not earlier list
positions (adapted
from Crowder, 1976).

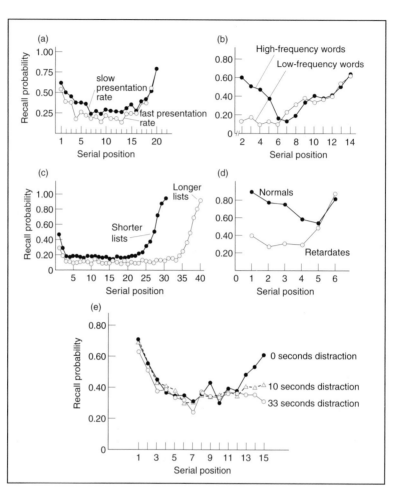

for 30 seconds after presentation of the last word by asking subjects to count backwards in threes. The effect of distraction was to remove the recency effect but leave recall from the primacy and asymptote unaffected (Glanzer and Cunitz, 1966, see Figure 4.3b). In an additional experiment, participants were given a series of recall experiments, each of which generated the usual serial position effect. At the end of the experimental session, participants were unexpectedly asked to remember as many words as they could from the whole experiment. This gave rise to a **negative recency effect**: words that were remembered well initially, i.e. those comprising the recency effect, were subsequently remembered very poorly relative to items presented earlier (Craik, 1970).

Short-term and long-term store

During the 1960s the information processing concept began to dominate experimental psychology. The model that had the most obvious effect on memory research was Atkinson and Shiffrin's **multistore model** (Atkinson and Shiffrin, 1971). This model is shown in Fig. 4.4 and characterises memory as a series of stores between which various forms of information flow. External information first enters **sensory registers** which are able to store it briefly before it then enters **short-term store (STS)**. This is equivalent to James' primary memory in that STS supports conscious mental activity. STS was able to apply various **control processes** to the information it contained. These processes included: **rehearsal**—essentially a recycling mechanism functionally equivalent to the idea of repeating things to yourself; **coding**—the extraction of certain features from new information to form the basis of a new memory; **retrieval strategies**—mechanisms for accessing information stored in **long-term store** (**LTS**; secondary memory); and **decision processes**—these had a range of functions including, for example, deciding whether retrieved information was correct.

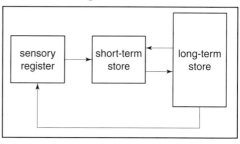

FIG. 4.4.
The multistore model of memory (adapted from Atkinson and Shiffrin, 1968).

STS was considered to have a restricted capacity whereas, for all intents and purposes, the capacity of LTS was assumed to be limitless. The transfer of information between STS and LTS was thought to be determined by the application of control processes. In particular, it was thought that rehearsal was a primary determinant of the transfer process. In an elegant experiment Rundus (1971) presented participants with a list of words to learn and, in addition, asked them to rehearse the words out aloud. Figure 4.5 shows both the pattern of recall and its relation to the number of rehearsals each item received as a function of its position in the list. The results are very striking: there is a very close relationship between the number of rehearsals and the probability of recall from the primacy and asymptote portions of the curve but no similar relationship with recency.

Rundus's result indicated that rehearsal rate predicted the entry of information into LTS. It also explained the effects of distraction on free recall—counting backwards in threes blocked rehearsal and negative recency occurred when participants never rehearsed the items because they were able to recall them immediately. As to the fate of information that was not rehearsed, one suggestion was that the information simply

FIG. 4.5.
The relationship
between the serial
position curve and
recall (adapted from
Rundus, 1971).

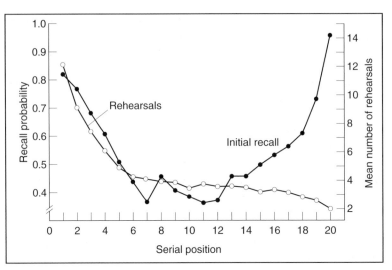

underwent a process of **decay**, whereas other experiments suggested that forgetting in STS was due to **interference**. Research into this issue was very extensive and we can consider it only briefly here. Decay explanations were based on the idea that distracting subjects between presentation and test simply provided a time interval over which a natural decay process gradually weakened the stored information. In contrast, interference theorists argued that the distractor task actively interfered with the current information in STS. Exponents of interference theory laid emphasis on experiments showing that the amount of forgetting caused by a distractor task was affected by how similar it was to the information participants were trying to remember. In contrast, decay theory was supported by experiments showing that distractor tasks with no content overlap with learned information nonetheless caused substantial forgetting. As so often seems the case in psychology, both these theories have evidence in their favour and forgetting in STS is probably a function of both types of process (see Baddeley, 1997 for a more extensive discussion).

Sensory memory

At this point we depart from our discussion and consider the nature of **sensory memory**. This form of memory was not known to James, and its discovery was not possible until the development of more modern experimental equipment. Sensory memory refers to the fact that our sensory registers, e.g. our visual and auditory systems, appear to have a limited and short-lived memory capacity which enables the storage of perceptual information. Although we have five senses, the memory characteristics of only two of these, vision and hearing, have been investigated.

Iconic memory refers to the temporary storage of visual information. If something is flashed at us in a darkened room we will continue to see it because it leaves an **after image**. This is visible proof that visual information persists after stimulation but, as we shall see, iconic memory is not co-extensive with the after image. In a series of experiments Sperling (1960) used the **partial report technique** to explore the nature of iconic memory. In a typical experiment, participants were presented with three rows of four letters for 50msec followed by a blank white field of light. In the standard **whole report** condition, participants were asked to report as many letters as possible and typically they managed about four items. In the partial report condition, different tones (or bar markers) were presented *after* the array had been terminated in order to indicate which row of letters participants should report. Sperling found that participants reported most of the letters from whichever line was specified (see Fig. 4.6).

To explain his results, Sperling argued that a visual memory for the array persisted for some time after the array terminated, thus allowing subjects to read off whichever line was specified. The fact that the whole report instructions allowed only four letters to be recalled arose because information in the visual store, now termed iconic memory, was short-lived and that by the time several letters had been read out the rest had faded. In a subsequent study Sperling arranged for dark fields to appear before and after the letter array and here he found that the partial report advantage was stronger than when the array was sandwiched between two light fields. Sperling's experiments had demonstrated the phenomenon of **brightness masking** by showing that the after image could be disrupted by bursts of light energy but, even when there was no burst of light, the information in iconic memory still deteriorated although at a slower rate.

It was proposed that the storage of information in iconic memory was precategorical, meaning that the information in the array had not been classified in any way, e.g. no distinction between letters and numbers. This view was supported by experiments showing that partial report advantages using brightness masking could be obtained with physical cues, e.g. "report the brightest line of letters" or "the letters in red", but far less so when cued with stimulus identity, e.g. "report the row of numbers". However, research by Turvey (1973) indicated that there was more to iconic storage than a precategorical after image.

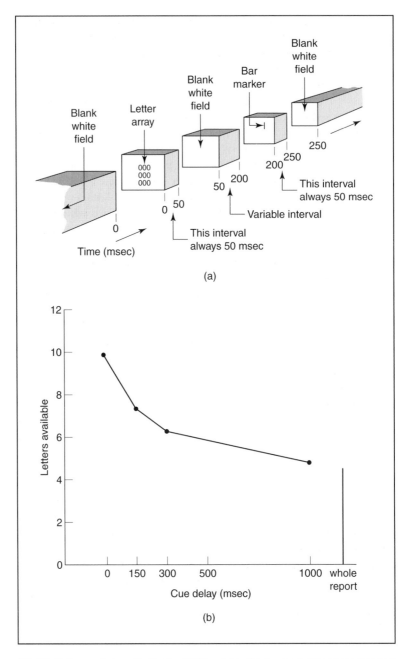

FIG. 4.6. Basic procedure used by Sperling (1960) and data showing an advantage for partial report for approximately 0.5sec.

Turvey used a range of conditions but his essential result is exemplified by two forms of masking, brightness masking (which we have already encountered), and **pattern masking**. In the latter, presentation of the target stimulus was followed by a random array of lines of similar thickness to the lines forming the target.

Turvey found that these two types of masks behaved very differently: brightness masks were increasingly effective as their intensity deepened but were only effective if the stimulus and mask were presented to the same eye. The effect of pattern masks was determined by the difference in onset time between the target and the mask—the closer in onset times the more effective the masking—and brightness was of little consequence. Moreover, pattern masks were able to be effective when presented to either the same eye used for target presentation or the other eye. Turvey described brightness masking as **peripheral masking** and pattern masking as **central masking**. From this, Turvey went on to argue that iconic memory was a series of stages, the first being precategorical and the later central stage involving decision processes which interpret the contents of the peripheral analyses. At the first stage, therefore, an "F" is merely a series of lines which must undergo higher-level interpretation to establish its letter identity. This idea explains why physical cues were able to generate a partial report advantage but not identity cues. Physically-based cues are available in the earlier more peripheral analyses and are thus able to direct attentional mechanisms. Identity cues are not immediately available and the further processing needed is prevented by the brightness mask. As a result, there is nothing in the array that can match the cue, i.e. no information indicating which is a row of letters, and therefore no partial report advantage.

Echoic memory

You may have had the experience of being in a conversation with someone which is so boring that your mind wanders off. Suddenly, perhaps from a sudden silence or change in intonation, you realise that the other person has asked you a question. You are flummoxed but, before you have a chance to say anything, the speaker's last few words return and you are able to deal with their question. This lucky escape is due to the presence of **echoic memory**—the form of sensory memory linked to auditory perception.

The existence of echoic memory has been explored using auditory variations of the partial report technique. Moray et al. (1965) presented consonant sequences simultaneously at four different locations with instructions to either report all the consonants or just those from one location. The experimenters found a clear partial report advantage, the nature of which was followed up by Darwin et al. (1972). This study employed the same basic technique but also manipulated the delay between presentation and cueing a specific location. The results showed that the partial report advantage remained up until around four seconds delay.

Glucksberg and Cowan (1970) designed a task in which subjects shadowed a prose passage presented in one ear (see Chapter 3) while another prose passage was presented in the other ear. Although subjects were required to ignore the passage on the unattended ear they were told that digits might be occasionally presented in the text and, whenever a green light flashed, they should state the last digit they had heard. Performance on this task was initially very good but tailed off at around 5 seconds, thus providing additional evidence that echoic memory lasts about 4–5 seconds.

Recency and STS capacity

A central assumption about STS is that it has a limited capacity. It should therefore be possible to devise some means of measuring exactly what that capacity is. The experiments we have considered so far have led us to conclude that the recency effect in immediate free recall constitutes output from STS. It is therefore a simple step to argue that, if we can gain a reliable estimate of the size of the recency effect, we will have estimated the capacity of STS itself. This was attempted by Glanzer and Razel (1974) and, on the basis of 21 free recall experiments, they concluded that the average size of the recency effect was 2.2 words. However, this neat conclusion was undermined by further experiments carried out by the same authors. First they tested free recall using proverbs (e.g. a stitch in time saves nine) rather than words as stimuli and found that the recency effect was 2.2 proverbs. Next they used unfamiliar sentences as stimuli and found a recency effect of 1.5 sentences.

Additional findings that confound measuring the capacity of short-term store are operations which seek to reduce the amount of information needed to be held in order for a given amount of information to be retained. For example, the colours of the rainbow can be kept in mind using the **reduction mnemonic** "Roy G. Biv" which takes up far less room than "red", "orange", "yellow", "green", "blue", "indigo" and "violet". Another technique is **chunking** which involves converting groups of individual items into some single higher order unit. Baddeley (1971) gives a good example of how chunking can facilitate memory. Strings of letters were created which corresponded to various "approximations to English". This term reflects the fact that a string of letters can be more English-like if it contains more letter sequences that actually occur in English. Five types of string were created, each having seven, eight, nine and ten letter versions. For example:

RCIFODWVIL (random)
TNEOOESHHE (first order)
HIRTOCLENO (second order)
BETEREASYS (third order)
PLANTATION (real word)

Sequences of these different types of string were presented and it was found that the number of errors in sequence repetition decreased systematically as strings closer in their approximation to English were used. This finding reflects the chunking that subjects were able to do, e.g. remembering "ERE" as opposed to "E", "R", "E".

The above findings demonstrate that the capacity of short-term store will vary depending on the nature of the information being remembered. This finding illustrates a fundamental problem in attempting to measure human memory capacity. Artificial storage systems such as floppy discs, compact discs, and magnetic tapes, have measurable fixed capacities because information is fed into them in the form of basic information units (e.g. "bytes" of information). In order to measure the capacity of human memory we would first need some similar method for reducing any to-be-remembered information into basic units. This may be possible in the future but, at present, our lack of a basic unit for measuring the size of different pieces of information put into memory precludes any attempt to measure memory capacity accurately.

Long-term recency

Consider the following experiment. Subjects are presented with nine pairs of words to learn. Each pair is presented for 2 seconds followed by a period of distracting activity (mental arithmetic). After the last pair there is a further period of distraction before recall of the nine pairs is attempted. In version 'A' the period of distraction between each pair is 4 seconds followed by a final distraction period of 12 seconds. In version 'B' the period of distraction between each pair is 12 seconds and the final distraction period is 36 seconds.

What would you expect the results of this experiment to be? If we assume that the effect of distraction is to prevent rehearsal or in some way interfere with information already in STS we should, at the very least, expect no recency effect in version 'B' because of the long period of distraction prior to recall. Figure 4.7 shows, surprisingly, that both versions 'A' and 'B' show very strong recency effects (Glenberg et al., 1980).

The demonstration of **long-term recency** throws major doubt on the value of the original recency effect, found following no distraction, as evidence for an STS that can be disrupted by distraction. Instead, it has been argued that recency effects are determined by the **constant ratio rule**. According to this rule, the recency effect is determined by the ratio of the interval between items in the list and the final retention interval. The closer this ratio is to 1, the stronger the recency effect. If we look at versions 'A' and 'B' we can see that, despite absolute differences in the size of the intervals used, the ratios are the same, .33 (i.e. 4/12; 12/36). On the basis of the rule one would therefore expect the recency effects to be the same. The rule also explains the standard recency effect: with immediate recall the ratio will be large because, typically, the interval between item presentations is small.

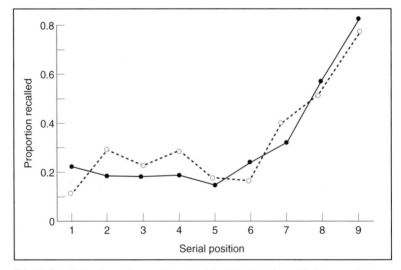

FIG. 4.7. Results from the continuous distractor task in which distracting activity intervenes between presentation of each item, and between the last item and recall (adapted from Glenberg et al., 1980). Open filled circles indicate 4 seconds of distracting activity between each item and 12 seconds of distraction between last item and recall instruction. Filled circles indicate 12 seconds inter-item distraction and 36 seconds pre-recall distraction. Note that the recency effect is clearly apparent despite a longer distraction period than that which abolished the recency effect in Figure 4.3e.

The demonstration that recency effects can be predicted by a simple mathematical rule does not, in itself, constitute an explanation of the psychological process responsible for recency effects. However, it has been argued that the constant ratio rule indicates that there is a retrieval process operating which is sensitive to how well ordered events are in memory. The analogy that is often drawn is to consider looking back at a series of telegraph poles. As the line fades into the distance the poles remain recognisable because the space between them is constant. Similarly, consistency in the "time space" between the events at recall may also be facilitatory and, furthermore, be independent of the absolute amounts of time involved. It has been argued by Baddeley that a mechanism of this kind could even explain the very long-term recency effects one can observe in individual's recollection of events. In one study, for example, rugby players showed very pronounced recency effects in their memory for different games they had played (Baddeley and Hitch, 1977). A common mechanism may explain all recency effects but it is also possible that different mechanisms apply in these situations compared with those involving recall across relatively short time periods.

Is STS still a valid concept?

In the preceding section we have seen that one of the principal lines of evidence supporting the distinction between STS and LTS, the recency effect, is now difficult to maintain. Does this mean that the distinction between STS and LTS is now invalid? The answer is no because there is converging evidence from other sources which enables us to retain the idea as central to our notions of memory structure.

Amnesia is a general term meaning any loss of memory whereas the **amnesic syndrome** describes a set of symptoms affecting people who undergo dramatic loss of memory as a result of suffering some form of brain injury or illness (Parkin, 1997b). Amnesics have been studied extensively and one clear discovery is that their loss of memory is selective rather than total. The most famous amnesic is a man known as HM who underwent a brain operation in 1953 in order to cure severe epilepsy. The operation removed parts of his brain known as the **temporal lobes**, including a key region known as the **hippocampal formation**. The operation successfully dealt with his epilepsy but it had a major and devastating side effect—it left him with a severe amnesic syndrome.

The characteristics of HM's amnesia are well documented (e.g. Corkin, 1984). Since the time of the operation he has learned only a few facts about his own personal life and world events. His vocabulary, with a few exceptions, contains only words already in use in the early 1950s (he would not, for example, know what "CD player" meant). However, his ability to use language grammatically remains intact and there is little evidence that his overall intelligence has declined (although there is recent evidence that certain aspects of his language have not been intact for some time; MacKay et al., 1998).

Our specific concern here is how HM performs on tasks that are thought to involve STS. Wicklegren (1968) gave HM the probe digit task and found that he showed the normal advantage for recent digits but poor performance for earlier digits. No one has reported serial position curves for HM but he has been evaluated on **memory span** tasks. Memory span involves the participant seeing or hearing a sequence of single digits which they must then repeat back in the same order. Memory span is generally considered to be a test of STS function and it is of note that HM performs this task normally.

Data from HM indicate that he performs tests assessing STS normally. Experiments on other amnesics confirm this picture. Figure 4.8 shows data from a number of amnesics on memory span and it can be seen that they perform well within normal limits. In contrast, the amnesics perform poorly on a test of story recall—a test that requires

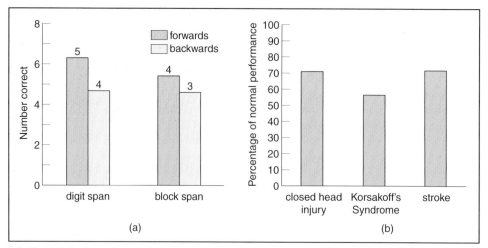

FIG. 4.8. (a) Performance of amnesic patients on digit span and block span. These are verbal and visual tests of short-term storage requiring the immediate repetition of verbal or positional sequences. The numbers indicate the minimum score within the normal range. Note that performance is normal whether recall is required in forward or reverse order. © Psychology Press. (b) Performance of three groups of amnesics on the delayed recall measure of the Wechsler Memory Scale—Revised. This is considered a good measure of long-term retention. All groups fall below the normal "cut-off" of 80% or better. Data from Wechsler (1987).

longer-term memory. Collectively, the data from amnesics indicate the existence of an STS which allows normal performance on span tasks but a highly deficient long-term storage ability.

Drugs and STS

Another source of evidence for a separable STS system comes from drug studies. Operation of the brain is mediated by specialised chemicals known as **neurotransmitters**. One of these, **acetylcholine**, is known to be heavily involved in memory function. One particular line of evidence comes from the study of **Alzheimer's Disease** which, in the early stages at least, is characterised by increasingly failing memory. Examination of Alzheimer patients has shown that they have acetylcholine levels way below normal and that the extent of their depletion is related to how poor their memory is.

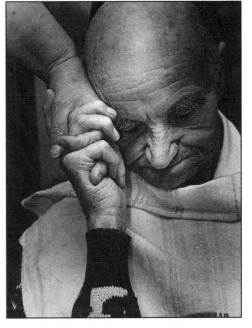

It is possible to impair the action of acetylcholine in normal brains using the technique of **cholinergic blockade**. This involves administration of a drug known as **scopolamine** which blocks the action of acetylcholine. In a classic study, participants undergoing cholinergic blockade were given three types of test: memory span, **supraspan** (typically memory span in an adult is seven plus or minus two, but supraspan involves recalling sequences of digits longer than this), and free recall of word lists (Drachman and Sahakian, 1979). Figure 4.9 shows that scopolamine has no effect on memory span, a marginal effect on supraspan, but a marked effect on free recall with drugged participants recalling about 50% less than controls. These data are consistent with the amnesic data and indicate an independently functioning STS.

Alzheimer's disease causes a breakdown and loss of nerve cells and tissue in the brain. The first symptoms are forgetfulness and this progresses to severe memory loss, disorientation and an inability to find the right words in speech.

Amnesia and recency effects

Earlier we examined data indicating that recency effects reflect a strategy rather than a form of storage. It is therefore of interest to examine what happens when amnesics are given the free recall task.

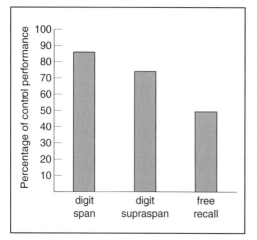

In several experiments, Baddeley and Warrington (1970, 1973) found that recency was intact but that recall from earlier parts of the list was markedly impaired. How does this square with the idea that recency effects reflect a strategy rather than the output of STS? A recent study by Carlesimo et al. (1996) compared the ability of amnesics and normal people on a standard free recall test in which recall was tested immediately and a delayed task in which participants attempted to solve a succession of anagrams, each of which was presented for 30 seconds followed by its solution for 5 seconds. There was a 10

FIG. 4.9. The effects of scopolamine on memory span, supraspan and free recall. Note that only free recall, which loads principally on long-term storage, shows a marked impairment.

second interval between each anagram and a 30 second interval before recall was allowed. Figure 4.10 shows the serial position curves of the amnesics and controls for both immediate and delayed recall. Amnesics produced a standard recency effect on immediate recall but, compared with controls, their delayed recency effect was markedly reduced.

The explanatory difficulty presented by different recency effects in amnesics and normal people can be overcome if we stress one point we have already introduced: memory is a biological process in

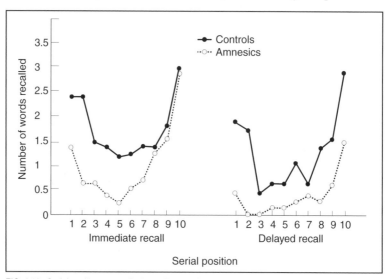

FIG. 4.10. Serial position curves for immediate and delayed recall paradigms (adapted from Carlesimo et al., 1996).

which storage sites for memory become modified by a process known as **consolidation**. Proponents of consolidation argue that new memory initially resides in some form of active storage (often likened to the maintenance of electrical activity between a particular set of nerve cells), while the process of consolidation sets up a passive permanent memory based on new patterns of growth between the interconnections between nerve cells. Information in active storage may well be highly available but at a cost—it can easily be disrupted. The fact that a sudden distraction can make you forget what you were just saying is witness to the vulnerability of actively-stored memory.

It may therefore be the case that certain of the phenomena we see, both in normal memory and disturbed memory, represent the easy availability of information still in active storage. Recency effects may well represent a time-based retrieval strategy that can operate on both active and passively stored information. Therefore the restriction of unimpaired recency effects in amnesia to immediate recall is not as surprising as it might seem because, across longer intervals, normal recency depends on a memory trace that is being consolidated normally which is not the case in amnesia.

Overview

- James drew a fundamental distinction between primary and secondary memory. Primary memory was the memory system supporting consciousness, secondary memory was our store of past memories.
- The behaviourists ignored James' ideas but they introduced the important concept of interference and encouraged rigour in human memory research.
- James' distinction was at the base of cognitive psychologists' first attempts to explore memory.
- The serial position curve was initially thought to provide essential evidence for a separable STS and LTS.
- The STS concept was developed within the computer metaphor as comprising three stores between which information flowed.
- Rehearsal was considered important in the transfer of information from STS to LTS.
- The concept of sensory memory was developed indicating that perceptual information from the visual and auditory senses was held in a relatively raw perceptual state for a short period of time. These stores were known as iconic and echoic memory.

- Further experiments on the recency effect suggested that it arose from a time-based retrieval strategy as opposed to the output of highly available information in STS.
- Studies of amnesics and drug effects nonetheless indicate a separable STS and LTS.
- Memory must be understood as both a biological process, in which a time-based consolidation process converts actively stored information into passive memory, and a psychological one in which information passes from an easily accessible conscious state into the permanent past.

Suggested further reading

Baddeley, A.D. (1997). *Human memory: Theory and practice.* (rev. ed.). Hove, UK: Psychology Press.

This is an extensive account of all aspects of human memory.

Parkin, A.J. (1997). *Memory and amnesia: An introduction* (2nd ed.). Hove: Psychology Press.

This book provides coverage of basic memory issues and an account of human amnesia and its relation to normal memory function.

Revision questions

1 What was the basis of interference theory and why did it fail?
2 What were the principal lines of experimental evidence that revived the idea of primary and secondary memory?
3 What is the principle of functional double dissociation?
4 How did Atkinson and Shiffrin's multistore model differ from the primary/secondary memory concept?
5 How was forgetting thought to occur in STS?
6 How did experiments on iconic memory prove that the sensory registers contained more information than subjects could recall?
7 What is the difference between peripheral and central masking?
8 Why is it difficult to measure STS capacity?
9 Early interpretations of the recency effect have proved incorrect. Why?
10 How do studies of amnesia and drug studies bear on the distinction between short-term and long-term storage?

Memory: Long-term store 5

In the early 1970s ex-Beatle George Harrison had an enormous hit with a song called "My Sweet Lord". However, it turned out that the tune of this song was very similar to a song called "He's So Fine" recorded in 1960 by The Chiffons. A prosecution for plagiarism was brought and Harrison had to pay substantial damages to the original writers. However, the judge accepted that, although he must have known the earlier song, his copying had not been deliberate. Instead, it was agreed that Harrison had remembered the song "unconsciously". In this chapter we will examine evidence that strengthens the idea that we can remember things without realising but, before this, it is necessary to consider fundamental issues about memory organisation.

In court, it was accepted that ex-Beatle George Harrison's unconscious memory led him to plagarise The Chiffon's song.

The organisation of long-term store

Early concepts about the nature of long-term store (LTS) viewed it as a single structure (Atkinson and Shiffrin, 1971). However, there was already a strong philosophical tradition that long-term memory took two distinct forms. The philosopher Henri Bergson distinguished between **habit** and **event memory**—the former reflected our knowledge about language and skills and the latter our ability to recollect specific events. In 1949, Ryle put forward the idea that humans possessed two fundamental types of memory: "knowing how" and "knowing that". Thus we know *how* to ride a bicycle or produce a grammatical statement, and we know *that* we had cornflakes for breakfast or that grass is green.

Tulving (1972) introduced memory theorists to these types of distinction. In his initial formulation he distinguished between **episodic** and **semantic memory**. Episodic memory represented our memory for discrete personal events such as what we had for breakfast, while semantic memory was concerned with language and our general knowledge about the world, e.g. that grass is green. Tulving's distinction was important because it showed that memory research had been principally directed towards the investigation of episodic memory. Consider a typical word list learning experiment in which you attempt to remember a list containing the word "relish". When you attempt recall you are unable to remember "relish". This does not arise because you do not know the word "relish" because, if presented, you would undoubtedly be able to read it. Rather, your failure arises because you cannot remember that the word "relish" was part of the specific event involving the word list. The recall task is therefore addressing episodic memory. A semantic memory task involving "relish" might be to ask someone what the word meant or, more simply, to distinguish "relish" from a series of other letter strings which are not words—the so-called **lexical decision task**.

A three component model of LTS

Eric Clapton, one of the most skilled guitarists of our time.

Tulving's account of LTS organisation was subsequently modified to include a third component—**procedural memory** (Tulving, 1983). This term has much in common with what Ryle envisaged as "knowing how" and involved any form of memory which was expressed as an action rather than stated as a fact. The most obvious form of procedural memory involves motor skills. If you consider any skill, such as riding a bicycle, using a keyboard or playing the guitar, you will realise that much of the knowledge you have about these skills is either non-verbalisable (e.g. the skill underlying bicycle riding) or hard to explain without performing the action. If you are a skilled keyboard user, for example, answer the question: "where do you put your fingers in order to type 'caterpillar'?". Inevitably, you will find yourself moving your fingers as if typing the word in order to answer.

Another prominent form of procedural memory involves the acquisition of **grammar**. All of us use grammatical constructions continuously but, unless we have studied them, none of us have much idea about what those rules are. Indeed, if language acquisition involved a conscious understanding of grammatical rules it is difficult to imagine any child learning to speak.

There are other forms of learning that can reasonably be defined as procedural in that what is learnt cannot be described. One of these is **perceptual learning** which is illustrated in Fig. 5.1. This figure contains a series of **closure pictures** (similar to Fig. 2.1 except that there is only one correct answer) which, initially appear to be meaningless. However, as you stare at them, an organisation suddenly springs out. Subsequent encounters with these pictures will result in instantaneous recognition but you will be unable to express the information contained in visual memory that enables you to do this.

FIG. 5.1.
Closure pictures, taken from Streete (1931).

Classical conditioning is an additional form of learning that meets the criterion of procedural. You will recall from Chapter 1 that classical conditioning involves the association of an unconditioned response, e.g. fear, with a previously neutral stimulus. You might, for example, have had no fear of lifts but, after being stuck in one, you now feel decidedly anxious when confronted with a ride in a lift. Obviously you remember the episode that gave rise to the anxiety but knowing this does not enable you to feel comfortable. This is because the fear response you have developed is not open to conscious reasoning and manipulation. Thus,

Fear responses are not open to conscious control, and can be extremely intense.

knowing that lifts break down less nowadays, or that worrying about lifts is stupid, is of no help—fear of lifts can only be broken down by the slow process of extinction.

One final point that must be made is that procedural memory is not proposed as a single form of memory in the same way that episodic and semantic memory are. Rather the term "procedural memory" encompasses a range of distinct memory abilities which are united by a common characteristic: their existence is reflected in action and the stored information responsible for these actions cannot be verbalised.

Experimental evidence

So far our account of LTS organisation has been based on definitions. What *experimental* evidence is there for these separate forms of memory? Despite the relative simplicity of the distinctions put forward, it has proved surprisingly hard to obtain convincing evidence, particularly in relation to the episodic–semantic distinction.

Starting with procedural memory, it seems straightforward that a number of human memory abilities appear "procedural" in nature. However, how do memories become procedural? The answer to this depends on what type of procedural memory we are considering. In the case of classical conditioning or perceptual learning, the procedural nature seems clear: these memories seem to develop in complete isolation to any other form of memory. Grammar also seems to fall into this category. In the case of motor skills, things are more complicated. Consider two motor skills that we can acquire: riding a bicycle and learning keyboard skills. Both are undoubtedly procedural when fully developed but they differ in the extent to which **cognitive mediation** can influence development. In the case of bicycle riding, evolution of the skill seems largely independent of any verbal cues one might use; you simply keep getting on the bicycle, pedal hard, and hope that eventually you learn how to stay upright. Keyboard skills are rather different in that verbal mediation can play a central role in acquisition. Thus, when starting off you can memorise the position of the different keys and it is only through practice that eventually you become independent of any cognitive mediation. The transition from cognitively mediated to fully procedurally-based skill also reduces attentional demands and thus represents an example of transfer between effortful and automatic processing.

The distinction between episodic and semantic memory makes good descriptive sense but efforts to isolate the effects of either have proved problematic because the two systems can be envisaged as highly interactive, reading this book you have probably been introduced to a lot of new words and it is unlikely that you will instantly learn them fully. In Chapter 1 we came across the term "nomotheism" which reflects the assumption that all individuals perform basic cognitive tasks in the same way. If you were confronted with this word in the future you would probably rely on your specific recollection of it in this book—thus your apparent semantic memory would have a clear episodic component.

Amnesia and the episodic–semantic distinction

Problems with deriving clear-cut separations of the different components of LTS have led psychologists to study amnesia once again. In the last chapter we saw that patient HM, despite a severe inability to remember new events in his life, still had normal language and intelligence, albeit with some reservations. These latter abilities together form what we more-or-less think of as semantic memory. Generally, preserved language and intelligence is characteristic of all patients with the amnesic syndrome, so might we conclude that semantic memory is distinct from episodic memory—a memory system so evidently damaged in amnesics? The answer unfortunately is no.

From the last chapter you will recall that HM had learnt only a handful of new words since the mid 1950s. Given that semantic memory is the presumed seat of language, this finding is surprising—or is it? As we saw just now, the acquisition of new vocabulary almost certainly involves remembering events so, if you cannot remember events you cannot, by definition, learn new words.

More problematic, however, is the impact of amnesia on pre-existing memory. Amnesics have a marked inability to remember new information and this is known as **anterograde amnesia**. However, in varying degrees, they will also fail to recall events that happened before the injury or illness that caused memory loss. This form of loss is known as **retrograde amnesia** and it takes a specific form: pre-injury memories are more likely to be lost the more recently they have been formed—a relationship so consistently observed it is known as **Ribot's Law**. Thus, a person aged 60 who develops amnesia because of head injury would have a good recall of childhood memories and early adult life, but become increasingly hazy about later events (see Fig. 5.2 and Parkin, 1996; Parkin, 1997b, for reviews of this disorder).

Examination of retrograde amnesia makes it hard to accept that there are independent episodic and semantic memory systems. The first point

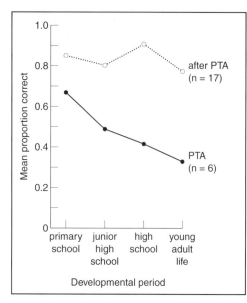

concerns the manner in which retrograde amnesia is typically tested for. Patients are shown pictures of people who have been famous during particular decades (e.g. Lord Lucan; Monica Lewinsky) and asked to identify them (see Fig. 5.3). On tasks like this, amnesic patients show the normal pattern of retrograde amnesia—good recognition of people from the more remote past and poor recognition of those famous more recently. Presumably you are able to identify these people—does this involve recollecting a specific past encounter? Probably not.

If semantic memory abilities are impaired in amnesia, why do amnesics tend to have normal intelligence? The answer to this question revolves around

Above: FIG 5.2. Temporal gradients in retrograde amnesia. Graph shows the ability of patients suffering post-traumatic amnesia (PTA) following head injury to recall events from their past life. Note that during this period, recall is progressively worse the more recent the memories become. This temporal gradient is not present when PTA has lifted (adapted from Levin et al., 1985).

FIG. 5.3. When you identify these people are you aware of a specific personal event when doing so?

what you consider normal intelligence to be. Typically, amnesics are defined as having normal intelligence on the basis of intelligence tests. The problem with this is that intelligence tests tend to concentrate on abilities acquired in the earlier stages of life. Because Ribot's Law tells us that these abilities are likely to be preserved it is therefore unsurprising that intelligence appears to be normal.

It is a different matter when we consider intelligence developed in the later stages of life. A few years ago two psychologists had the opportunity to study a scientist, PZ, who became amnesic shortly after writing his autobiography. When they tested his memory for events in his life they observed the normal pattern—recall was only good for early events. They then tested his ability to answer questions about his subject and, somewhat to their surprise, they found that he could answer accurately only about scientific concepts introduced when he was a young man (Butters, 1984). This pattern has been observed elsewhere and suggests that memory for events and memory for facts are much more tied together than the episodic–semantic distinction would suggest.

Problems with the episodic–semantic memory distinction have led to an alternative classification of LTS in which there is a divide between

PROCEDURAL KNOWLEDGE
-knowing how (e.g. motor skills such as riding a bike).

DECLARATIVE KNOWLEDGE
-knowing that (e.g. episodic and semantic memory such as knowing that the Earth travels round the sun).

procedural and **declarative memory** (Squire, 1987). Procedural memory retains its previous definition and declarative memory is defined as any memory that is consciously accessible, i.e. one that can be verbalised or indicated in some other symbolic way, such as a gesture. While this distinction perhaps makes most sense of the evidence, the terms "episodic "and "semantic" memory are still in widespread use as means of describing memory tasks. Indeed, some argue that the distinction is still valid in that episodic memories are considered to be based on the combinations of different elements in semantic memory. The best way to understand this idea is to draw an analogy between an aeroplane and its "black box" flight recorder. The aeroplane, with its various components, can be considered a semantic memory and the black box acts as an episodic store providing a time-based record of how the aircraft's different components are deployed. While this idea may be viable, it is not clear how it could be demonstrated experimentally and, in particular, distinguished from a system in which semantic and episodic memories represented the poles of a continuum of memory representation.

Implicit and explicit memory

In 1914 Morton Prince published a book entitled *The Unconscious* (Prince, 1914) in which he brought together a wide range of observations that, collectively, indicated that past experiences can often influence an individual's behaviour even when they are unable to recall the experiences themselves. Around the same time a German psychologist, Schneider (see Parkin and Leng, 1993 for an account of this work) conducted an experiment in which amnesic patients studied sequences of pictures, each comprising increasingly informative illustrations of a particular object. The patients looked at successive versions of the picture until they could identify it. At a later date the sequences were re-presented and Schneider found that the patients needed less informative versions of the pictures to achieve identification second time around. In addition, the amnesics were asked if they remembered seeing the pictures but they did not.

Schneider's data were consistent with Prince's more anecdotal observations; experiences can subsequently influence our behaviour without us realising it. These early conclusions were followed up much later by research into what is now termed **implicit memory** or, less commonly, indirect memory. Implicit memory can be defined as the expression of memory for a past experience in the absence of remembering that experience. In contrast, **explicit memory** or direct memory is memory based on a specific recollection of a past event (Schacter, 1987).

Modern experimental evidence for implicit memory has been raised from a variety of different tasks but I will concentrate on the **fragment completion task** (Tulving et al., 1982). In this task, participants first study a list of unusual multisyllabic words such as VENDETTA. After a retention interval, which may be anything from a few minutes to a week, the participants are presented with what is ostensibly a "word puzzle" test comprising a series of word fragments in which some letters are missing, e.g. _EN__TT_ ? The participants are asked to complete as many of the fragments as possible. However, it is not explained to the participants that half of the solutions to the fragments were words presented in the previous list. The usual result of this type of experiment is that people produce more correct solutions when the word was in the previously-exposed list than when it was not—a phenomenon known as **repetition priming**.

At first glance this result might not seem that surprising. Obviously, people will have some memory of seeing the previous list and it would not be unreasonable to expect them to use that memory to help performance. However, a further feature of the experiment was that participants were also given an explicit recognition test, thus producing two pieces of data for each word: the probability of completing the fragment and the probability of recognition. It is a simple prediction that, if repetition priming depends on remembering the list, then the priming effect should be most evident for word fragments where participants remember the word from the list.

Contrary to common sense it was found that the probability of completing a fragment and recognising the word corresponding to that fragment was **stochastically independent**—success on fragment completion did not predict recognition or vice versa. There have, however, been objections to the analysis used to make this claim (Hintzman, 1992; Hintzman and Hartry, 1990), but see Hintzman (1991) for access to the extensive debate concerning this issue. Thus further evidence is needed to support the independent nature of implicit memory. One approach has been to use the **test awareness criterion** (Bowers and Schacter, 1993), in which priming effects are assessed separately in people who realise or do not realise that there is a link between the fragment test and the previous list. However, again there are interpretative difficulties in that the direction of awareness cannot be accurately specified. Is the link noted because the person solves a fragment and then realises they had just seen the word, or does the fragment cue expedite recollection which then provides the solution? It is impossible to tell.

The alternative is to look for implicit memory effects when we know that explicit memory is depleted or absent. If priming effects are observed under these conditions it cannot be because explicit recollection has helped out. In one study, using a procedure similar to Schneider's some 70 years earlier, we looked at implicit memory in children of different ages plus a group of adults (Parkin and Streete, 1988). The experiment used a method similar to that pioneered by Schneider in 1912. In the first phase participants studied a series of degraded pictures which became increasingly more informative until a point was reached where the participant could identify the picture (see Fig. 5. 4). There was then a retention interval of either a few minutes or one week. The retention test involved presenting the picture sequences again and measuring at what point participants could now identify the picture. This allowed the calculation of **savings**, i.e. the extent to which participants needed less information to identify the pictures second time around. In addition we also asked participants whether they remembered seeing each picture before. All age groups, even the youngest, showed substantial savings, thus indicating that they had retained something about the original learning experience. For

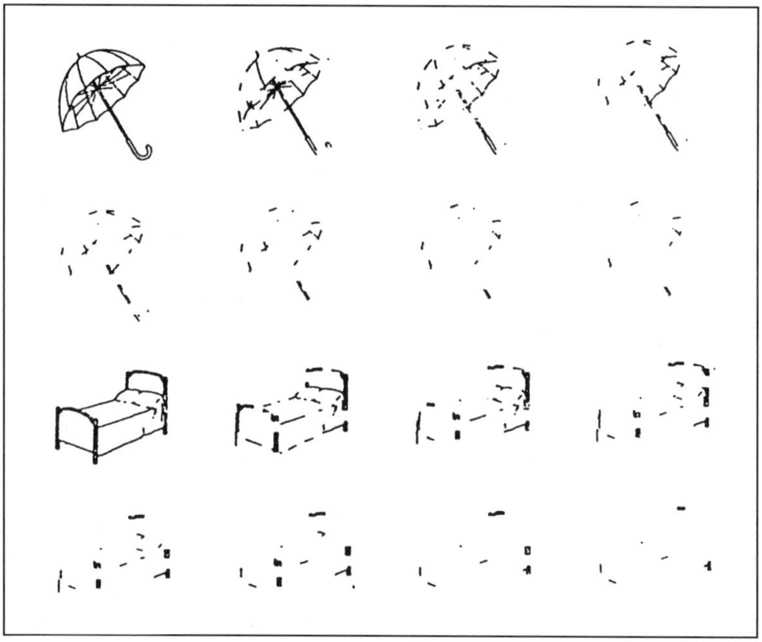

FIG. 5.4.
Pictures used by
Parkin and Streete
(1988).

the older groups it was clear that memory for the original presentation had helped them but this was not true in the youngest group who, despite showing savings, appeared to have little explicit recollection of seeing the sequences before. We also demonstrated similar effects with the elderly; older participants show reliable savings even though their explicit recall of the sequences was markedly impaired.

Several studies have also made use of the **infantile amnesia** barrier which reflects the fact that few of us can remember much about our lives prior to the age of four. In one experiment older children were shown photographs of children they had been at nursery with but with whom they had now lost contact. As they viewed each of these faces the experimenters measured their **galvanic skin response** (GSR)—this is simply a change in the electrical conductability of the skin and is the basis by which lie detector machines work. GSRs are known to increase when people encounter anything they are familiar with and it was found that the children's GSR's increased when they saw previous classmates even though they did not consciously recognise them (Drummey and Newcombe, 1995). In a similar type of study young children were allowed to explore a room and find a gift. Returning to that room several years later, post infantile amnesia, it was found that the children searched in the same place for a gift even though they did not remember being in the room before (see Parkin, 1997a, for a review of this area).

There is now abundant evidence that implicit memory can be demonstrated in situations that do not allow any explicit influences. However, the extent of this evidence should not make us think that there is an "implicit memory system"—rather it is the opposite. The multiplicity of tasks indicates that there are various components of the cognitive system, each having a memory capability that can be addressed in the same way. Thus word fragment completion and picture completion priming represent the implicit properties of two different systems. In this way, implicit memory has much in common with the term "procedural memory"—indeed psychologists tend to use the terms interchangeably.

While there is no doubt that implicit memory can be demonstrated, it is a different matter to explain what it is for. However, one recent experiment indicates that the effects of advertising may be mediated, at least in part, via implicit memory (Perfect and Askew, 1994). In this study, participants viewed adverts in colour magazines. One group was asked to look at them directly and rate how attractive they were. The other group encountered the same adverts incidentally by being asked to read parts of an article next to the advert. Participants were later tested on how well they remembered the pictures using a recognition test, and at the same time asked to rate how much they liked the adverts. The group who had studied the adverts recognised more of them correctly but there

For decades the mass media have taken advantage of our implicit memory for adverts.

was no difference in the extent to which both groups rated the previously exposed adverts as more attractive than those they had not seen previously—this is known as the **mere exposure effect**. This study thus suggests that our implicit memory for adverts may lead to motivating effects of which we are not consciously aware.

Implicit learning

Although similar in essence, there has been a separate research tradition in **implicit learning**. In an implicit learning task, participants are confronted with some sort of problem which they attempt to solve. The key aspect of these tasks is that participants are able to "solve" problems eventually, even though they are unable to explain what it is they have learnt. In perhaps the simplest type of task, participants were presented with a set of lights, each with a button below it. The lights go on and off in an apparently random fashion and the participant simply has to press the button under the light that has just come on. Unknown to the participant the lights are actually flashing in a sequence. Typically participants start to respond faster in this task as they learn the sequence but they are not able to explain what they have learnt (Nissen and Bullemer, 1987).

At a more complex level are studies that explore people's ability to operate simulated activities (so-called dynamic learning tasks). In one study, participants were presented with a simulation of a sugar production factory, and told that output of sugar could be controlled by the number of workers employed. They were told to try and maintain sugar production by manipulating the number of workers employed. Unknown to the participants there was an underlying rule determining optimal production related to both the number of workers and the output of sugar on the previous trial. It was found that participants were able to maximise output a lot of the time but, on questioning they could not report the underlying rule (Berry and Broadbent, 1984; Berry and Dienes, 1993).

The acquisition of rules without awareness is also highlighted by the learning of **artificial grammars** (Berry and Dienes, 1993; Reber, 1989) In these experiments, participants are presented with strings of letters which all conform to an artificially derived grammar in which only certain combinations of letters are "grammatical" (see Fig. 5.5). Following the learning phase, participants see strings of both "grammatical" and "ungrammatical" strings and have to classify them accordingly. Although performance on these tasks may not be particularly high, it has been reliably demonstrated that participants can derive the grammar even though they are unable to explain what it is. Even more surprising is the fact that participants can learn two artificial grammars in parallel and apply them strategically even though they cannot describe them (Dienes et al., 1995).

Although implicit learning is a robust phenomenon, controversy exists concerning the nature of the mechanism involved (see Berry and Dienes, 1997 and successive articles in the same issue). One idea is **instance theory** which supposes that memory for individual items indicative of correct and incorrect form the basis of what participants learn. This view has considerable support in the learning about dynamic systems (Dienes and Fahey, 1995b; Dienes and Fahey, 1998) and has also been proposed for artificial grammar learning (Vokey and Brooks, 1992). However, an alternative view is that participants build up a knowledge of artificial grammar by learning that certain fragments are correct (Perruchet, 1994; Perruchet and Gallego, 1997). Thus, in the above example the sequence TT is legal so its presence might encourage people to respond "correct" even though other parts of the string may be ungrammatical; this is not a very good strategy because it can lead to high error rates but might explain why the learning of artificial grammars is so poor. A particular problem for both the **fragmentary hypothesis** and instance-based accounts is that artificial grammar learning can be observed in cross modal

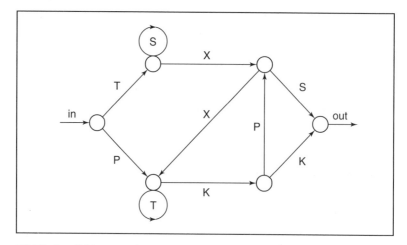

FIG. 5.5. An artificial grammar. Grammatical strings (e.g. TSXS; TSXXTKPS) are generated by entering through the "in" node and progressing to the "out" node. Each progression between nodes produces the letter associated with that link. A circle allows a letter to be repeated. Ungrammatical strings are created by changing at least one letter of a grammatical string (e.g. XSXS; TSSXK). Adapted from Cleeremans et al. (1998).

situations—subjects who learn a grammar based on letter patterns can successfully learn to discriminate correct from incorrect tone sequences based on the same grammar (Dienes and Fahey, 1995a). This shows a degree of abstraction in the representation governing artificial grammar acquisition, the nature of which has yet to be specified in detail.

Overview

- Initial formulations suggested that LTS had three separable components, episodic, semantic, and procedural memory.
- Procedural memory involves any form of memory whose contents are not consciously available. Included in this definition are motor skills, perceptual learning, the acquisition of grammar, and classical conditioning.
- Episodic memory is an assumed store of personal events; semantic memory comprises our knowledge of language, concepts and general facts about the world.
- Procedural memory appears to be a separable entity although there is not a single procedural memory system. Rather, a number of forms of learning have a procedural quality.
- The distinction between episodic and semantic memory is not clear. In particular, the evidence from the nature of retrograde amnesia argues against the distinction and supports the idea of a single declarative memory system representing all consciously accessible knowledge.
- Implicit memory is the expression of memory for an event without recollection of that event. It is contrasted with explicit memory which specifically involves event recollection.
- Implicit memory can be demonstrated across a wide range of tasks.
- Implicit memory is not a single memory system; different forms of memory all have an implicit dimension.
- Implicit learning is the gradual acquisition of knowledge without the ability to report what is being learned.

Suggested further reading

Baddeley, A.D. (1997). *Human memory: Theory and practice* (rev. ed.). Hove, UK: Psychology Press.

Provides more detailed coverage of some of the topics raised in this chapter.

Cleeremans, A., Destrebecqz, A., & Boyer, M. (1998). Implicit
learning: News from the front. *Trends in Cognitive Sciences, 2*,
406–416.

Provides a short but comprehensive and up-to-date view of implicit
learning.

Parkin, A.J. (1997). *Memory and amnesia: An introduction* (2nd ed.).
Hove, UK: Psychology Press.

Covers issues relating the nature of amnesia to the organisation of
memory.

Parkin, A.J. (in press). *Memory: Phenomena, experiment and theory* (2nd
ed.). Hove, UK: Psychology Press.

Provides a more extensive account of issues covered in this chapter.

Revision questions

1 What is the fundamental distinction between episodic and
semantic memory?
2 What is meant by procedural memory and how does it differ
crucially from declarative memory?
3 Why was it argued that the term declarative memory should
replace episodic and semantic memory?
4 What is the difference between tests of implicit and explicit
memory?
5 What sorts of evidence support the distinction between implicit
and explicit memory?
6 Why is it difficult to be fully confident that a test of implicit
memory is just that?
7 Why is it incorrect to think of a single implicit memory system?
8 What is implicit learning and how can it be explained?

Memory: Codes, processes, and loops 6

When we "remember" what exactly is it that we remember? It seems an obvious thing to say that when we memorise an object we do not store the object itself in our heads—we store a representation of that object, in other words a **memory trace**. As we saw in Chapter 1, information processing systems operate by deriving **codes**. A telephone message involves the translation of a voice into a series of electrical impulses which are then decoded by the receiver. So, in the same way, memory involves deriving a code from information we are asked to remember, and then decoding that representation when we wish to recall.

Memory codes

We can think of memory codes at two levels, biological and psychological. Neuroscientists are now confident that the basis of memory is the pattern of interconnections between neurones in the brain. However, this biological fact does not takes us very far if we ask the question, "What is stored in a memory trace?" Quite simply, at a biological level, memory all looks the same—connections between neurones. To answer our question, we need a psychological theory of the memory trace.

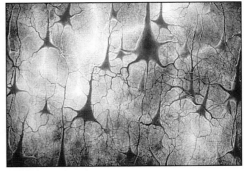

Groups of nerve cells (neurones) in the brain. Each cell has branching structures called dendrites and a larger axon carrying information as electrical impulses.

Earlier concepts of memory traces took an atomistic view of a memory trace. According to this idea, memory for a word, for example, involved activating a fundamental representation of that word which was the same regardless of the circumstances in which it was encountered. Thus, to learn the word "table" in one list and then in a subsequent list would involve activation of the same basic representation. All that would differ was the "tag" attached to the word indicating that it was now part of a different list.

The atomistic view of memory traces was challenged by **attribute theory**. According to this theory, something to be learned was viewed as a nominal stimulus from which the individual could choose to extract different forms of information. This idea is most readily understood if we consider how we go about remembering words but it is equally applicable to different and much more extensive situations such as remembering an event. Research on eye witnessing, for example, has highlighted how two or more people can have vastly differing views of an event and part of this discrepancy can be explained by the idea that the individuals have emphasised different attributes of the event in their memory (Davies, 1993).

Codes in verbal memory

One of the reasons why psychologists have studied memory via the use of word lists is because the idea of coding and attribute variation is easy to comprehend if we use words as stimuli. A word can be thought of as having three **encoding dimensions**:

- **orthography**: the visual characteristics of the constituent letters;
- **phonology**: the sound of the word;
- **semantics**: the meaning of the word.

Within this scheme, presentation of a word to a participant allows encoding on each of three dimensions with any degree of relative combination. Thus a word might be encoded principally in terms of sound, shape, or meaning. Of the three dimensions, meaning is the most flexible—even common words such as "table" have a multiplicity of meanings and associations when you think about it. This inherent flexibility gave rise to the **encoding variability hypothesis** (Melton, 1970) which proposed that no two encounters with the same word would result in exactly the same memory trace being formed.

The idea of encoding variability was most notably applied to explaining the **spacing effect**—the demonstration that repeated presentations of a word would result in better memory if these repetitions were separated by other activities—thus contradicting the commonsense view that repeating the same information without interruption is the best way to learn something. According to encoding variability theory, the spacing effect arose because separation of presentations increased the probability that the two memory traces of the word would encode different information and, collectively, make the memory trace more distinctive.

Levels of processing

In Chapter 4, we saw that the idea of STS ran into considerable trouble because the recency effect turned out to be much more complicated than people thought. Difficulties such as these led to a radical rethink about how memory should be studied which resulted in the **levels of processing** (LOP) concept (Craik and Lockhart, 1972). The basis of this idea was that the memory trace should be considered as the by-product of perception: what is perceived is what is remembered. To develop the idea, it was proposed that perception of a stimulus existed as a continuum ranging from "shallow" to "deep" processing. The concept revolved around verbal memory, with shallow processing characterised by concentration on orthographic features and deep processing represented by semantic processing, with phonology falling somewhere in the middle. Subsequently, the idea of a processing continuum was replaced with the idea that different aspects of stimulus processing were carried out in separate **processing domains** (Craik and Tulving, 1975).

LOP drew on an existing body of evidence concerning the effects of **orienting tasks** on human memory. An orienting task is an instruction to the participant to pay particular attention to one dimension of a stimulus. Take the word FROG in relation to the three domains of processing we have identified, is it in upper or lower case? (orthographic), does it rhyme with dog? (phonological) is it a living thing? (semantic). Many experiments had shown that the type of orienting task undertaken during learning greatly affected the amount people remembered in an unexpected memory test. Figure 6.1. shows data from an experiment carried out by Craik (1977). Orthographic processing is seen to produce the poorest level of memory, then phonological processing. Semantic processing produces the greatest level of retention and, interestingly, performance is as good as that found with intentional learning.

Craik and Lockhart explained the results of incidental learning studies by arguing that processing of a stimulus was under the control of a **central processor**, a system with limited but flexible capacity that dealt with the processing of new information. Retention of a stimulus depended on the way in which the central processor was deployed during learning—the deeper the level, the better the retention. Embodied in this idea was the **co-ordinality assumption** which stated that the nature of processing undertaken in response to an orienting task was directly related to the overt demands of the task. Thus, if you were asked whether the word TABLE was in upper or lower case letters, your processing was assumed to be restricted to the orthographic level.

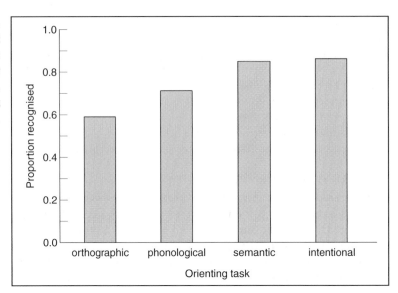

FIG. 6.1.
The effects of different orienting tasks on subsequent memory performance. Data from Craik (1977).

The co-ordinality assumption, in its most extreme form, is patently wrong. There is abundant evidence, for example, that when we look at a word, we are automatically aware of its meaning. A clear demonstration of this is the **Stroop Effect** (see Chapter 3). Phenomena such as the Stroop Effect led Craik and Tulving (1975) to propose that any stimulus first underwent a **minimal core encoding** which included a degree of semantic analysis which was followed by central processing in the appropriate domain (see Fig. 6.2).

Craik and Tulving (1975) confirmed the **depth effect** by showing, under a variety of conditions, that semantic orienting tasks always produced better retention than non-semantic tasks. However, they also made comparisons within the semantic domain and found that judging

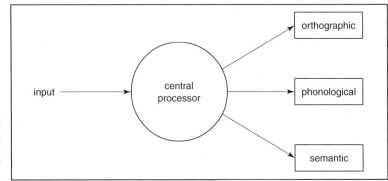

FIG. 6.2.
Schematic outline of levels of processing as proposed by Craik and Tulving (1975).

whether a word fitted the blank in a sentence (e.g. "He met a _____ in the street" FRIEND) produced better retention than judging whether a target item belonged to a particular category ("Is the word a type of fish" SHARK). Craik and Tulving explained this by arguing that the sentence frame task achieved its results because it produced a more richly encoded or elaborated memory trace. Further experiments showed that this **elaboration effect** only occurred in the semantic domain, thus suggesting that the effect is dependent on the participant's ability to set up increasing numbers of associations with the stimulus.

Problems with levels of processing

As more and more studies demonstrated orienting task effects a number of theorists became highly critical of the LOP approach (e.g. Baddeley, 1978; Eysenck, 1978; Nelson, 1977). The primary objection concerned the value of LOP as a **theory**. To be fair, Craik and Tulving (1975) never claimed specifically that LOP was a theory, preferring instead the term "framework for memory research". Nonetheless, it was evident that many people were treating it as if it were a theory and, as such, it was therefore a target for criticism.

The most important problem concerned the **circularity problem** inherent in the LOP approach to explain the relation between learning and retention. The demonstration that semantic processing typically produces better retention than non-semantic processing was explained by asserting that semantic processing is "deeper". However, the assumption of deeper processing under semantic orienting instructions was itself confirmed by higher levels of retention.

Craik and Tulving were well aware of the circular reasoning in LOP and attempted to break the circularity by devising an independent measure of depth, that is, some index which could be measured during orienting task performance that would allow different depths of processing across orienting tasks to be established independently of the differences in retention those tasks would be expected to produce. Craik and Tulving had noted that in all their experiments semantic orienting tasks always took the longest to perform. From this they reasoned that processing time might be an effective independent measure of processing depth, with longer processing times indicating deeper processing and therefore greater retention. To test this idea they devised a non-semantic task that took longer than a semantic task to perform. If processing time was a valid measure of depth, the non-semantic task should produce the best retention. Figure 6.3 shows that this was not the case. Despite taking less time to perform, the normal superiority of semantic processing was still found.

FIG. 6.3.
The relationship
between time taken to
perform an orienting
task and subsequent
retention. Note that
the semantic task is
quicker to perform yet
produces better
memory—time spent
studying the stimulus
does not therefore
predict retention.
Data from Craik and
Tulving (1975).

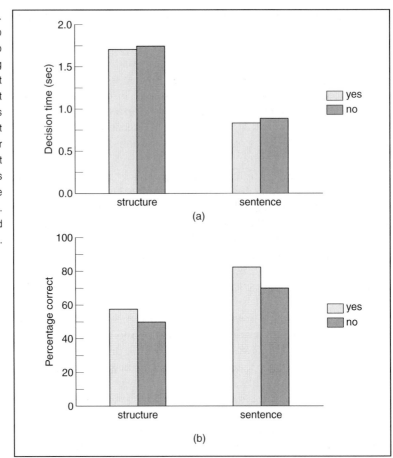

Failure to find a relationship between processing time and retention was in some ways fortunate for the LOP idea. If processing time had predicted depth effects it would have undermined the whole idea that memory can be affected by qualitative differences in the way information is encoded. Instead, it could have been argued that orienting task effects are merely one expression of the total time hypothesis which states that learning is a positive function of study time *per se*. Failure to find any relation between processing time and memory means that the relationship between learning and memory is determined by more than just how long is spent attending to the stimulus.

I tackled the circularity problem as the topic of my doctoral research (Parkin, 1979). The aim of these experiments was to examine whether semantic and non-semantic processing tasks could be distinguished in terms of their ability to evoke associative processing. It is well established that if two related words are presented sequentially, identification of the second word will be made easier if it is associatively related to the first, e.g. TABLE → CHAIR. This is known as **associative priming** and, logically, it must depend on processing of stimuli in the semantic domain. I reasoned that semantic orienting tasks should allow associative priming to occur because they direct conscious processing into the semantic domain. In contrast, non-semantic tasks, by definition, should preclude the possibility of associative priming.

In each trial of my experiment, participants first saw a single word and were asked to make either a semantic or non-semantic orienting decision about it. Following this, a second word written in coloured ink appeared which was either associated or unassociated with the first word. Participants had to name the ink colour of the second word as quickly as possible. The second part of the trial is therefore a variant on the Stroop Test we considered earlier, where the key factor influencing performance is the participant's ability to ignore the carrier word.

Participants in the semantic condition took significantly longer to name the ink colour when it was associated with the preceding decision words, whereas association between the two words had no influence in the non-semantic condition. The delay in naming the ink colour on the associated trials is evidence that associative priming has occurred; priming of the word in colour makes it more easily identified and thus more difficult for the participant to ignore. The fact that this **associative interference effect** occurred only in the semantic condition indicates that only this task directed processing to the semantic domain and that recall from this condition should be superior—which it was!

Transfer appropriate processing

In a LOP experiment, orienting tasks vary in the extent to which they force participants to regard the stimuli as words. If you have to judge whether "tiger" belongs to the category "mammals" you have to know what the target word is. But what if you were asked whether or not it had two syllables? You would probably still be aware that "tiger" is a word but this is irrelevant to what you are required to do. Thus you would probably find it no more difficult to make this decision if it was the nonword "riger". Morris et al. (1977) pointed out that orienting tasks vary in the extent to which they place emphasis on the "wordness" or lexical characteristics of stimuli but the retention tests always demand that words are remembered. Because semantic tasks always require word-based processing but non-semantic tasks do not, the superior memory following semantic processing could arise because the retention tests used are biased towards the type of information that semantic orienting tasks lead participants to encode.

Morris et al. designed an experiment in which participants first learnt target words under either semantic or non-semantic orienting conditions. The semantic task was a sentence verification task involving a highlighted word and the non-semantic task was a rhyming judgement. Two forms of retention test were used: a standard test of recognition (i.e. indicate which of these words you saw in the orienting phase), and one in which participants searched a list of words and indicated words that sounded similar to words used in the orienting phase. Figure 6.4 shows that, with standard retention conditions, the expected depth effect was found. However, on the rhyming recognition test, it was the non-semantic group that showed the best performance.

Morris et al. referred to their discovery as the principle of **transfer appropriate processing**. Stated simply this asserts that the most appropriate learning strategy is the one that most closely addresses the information required at testing. This principle, which is rather difficult to dispute, rather deflated the LOP approach which, until then, had asserted that semantic processing was always superior to non-semantic processing.

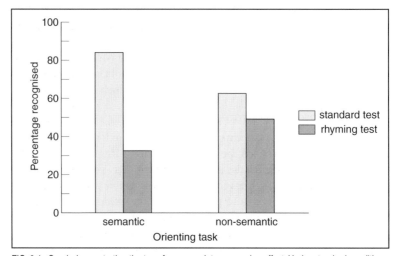

FIG. 6.4. Graph demonstrating the transfer appropriate processing effect. Under standard conditions there is the normal superiority for semantic processing but, when the retention test is directed more towards the demands of the non-semantic task, it is this task that produces the best memory performance. Data from Morris et al. (1977).

The aftermath of LOP

It is easy to think of LOP as somewhat of a blind alley in memory research but this would be wrong. Prior to the LOP concept, psychologists had not really emphasised the extent to which flexibility in the learning process could affect retention. After LOP, theorists were acutely aware that processing strategies, imposed or self-generated, were of major importance in determining the outcome of memory experiments. Also, concepts like transfer appropriate processing would not have been identified without pursuing the LOP idea.

Working memory

An alternative reaction to the problems with the STS concept was the development of the **working memory** model. In models such as that of Atkinson and Shiffrin (1971), STS is depicted as a single structure with a limited capacity. Baddeley and Hitch (1974) pointed out that there were data inconsistent with this idea. One intriguing source of evidence came from the study of a man known as KF who had suffered an injury to the left side of his brain (Warrington and Shallice, 1970). When tested he was found to have a digit span of only 2 compared to the normal 7. Span tasks are assumed to reflect the capacity of STS so this would indicate a severe impairment which would have the obvious knock-on effect of impeding LTS storage because all information must first be processed by STS. Yet, when KF was given a paired associate learning task, he performed normally.

It was argued that results such as these were inconsistent with a unitary STS and that, instead, selective disruption of the span task must reflect the operation of some kind of subsystem that has been independently disrupted. To test this hypothesis, it was necessary to devise a **dual task method** in which the participant performs a primary task whilst simultaneously carrying out a secondary task. In one study participants were given the primary task of learning lists of visually presented words while at the same time retaining either a sequence of three or six auditorally presented digits, or copying down pairs of digits as they were spoken. If digit span does reflect maximum STS capacity, we should expect subjects doing the list learning and retaining six digits at the same time to be quite impaired on the task because most of the available STS capacity is being used up. Figure 6.5 shows that the additional load of six digits did generally reduce performance but to nowhere near the extent one might expect if STS capacity was largely absorbed with digit span.

FIG. 6.5.
The effect of digit
preload on learning a
list of words. Note how
only the 6-digit
preload lowers
performance
(adapted from
Baddeley and Hitch,
1977).

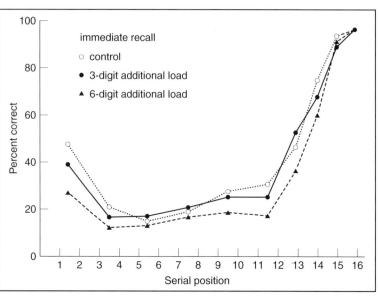

Below: Working in a
busy pizzeria will
cause the waiter to
develop various
strategies to
remember customers
and their orders.

Additional experiments confirmed the basic finding. In one study, participants were asked to verify sentences such as, "Canaries have wings", "Dogs have feathers". Before each of these sentences was presented, participants were given a sequence of digits to remember which ranged from 0 to 8 numbers. The participants had to repeat the sequence continually until they had verified the sentence in front of them. Even when participants were keeping in mind seven or eight random digits they could still perform a reasoning task in two seconds with 95% accuracy. It is extremely difficult to reconcile this and other similar results (e.g. Baddeley and Hitch, 1974) with a unitary concept of STS in which digit span is assumed to be a measure of capacity because, if so, one would have expected verification performance to be severely disrupted when participants were re-peating seven or eight digits.

The articulatory loop

The results of these early experiments led to the view that the system responsible for memory span—as measured in the digit span task—was not the same as the memory system supporting all our conscious mental activity. Instead, it seemed possible that the task of retaining short sequences of digits might, to a large extent, be carried out by a different system from that involved in tasks such as learning word lists and reasoning. Baddeley and Hitch (1974) suggested that the system underlying the retention of digits was a limited capacity speech-based mechanism initially named the **articulatory loop**. Systems such as this were referred to as "slave systems." A slave system is one which reflects the fact that, at least in Roman times, slaves were trained for specific purposes. Indeed, there were even slaves that specialised in memory skills; these were known as graeculi.

Evidence for the existence of an articulatory system underlying memory span came from an elegant series of experiments by Baddeley et al. (1975). The experiments were based on the observation that memory span for sequences of short words (e.g. *sum, wit*), is better than for long words (e.g. *aluminium, university, mechanism*). Baddeley et al. examined whether the **word length effect** depended on the number of syllables in short and long words, or differences in the spoken duration of each word type. To examine these two possibilities, Baddeley et al. compared memory span for items that have equal numbers of syllables but relatively shorter or longer spoken durations (e.g. *wicket* vs. *harpoon*). They found that memory span was lower for words with longer spoken durations and therefore concluded that the system underlying memory span was speech-based.

More evidence for an articulatory loop came from a second study where the word length effect was examined under conditions of **articulatory suppression**. In this secondary task, the participant has to repeat a meaningless spoken sequence (e.g. *the, the, the ....*) while carrying out a primary task. Figure 6.6 shows that articulatory suppression causes the word length effect to disappear. Note in particular that performance on short words is reduced to the same level as long words.

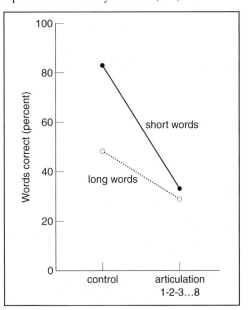

FIG. 6.6.

The effect of articulatory suppression on the word length effect in memory span. Data from Baddeley et al. (1975).

This is rather nice evidence that the advantage in recalling short words in a memory span task depends critically on the availability of an articulatory coding system. When this is not the case, as with articulatory suppression, short and long words are dependent on the same memory processes and are therefore recalled to the same degree.

These findings led to the first specific model of working memory which is illustrated in Fig. 6.7. It identifies three components: the articulatory loop; a **visuo-spatial scratch pad**; and a **central executive**. On the basis of experimental evidence, the articulatory loop was characterised as a structure capable of holding and recycling a small amount of speech-based information. The articulatory loop was assumed to underlie participants' ability to perform mental tasks relatively easily while simultaneously holding digits. The argument was that part or all the digit load could be placed in the articulatory loop thus making little or no demands on other components of working memory. The visuo-spatial scratch pad served as a medium within which spatially arranged information could be mentally manipulated, but further discussion of this idea will be postponed until a later chapter.

Within the model, the central executive is responsible for most mental activity but, in relation to the extensive amount of work examining the phonological loop, there is very little known about the executive. Baddeley has likened the idea of an executive to the function

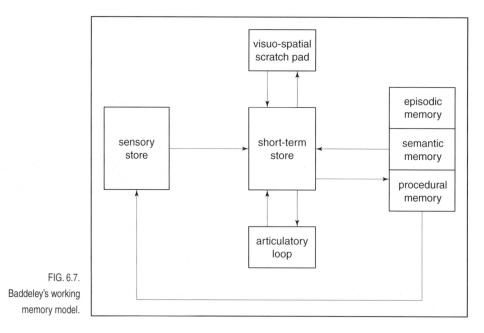

FIG. 6.7.
Baddeley's working
memory model.

of the frontal lobes and to the SAS model of attention proposed by Norman and Shallice (see Chapter 3). Several theories argue that the frontal lobes contain the highest control centres of the brain and this is backed up by evidence from people who unfortunately suffer frontal damage. As we saw earlier, patients with frontal lobe lesions have deficits consistent with inefficient supervisory processes. However, beyond saying that the executive is an all-purpose high-level decision making system with a certain degree of memory capacity, nothing more is known. Indeed, some have argued that there is no good evidence for a unitary central executive (see Parkin, 1998, and Baddeley, 1998 for a reply).

Before moving on, we must note a couple of refinements to the articulatory loop concept. First, the loop is now known as the **phonological loop** and is thought to comprise two components: a **phonological store** which holds speech-based information, and a **subvocal rehearsal process** which internally recycles a limited amount of speech-based information (Baddeley, 1997). This distinction is necessary to account for the fact that under conditions of articulatory suppression participants are still able to make certain judgements about phonology. Besner et al. (1981) for example, showed that participants undertaking articulatory suppression had no difficulty judging whether or not nonwords (e.g. PALLIS) sounded like real words.

What is the phonological loop for?

Although the working memory model describes different memory structures, it is also a functional model in that there is an attempt to identify structures with real life tasks. With this in mind, we can ask what the phonological loop is actually for. In adults, there does not seem to be much of a role for the loop. There are now a number of studies of patients such as KF, in whom digit span, and presumably the phonological loop, is severely impaired. Nonetheless, these patients have not experienced any great cognitive difficulties because of this (Vallar and Shallice, 1997). Findings such as these have led Baddeley and his colleagues to suggest that the phonological loop has its greatest influence in child development, in particular in the development of reading.

Baddeley et al. (1998) present a wide range of evidence consistent with the idea that the phonological loop is involved in

The phonological loop has its greatest influence in child development, in particular the development of reading.

reading development. One key finding concerns the **phonological confusion effect** in memory span. Conrad (1964) explored the ability of people to repeat back, in the correct order, visually presented sequences of letters that were either phonologically confusable (e.g. CTVG) or non-confusable (e.g. XVSL). He found that phonologically confusable strings were more difficult to remember even when potential confounding influences of visual similarity were controlled for. Conrad's finding strengthens the view that the phonological loop is heavily implicated in memory span. When this experiment was repeated in dyslexic children it was found that they showed a reduced span and far less evidence of phonological confusion, suggesting that the phonological loop was not operative.

Baddeley et al. consider a large number of studies that have looked at the relation between phonological memory and vocabulary development at different age points. Two measures of phonological memory are taken: memory span and a task involving the repetition of nonwords. A strong relationship is found between children's vocabulary scores and their phonological memory scores. Further analysis suggests that it is phonological memory that determines vocabulary, not vice versa. Discussing these results, they conclude that the phonological loop acts as a storage mechanism for new sounds while a more permanent representation is established.

An alternative conception of working memory

Baddeley's concept of working memory can be classified as a structural model because the aim of research has been to identify different components of the working memory model and attempt to define their properties. An alternative approach has been to approach working memory in terms of capacity limitations. This is not to say that Baddeley's model does not accept capacity limitation, rather that it has not been the central focus of research.

The capacity approach has centred on experimental techniques aimed at measuring the amount of information that people can hold "in mind" at one time. In Chapter 4 we saw that certain strategies, such as reduction mnemonics and chunking, can considerably increase the amount of information we can hold in mind and thus distort the measurement of capacity. An early approach to the capacity idea was the work of Daneman and Carpenter (1980) who were interested in the relationship between working memory and reading ability (see also Just and Carpenter, 1992). They devised a working memory task in which participants listened to sentences and had to remember the last word of each one. At the end of the session, recall ranged from between two and five correct words and the participants' score on this test correlated positively with reading ability.

Daneman and Carpenter's data indicate that the average working memory capacity of their participants was between three and four items. Interestingly, this figure corresponds well with other attempts to measure the capacity of working memory when enhancing strategies such as chunking and reduction mnemonics are ruled out (Cowan, 1998). In one study (Luck and Vogel, 1997) participants viewed two arrays of coloured squares and decided whether the second array was identical to the first array, or whether it differed in the colour of one of the squares. The arrays were presented sequentially with a gap of just under a second, thus requiring that the first array had to be memorised in order to do the task (see Fig. 6.8a). The key manipulation was the number of squares in the arrays and it was found that performance was very good with arrays up to four in size but then performance deteriorated with further increases in the number of squares.

Vogel and Luck's work also highlighted the difficulty of deciding what "an item" is in relation to measuring working memory capacity. In a follow-up experiment, they presented arrays of lines where the difference between presentations could be that either an orientation had

FIG. 6.8. Procedures and results adapted from Luck and Vogel (1997). (a) Ability to detect a change in colour of a square (i.e. single feature) is good for arrays of up to four items; (b) performance on the conjunction condition is no different to when participants detect differences relating to only one stimulus feature.

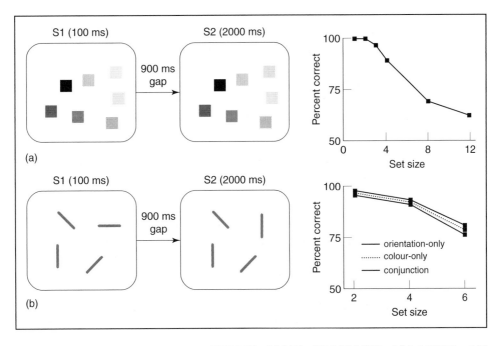

changed or that one line was a different colour (see Fig. 6.8b). They found that when participants were asked to detect whether a line had only changed colour or only changed orientation there was little fall off in performance with set sizes up to four. However, in a "conjunction" condition, in which participants had to decide whether a line had changed orientation *or* colour, thus requiring twice as much information to be remembered, they showed an identical pattern of results to the single feature condition. To account for this, Vogel and Luck propose that the input to working memory from the perceptual system has already integrated the two features of each line (orientation + colour) into a single representation.

Another issue within this field of research is what exactly constitutes working memory? The capacity studies we have looked at so far suggest that it comprises a temporary store holding just a small amount of information. However, researchers such as Cowan (1998) and Ericsson and Kintsch (1995) have suggested that working memory comprises both a limited capacity focus of attention and a partial activation of those aspects of long-term store relevant to the ongoing task, or the so-called long-term working memory (see Fig. 6.9). The latter are made accessible via the availability of fast-acting retrieval cues. This form of working memory is considered necessary to explain abilities such as text comprehension (because this will often require reference to events some considerable distance back from the text currently being handled), and in the development of expert memory skills (in which complex strategies beyond the immediate focus of attention can be brought to bear on a problem). As an example of this, see the chunking skills used by chess experts, described in Chapter 14.

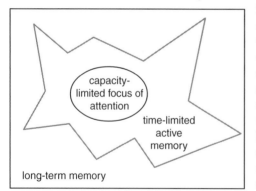

FIG. 6.9.
Outline of a working memory model in which a focus of attention is combined with high speed retrieval links to a long-term store containing task-relevant information (adapted from Cowan, 1998).

Overview

- The memory trace comprises a code derived from what it is we are trying to learn.
- Information can be encoded along different dimensions and the same thing may be encoded in different ways at different times.
- Levels of processing proposed that memory was the by-product of perception with meaningful analysis representing a deeper level than a physically based analysis.

- Levels of processing suffered, to some extent, from a circularity of explanation although this problem was partly overcome.
- Transfer appropriate processing states that memory will be maximised when the goals of learning and retrieval are most similar.
- The working memory model comprises a central executive linked to two "slave systems"—the phonological loop and the visuo-spatial scratch pad.
- Only the phonological loop concept has been extensively developed and it is thought that its role is to facilitate the learning of new spoken vocabulary.
- An alternative idea of working memory is to approach it in terms of capacity limitation. It has been suggested that working memory has a very limited capacity but other approaches suggest that working memory is a dual component mechanism comprising a limited focus of attention plus a partial activation of long-term store.

Suggested further reading

Baddeley, A.D. (1997). *Human memory: Theory and practice* (rev. ed.). Hove, UK: Psychology Press.

This provides an up-to-date account of working memory.

Cowan, N. (1995). *Attention and memory: An integrated framework.* Oxford: Oxford University Press.

A good place to read about capacity-based approaches to working memory.

Parkin, A.J. (in press). *Memory: Phenomena, experiment and theory.* (2nd ed.). Hove, UK: Psychology Press.

This book contains a detailed account of the LOP concept and a discussion of coding.

Revision questions

1 Why is our knowledge about the biological substrate of memory insufficient to answer key questions about how memory works?
2 How do psychologists currently think about the structure of memory traces?
3 What is the levels of processing approach to memory, why did it come about, and what evidence was it based on?

4 What critical problems did the levels of processing approach encounter?

5 Was the levels of processing approach a waste of time? If not, why?

6 What is the basic concept of working memory as defined by Baddeley and Hitch?

7 What sorts of evidence led Baddeley and Hitch to propose their model?

8 What is the evidence for the articulatory loop?

9 How good a concept is the notion of a central executive?

10 What functions have been proposed for the articulatory loop, now known as the phonological store.

11 How do capacity models differ from Baddeley and Hitch's approach to working memory?

Memory: Remembering and forgetting 7

Intuitively, we all probably think that the better our memories are, the more successful we will be in life. While there is no doubt that having a superior memory can be useful in certain situations, such as learning a language or remembering strings of unrelated facts, there is more to it than that. It is often overlooked, for example, that an efficient memory depends as much on the ability to forget unwanted information as it does on the capacity to remember useful information. This point is aptly illustrated in A.R. Luria's (Luria and Solotaroff, 1987) famous account of "S", a man with an apparently phenomenal memory. In his book, *The Mind of a Mnemonist*, Luria describes outstanding feats of memory carried out by "S". In one case, for example, "S" was shown a blackboard full of rows of random numbers for a minute. Ten years later he was able to recite those numbers entirely accurately in any direction specified by the experimenter. This incredible memory stemmed from the fact that "S" had **eidetic imagery**—photographic memory—something that is rare in adults (see Chapter 9). He also experienced **synaesthesia**; his senses overlapped to the point where he could hear colours and see sounds, all of which contributed to the richness of his memory. One might suspect that a memory like this would lead to great things but it did not for two reasons. First, "S" had trouble forgetting what he had learned and, when attempting to remember something important, he would be overwhelmed by irrelevant details coming to mind. The second problem was that his memory was unstructured, resembling a pile of photographs that had not been catalogued in any way. Each memory was, in itself, rich but it did not relate to any other memory. The consequence of these problems was that "S" eventually became a "memory man" in the theatre.

6	6	8	0
5	4	3	2
1	6	8	4
7	9	3	5
4	2	3	7
3	8	9	1
1	0	0	2
3	4	5	1
2	7	6	8
1	9	2	6
2	9	6	7
5	5	2	0
x	0	1	*x*

The random table of numbers learnt by S.

How do we know memory is selective?

Some of the earliest work on **forgetting rate** was carried out by Herman Ebbinghaus (1885). Although not averse to a bit of theorising, Ebbinghaus's principal contribution was to provide very accurate data on the rate at which we forget. Ebbinghaus used a technique known as **savings**, which we encountered in Chapter 5. In his experiments, which were principally done on himself, he learned lists of nonsense syllables (e.g. VIK) until he could recite them back faultlessly. He would then wait various periods of time and then measure how many repetitions of the list he needed before his recall was once again perfect. Using this technique, Ebbinghaus established that forgetting is initially very rapid and that within 20 minutes we will have forgotten 40% of what we have learned. After eight hours this value has dropped to 65% and after a month it is around 75%. Ebbinghaus's results, which are not disputed by much more recent work, indicate that the various factors affecting what is retained and what is lost operate at a very early stage.

Despite Ebbinghaus's findings, not everyone agrees that memory is a selective process. We shall see later that certain "reconstructivists" believe that all memories are stored away and that, via hypnosis, apparently forgotten memories can be "unlocked". The idea that memory is complete and non-selective is derived from a series of unusual experiments carried out in the 1940s and 1950s by the neurosurgeon Wilder Penfield (Penfield and Roberts, 1959). Patients were undergoing brain surgery to remove parts of their brain which were causing severe epilepsy. These operations could be performed while the patient was conscious because the brain itself feels no

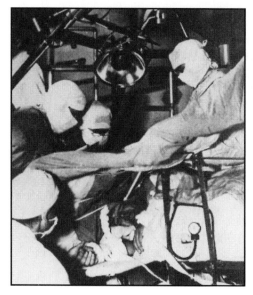

'Open-head' surgery taking place, with the patient awake.

pain. Once the brain was exposed, the surface was stimulated with an electrode with the aim of determining which areas of the brain did what. In particular, surgeons wanted to avoid removing areas concerned with speech. While doing this, Penfield noticed that much of the speech people produced was in the form of memories and, furthermore, these memories were trivial. This led Penfield to claim that he had located the stream of consciousness—all memories were available and forgetting was simply a problem of accessibility.

Penfield's claims went unchallenged for 30 years until Loftus and Loftus (1980) re-examined them. They found that most of the patients did not appear to be retrieving memories at all and that, even when they did, these apparent memories were fabrications—in short they found little support for the stream of consciousness idea. Yet, to this day, people still cite Penfield's work as supporting the existence of vast untapped memory, the consequences of which have sometimes been disastrous as witnessed by the **false memory syndrome** (see below).

"The Things I Always Remember Are the Things You Always Forget", a famous tune written by Dave Brubeck, sums up what one might see as the opposite view: memory is highly selective with no two people able to agree on anything they witnessed jointly. We are, of course, acutely aware that this often appears to be the case, even in our own lives. In addition we will be reviewing many experiments which show how people can be remarkably biased in what they remember. Unfortunately, demonstrating effects of this kind is only consistent with the idea of a selective memory; we cannot, with absolute certainty, rule out the possibility that selectivity operates at the point where information is retrieved from memory rather than when it is stored. At the end of the day, selectivity in memory is something we assume on intuitive grounds in that it does not make sense for any organism, human or animal, to store away vast amounts of inconsequential detail about our experiences. Moreover, evidence purporting to show total storage does not stand up to scrutiny.

Theories of remembering

In trying to understand remembering, we are involved in constructing a **retrieval theory**: some formal account of how information from the past is accessed and restored to consciousness. The essential point about retrieval is that it is a **reconstructive process**; memories are accessed by an interactive process in which there is an initial proposition about what a memory trace might be that is then matched with the contents of memory. If a match is found, further propositions along that line are examined until retrieval occurs.

We have all experienced reconstruction in memory. Thus, if asked what is the capital of Peru, we may initially be unable to answer but, when given the clue "begins with L", we can construct a restricted candidate list which hopefully will contain the correct answer "Lima". In producing accounts of retrieval, some psychologists have sought to capture this reconstructive process.

An important aspect of reconstructive memory is that it allows for incorrect information to be introduced. Very often this takes the form of a "normalisation" process in which the contents of an event are restructured according to some general idea as to what might have happened in a given situation. This was famously demonstrated by Bartlett (1932) in his book *Remembering*. Bartlett described an experiment in which participants heard an unfamiliar folk story and were then required to remember it on a number of successive occasions. Bartlett found that, as time progressed, participants introduced more and more of their own knowledge as a means of filling gaps created by forgetting the original information. Thus if the story had mentioned "canoes", participants would actually recall "boats". Similarly, unfamiliar phrases such as "something black came out of his mouth" would be replaced with the more common phrase "foamed at the mouth".

To account for these results Bartlett made use of the term **schema** (pl. schemata). This had first been used by the physiologist Henry Head to explain how various parts of our body are co-ordinated to achieve a certain goal, thus there might be an overall "body image" for sitting, standing and so on. Bartlett argued that schemata could also exist in psychological terms. Thus, in trying to remember a particular situation one might evoke a schema typical of that situation, to guide remembering. Thus, in recalling the *War of the Ghosts*, various schemata were employed to fill in the missing memories. The idea of schema had an immediate impact on the psychology of memory (see Parkin, in prep.). We will return to the idea of schemata in a later chapter.

Clarifying our terms

Up until now we have used terms like "recall" and "recognition" fairly freely but for this chapter we must use sharper definitions. Essentially there are three types of conscious, explicit, remembering:

free recall: participant attempts to remember the target information without any assistance from the experimenter.
cued recall: participant attempts to remember the target information in the presence of some specific cue (e.g. an associate of the word they are trying to remember).
recognition: participant is presented with a stimulus and must decide whether it is a target in either a yes–no procedure in which each item is judged individually or by forced-choice in which one item from an array of stimuli must be selected as the target.

Generation–recognition

The first systematic attempts to explain retrieval as a reconstructive process were **generation–recognition** (GR) models (see Watkins and Gardiner, 1979 for a detailed account). Although there is variation, the models all operate in essentially the same way. At the outset of retrieval, the system **generates** possible candidates for the memory that is being sought. These candidates are then subjected to a **recognition** process which, if successful, results in that candidate being retrieved as a memory.

The most well-known examples of GR models are those of Anderson and Bower (1972) and Kintsch (1970). These models specifically address how participants retrieve words in a verbal learning experiment but it must be borne in mind that the intention was to produce a general account of how retrieval happens. These models assume a structure rather like semantic memory in which each known word is represented by a node. When a word is studied, it is assumed that some form of "tag" is set up to indicate that the word was part of the target list. When recall is attempted, various candidates are generated and the corresponding nodes examined for markers which, if detected, result in recognition and hence retrieval. In recognition, access to the node was considered to be automatic and the recognition was dependent simply on detection of a marker.

Earlier we saw that conscious, explicit, memory can be tested in three ways: free recall, cued recall, and recognition. Under normal conditions these three types of task behave in an orderly way. Free recall will always produce poorer retrieval than cued recall which, in turn, is inferior to recognition. Any model of retrieval must therefore account for this consistently observed relationship. GR models explain the natural ordering of these tasks on the grounds that, in free recall, the generation phase has less information to guide generation than that available when a cue is present. Recognition produces even better performance because the fallible generation stage is bypassed altogether and the participant simply has to detect evidence that the presented item is a target.

GR models were able to account for a number of other findings as well. A well-established finding is that words of high frequency in the language (e.g. TABLE, DOG) are easier to recall than low-frequency words (e.g. BARGE, PINE) whereas the reverse occurs in recognition memory. The better recall of high-frequency words can be attributed to the greater probability of them being generated as candidates for recognition. Poorer recognition, in turn, arose because higher frequency words might be expected to be associated with a greater number of occurrence markers, making it more difficult to decide whether that word was presented in a specific list.

Another important finding explained by GR models was the influence of **extra-experimental association** on cued recall. If participants are given a stimulus word (e.g. TABLE) and asked to free associate, they will produce some words (e.g. CHAIR) far more often than others (e.g. GLUE). A number of studies showed that this measure of extra-experimental association was an accurate predictor of cued recall performance in that cues with a strong extra-experimental association with their target word were far more effective than cues where this relationship was weak (e.g. Bahrick, 1970). In terms of GR theory, this effect of extra-experimental association arises because the generative process is itself governed by the same principles that operate in free association.

The encoding specificity principle

The GR theory gave rise to a testable prediction: recall of an item involves both successful generation and recognition whereas recognition involves just the latter stage of the retrieval process. From this, it follows that any item we are able to recall must be capable of being recognised because the recognition process must have been involved in recall.

This prediction was the subject of a series of experiments carried out by Endel Tulving and his colleagues (e.g. Tulving and Thomson, 1973). The basic experiment consisted of four phases. In Phase 1 participants were presented with a target word along with a "cue" word which they were asked to attend to but not try to remember. The target and cue word pairings were not closely associated with one another, e.g. ENGINE—black. In Phase 2 participants were given another list of words each of which was a strong associate of one of the target words in the learning list (e.g. STEAM). For each of these Phase 2 words, participants had to generate several associations and, because of the way in which the lists were constructed, there was a high probability that participants would produce target items from the list as associations (e.g. STEAM → ENGINE). In the third phase of the experiment, participants were asked to indicate whether any of the words they had generated were target words from the list presented in Phase 1. Finally, participants were given the low value cue words and asked to recall which items were paired with them during Phase 1.

According to GR theory any target word recalled successfully in Phase 4 should also have been recognised in Phase 3: this follows on the assumption that the recognition process undertaken as part of cued recall in Phase 4 is the same recognition process as carried out when only recognition was required in Phase 3. The results contradicted this prediction in that words recalled in Phase 4 were often not recognised in Phase 3—a phenomenon that has been termed "recognition failure of recallable words" or, for short, recognition failure.

On the basis of these recognition failure results, Tulving and Thompson (1973) put forward the **encoding specificity principle** (ESP). This proposed that recall and recognition were different manifestations of a single retrieval system and that the retrieval of information depends critically on the degree of overlap between the features encoded in the memory trace and the features present in the retrieval environment (e.g. the information provided by a recognition probe or a cue). To explain their own data, Tulving and Thompson proposed that the learning manipulation in Phase 1 resulted in an encoding of the target word, which emphasised its featural overlap with the low associative cue. When recognition was tested in Phase 3, the target was presented in a retrieval environment specifying a different pattern of featural overlap to that encoded during learning (i.e. one emphasising the target's relations with a strong association), with the result that insufficient overlap existed for a successful recognition response to occur. In contrast, the potentially more difficult cued recall task was in fact easier because the cues had a high degree of featural overlap with the target memory trace. Recall and recognition were thus independent of one another because they had differing featural overlap with the target as encoded.

Other findings also seemed consistent with ESP. The superiority of strong associates over weak associates as retrieval cues could be explained by assuming that, without any constraints imposed, participants will tend to encode the dominant meaning of a stimulus during learning. Now, because pre-experimental associative strength and semantic overlap are highly confounded (e.g. TABLE is not only the commonest associate of CHAIR, it also shares a large number of semantic features), it follows that any strong associative cue will also have a high degree of featural overlap.

ESP also accounted for the general relationship between recall, cued recall, and recognition by arguing that, on average, recall tests provide a more impoverished retrieval environment than cued recall tasks which, in turn, provide less information about target memory than a recognition test (see Fig. 7.1). The essential proposal, however, is that the contrast between recognition and recall is not one involving qualitative differences in the underlying memory system. Rather, it reflects the operation of a single retrieval system whose prime

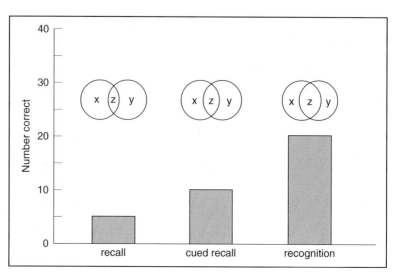

FIG. 7.1.
The typical
relationship between
recall, cued recall,
and recognition.
According to the
encoding specificity
principle this pattern
reflects the typical
increase in overlap (Z)
between memory
trace content (X) and
retrieval environment
context (Y).

determinant is featural overlap between memory trace and retrieval environment. Recognition superiority is therefore the norm because, as a form of testing, it usually provides the most featural overlap with a target trace. However, as Tulving and Thompson's demonstration shows, memory can be manipulated so that cued recall for an item can be better than recognition.

Forgetting

As we have already noted, forgetting is a vital aspect of human memory but explanations of how it occurs still elude us. It is traditional to think of forgetting as occurring for one of three reasons: encoding failure, storage failure, or retrieval failure. Encoding failure reflects forgetting due to a failure in the consolidation process—information simply fails to enter long-term storage in the first place. Encoding failure can be observed anecdotally. If, for example, you are interrupted while speaking to someone, you may be unable to pick up the thread of what you were saying—the contents of your mind have been "lost". At a more formal level, drugs can also interfere with the consolidation process. Under these conditions people have no difficulty remembering information prior to drug administration but are poor at remembering post-drug information (e.g. Calev et al., 1989).

Forgetting due to storage failure assumes that information, once consolidated, can be vulnerable to the effects of information already in memory or be affected by new information entering memory. In his thoughts about memory, Aristotle drew an analogy between memories and wax tablets. According to his idea, each memory was a tablet and this could be compressed by other memories (tablets) already in memory or entering memory at a later point. He also considered that the longer a tablet remained in memory the harder it became and therefore the less vulnerable to distortion.

Aristotle's analogy is interesting for two reasons. First, his notion about varying "hardness" predicts that early memories are less vulnerable to disruption, a fact we saw confirmed in Chapter 5. It is also an ancient forerunner of **associative interference theory.** Developed during the behaviourist era, this is the only major attempt to *explain* how forgetting occurred. According to interference theory, forgetting arose because two responses became potentially associated with the same stimulus. Perhaps the most important point about interference theory was that it was a dynamic theory of forgetting; that is, forgetting arose because of processes occurring in memory. This contrasted with the more "passive" explanation of memory characterised by the law of disuse. This specified that a memory deteriorated across time if it was not refreshed by use. Psychologists were at pains to point out that "time" itself is not an explanation of anything; rather, it was what happened with time that was the issue. Thus in the same way that we need the concept of "rusting" to explain why a nail gradually deteriorates in water, it was also necessary to propose a process that occurred across time to explain loss of memory.

To test interference theory experimentally, psychologists devised the A→B, A→C paradigm in which participants first learnt a series of word pairs, e.g. (A) "farm" → (B) "biscuit", and then a second series in which the B words were replaced by new words, e.g. (A) "farm" → (C) "pen". Following this, recall of the A–B pair could be tested, i.e. what was "farm" paired with on List 1? Within a paired assoicate (PA) learning task one can observe two forms of interference:

proactive interference (inhibition): this occurs when learning of the A → C pair is impaired because of prior learning of A → B.
retroactive interference (inhibition): this occurs when learning of the A → C pair impairs subsequent relearning of the A→ B pair.

Large numbers of experiments were conducted using PA learning, along with other similar methods, in an attempt to explain forgetting. Despite the extent of the enterprise, interference theory failed to produce any coherent explanation of forgetting, even within the PA learning method itself (Baddeley, 1976 provides a good overview of this work).

In addition, even if associative interference theory had succeeded in explaining forgetting in the A → B, A → C task, it is doubtful if a great deal would have been solved. The essential problem is that it is difficult to envisage either the acquisition or forgetting of information in response competition terms. Giving your old telephone number when you have just changed to a new one is an example, but how would the A → B, A → C framework explain what you forget about a film you have just seen or a book that you had read?

It is easy to "write off" the behaviourist era as a blind alley in memory research but this would be a mistake. First, terminology such as "proactive and retroactive interference" is still used widely independent of its original experimental context. Also, many of the phenomena studied are still of considerable interest today. Among these is the spacing effect (the tendency for repeated information to be more memorable if repetitions are separated by other activity) and the reminiscence effect (the demonstration that retention of information will increase across time without any intervening practice). Added to this, behaviourism provided those psychologists charged with taking memory research into the cognitive era with a rigorous methodological training (Baddeley, 1976 provides an extensive account of interference theory).

The final cause of forgetting, retrieval failure, has proved the most tractable from an experimental point of view in that all that is required is the demonstration that information can be retrieved in one set of circumstances but not another. In the following sections we see an impressive array of factors which determine the retrievability of information. What you must bear in mind, however, is that these experiments only demonstrate the various conditions that affect retrieval—they do not offer up either a theory of retrieval or forgetting in terms of the actual mechanisms involved.

Context

ESP experiments were important because they alerted theorists to the importance of **context** in determining remembering and forgetting. Context is a much used and, according to some, much abused term which can be defined in a number of ways. One useful approach, first put forward by Hewitt (1973), draws a distinction between **intrinsic** and **extrinsic context**. Intrinsic context refers to various features that are an integral part of a target stimulus. For a word, the intrinsic context constitutes the particular sub-set of features encoded about that word at the time of learning (e.g. those features that associate

TRAIN with BLACK). Extrinsic context represents those features that are present when the target is encountered but are not, themselves, an integral part of the stimulus. Examples of this include the place and time where the stimulus was encountered. Modern theorists have tended to replace the terms intrinsic and extrinsic context with the concept of **interactive** and **non-interactive** context (Baddeley, 1982) or **context beta** and **context alpha** (Wickens, 1987). The distinction, however, remains the same.

The encoding specificity results were thus obtained by manipulations of intrinsic context. In this respect it also becomes apparent that a modification of generate–recognise theories could accommodate Tulving and Thompson's result. Prior to the encoding specificity experiments, GR theorists had operated under what we will term the **trans-situational identity assumption**. This asserted that words were represented by "atomistic" nodes and that whenever a given word was learned in an experiment this node, representing all aspects of the word's meaning, was activated. In Chapter 6 we saw that attribute theory argued against this idea and this was reinforced by the encoding specificity results. It was, however, a small step to provide a modification of GR theory to accommodate the effects of intrinsic context. All that was needed was to modify the model so that it operated at the level of individual word features rather than atomistic word units (Reder et al., 1974).

A feature-based GR model could therefore handle the data from encoding specificity experiments by arguing that, under certain cued recall conditions, the cue can generate more features in common with a target than a recognition probe presented under conditions designed to de-emphasise its relationship with the target. A problem, however, is that this modification brings to the GR model a major theoretical weakness of the ESP—**circularity of explanation**. Consider a hypothetical experiment in which a subject learns some new information. Two cues, X and Y, are then presented successively but only Y results in correct recall. ESP asserts that Y must have an overlap with the target trace whereas X does not. However, if X were singularly successful the opposite conclusion about the nature of the memory trace would be reached. A modified GR theory falls into the same trap in that successful recall would be attributed to the featural similarity between target and retrieval environment which, in turn, is inferred from whether or not recall is successful.

Although ESP and GR accounts of retrieval seem much more similar than when we started out they still differ in one important way. The ESP account proposes that retrieval is a direct result of the interaction between the retrieval environment and the stored trace and that recall and recognition are different manifestations of a single retrieval process:

$$TRACE \longleftrightarrow RETRIEVAL\ ENVIRONMENT$$

Within this arrangement, retrieval is achieved when the overlap between the stored trace and the retrieval environment reaches some critical value. The important point to note is that only information in the retrieval environment can facilitate trace retrieval.

GR theory specifies a different relationship between trace and retrieval environment. Information in the retrieval environment forms the stimulus for a generative process whose output is tested against the contents of memory. Recall occurs when a recognition match between the generated information and the trace reaches a critical level; recall and recognition are therefore separate stages in retrieval:

$$TRACE \longleftrightarrow GENERATIVE\ MEDIATION \longleftrightarrow RETRIEVAL\ ENVIRONMENT$$

Under these conditions the information provided by the retrieval environment could influence retrieval directly because part of what it represents is generated in an attempt to contact the target trace. However, the retrieval environment can also facilitate retrieval indirectly by causing the generative mediation stage to produce information that, although not specified by the retrieval environment, does overlap with the trace.

GR thus imparts a degree of flexibility to the retrieval process that is not possible in the ESP account because GR enables entirely novel information to enter the retrieval process effectively. This flexibility would certainly be an advantage to any organism because its ability to retrieve information would not be strictly bound by its immediate external environment. At the end of the day, it is probably a combination of the two theories that provides the best way of thinking about retrieval. GR emphasises the reconstructive aspect of retrieval and the possibility that novel cues can intervene in the process. ESP stresses the central role of context and the dependence of retrieval on an overlap between the actual trace and the current candidate information.

Components of recognition memory

In our models of retrieval we have assumed that recognition is a single process. However, there is now abundant evidence that this view is incorrect and that recognition itself should be thought of as comprising two separable components: **familiarity** and **recollection**. This concept of recognition was first stated formally by Mandler (1980) who described the typical experience of meeting someone in the street, becoming aware that you know them, but initially being unable to identify them. Subsequently, you finally remember who they are. Mandler attributed the first experience to a feeling of familiarity ("something previously encountered") and the latter to recollection in which a specific context is retrieved.

The history of recognition research has centred largely on trying to find out more about these two forms of recognising. Mandler and Boeck (1974) asked participants to sort a hundred randomly selected words into categories and found significant variation in the number of categories individuals used for doing the task. In line with earlier studies, they found that participants who used more sorting categories achieved better recall and recognition performance and this was attributed to better initial organisation and differentiation of the words. A recognition test was then given a week later in which the speed of participants' recognition responses was recorded. Each participant's reaction times were divided into slow and fast before examining how initial organisation affected recognition speed. For slow responses the effect of organisation was again evident, in that participants who sorted the words into fewer categories produced longer reaction times. However, for the fast responses, the organisational factor had no effect. Mandler and Boeck concluded that the slow recognition responses were indicative of the context retrieval process operating in recognition and that this was slower for memories that were less well organised. Faster responses, in contrast, were assumed to reflect familiarity responses and for this reason were not sensitive to the organisation factor.

Subjective differences in recognition memory

Tulving (1989) introduced a new methodology for understanding the nature of recognition. In many ways this methodology addressed Mandler's original distinction, but the major difference was that the experiments involved participants making subjective judgements about their memory experiences. Tulving's approach emerged from his own conviction that memory for an event could be derived either from its representation in semantic memory or from episodic memory, an issue that we now know is controversial. Tulving demonstrated that participants could reliably classify their recognition responses as ones either based or not based on conscious recollection of a specific event. Following a learning phase, participants were given a recognition test and required, on recognising a stimulus, to classify their response as either **remember** (R) or **know** (K). An R response represented contextual recognition in which the response was associated with some episodic recollection of the word's prior occurrence (e.g. an image or emotion it evoked) whereas a K response represented recognition without any specific recollection.

Despite its subjective nature, the "R/K task" has shown some surprisingly consistent and interesting results. R responses seem sensitive to a wide range of factors including attentional resources, levels of processing, intentional learning instructions, and tranquillisers that affect our conscious processing resources. In addition, several studies have now identified variables which have opposing effects on R and K responses. Parkin and Russo (1993) examined how spacing influenced the distribution of R and K responses. For items classified as R, there was a conventional spacing effect but for items classified as K there was a "reverse" spacing effect with more items being classified as K when repeated immediately (see also Parkin et al., 1995). Age also has contrasting effects on R and K; as we get older the number of R responses decreases and the number of K responses increases (Parkin and Walter, 1992). In addition, dual task performance during learning was found to affect R responses but not K responses (Gardiner and Parkin, 1990, and Fig. 7.2).

FIG. 7.2.
The differential effect of various factors on the proportion of R and K responses. (a) The demonstration that R responses increase with spacing whereas K responses increase with massed presentation. (b) Increased aging leads to a decrease in R responses and an increase in K responding. (c) Applying divided attention during learning reduces R but leaves K unaffected.

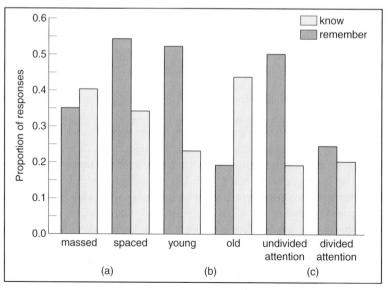

There has been a general tendency to accept R/K experiments as indicative of responses arising from different forms of memory, one responsible for familiarity and the other for recollection. However, Donaldson (1996) has proposed that R and K responses reflect a decision criterion based on the "strength" of the memory trace, i.e. how well it is represented in memory. Thus once an item passes the criterion for "recognised", its strength is assessed again with stronger traces being classed as R and the weaker ones classed as K. A problem with this account, however, is that some experiments have directly compared R/K judgements with measures of confidence. The Parkin and Walter study, for example, was repeated using sure–not sure as the basis for classifying "yes" responses. This showed that older participants classified 93% of their yes responses as "sure" compared with the younger participants' 91%. On the basis of this result, it is difficult to argue that the increase in K responses with age reflects weaker memory traces.

Process dissociation framework

Recently Jacoby (1991) has proposed the **process dissociation framework** as a means of measuring the extent to which a participant's recognition response is determined by familiarity or contextual retrieval. In a typical experiment, participants are presented with two successive lists of words, one spoken and the other visually presented. Two types of recognition test follow: In the exclusion condition, participants were required to make a contextual recollection in that they were required to identify only words from list 2. In the inclusion condition, no contextual demands were imposed, participants were just told to recognise words they had seen before. The assumption of this methodology is that recognition of a list 1 word in the exclusion condition indicates that the participant has forgotten the context of that word's presentation. By the use of simple equations it is then possible to estimate the amount of recognition based on recollection as opposed to that based on familiarity.

One of the crucial assumptions underlying the use of the process dissociation procedure (PDP) is that the probability of recognising an item on the basis of familiarity is stochastically independent of recognition based on recollection, i.e. it assumed that an item cannot be recognised on the basis of both familiarity and recollective information. Support for this independence assumption came from divided attention experiments which showed that distracting participants during learning reduced the recollective component of memory but not the component based on familiarity (Jacoby et al., 1993). However, subsequent experiments have indicated that this independence assumption is incorrect and that the interpretation of PDP findings is not as straightforward as once thought (Russo et al., 1998).

Bottom-up vs top-down processes in recognition

One influential idea about recognition is that familiarity and recollection differ in terms of their reliance on bottom-up vs top-down processing. This idea was formalised in an experiment by Johnston et al. (1985). In the first part of this experiment participants were required to read some individually presented words. In the next phase these "old" words were presented together with an equal number of "new" words. At first these words were severely degraded, but gradually they became clearer until a point was reached where subjects could name them. Following naming participants also had to indicate whether each word was "old" or "new". The independent variable of interest was the speed of naming as a function of whether the words were "old" or "new" and whether the recognition decision was correct. It was found that naming speed for "old" words was faster irrespective of whether the recognition response was correct. Johnston et al. (1985) described this faster reading of "old" words as **perceptual fluency**; the idea was that a recognition response could be cued on the basis that perception of a previously-seen item was easier relative to an unseen control item. Central to the idea of fluency is that it is context-free information regarding recollection which emanates entirely from how the stimulus interacts with the perceptual system.

Recently, Parkin et al. (in press) tested this idea using a different type of task. Participants were first presented with a list of words and then a yes–no recognition test in which list words had to be discriminated from distractor words. There were two conditions: overlap, in which the targets and distractors were chosen at random, and non-overlap. In this second condition, target and distractor words were constructed from different portions of the alphabet. Thus, one half of the alphabet was used to construct the learning list words and the other half the distractor list. The results showed that false alarms (misidentification of distractors as targets) occurred less in the non-overlap condition. This effect was attributed to the greater difference in bottom-up information provided by the non-overlap condition. Interestingly, no participant noticed what the difference between the types of list used was, thus indicating that the effect was mediated at a level that did not impinge on conscious awareness.

Context effects

There are many formal demonstrations that context exerts powerful effects on our ability to recognise stimuli. Light and Carter-Sobell (1970) required participants to study simple sentences which biased participants towards encoding one particular meaning of an ambiguous word (e.g. *They were stuck in a traffic* JAM). Retention testing involved participants identifying the target words which were again embedded in biasing sentences but, in half of these, the sentence was biased toward a different meaning to that used at learning (e.g. *They enjoyed eating the* JAM). Recognition was substantially reduced when the bias changed between learning and test, thus indicating a strong effect of intrinsic context.

In many ways we should not be surprised at the Light and Carter-Sobell result. What has been demonstrated, in effect, is that if you learn one thing and test for another you get impaired memory; a good example of transfer appropriate processing. What is far less clear is what we should expect when the extrinsic context is manipulated because, here, the contextual changes have no apparent relevance to what has been learned.

Environmentally dependent memory

The idea that the environment within which we learn might have an impact on how we remember has a long history. Dulsky (1935) showed that paired associate learning was impaired if the background colour in the learning phase is altered at test. Abernethy (1940) showed that classroom learning was affected when testing took place in a different room and reduced further when a different teacher was present. The most well-known example of **environment dependent memory** comes from a study by Godden and Baddeley (1975) who examined memory performance in two distinct environments: on land and underwater. It was found that free recall was better when the learning and test environments were the same than when they were different. However, Godden and Baddeley found no similar effect when a recognition test was used.

Smith (1986) reports a similar study in which participants undertook a number of memory span trials either in a room or while immersed in a flotation tank. They were then given an unexpected final memory test for the items and a significant environment-dependent effect was found for both recall and recognition. A subsequent study examined whether changing rooms could exert environment-dependent effects on recall and recognition. Memory span again served as the basic task but half the participants were also told that their memory for the words would be tested again later. Here it was found that an environment-dependent effect only occurred when participants did not know that recognition would be tested at a later point (see also Smith and Vela, 1992).

State-dependent memory

State-dependent memory refers to the idea that various psychoactive drugs can influence the memory process in contextual manner, although recently it has been shown that variations in aerobic state can exert similar effects (Miles and Daylen, 1998). Thus, it has often been claimed that information learned in an intoxicated state will be better remembered if that intoxicated state is also present at test as opposed to a sober state. In an early study of this type, Goodwin et al. (1969), participants undertook recall and recognition tasks having either recently consumed a soft drink or a substantial amount of high-strength vodka. The next day they were required to perform the same tasks again either in the same state or a different state. A change in state (e.g. learn sober, test intoxicated) produced reliably lower recall performance but there was no state-dependent effect on recognition.

During the next decade there was considerable interest in the ability of various drugs to induce state-dependent effects but the results were very inconsistent. Analysing these studies, Eich (1980) noticed that 88% of studies showing evidence for state-dependent effects had measured free recall, while 90% of the studies failing to show state-dependency had used either cued recall or recognition.

Why do environment- and state-dependent effects occur?

There has not been a great deal of research into this topic although one clue as to why these effects occur is provided by Block and Wittenborn (1985) in a study involving marijuana, a drug that is known to produce state-dependent effects similar to alcohol. In an earlier chapter we saw that associations made during learning are part of what we remember and that memory is promoted if those associations are also present at test. Block and Wittenborn (1985) showed that the types of association made when people were high on marijuana were, not surprisingly, rather different to those made when they were not drugged. A state-dependent effect might therefore arise because, when drugged again at test participants are more likely to think of these unusual associations as retrieval cues compared with when they are not drugged. Similar explanations could also be offered for other drugs and might even extend to explain environment-dependent effects: a particular context might make people think about information in specific ways that would not occur elsewhere.

It should also be stressed that environment- and state-dependent effects are often rather small and this may explain why the effects only seem obtainable with recall. Recognition, as we have seen, is considered to be a dual component process based on recollection and familiarity. We can reasonably assume that context only affects recollective memory so, if a considerable extent of recognition is based on familiarity, there is far less scope for any effect to appear.

Mood and memory

The effects of mood on memory have received considerable attention (Blaney, 1986; Mineka and Nugent, 1995). Bower (1981) asked participants to keep a diary of the emotional aspect of their lives. After one week, they were subjected to a **mood induction** procedure in which hypnotic suggestion was used to make them either "happy" or "sad". They were then required to recall events and it was found that there was a **mood congruency** effect, with participants in a pleasant mood recalling more pleasant memories and those in an unpleasant mood recalling more unpleasant memories. A second study by Bower et al. (1981) again used mood induction to create "happy" or "sad" participants who then listened to a story about Paul Smith. Half the events happening to Paul were positive and half negative, and again a mood congruency effect at recall was found. Findings like these were incorporated into a network model in which mood state was selectively biasing which aspects of an experience were remembered (Bower et al., 1981). However, since then there has been controversy as to whether mood congruency effects reliably occur. Also, as we shall see, the use of hypnosis as a means of inducing mood adds a further degree of uncertainty to the interpretation of positive mood effects.

Eich and Metcalfe (1989) reasoned that "internal events", events that originate from mental operations such as reasoning and imagination, might be more influenced by current mood state than externally mediated events. If true, memory for these internal events should be more susceptible to mood congruency effects than external events. To test this idea, participants were first placed in either a good or bad mood by listening to appropriate classical music (e.g. Mozart's *Eine Kleine Nachtmusik* or Albinoni's *Adagio in G Minor*). During the learning phase participants either read a target item paired with a category name and a related example (e.g. milkshake flavours: chocolate—VANILLA), or they generated the target item with a high probability when given the initial letter (e.g. milkshake flavours: chocolate—V___?). The authors assumed that production of the response under generate conditions would correspond to an internal event whereas read conditions would

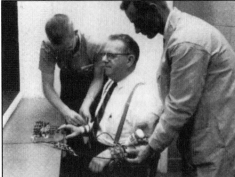

Stanley Milgram (1963) set up a mock situation to test whether a "teacher" would do as instructed and give electric shocks of increasing intensity to a "learner" every time a wrong answer was given. He found that, alarmingly, 65% of the participants were willing to deliver a lethal shock if instructed to do so by the experimenter. This study, intended to investigate the concept of obedience to authority, may have been affected by the demand characteristics of the experimental situation.

be perceived as external. A subsequent retention test in which either the same or different mood to learning was induced revealed two principal findings: mood congruency effects were much more substantial for generated than read items, but only when free recall was measured. No effect of mood emerged with recognition testing.

One problem with mood and memory experiments is that they may be sensitive to **demand characteristics**. This term refers to the fact that participants may grasp what an experiment is trying to prove and then shape their responses accordingly. In connection with this, one study showed that mood congruency effects such as those found by Bower (1981) could be found in subjects who were simply instructed to behave *as if* they were happy or sad (Perrig and Perrig, 1988).

Doubts about possible compliance and demand characteristic factors present in hypnotic induction procedures did not deter Rinck et al. (1992) from trying to demonstrate mood congruency effects. After becoming either "happy" or "sad" participants rated words on a seven point scale ranging from –3 (very unpleasant) to +3 (very pleasant). Four types of words were used: strongly unpleasant (e.g. ulcer), slightly unpleasant (e.g. dirty), slightly pleasant (e.g. avenue), and strongly pleasant (e.g. beauty). Next day, free of induced mood, participants were given an unexpected recall test and the results are shown in Fig. 7.3. For strongly toned words there is a mood incongruency effect but for slightly toned words there is a mood congruency effect: participants recalled more words incongruent with the mood they were in during learning.

Rinck et al.'s data are difficult to explain in terms of demand characteristics because it is quite implausible that participants could have noticed the difference between strongly and slightly toned words and responded accordingly. Instead, the authors suggest that mood does have an effect but is dependent on the emotional valence of the stimulus. Strongly toned words exert a mood congruence effect whereas a slightly toned word will result in either no effect or a mood incongruency effect. However, the manner by which the latter is held to come about is not very well specified by the authors.

While we may have some doubts as to whether mood can affect memory in normal people, there seems little doubt that abnormal mood

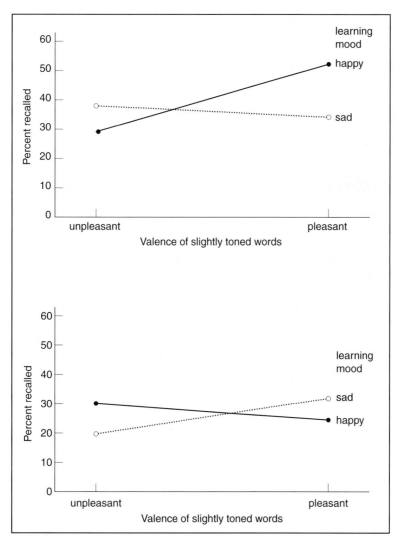

FIG. 7.3.
Data from Rinck et al. (1992) showing that mood effects occur with strongly toned words (top) but not with slightly toned words (bottom).

states do have a profound effect on memory. Lloyd and Lishman (1975) found that time taken by depressed patients to recall negative experiences decreased as they became more depressed. Clark and Teasdale (1981) exploited the natural mood swings of depressed patients. When the patients were relatively happy they recalled more pleasant than unpleasant memories, but when they sank into deeper depression unpleasant memories dominated their recall. Williams and Broadbent (1986) found that depressed suicidal patients found it more difficult to retrieve memories when prompted with positive cue words and, even when successful, these memories were less specific. In a similar kind of study, Burke and Mathews (1992) presented clinically anxious and non-anxious participants with neutral cues and found that the anxious subjects produced more anxiety-related memories. Collectively, these studies indicate that clinical mood states do exert important influences over the pattern of memories retrieved—findings that may have significance for understanding the nature and maintenance of these disorders.

Repression, false memory and hypnosis

In various writings, Freud put forward the view that forgetting could be caused by **repression** (Freud, 1901). In the Freudian sense, the idea of repression is linked directly to Freud's psychosexual theory of personal development. According to Freud, people pass through various stages of personal development including, crucially, the oedipal phase. In the case of boys this involves a period when a boy is thought to be sexually attracted to his mother. In most individuals this oedipal complex is resolved via fear of castration, and personal development continues normally. If the complex is not resolved, the person regresses to the earlier anal or oral stages of development and unresolved oedipal conflict is repressed. Freud's psychoanalytical techniques were aimed specifically at rooting out repressed memories.

A few experiments have examined whether Freud's concept of repression has any scientific value and the answer is clearly no. However, the concept of repression considered more broadly—i.e. the general idea that our memory system can in some way block particular forms of memory—needs to be taken seriously. Within the clinical field there are numerous examples of what we can term **psychogenic** or **functional amnesia**. People suffering these disorders have not suffered any brain damage but have experienced highly traumatic incidents which they cannot now remember. Most common is combat amnesia where soldiers return from battle unable to remember what has happened to them. Amnesia for crime is also quite common where extreme violence has been involved. For example the Moors Murderer, Ian Brady, repressed memories of his hideous crimes for years before finally remembering where he had buried his unfortunate victims (Parkin, 1997b).

Recently there has been an enormous controversy concerning false memory syndrome with large numbers of (most commonly) female adults suddenly recovering memories that they were sexually and

physically abused during their childhood. In addition, there have been a remarkable number of studies in which young children claim to have witnessed satanic rituals, including ritual human sacrifice. If correct, the frequency of these claims suggests a very unpleasant world with untold numbers of people suffering. Fortunately, as we shall see, these phenomena are not at all what they seem (for detailed criticism of the concept of recovered memory see Loftus, 1993; Loftus and Ketcham, 1994; Ofshe and Watters, 1995, and for a compendium of different views see Conway, 1997).

Recovered memories of sexual abuse began to appear more frequently after the publication of a book which claimed that if you were mentally unwell it was most likely that you had been sexually abused as a child (Bass and Davis, 1988). Many therapists received this idea enthusiastically and introduced "memory work" as part of their therapeutic strategy. Usually, memory work involved the use of hypnosis under the false assumption that hypnosis can unlock forgotten memories. There has been a steady stream of experimental studies exploring the possibility that hypnosis can facilitate memory but all have showed negative results (see Parkin, 1997b for an overview).

How, then, does hypnosis lead to false memory? The answer lies in the fact that hypnosis induces a state of **compliance** in the hypnotised person. When this is combined with leading questions, a

When the Herald of Free Enterprise ferry capsized off the coast of Belgium in 1987, many people lost their lives. Survivors of the disaster were prone to suffer from post-traumatic stress disorder (PTSD), a psychological disorder caused by the memories of a traumatic event.

false belief that hypnosis can unlock forgotten experiences (Yapko, 1994) and a presumption that sexual abuse lies at the heart of a person's difficulties, it is not difficult to see how the false memories come about. In the case where children believe they have seen satanic rituals, the form of questioning used by counsellors seems to be the primary cause. In a recent detailed investigation of one such incident it was shown that the questioning techniques used very obviously pressured the children into manufacturing false memories. Techniques included repeated questioning if the child did not concede that abuse had taken place and coercion based on telling the child that older children had witnessed the alleged events (Garven et al., 1998). These types of problem have also been evident when children have been questioned in courtrooms (Ceci and Bruck, 1995).

Overview

- Memory is a selective process.
- Remembering is a reconstructive process.
- The reconstructive process is thought to be guided by schemata.
- Generation–recognition models propose that retrieval involves two stages: generation of candidates and a recognition check to determine which candidate is the sought-after memory.
- Generation–recognition predicted that any word that could be recalled could also be recognised. Experiments on encoding specificity refuted this claim.
- Encoding specificity proposed that recall and recognition were different dimensions of a single retrieval process.
- Encoding specificity emphasised the importance of context in remembering.
- Context can be divided into intrinsic (interactive) and extrinsic (non-interactive) contexts.
- Recognition is considered to be a two-component process comprising both familiarity and recollection.
- Changes in intrinsic context have very strong effects on memory.
- Changes in extrinsic context, such as environment and psychoactive state, can also influence remembering.
- Mood appears able to influence memory in a state-dependent manner but the exact conditions under which this occurs are somewhat controversial.
- Repression, in its general sense, appears to be a genuine form of forgetting.

- False memory appears to arise as a consequence of hypnotically-induced compliance and the use of leading questions.

Suggested further reading

Baddeley, A.D. (1997). *Human memory: Theory and practice* (rev. ed.). Hove, UK: Psychology Press.

Provides a detailed review of all aspects of remembering and forgetting including more peripheral topics not covered here.

Parkin, A.J. (1993). *Memory: Phenomena, experiment, and theory*. Hove, UK: Psychology Press.

A slightly older alternative to Baddeley.

Parkin, A.J. (2000). *Memory: A professional's guide*. Chichester: Wiley.

Although aimed at professionals other than psychologists, the chapter on false memory may be useful.

Schacter, D.L. (1996). *Searching for memory*. New York: Basic Books.

Although written as a "popular" book, Schacter's book contains thorough discussions of many of the topics in this chapter, particularly false memory.

Schacter, D.L. (1999). The seven sins of memory: Insights from psychology and cognitive science. *American Psychologist, 54,* 182–203.

This is a thorough review of the various ways that our memory system can let us down and covers many of the issues raised in this chapter.

Revision questions

1 Why does it make more sense to have a selective memory?
2 Why did some people come to believe that our memory stored away all our experiences and why were they wrong?
3 What does it mean to say that retrieval is a "reconstructive process"?
4 What is a schema?
5 Outline the generation–recognition model of retrieval and explain why it predicted that any word that could be recalled must also be capable of being recognised.
6 What sorts of phenomena was the generation–recognition model of retrieval able to account for?

7 Why was the generation–recognition model unable to explain the results obtained by Tulving and Thompson?

8 What is the encoding specificity principle?

9 What are the principal differences and similarities between the generation–recognition model and encoding specificity?

10 What are the three different causes of forgetting?

11 What is the difference between familiarity and recollection, and how have psychologists attempted to distinguish these two forms of recognition memory?

12 What is meant by context and what sorts of influence can it have on memory?

13 Why do various forms of context affect recall more than cued recall and recognition?

14 What evidence is there that mood state affects memory?

15 What is meant by "repression" and does it really occur?

16 What is "false memory syndrome" and how might it arise?

Knowledge 8

The English scientist Francis Galton tackled many different issues during his long career. One problem he considered was the notion of "typicality" and his particular concern was "what does the average criminal look like?". Galton's idea was to collect together the negatives of photographs of known criminals, lay one on top of another, and print the resulting photographic collage. Galton believed that "typicality" was represented by taking some kind of average of all the **exemplars** of a category. Galton may have been misguided in thinking that there was a "criminal look"—although not that long ago British policemen were advised to attend courts in order to learn what criminals look like. In this chapter, we will see that what determines typicality is a central issue in the representation of knowledge and that Galton's idea of a cumulative average is still an influential concept.

In *Get Carter*, Michael Caine played the anti-hero Jack Carter, a London gangster avenging the murder of his brother. Do you think that he looks like a "typical" gangster?

Experimental evidence

Imagine an experiment in which participants sit in front of a screen and view a series of simple sentences such as:

(1) "A canary is a bird."
(2) "An ostrich is a bird."
(3) "A potato is a tree."
(4) "A rifle is a tree."

The participants' task is to decide whether or not each sentence is true. Tasks such as **sentence verification** have been used extensively in research about the representation of knowledge. By examining the relative degree of difficulty posed by different sentences, it is hoped that some insights can be gained about how knowledge is represented in the brain.

Returning to our experiment, we can observe two effects. The first of these is the **typicality effect** illustrated by faster "yes" decisions for sentence (1) compared with (2). This effect indicates that our knowledge system is in some way sensitive to the fact that a canary is a better example of a bird than an ostrich (Rosch et al., 1976). The second effect concerns the fact that participants take longer to reject (3) as untrue compared with (4). This is known as the **category similarity effect** and indicates that our knowledge system is organised so as to pick up the less distant relationship between "tree" and "potato" compared with "tree" and "rifle".

Meaning in terms of defining attributes

An early approach to knowledge representation centred on the idea of **defining attributes**. According to this, objects can be grouped together in terms of certain attributes (features) that are common to all of them in order to form a concept. Thus our concept of a horse is that it has four legs, hair, a tail, and it neighs. Other attributes can also be associated with "horse" such as "can be ridden", "piebald", but because these attributes only apply to some horses, they are not defining.

Collins and Quillian (1969) put forward a **network theory** of how we might represent concepts in this way. This theory was an early example of **computational modelling** in that the idea was initially developed as a computer program and only subsequently tested on humans. Collins and Quillian's network is illustrated in Fig. 8.1 and it is essentially based on the idea of defining attributes. The basic organisation of the model is that each concept we possess is represented by a node which has a number of attributes associated with it, e.g. "bird" → "has feathers, can fly". The network is organised as a hierarchy with more specific concepts subsumed under less specific ones, e.g. the concept "animal" is a **superordinate** of "bird" and "fish" which, in turn have the **subordinates** "canary" and "salmon". The network also employs **cognitive economy** in that only those attributes that distinguish a concept from its superordinates are stored at the concept itself. Thus the node "bird" has attributes such as "can fly" but the attribute "breathes" is represented at the "animal" node. Similarly, the "canary" node has the attribute "yellow" but the fact that it is a bird is embodied in its link with the higher level node "bird".

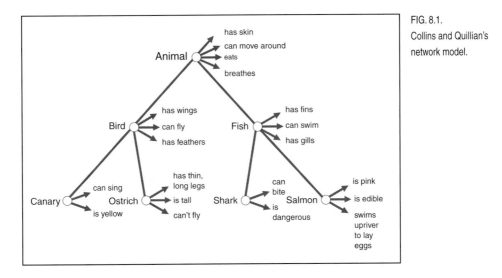

FIG. 8.1.
Collins and Quillian's
network model.

Collins and Quillian's model made some straightforward predictions about how participants might respond in a sentence verification task. According to the model, decision time should be a function of the "distance" between the accessed node and the node that contains information regarding the answer. Thus for the three questions:

(1) "Is a canary yellow?"
(2) "Is a canary a bird?"
(3) "Is a canary an animal?"

the ordering of response times in terms of fastest to slowest should be (1) < (2) < (3).

Initial experiments produced the expected results but there were many problems. First the model, although able to deal with category similarity effects, was not able to explain the typicality effect. The distance between "ostrich" and "bird", and "canary" and "bird", is similar so one would predict similar response times but, as the typicality effect predicts, "robin" was verified faster. In addition, some verification experiments produced findings at odds with the network account in that statements reflecting greater distances between nodes were verified more quickly than closer relationships, e.g. "chicken is an animal" was verified faster than "chicken is a bird".

These experimental data were complemented by philosophical objections, particularly the view that not all concepts have defining features. The classic example of this was Wittgenstein's (1953) discussion of the word "game". We all know what games are but it is impossible to think of one attribute that is common to all games. Instead, members of the concept "game" share some **family resemblance** that cannot be pinned down to a specific feature. Another problem is so-called linguistic hedging in which instances can change categories depending on the context. Thus, in biological terms, a tomato is a fruit but, in relation to cooking, a tomato is conceptually dealt with as a vegetable.

Feature comparison theories

In a **feature comparison model**, concepts are represented as lists of features. These are divided into defining features and **characteristic features**. A defining attribute is one possessed by all members of a category, e.g. all birds have feathers, and characteristic features are attributes possessed by most members of a category. Within this model, verification involves two stages. First, all the features associated with each concept are compared and, if the overlap is sufficient, a "yes" response is made. If there is not sufficient featural overlap a second comparison is initiated based only on the defining features (Hollan, 1975).

Feature comparison theory dealt with the typicality effect by proposing that an atypical member would not share sufficient features with a category in the first comparison, thus necessitating a second and more time-consuming comparison of only the defining features. The category similarity effect was also explained on the grounds that a distant related pair of concepts ("potato" "tree"), would show some overlap and thus delay responding compared with completely non-overlapping pairs ("potato" "rifle").

Although feature comparison theory had advantages it still had major problems. First, because it still makes use of the defining feature concept, it has the limitations we have just discussed in relation to defining feature theory. In addition, it is a theory aimed at explaining how we verify statements as proposed to a more general theory of how we extract the meaning of what we see or hear. As a result, it makes absurd predictions; e.g. "a canary is a bird" and "a bird is a canary" would both be classed as true. However, it cannot explain how we verify statements involving concepts that have no featural overlap, e.g. "the man has a brick".

Prototype theory

A completely different way of conceptualising knowledge representation is in terms of **prototypes.** In many ways, prototypes can

be thought of as a modern expression of Wittgenstein's idea of family resemblance (Rosch and Mervis, 1975). A prototype thus represents a form of "average" in which the individual features of instances or exemplars of a category somehow coalesce into a single representation of what the category typically looks like. This averaging process sidesteps the awkward problem of specifying defining features, and typicality effects are explained in terms of the extent to which any exemplar of a category deviates from the average; thus an ostrich is a "less average" bird than a robin.

When considering the category of birds, a pigeon is a more "typical" bird than a flamingo.

There is abundant evidence that people behave as if they store knowledge in a prototypical way. In one experiment, participants studied geometric patterns, each of which was a distortion of a basic prototype that was not presented. A recognition test followed in which participants had to identify which figures they had seen before. Of most interest were the **false alarms**—occasions when people incorrectly thought they had seen a figure before. This was most likely when the figure presented was the prototype from which the studied figures had been derived and became systematically less likely as the deviation of the non-seen items from the prototype increased (Franks and Bransford, 1971, and see Fig. 8.2).

The above study shows that participants might make use of prototypes if required to in an experiment, but what about pre-existing knowledge? When people are asked to produce examples of a category, they consistently give typical examples first (Barsalou, 1985). Similarly, we can observe a typicality effect for pictures; good examples of a category are identified faster than unusual ones (Smith et al., 1978). Finally, if told that a common member of a category has a particular property (e.g. a robin has a contagious disease), people will assume that

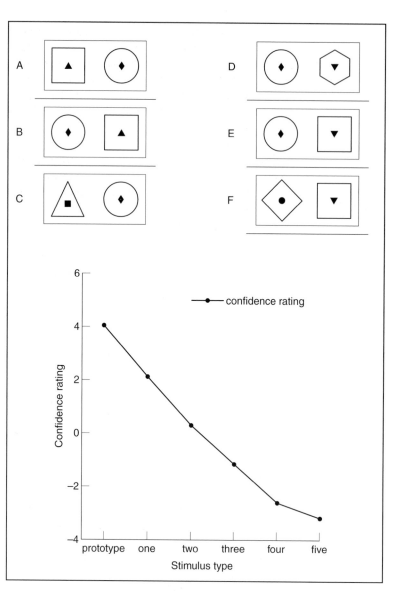

more members of that category are also affected than if the property is
attributed to a less typical member (e.g. a duck (Rips, 1975).

Exemplar based models

It is generally assumed that prototypes emerge through the process of
categorisation, i.e. that successive encounters with different exemplars

of a category enable the common features of that category to become assimilated. Exemplar theory differs substantially from prototype theory by arguing that no prototype is stored, just exemplars of concepts that are all considered members of the same category. If we consider how this would work, it becomes clear that our list of exemplars would be dominated by typical examples, e.g. for birds there would be sparrows, tits, robins, but very few large flightless examples such as emu, ostrich. In order to assess similarity, it is proposed that the system retrieves an exemplar to match with a new item. Because of the predominance of typical exemplars, it is more likely that one of these will be retrieved. Thus when presented with another typical bird, e.g. chaffinch, a high typicality judgement is far more likely than if an atypical bird is presented, e.g. a penguin (Estes, 1993; Shin and Nosofsky, 1992).

Both prototype theory and exemplar theory explain typicality effects, so how might these theories be distinguished? One argument in favour of exemplar models is that they preserve information about the variability within a concept. For any category we know, we can also answer questions about variability. We know, for example, that pine trees vary in size, ranging from your typical Christmas tree right through to the giant sequoia. If our knowledge of pine trees is just an abstracted average, how would we know that? In contrast, a range of exemplars easily provides the basis for such knowledge.

There is also the issue of correlation between features. Because the notion of a prototype is held to be an averaging process, it does not embody specific relationships that might exist between particular features that go to make up that prototype. For example, it is generally the case that flightless birds are bigger than their aerial counterparts but this would not be apparent in a simple averaging procedure. One could, of course, start to argue for more specific prototypes such as "flightless" bird which, when compared with the "flighted bird" prototype, would provide information about relative size. However, this would still be a misleading way to go about representing information because variability within those categories is hidden, i.e. some flightless birds are actually quite small. If one follows this path, it becomes apparent that the full range of knowledge can be expressed only by assuming continued access to exemplar-based knowledge.

Another problem with prototype theory concerns **ad hoc categories**. Barsalou (1983) presented participants with short vignettes, such as the case of "Roy" who was living in Las Vegas but, as a result of double-crossing the Mafia, now had a "contract" out on him. The participants were given a sheet of various statements, e.g. "change your identity and move to the mountains of South America" and asked which ones belonged to the category "Ways to escape being killed by the Mafia". Barsalou found typicality effects with these ad hoc categories; findings that are difficult to attribute to prototype theory on the grounds that it is unlikely that people would have entered the experiment with a pre-existing prototype concerning Mafia avoidance. Instead, Barsalou argued that ad hoc categories arise by the implementation of goal-specific operations that search through our knowledge with a particular aim in mind. In the case of the Mafia example, each statement is assessed in relation to a dimension representing anonymity. Thus the same set of exemplars might be assessed in different ways depending on the question. Taking items stored in your loft, for example, different lists would be produced to the category "things that could fall on your head" as opposed to "things you could sell in a garage sale".

While one can see some distinct advantages for the exemplar model, there are some problems. First, there is the practical issue of storing so much information. Also, exactly what is an exemplar? Is it a literal collection of all encounters with a particular item or some abstraction? If it is the latter, then we seem to be heading back towards prototypes. Another problem is that a range of exemplars needs to be organised in some way. If the theory is correct, the question "is a canary a bird" must be addressed by locating a range of "bird" exemplars and the question arises as to how these exemplars are grouped together. One solution might be to take Barsalou's suggestion that we use dimensions to search our knowledge base. Thus, when asked to locate birds we use a dimension "has a beak?" which would locate all birds without the necessity of bird exemplars being formally linked as birds.

Schema

We have already encountered the concept of **schema** (pl. **schemata**) in our consideration of Bartlett's approach to remembering (see Chapter 7). In this section we will see how the idea of a schema and its derivatives have played an important role in attempting to understand how we represent knowledge. In principle, a schema is a framework for understanding any particular situation in the world. It will have a fixed core and a range of variables. The schema of a football match, for example, would have core information such as involves two teams, "uses a ball", and a range of variables: can result in a win or a draw, the teams taking part, the result, and the type of competition involved (league, cup). By their nature, schemata can have unspecified variables that enable gaps to be filled. Thus the sentence "Rangers were pleased to be through to the next round" is taken to mean that Rangers won the match, because the schema assumes that progress to the next round requires winning as opposed to a less likely possibility that the other side did not turn up.

The idea of schema allows for selectivity in learning and was neatly demonstrated in a study in which participants were asked to look around a house, either from the perspective of a burglar or an estate agent (Anderson and Pichert, 1978). Recall of the groups was very different, with the "burglars" noting open windows and broken locks, and the estate agents noticing decorative problems and room sizes. Here it appears that different schema have been applied to the same basic information to achieve different goals.

Scripts

The idea of schema was developed by Schank and Abelson (1977) in their **script** theory. As the name implies, a script is an account of events that typically happen, in particular situations such as going to a restaurant. Scripts represent another example of cognitive economy in that they enable generally similar things to be stored only in terms of what differentiates them. In the case of a restaurant, the script would provide general information that you ate food and paid the bill but a specific memory would recollect that the food was prawn curry and that it was over-priced. Support for script theory was provided by Bower et al. (1979) who showed that, when asked to describe typical events such as a visit to a restaurant, people tended to agree on what typically happened.

In its original form script theory did not handle real world data very well. If, for example, you were in a restaurant and discovered a cigarette end in a pizza it is highly unlikely that you would forget the incident, yet script theory, with its emphasis on storing typical events, would suggest the opposite. Problems such as this led to a revision known as the **dynamic memory theory** (Schank, 1982). The initial motivation of this theory was the observation that participants' memory for one distinct event, e.g. a visit to the doctor, was often confused with details from another event, e.g. a visit to the dentist. Standard script theory would not predict this because the events should be represented as separate schema.

Schank proposed a number of additional concepts in his revised theory. Plans represent the goal that underlies a given sequence of events and this can be flexible. Thus the goal of being in a restaurant may not simply be to eat, it might involve an attempt to impress a new partner, or a means of winning over a new client. A plan like this might, therefore, enable the statement "he chose a very expensive wine" to be more clearly interpreted. Memory organisation packets (MOPs) are

The Magnificent Seven, a very famous Western, was actually based on the same story as *The Seven Samurai.* generalised representations of particular actions or **scenes**. Schank gives as one of his examples visiting a health professional (see Fig. 8.3). This would involve three MOPS, each of which has a number of associated scenes. MOPS are configured so that they can apply to any range of events. Thus the MOP "PROFESSIONAL–OFFICE–VISIT" could apply to any visit to a professional and thus accounts for why people might muddle up visits to the doctor and dentist.

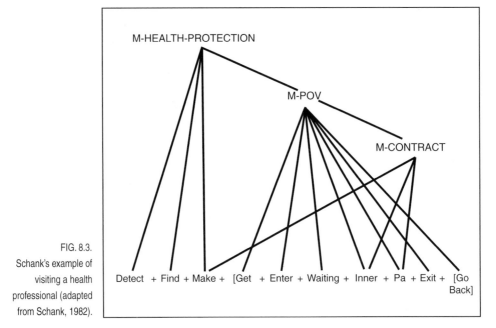

FIG. 8.3. Schank's example of visiting a health professional (adapted from Schank, 1982).

The idea of scripts certainly has intuitive appeal and is consistent with a number of experimental findings. The problem, however, is that the concept appears to be infinitely extendible so that it can deal with any expression of knowledge. Thus my cigarette-end-in-the-pizza example could be explained by combining a restaurant scene with a "finding things" scene and a "revulsion" scene. In addition, **thematic organisation units** (TOPS) have also been proposed in which general "theme" information is available. Information at this level, for example, might be used to realise that the classic Western *The Magnificent Seven* is based on the same story as Kurosawa's *The Seven Samurai*. While this apparent level of explanatory power appears impressive, the power to generate increasingly abstract representations of human knowledge without specifying how these units arise and how they are constituted undermines this approach as basis for the scientific study of knowledge.

Overview

- Attempts to define concepts in terms of defining features are not satisfactory because too many concepts do not have defining features.
- The Collins and Quillian network model introduced the idea of cognitive economy but it failed to predict how people performed in certain sentence verification tasks, especially the typicality effect.
- Feature comparison theory was an improvement in that it handled the typicality effect but it was undermined because it still relied on the assumption of defining features. It was also a model aimed at explaining verification rather than the representation of knowledge more generally.
- Prototype theory asserts that categories are represented by prototypes which represent the average of exemplars of that category.
- Prototype theory has been criticised because a prototype does not allow information about variability in a concept to be expressed, nor does it represent correlations that may exist between features of a concept.
- Exemplar theory states that typicality judgements are made by comparing a new item with an exemplar. Typicality effects arise because the exemplar is more likely to be typical. Exemplar theories have the advantage of allowing variation and correlation to be expressed but they do require a large amount of storage. There is also the problem of how information from exemplars is represented and how that information becomes grouped together into categories.

- A schema represents a framework for understanding some aspect of the world. It is thought to have an invariant core and a range of variable values.
- Schema introduce economy into memory in that only information differentiating two similar events needs to be remembered.
- Script theory is a variant on schema which allows for greater flexibility in the representation of knowledge. It suffers from being scientifically untestable.

Suggested further reading

Kellog, R.T. (1995). *Cognitive psychology*. Thousand Oaks, CA: Sage.

Stevenson, R.J. (1993). *Language, thought and representation*. Chichester: Wiley.

Both these books contain detailed accounts of topics raised in this chapter.

Revision questions

1 The typicality effect and the category similarity effect must be accounted for by any theory of knowledge organisation. What are these effects?
2 What was the Collins and Qullian network theory and how did it embody the concept of cognitive economy?
3 What is meant by family resemblance?
4 What were the advantages and limitations of the feature comparison theory?
5 What is meant by a prototype and how is knowledge of a prototype built up?
6 What is a schema, what evidence supports the concept, and to what extent is it an explanatory construct?
7 What is script theory and what is its limitations?

Imagery 9

The idea of mental images seems so natural to us that it is hard to believe that the whole concept of mental imagery has proved so highly controversial. To begin our account, we must distinguish between two forms of imagery, **eidetic** and internal. At a subjective level we can define eidetic imagery as the experience of images as if they were actual percepts, i.e. they appear in front of us and when we use them it is as if we are actually "seeing" them. In adults, eidetic imagery is exceptionally rare but it is thought to be more widespread in children. According to Haber and Haber (1964) eidetic imagery is thought to be present in around eight percent of children but only 0.1 percent of adults. In a famous study of eidetic imagery, Allport (1924) briefly presented English children with the German word *Gartenwirthschaft* (meaning "market garden"). After only a brief exposure Allport found that the children could accurately repeat the sequence of letters backwards! In contrast, internal images are what we all experience; thus if asked to imagine something in our mind's eye we are perfectly capable of doing so.

However, not all attempts to show enhanced eidetic imagery in children have yielded positive results. Gummerman et al. (1972) used three different procedures to assess possible eidetic skills. One task involved the sequential presentation of two checker board patterns which, when combined, produced a figure (see Fig. 9.1). If eidetic imagery existed then sequential presentation of the two patterns should produce the third patterned image. No "eidetikers" were found with this task although one similar task did reveal two retarded children who showed some eidetic skills.

At first glance it might seem surprising that such a phenomenal memory ability as eidetic imagery should disappear but, with further thought, this is not so surprising. For the moment we can think of an image as something rather like a photographic image, a picture of some aspect of the world. However, images, just like photographs, need to be interpreted. Look at Fig. 9.2. You can obviously see and perhaps

FIG. 9.1.
Stimuli used by
Gummerman and
Gray (1971) to test for
eidetic imagery.

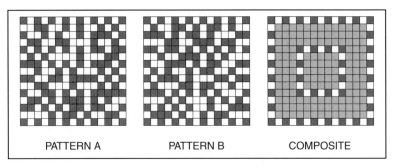

PATTERN A   PATTERN B   COMPOSITE

remember the image but only some additional interpretative process enables you to understand the meaning of the picture. Given that we interpret images and derive information from them, does it make sense to store those images away? Is, for example, recollecting the famous image shown in Fig. 9.2 needed for us to remember the facts leading to President Clinton's impeachment trial? The answer, on logical grounds, would appear to be "no" because the information we have derived from it is sufficient.

FIG. 9.2.
This picture of
President Clinton and
Monica Lewinsky
taken in 1996 was
used by the media to
fuel the sex scandal
that led to the
President's
impeachment trial
in 1999.

Given its infrequency there has been little experimental investigation of eidetic imagery and some debate as to whether apparent eidetikers were really using eidetic imagery. We have already encountered Luria's famous case of "S" (see Chapter 8) in whom the presence of eidetic imagery seems highly likely. More recently, Stromeyer and Psotka (1970) reported the case of Elizabeth, a university teacher who appeared to have remarkable eidetic abilities. She claimed to be able to mentally project beards on to men's faces and leaves on to barren trees. Her eidetic imagery was tested more formally using **random dot stereograms;**

these consist of a pair of apparently random patterns of dots. However, when presented using a stereoscope so that one pattern projects only on to the left eye and the other onto the right eye, a figure can be seen in depth. One half of a 10,000 dot stereogram pair was projected to Elizabeth's right eye and, 10 seconds later, the second pattern was presented to her left eye. She was asked to superimpose the eidetic image from her right eye on to the pattern she could see in her left eye and, without hesitation, correctly identified the pattern produced by combining the stereograms.

Another famous case was "Sue d'Onim" (Coltheart and Glick, 1974) who could visualise words and sentences then spell them backwards. In addition, she also had much higher recall in the iconic memory task than normal subjects (7.4 vs a control average of 4.8). However, the authors concluded that Sue d'Onim was not an eidetiker for a number of reasons, including the fact that she only visualised material when she was recalling it and relied on verbal rehearsal to retain information prior to recall, and because her ability to visualise memory was directly related to her verbal memory for the same material. Nonetheless, Sue d'Onim was regarded as unusual in that she formed particularly vivid images; this contrasted with views that she had a highly developed skill that, with practice, can be acquired by anyone (e.g. Ericsson and Faivre, 1988). Gummerman and Gray (1971) present a similar interpretation in relation to a student who had peculiarly good memory for visual scenes. Eidetic imagery therefore appears to be a rather elusive phenomenon (Wilding and Valentine, 1997).

Knowledge as propositions

On logical grounds, therefore, it does not make sense to store information as images; what we need to store is the information images convey and it is probably for this reason that eidetic imagery disappears so rapidly during child development. Dismissal of imagery has given rise to the idea that all our knowledge is represented in the form of **propositions**. A proposition represents the smallest unit of meaning to which we can answer "true" or "false". Thus "gerbils are common pets" is a proposition whereas "gerbil" is not. According to this idea, our knowledge of anything is built up by increasingly complex lists of propositions. It should be noted that, although propositions are expressed verbally, it is not intended that propositions are inherently verbal—rather they are thought to be held in some more abstract form.

So far we appear to be giving the idea of imagery rather short shrift, but consider the following mental task. I would like you first to imagine your bedroom. Once you have done this I would like you to answer a few questions:

(1) Where is your bed in relation to the door?
(2) Where is the door in relation to the window?
(3) What colours are the walls?
(4) Is there a TV in the room and, if so, where?

Unless there is something strange about you, almost certainly you will have used some form of internal image to answer these questions. Now, how do we reconcile this apparent use of imagery with our earlier conclusion that it makes no sense to store away images? This issue lies at the heart of modern debates about imagery which began when imagery was rediscovered after the behaviourist era ended.

Imagery as an experimental variable

The revival of imagery as an experimental issue is largely attributable to the work of Allan Paivio (Paivio, 1971; Paivio, 1986). Paivio's approach was to show that mental imagery could be studied within an experimental framework that behaviourists would find acceptable (Richardson, 1999). In early studies, Paivio (1969) used the **paired associate** (PA) learning task to explore the value of imagery as a factor in verbal learning. The PA task is a stimulus–response method for investigating memory and was used extensively by the behaviourists in their attempts to understand forgetting (for a full description of PA learning, see Chapter 5). Paivio examined the ease with which participants could learn associations when the stimulus and response terms were either concrete or abstract words. A concrete word is one that can be assumed to evoke a visual image (e.g. piano) and an abstract word is one that does not bring an obvious image easily to mind (e.g. justice). The results showed that participants found it much easier to learn associative pairs based on concrete words compared with abstract words.

Paivio's initial studies were supported by other investigators who examined the effect of instructing participants to use mental imagery while they were learning. Bower (1970) required participants to learn a list of 30 word pairs of concrete words (e.g. piano–cigar) under one of three kinds of instruction:

Rote learning: Repeat word pairs aloud as they appear.
Interactive imagery: Imagine the objects defined by the words acting together in some way.
Separate imagery: Make separate images of the two objects defined by the words.

The three types of instruction had no differential effect on recognition but interactive imagery produced far better recall. The benefits of interactive imagery were particularly evident in a study by Schnorr and Atkinson (1971) who found that the technique allowed participants to recall around 75% of the 96 stimulus response pairs they had been instructed to remember.

The dual coding hypothesis

To account for the effects of imagery on verbal learning, Paivio put forward the **dual coding hypothesis**. According to this hypothesis, mental activity involves the interaction of two interconnected but functionally independent subsystems: a non-verbal imagery system which processes visual information about objects and events and a verbal system specialised for handling speech and writing (Paivio, 1986). Within the verbal system, each known word is assumed to be represented by a **logogen**—a concept borrowed from Morton's (1969) recognition model. Images are represented in a similar discrete unit system in which the image associated with a specific object related to a particular **image**. Logogens and images are assumed to be connected by **referential links** that allow a word to be associated with its relevant image and vice versa.

The dual coding hypothesis provides a convenient account of various experimental findings. The better learning of concrete words can be attributed to their ability to induce both verbal and non-verbal codes, whereas abstract words are more poorly recalled because only a verbal code is available. It is also known that pictures are easier to memorise than words representing those pictures (Paivio, 1971). This finding can be explained by arguing that presentation of a picture is more likely to elicit a verbal code in addition to an imaginal one compared with word presentation in which imagery might be less likely to occur. However, the theory was not explicit as to what images were exactly.

Exploring the properties of the mental image

One way of defining a mental image is to think of it as an "internal percept" i.e. some embodiment of what it is like to see the object we are thinking about (one can, of course, have images related to our other senses but these are far less investigated and we will not consider them here). Images are therefore assumed to be dependent, to some extent, on the same system that underlies perception itself. In particular, images and percepts are thought to share one important quality in that both are **analogue representations**.

An analogue representation is one in which each part of the depicted object is represented once and only once. This is the reason why we describe a conventional clock face as an analogue dial; each time represented by the dial involves a unique combination of the two hands which cannot represent any other time. Another property of an analogue representation is that the spatial relationships between different elements of the representation correspond, in proportional terms, to the same relationships in the object itself—the image is therefore depictive. This idea can be understood if you imagine a map of Great Britain. As well as the general shape, various towns will be identifiable and the distances between them on the map are proportional to the distances in real life. Thus, the distance between London and Brighton in the image will appear less than the distance between London and Edinburgh.

A third property of a mental image is that it can be rotated in a way similar to rotation of the object itself in space. If you hold a pencil horizontally in front of you and rotate it around its central point you observe a continuous transformation of the object. You can also imagine the same thing and observe the same continuous transformation in your mind's eye.

Images are therefore assumed to be analogue representations of objects which can undergo transformation. The ability of mental images to undergo **mental rotation** was explored in a series of classic experiments by Roger Shepard and his colleagues (e.g. Shepard, 1978; Shepard and Metzler, 1971). In the first of these experiments, participants saw pairs of two-dimensional drawings (see Fig. 9.3) and had to decide whether the drawings showed the same object from different orientations (if you have ever played the computer game *Tetris* you can get some idea of what it is like to perform mental rotations). The graph shows the time it took participants to decide that two drawings were of the same object as a function of the angular disparity between them (angular disparity represents the amount one object would have to be rotated so as to be at the same orientation as the other). Correct reaction time has a linear relationship with angular disparity—the more rotation needed, the longer the reaction time.

One problem for the image-based account of mental rotation experiments is that, in order to explain the linear relationship between angular disparity and reaction time such as that shown in Fig. 9.3, the participant must always choose the correct direction in which to rotate the image. Thus if an image has disparity of 240 degrees it should be rotated clockwise, but with a disparity of 60 degrees the rotation should be anti-clockwise. How does the person know which way to rotate? If only imagery is involved there is no way of knowing in advance whether or not the quickest rotational direction has been chosen. This emphasises the point that images alone do not provide information— they need to be interpreted. Thus, although it can still be argued that an analogue representation is used in performance, the mental imagery account must accept that other knowledge, not based on imagery, also contributes to task performance.

Mental rotation experiments were interpreted as showing that participants imagine the located objects within an internal three-dimensional space and that one object is rotated until it matches the other. The demonstration of a linear relationship between reaction time and angular disparity also suggested that the image rotation process itself operated at a constant speed. Shepard's mental rotation experiments were enthusiastically received and it was generally considered that no explanation, other than one proposing the existence of mental images, could explain what was going on.

A computational model of imagery

The concept of mental imagery has been actively developed in Kosslyn's (1980) computational model. This theory assumes that mental images exist in a **spatial medium** which has a number of essential properties. Like physical space, the spatial medium has a limited extent which, in turn, limits its capacity to hold information. It resembles the visual field by having its highest resolution in the centre and the medium also has "grain"

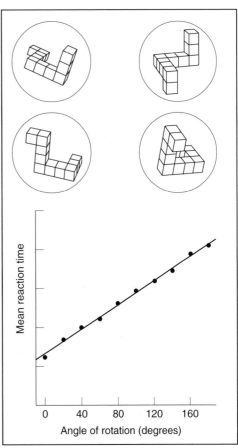

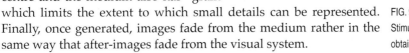

which limits the extent to which small details can be represented. Finally, once generated, images fade from the medium rather in the same way that after-images fade from the visual system.

Within Kosslyn's model there are two permanent stores of information about objects: **image files** and **propositional files**. Image files contain information about how the image of part or whole of a particular object is represented in the spatial medium. Certain image files, known as skeletal files, describe the basic shape of the object but not any specific details. Information about specific visual details is obtained from other image files. The basic shape of a bee, for example, can be enhanced by the addition of certain features, such as a black and yellow striped body.

Propositional files are not linked to a specific sensory modality (**amodal**) and only contain information about meaning. The files are

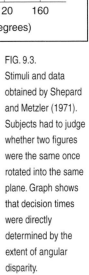

FIG. 9.3. Stimuli and data obtained by Shepard and Metzler (1971). Subjects had to judge whether two figures were the same once rotated into the same plane. Graph shows that decision times were directly determined by the extent of angular disparity.

collections of propositions which list the various properties of an object in relation to a foundation part, e.g. BLACK AND YELLOW STRIPES–LOCATION–SIDES–BODY. Information in propositional files is linked directly to the relevant image file. Thus a foundation propositional file describing a bee would be linked to the appropriate skeletal image of that object. Additional information about the bee would be stored in associated propositional files which, in turn, would be linked to the image files containing information about how to depict those details.

When asked to produce an image of an object the system first establishes whether there is a propositional file corresponding to a skeletal image. If located, the skeletal image is placed in the area of the spatial medium with the highest resolution. Additional processes then access further propositional information about the object and additional parts of the image are constructed in the spatial medium from associated image files. Once fully established, the image can then be operated on in various ways using processes such as SCAN, ZOOM and ROTATE.

Kosslyn and his colleagues (see Kosslyn, 1975; 1978; 1980; 1983) conducted a series of experiments on mental imagery. In an image scanning study, participants were asked to memorise a fictitious map of an island on which were several prominent landmarks (see Fig. 9.4). In the next phase, participants were asked to form an image of the map and focus on one of the landmarks. Having done that, a second landmark was named on which participants had to focus, and the time taken to do that was recorded. Figure 9.4 shows that the time taken to focus on a second landmark was a linear function of its distance from the first landmark. The participants' performance therefore suggested that the image of the map formed was an analogue of the actual map because processing operations performed on it appeared governed by the actual distances depicted on the map itself.

A second set of experiments examined how the assumed limited size of the spatial medium affected participants' ability to "see" detail in mental images. The participants were asked to imagine pairs of animals standing next to each other. One animal, the critical animal, was always imagined alongside another animal that was either much bigger or much smaller. A rabbit, for example, might be imagined alongside a bee or an elephant. The assumption was that when imaging a rabbit next to an elephant, the amount of spatial medium available for representing the rabbit would be small because of the large space taken up with the elephant. In contrast, a rabbit imagined next to a bee would have much more spatial medium allocated to it. On the assumption that the spatial medium was also granular, i.e. there was a finite limit to its powers of

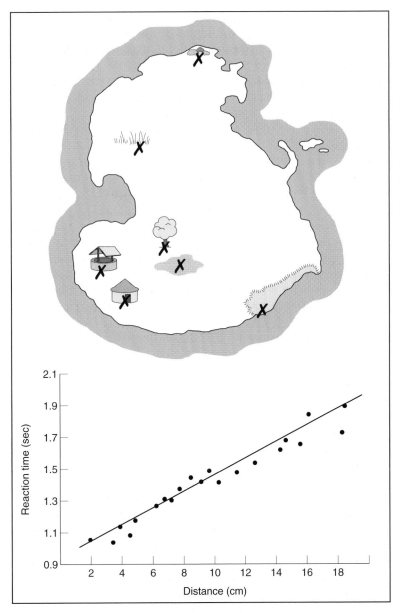

FIG. 9.4.
Kosslyn's fictitious island and graph showing time taken to scan mentally from one location (e.g. hut) to another (e.g. rocks). Note that scanning time appears directly proportional to actual distance between locations on map.

resolution, it followed that more details about a rabbit should be available when imaged alongside a fly compared with a rabbit. To examine this hypothesis, Kosslyn asked participants to indicate when they could "see" a specific feature of an imagined rabbit and he found that participants took longer when the rabbit was imaged alongside an elephant; this finding Kosslyn attributed to the poorer resolution of the rabbit image in the spatial medium. This finding represents an example of a privileged or emergent property of an image i.e. a property that is not stored as a proposition. The only way in which we know that a rabbit is less visible alongside an elephant is because this is evident from the depiction provided by the image.

The findings we have considered so far appear to make a fairly convincing case for the existence of mental images as functional representations. Under varying conditions it appears that participants are responding on the basis of internal analogue representations that share many of the qualities of percepts. This positive view of mental imagery is not, however, universal.

Arguments against mental imagery

Pylyshyn (1973; 1981) has put forward a number of criticisms of mental imagery. A primary argument is that images are **epiphenomena**, i.e. experiences that are the end result of rather than the basis of mental activity (see Chapter 1 for a review of this idea). Thus images are perhaps like the exhaust fumes of an engine: they tell you that the engine is working but not how it works.

We saw in our discussion of mental imagery experiments that it is necessary to propose the existence of knowledge other than an image to explain mental rotation findings. Pylyshyn's argument is an extreme form of this view in that he ascribes all phenomena attributed to mental imagery to the operation of a representational system based exclusively on propositional knowledge. The basis of this argument is as follows: If it is accepted that we can have a propositional representation of an object, it is also possible to have propositional knowledge about how we might respond if we had an analogue representation of that object. To understand this, let us return to Kosslyn's image scanning experiment described earlier. It is not difficult to argue that the information contained in that map about the distances between landmarks could be represented in propositional terms. Pylyshyn argued that people could use this distance information as a basis for responding *as if* they actually had a functional image—the greater the computed distance between objects, the longer the response time should be. Similar arguments could also, of course, be made about other imaginal judgements apparently influenced by perceived distance or size.

Pylyshyn's argument seems plausible but why do people decide to behave in this way? One strong possibility is that results obtained in image scanning and other similar studies are due to the demand characteristics of the experimental procedures. The idea is that participants "see through" the experiment and respond in order to satisfy the experimenter's predictions. Indeed, Kosslyn et al. (1978) did concede that their scanning results may have reflected "nothing more than the enthusiastic co-operation of our subjects".

Richman and Mitchell (1979) employed the "non-experiment" technique to establish the extent to which demand characteristics might explain the image scanning results of Kosslyn. Participants were presented with the written instructions used in the experiment and information about the relative distances on the fictitious map, but not the map itself. They were then asked to estimate what their scanning times would be and it was found that they produced significantly longer estimates for scanning between landmarks that were furthest apart. Pylyshyn (1981) also provided evidence supporting a demand characteristics interpretation of image scanning studies. Using experimental instructions similar to Kosslyn et al., in which participants were required to imagine a spot moving from one specified landmark to another, Pylyshyn found the familiar linear relationship between scanning time and map distance. However, when the instructions asked participants to focus on one landmark and then decide as quickly as possible what the compass bearing of a second landmark was, there was no relationship between map distance and response time.

How exactly do demand characteristics exert their influence on the pattern of results obtained in imagery experiments? Intuitively it seems unlikely that participants could have consistently devised conscious processing strategies for generating the systematic relationships evident in mental rotation and image scanning experiments. To solve this difficulty, Pylyshyn proposes that people also possess tacit (i.e. unconscious) propositional knowledge of how their visual systems behave and, in response to the demand characteristics of the experimental situation, allow this knowledge to simulate image-based responding. Thus, in a mental rotation experiment, participants tacitly know that when they actually see an object rotating it will do so continuously and take an amount of time directly proportional to the angle through which it has to rotate. This tacit knowledge then provides the basis for determining the participants' reaction times.

The tacit knowledge theory can account for all apparent instances where participants' response patterns suggest that an image is the basis of performance. Furthermore, much of this knowledge is held to be unconscious, making it impossible to establish independently whether or not any particular person does possess that knowledge. The propositional knowledge account of mental imagery cannot, therefore, be refuted by any experiment involving normal participants and mental imagery.

Kosslyn (1994) has defended the data from mental imagery experiments by arguing that demand characteristics cannot be the sole explanation of what is going on. In one study by Finke and Pinker (1983), participants viewed a random array of dots that were then replaced by an arrow. Their task was to decide whether the arrow, if combined with the display, would point directly to a dot. It was found that response times increased linearly as the distance between the arrow and its "target" dot increased. In this experiment, participants were not told to scan or use any image-based strategy although in fact some of them did. Jolicoeur and Kosslyn (1985) tackled the demand characteristics approach head on in a series of experiments that attempted to use demand characteristics as a means of influencing response times. Using the map task, for example, they told participants that scanning times would vary depending on the proximity of the objects. This, and no other manipulation, resulted in any significant deviation from the original findings.

This aspect of the imagery debate ended rather unsatisfactorily. Opponents of the imagery idea felt that the degree of transparency in imagery experiments made them unacceptably vulnerable to demand characteristics. Proponents, on the other hand, viewed the consistency of the effects and their own attempts to control demand effects as sufficient to pursue the issue at another level.

Imagery as perception

More recently, the concept of mental imagery has been supported by experiments showing that acts of imagery have much in common with the mechanisms of perception itself; if one can show that imagery and perception have common properties, then the case for functional analogue images becomes stronger. In one study by Rouw et al. (1997), participants were presented with simple line drawings and asked to decide whether each of the pictures contained a range of different features. Some of these were "high" level features (e.g. is the object symmetrical?) and others were "low" level (e.g. is there a T-junction present?). There were two versions of the experiment. In the first the picture remained present while participants made the decision; in the second participants had to form an image and rely on that for their decisions. As one might expect, the task was easier with the picture present and high level features were more easily detected than low level features. However, the extent to which high level features were detected better did not vary across the picture present/imagery manipulation. From this it was argued that images retained low level features and were not, as some had claimed, more abstract patterns containing little detail.

Neuropsychological evidence for mental imagery

Farah (1988) has produced various arguments in favour of mental imagery based on neuropsychological evidence. Goldenberg et al. (1992) compared the patterns of **regional cerebral blood flow** (rCBF) while participants tried to answer questions that either did or did not require the use of imagery. rCBF involves the injection of a radioactive isotope of oxygen into the blood stream. When blood containing this isotope reaches the brain it can be detected by a scanning process known as **positron emission tomography** (PET). The PET process indicates which areas of the brain contain most radioactive oxygen and, from this, it can be inferred which parts of the brain are most active. The imagery questions were of comparable difficulty to the non-imagery questions but they evoked significantly different patterns of regional blood flow. Imagery questions resulted in increased brain activity in the visual areas of the brain such as the occipital lobes but this was not the case with non-imagery questions. A more recent study confirmed the association of increased activation of visual cortex during imagery task with the distribution of the blood flow being linked to the topographical configuration of the stimulus.

Psychometric tests have also been devised to estimate the degree to which a person can use imagery to carry out a mental task. Charlot et al. (1992), for example, used two tests to classify participants into low and high imagers and then measured rCBF while they performed an image scanning task or a verb conjugation task. The results showed a number of differences between the high and low imagers; in particular, low imagers showed a general increase in rCBF during both tasks whereas high imagers showed a specific increase in rCBF to the right visual association cortex. While it is not clear why the right visual association cortex should be particularly active during verb conjugation, the data nonetheless point to markedly different patterns of brain activity in high and low imagers with the former appearing to be more reliant on visual areas of the brain.

However, can we conclude from experiments like those above that images must therefore have the same properties as the percepts that are also processed by these brain regions? This is certainly one interpretation, but an alternative is that this activation in visual areas corresponds to the epiphenomenal aspect of imagery, i.e. it is an index of what we experience as a consequence of carrying out image-based tasks rather than an indication that the visual areas of the brain are the neural substrate of the processes leading to responses in an imagery-based task.

Farah argues that this epiphenomenal argument can only be countered by demonstrating that damage to the visual areas of the brain produces deficits in mental imagery that parallel the nature of the perceptual deficits we observe in the unfortunate patient. The argument being that if activation of visual areas during image-based responding is epiphenomenal, damage preventing that activation should not preclude performance of the task because presumably this depends on structures elsewhere in the brain.

Visual neglect is a relatively common neuropsychological disorder caused by damage to the right parietal lobe of the brain (Parkin, 1996). The result of this is that the patients fail to see objects on their left side unless their attention is drawn to them. In a well-known case, it has been shown that internal images can also show neglect (Bisiach and Luzatti, 1978). A man with neglect was asked to imagine the Piazza del Duomo in Milan first from one perspective and then from the perspective directly opposite. From one perspective he described only the buildings on his right. This was also true when he adopted the other perspective, even though these were the buildings he had just described when he was viewing from the first perspective.

Farah (1988) reviews a range of studies which show a relationship between visual and imagery deficits. Several studies, for example, demonstrate that patients with colour blindness also lose the ability to make comparable colour-based imaginal judgements such as what is the colour of cement (De Vreese, 1991). In an unusual study, Farah et al. (1988) and her colleagues used Kosslyn's "mind's eye" task with a woman known as MGS, a patient about to have an operation to remove part of her occipital lobe in order to control epilepsy. Based on the task devised by Kosslyn (1978), the experiment involved MGS imagining a 12in ruler coming towards her and indicating, by a forward arm movement, how close it could get but still have the ends in view. This task was done with the ruler in both a horizontal and a vertical position. The task was then repeated post-operatively; the visual angle in the vertical remained similar but that in the horizontal was dramatically reduced. These changes mirror the effects that occipital lesions can have on actual vision and thus support the view that imagery and perception share similar processes. Cohen et al. (1996) show that lesions that disrupt mental rotation performance also result in deficits involving the perception and manipulation of real objects in space—again suggesting a common neural substrate for imagery and perception. In addition, Butter et al. (1997) reported a patient who had imagery deficits that exactly mirrored his field defects in vision.

Put together, these studies suggest that the neural substrates underlying visual processes are also involved in imagery. Thus, when colour vision is affected, colour imagery is also impaired and when our spatial vision is damaged, we also have difficulty in manipulating images in space. Neuropsychological data therefore allow us to conclude that people certainly seem to be doing something different when performing mental imagery tasks compared with tasks that do not demand imagery. However, can we further conclude that images are therefore analogical? This conclusion would only be valid if our additional assumption that percepts are analogical is also valid. At present, that is an unanswered and very difficult question.

Conclusion

What, then, can we conclude about this controversial area of cognitive psychology? First, there seems to be no doubt that instructions to use imagery greatly improve memory—indeed many memory aids (**mnemonics**) make specific use of imagery as a means of improving memory (Parkin, 1997a; Wilding and Valentine, 1997). Second, although there are logical objections to a system of memory based solely on images (the interpretation problem), there appears to be a substantial amount of data indicating that, under certain conditions, people appear to be using an image-type representation to carry out a task. Some people have argued that imagery experiments can be explained by the operation of a propositional system, particularly if there are strong demand characteristics. However, because a propositional system can simulate any behaviour, it is difficult to see how it can be refuted. Further evidence indicates that there is a strong correspondence between the properties of images and percepts, in both psychological and neurological terms, and that damage to the visual areas of the brain has a corresponding selective effect on individuals' ability to perform image-based tasks. Imagery thus appears to be a special type of mental process in which representations are created in relation to their perceptual characteristics. It is most likely that these images are produced in an *ad hoc* manner from underlying propositional knowledge in order to deal with specific tasks rather than representing a permanent store of images *per se*.

Overview

- Imagery has re-emerged as a major area of experimental psychology.
- Internal imagery, "seeing in the mind's eye", needs to be distinguished from the rare eidetic imagery in which participants appear to have a photographic memory.
- The imagability of material greatly influences how well something will be remembered and instructions to use imagery greatly enhance retention.
- An internal image is defined as some representation of the processes used to perceive an external stimulus. It is assumed to be an analogue representation in which the spatial characteristics of the stimulus are depicted in the structure of the image itself.
- The depictive quality of images is supported by mental rotation and scanning experiments.
- An alternative view is that all knowledge is represented as propositions. Apparent demonstrations of imagery are merely a consequence of the propositional system operating as if it had an image. This may have been enhanced by demand characteristics of certain experimental techniques.
- Because there are no constraints on what a propositional system can do it is, in effect, an untestable theory.
- There is, however, considerable evidence that when participants use imagery they make use of the visual areas of the brain whereas non-imagery tasks maximally activate other regions.
- Damage to visual areas of the brain has a parallel effect on imagery ability, e.g. loss of colour vision → loss of colour imagery. These two facts together indicate that imagery makes selective use of visual areas of the brain.
- We can therefore define an image as some mental representation making use of the visual system but its ultimate mechanics, propositional or analogical, is still a mystery.

Suggested further reading

Kosslyn, S.M. (1994). *Image and brain: The resolution of the imagery debate*. Cambridge, MA: MIT Press.

As the title suggests, an account of the pro-imagery position.

Jolicoeur, P., & Kosslyn, S.M. (1985). Is time to scan visual images due to demand characteristics? *Memory and Cognition, 13,* 320–332.

A good but much briefer overview of the pro-imagery viewpoint.

Richardson, J.T.E. (1999). *Imagery.* Hove, UK: Psychology Press.

An account of all aspects of imagery, including the debate about the nature of imagery and its value in mnemonics.

Revision questions

1 What is eidetic imagery and how reliably can it be demonstrated?
2 How does imagery affect memory?
3 What is the dual coding hypothesis and how does it explain imagery effects?
4 Mental images are described as "analogue representations"—what does this mean?
5 What were the key findings of mental rotation and mental scanning experiments?
6 What are the key features of Kosslyn's computational theory of imagery?
7 What objections has Pylyshyn raised to the concept of mental imagery and is there experimental evidence to support his view?
8 To what extent do mental images have the same properties as visual percepts?

Language: Speech recognition 10

In this chapter we will be specifically concerned with the nature of speech recognition. However, as this is our first encounter with the topic of language, perhaps it is appropriate to first consider what defines something as a "language".

The nature of true language

For many people, language is considered to be the ability that distinguishes us from other animals. For this reason, the study of language has been one of the fundamental areas of cognitive psychology. There has, of course, been considerable debate in recent times as to whether other animals can also demonstrate language-like skills. Thus it is claimed that animals ranging from chimpanzees to parrots have shown the ability to both comprehend and produce language. There is neither the space nor the scope to go fully into this issue here. Nonetheless, possibility of animal language is helpful in our attempts to understand what "true language" is.

Defining true language

It is possible to train a dog to obey various commands such as "sit" and "stay". It would be a mistake, however, to conclude that the dog now understands language. To explain the dog's behaviour, one merely needs to argue that the dog has learned that a pattern of speech sounds corresponds to a particular action and that failure to obey may have adverse consequences. There is no requirement for "stay" or "sit" to be represented as concepts; they are simply sounds that are associated with responses. Unfortunately, there is a pervasive **anthropomorphism** in the world in which people, particularly pet owners, are all too willing to attribute human-like features to animals and the issue of animal language is no exception.

A good example is the dolphin, who some believe actually has a superior intelligence to humans (for a balanced review of dolphin capabilities, see Reiss et al., 1997). Part of this claim is that the dolphins can communicate linguistically with each other. A TV programme screened in the early 1970s showed a male and female bottle-nosed dolphin in adjacent enclosures. The female's enclosure contained two lights, red and green, and the male's contained two paddles, left and right. There is a simple relationship between the lights and the paddles. If the green light is on, pressing the left paddle will deliver food to both dolphins. If the red light is on, pressing the right paddle delivers food. The dolphins learned this pretty quickly and it led many to believe that the dolphins were communicating linguistically, e.g. "green light on".

There is, however, a simpler explanation. Dolphins tend to emit noises regularly so it is likely that emission of a particular noise will coincide with one of the lights being on. Now, if at the same time as this noise is emitted the other dolphin pushes the correct paddle, both dolphins obtain a reward. Given that dolphins learn fast, this association between a given noise and a paddle might become rapidly established across a few essentially random pairings.

Do dolphins communicate linguistically, or can the patterns of behaviour where dolphins appear to "talk" be explained by other means?

However, the level of communication established is not linguistic in any sense; a fact reinforced by the demonstration that the same effect can be shown in the lowly pigeon. Rather, one dolphin has learned that a particular sound indicates a leftward movement and another a rightward movement (Boakes and Gaertner, 1977).

What then is true language? For a communication system to be a true language, its elements must be **symbolic** in that they are represented independently of any actions they might provoke. On responding to the command "go left" a human is not just producing a response, they are also aware of the concept of "direction" and that alternatives such as "go right" or "straight on" are also possibilities. Thus, if the person issuing the command makes a mistake, the other person readily corrects them. In the case of the dolphin, however, there is no need to argue that the dolphin has any such parallel conceptual awareness; its response in a particular direction is simply the expression of an association devoid of any conceptual content.

Another essential feature of language is that the symbols it comprises can be combined to form new expressions that have never been heard or seen before. This has been the acid test for attempts to demonstrate animal language. If an animal only produces symbol sequences it has seen before then these could have been acquired merely by imitation. Chimps have been trained to "speak" using American Sign Language because they are not vocally capable of human-type speech. These studies have been controversial in that some have claimed that apparently meaningful sequences of symbols arise either by imitation or pure chance. However, on balance, it seems that signing chimps and their close relations, the bonobos, do have a form of language similar to humans in that they can manipulate symbols in order to communicate simple conceptual information (e.g. Brakke and Savage-Rumbaugh, 1996; Canfield, 1995; Langs et al., 1996).

Speech recognition

We can therefore define language as a signalling system that enables concepts to be conveyed between two members of the same species. In the case of humans there are two main signalling systems, speech and writing, although we can also communicate via symbolic gesture (see Fig. 10.1 for an example). The latter should not be confused with the much discussed topic of "body language" in which various postural cues are thought to convey social signals such as social attractiveness and dominance. In all but the most devious, body language appears to operate at an unconscious level and there is no indication that it operates on a conceptual basis.

In this chapter we will be concerned with the first form of language to develop: speech. At this point it will be useful to introduce a few terms. The individual sounds that comprise a language are known as **phonemes** and together they make up the **phonology** of a language. Phonemes are combined to form **morphemes** which can be defined as the smallest units of language that have meaning. Most morphemes correspond to particular words but there are some that perform specific linguistic functions such as "s" which adds a plural and "ed" which turns a verb into the past tense.

Phonemes represent two basic types of sound, vowels and consonants. As a basis for understanding speech recognition it has been essential to discover the acoustic properties of these two types of sound. Speech sounds are analysed along two dimensions: **frequency** and **amplitude**. Any sound, vocal or otherwise, generates a pressure change in the air that will tend to be cyclical. The cycle of any sound will vary in frequency and it is this that determines the **pitch**—the higher the frequency the higher the sound.

Amplitude is a measure of the loudness of a sound. The basis of sounds can be demonstrated using a **spectrogram**. Figure 10.2 shows the spectrogram of the sentence "Joe took father's shoe bench out". The

FIG. 10.1.
A hand signalling
system used in the
Futures Exchange of
the London Stock
Market.

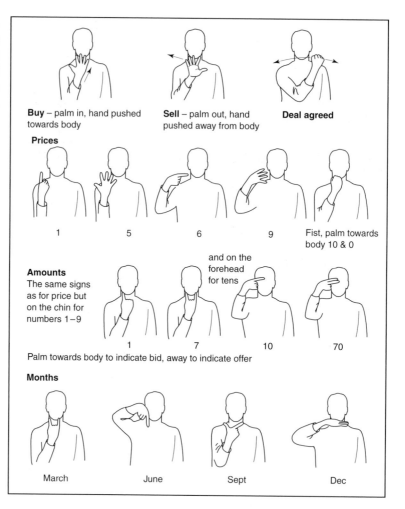

Buy – palm in, hand pushed towards body

Sell – palm out, hand pushed away from body

Deal agreed

Prices

1   5   6   9   Fist, palm towards body 10 & 0

Amounts
The same signs as for price but on the chin for numbers 1–9

and on the forehead for tens

1   7   10   70

Palm towards body to indicate bid, away to indicate offer

Months

March   June   Sept   Dec

vertical axis represents frequency and the horizontal axis represents time. Darker areas of the spectrogram indicate frequencies of higher amplitude. We can see, therefore, that even a single word is represented by sounds of varying frequency and amplitude. Another point to notice is that the spectrogram is continuous—there are no blank spaces between the words. This might seem odd because we certainly do not hear speech as a continuous stream of sound. This is because our speech recognition system is able to segment the stream of speech into words.

Figure 10.3 shows that vowel sounds have a characteristic quality when analysed by spectrogram. The sound of vowels is determined by specific changes in the way our vocal tract is configured so as to produce

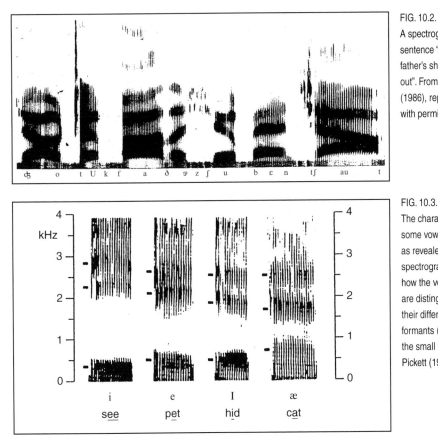

different sets of **resonant frequencies** for each vowel. These sets of frequencies are known as **formants** beginning with F1, the lowest frequency, and progressing to F2 and F3 with increased frequency. Some vowels have additional higher formants. However, the basis for distinguishing vowels is the positions of just F1 and F2.

The production of consonants is far more complex and they are less easy to distinguish on the basis of spectrogram analysis. Crucial in the understanding of consonant production are both the **manner of articulation** and the **place of articulation**. In relation to manner, consonants that arise from the vibration of the vocal cords are known as voiced (e.g. "v" and "n") and those that do not are known as unvoiced (e.g. "f" and "s"). Place of articulation is more complex. Some consonants, e.g. "b" and "p", are produced with your mouth closed (bilabial); consonants such as "v" and "f" involve placing your top teeth near your bottom lip (labiodental); interdental consonants, e.g. "th", involve placing the tongue between the teeth; alveolar consonants, e.g. "t" and "d" are produced by placing your tongue behind your upper teeth, and velar consonants, e.g. "k", come from the back of the mouth. Consonants can also be **stopped** in that airflow ceases as the sound is produced, as in "p" and "d", or they can involve continuing airflow, e.g. "f", "r".

Perceiving vowels

Figure 10.3 presents a rather ideal situation in which vowels have been produced by **artificial speech synthesis** in the absence of any other sounds. This represents the steady state of the vowel but it is something rarely encountered in normal speech. Normally we hear vowels in association with consonants, and it has been shown that it is the **formant transitions** that arise as speech goes into and out of vowels that seems particularly important in vowel identification. In a series of experiments by Strange (1989a; 1989b) short nonsense syllables were synthesised based on the structure "b" + vowel + "b" (e.g. "bab"). Various versions of these nonsense syllables were then created, including a silent centre and a variable centre version. In the silent centre, the part of the sound corresponding to the steady state vowel was removed, and in the variable centre only the steady state of the vowel was present. Participants were asked to identify the vowel they heard; compared with a control condition in which no deletion had occurred, the variable centre condition expectedly produced poorer performance. However, on the silent centre condition, where the vowel information had been removed, performance was as good as the undeleted control.

This experiment provides a clear demonstration of how the pattern of transition between consonants and vowels provides a vital cue to vowel recognition. To understand how this might work, consider an analogy with the semaphore signalling system. Each letter is signalled by a particular pattern of arm placement. As the sender moves from one letter to another (i.e. from one steady state to another) the arms must move. An efficient reader of semaphore may well know what the next letter is going to be from the intermediate arm positions before the next signal is indicated. In the same way, the variations in the speech signal as a consonant transforms into a vowel acts as a powerful cue as to what the vowel will be.

Perceiving consonants

Consonants can de divided into two types: those that can be identified in isolation and those that must be paired with a vowel for them to be perceived. Only the stop consonants "b", "d", "g" (all voiced) and "p", "t", "k" (unvoiced) require pairing with a vowel for identification. Thus "b" can only be perceived in the context of "ba", "be", etc. In fact, if stop consonants are presented in isolation they come over as non-speech like chirping sounds. The fact that stop consonants require binding with a vowel for perception is attributed to a process of parallel transmission in which information about the consonant and the vowel becomes available within the same acoustic segment.

Within research, most attention has been paid to perception of the six stop consonants. These can be thought of as three pairs, "b" and "p", "d" and "t", and "k" and "g", in which each pair differs in that the first one is voiced and the second unvoiced. It is thought that the **voice onset time** (VOT) provides a valuable cue for discriminating between voiced and unvoiced consonants. VOT is defined as the time elapsing between the onset of a word and the vibration of the vocal cords. To understand this, consider the two syllables "di" and "ti". Both of these syllables begin with a stop consonant but one, "d" is voiced and the other "t" is unvoiced. It has been shown that these two consonants are associated with different VOTs because the voiced "d" activates the vocal cords whereas no vibration occurs with the unvoiced "t" until the vowel commences. Thus, in the case of "di" the VOT is extremely brief, about 10msec, whereas with "ti" the onset is considerably longer, 60msec (see Fig. 10.4).

Categorical perception

In order to explore how VOT influences consonant perception, experimenters have again used artificial speech sounds. Starting with two ends of the VOT continuum, e.g. a 0msec VOT and an 80msec VOT, experiments have examined how tolerant the hearing system is to intermediary values such as 10, 20 and 30msec. In one experiment, participants hear a range of sounds varying in their VOT and are asked to say whether they heard "da" or not. As the manipulation is gradual, you might expect the participants' response to show this with, for example, a steady decrease in the proportion of "da's" identified as the VOT increases (remember that "da" is voiced). Figure 10.5 shows that this is not what happens at all. From a VOT of zero up to about 30msec, identification of stimuli is almost 100% "da". After this there is a narrow band of uncertainty until 50msec, after which further increases in VOT elicit virtually no "da" responses.

The phenomenon shown in Fig. 10.5 indicates that our speech recognition system can tolerate variation in the manner in which sounds are produced. Thus across a range of VOTs the same sound will be

FIG. 10.4.
Spectrogram
indicating the differing
voice onset times for
the voiced and
unvoiced consonants
"di" and "ti". The thin
vertical line to the left
represents the burst of
air associated with
the onset of
pronunciation. Note
that the gap between
the burst and the
onset of the first
formant (voice onset
time) is very brief
whereas in the case
of "ti" this distance is
considerably longer.

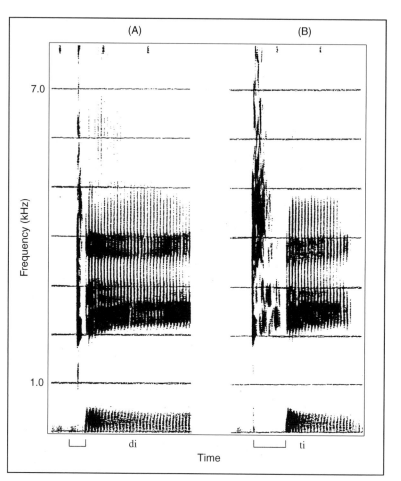

perceived with equal frequency. Participants are therefore hearing exactly the same thing at these different intervals, a conclusion that has led to this phenomenon being described as **categorical perception** (Eimas and Corbit, 1973). Thus, until a critical VOT is reached, all "da's" seem to sound alike.

Theories of lower level speech perception

So far we have seen that speech has a range of properties, and it seems reasonable to suppose that identification of those properties plays some role in the speech recognition process. In our discussion of visual object recognition (see Chapter 3) we encountered the idea of using invariance as a means of identifying an object; identifying features that remain constant regardless of the angle from which we view the object. Theories of speech recognition have also attempted to find invariant properties to explain how the system deals with distortions in the speech signal.

A major source of distortion comes from the phenomenon of **co-articulation**. To understand this, consider the two phrases "foolish dancer" and "fearless dancer". Although the second word is the same, we perceive the initial "d" differently (try saying the phrases to yourself while looking in the mirror if you are not sure what I mean, and see also Fig. 10.6). To account for this lack of invariance problem, the **motor theory of speech perception** (Liberman et al., 1957; 1967 and Liberman, 1970), proposes that infor-

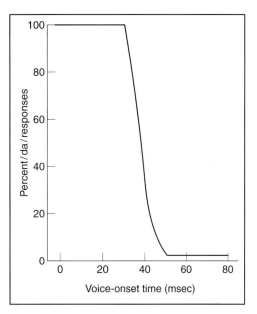

mation about how sounds are articulated plays a crucial role in determining how sounds are heard. Thus, although in our example the "d" phoneme has variable characteristics, knowledge of its overall articulation pattern is able to identify a similarity and allow the same consonant to be perceived.

FIG. 10.5. Categorical perception. Note that an increase in VOT does not lead to any reduction in the number of stimuli identified as "da" until a critical threshold is reached, after which very few stimuli continue to be identified as "da".

Unfortunately, the motor theory has a number of problems. One of these surrounds the assumption of **motor invariance**, i.e. that phonemes are associated with consistent articulatory movements. It now appears that there is substantial variety in the way in which phonemes are articulated (MacNeilage, 1972). Another difficulty stems from the fact that infants, who have very limited speech production abilities, can nonetheless distinguish speech sounds very well. Despite these difficulties, it has been argued that motor theory is important because it has stressed that speech perception is distinct from the perception of non-speech sounds. This may be true, but even this conclusion can be criticised on the grounds that speech-like perceptual effects can be found in non-humans. Monkeys, chinchillas, and quails, for example, have all been shown to have marked categorical perception (e.g. Kuhl, 1986).

An alternative theoretical approach to speech perception has been described by Massaro (1992; 1998) in his **Fuzzy Logic Model of Perception** (FLMP). The primary emphasis of this model is that various sources of evidence contribute to speech perception. Three basic stages of processing are identified: evaluation of the input; integration of the

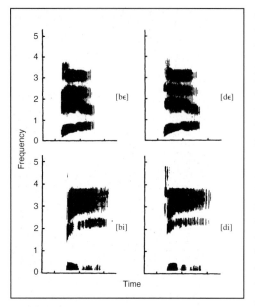

FIG. 10.6
Spectrograms of "di"
and "do". Despite
beginning with the
same phoneme note
the very different
overall sound pattern.
This is the
phenomenon of
corticulation where
the preceding
consonant affects the
way a vowel is
produced.

evaluation results; and a decision based on that integration. The theory makes use of the idea of prototypes, an idea we have already encountered in our discussion of knowledge representation. According to this model, a given phoneme is compared with an ideal representation of that phoneme and a "goodness of match" value is computed.

Although Massaro's model is a general one his research has concentrated on how two particular sources of information are integrated in order to achieve a phoneme: the acoustic signal itself and the visual cues provided by a speaker's face. We are all aware of how well deaf people can make use of lip reading but it is also the case that visual speech also influences normal speech perception. The influence of visual cues of speech is evident from the **McGurk Effect** (McGurk and MacDonald, 1976). This demonstrates that pairing the video of someone saying "ga" with a synchronised production of /ba/ results in subjects hearing the intermediary sound "da". Massaro developed this finding using animated faces (see Fig. 10.7) and synthesised speech. Both face and speech information were systematically varied between clearly being the syllable "ba" or "da". When both sources of information concurred there was no problem identifying the syllable but with other combinations syllable identity was less obvious.

"Top-down" effects in speech recognition

In our discussion of visual perception, we saw that basic perceptual analyses can be influenced by prior knowledge—so called top-down effects. It should come as no surprise that top-down influences also affect speech perception. Consider the sentence "Ice cream every time". Here the segmentation we perceive would be conceptually driven because the same sentence could be heard as "I scream every time". Top-down effects are also evident in the recognition of single words. In one study, participants had to listen to sentences in which certain words had been altered by substituting a coughing sound for a phoneme. The participants were asked to locate the cough. They rarely noticed that the cough occurred within a word, deciding instead that it occurred in the background. Warren termed this effect the **phonemic restoration**

effect on the grounds that participants appeared to have somehow replaced the missing phoneme (Warren and Warren, 1970).

Another technique for investigating top-down processes involves asking participants to comprehend sentences which end in a word that can vary in its phonemic distinctiveness. In one study an artificial speech continuum was constructed involving 16 syllables, all based on initial consonant plus the vowel sound /a/. The continuum embraced three stop consonants "b", "d", and "g", and at various points the sequence yielded the unambiguous words, "bait, "date" and "gate". However, at other points in the continuum it was less clear which word was actually heard. All 16 variants from the continuum were placed at the end of sentences and participants were asked to identify what they heard at the end. When the unambiguous words were presented the sentence had no effect on word recognition. However, when less distinct versions of the words were used identification was influenced by the sentence context. Thus exactly the same poorly formed word would be heard as "bait" after the sentence "Here's the fishing gear and the...." but as "date" following the sentence "Check the time and the..." (Garnes and Bond, 1976).

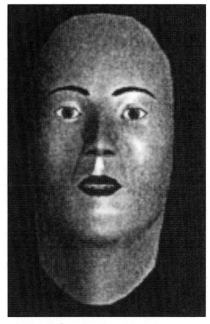

FIG. 10.7.
Animated face used by Massaro.

A further issue concerns the locus of top-down effects in spoken word recognition: are these effects even across all parts of the word or are some places more affected than others? Using another variant of the mispronunciation task, participants heard words in which incorrect phonemes had been inserted into either the beginning or ends of words. Detections were over twice as likely when the change involved the beginning than the end of the word. This, combined with many other findings, indicates that top-down influences are more apparent for the later portions of words, and that identification of spoken words is centred on the early part of the word (Marslen-Wilson, 1987).

Models of spoken word recognition

Perhaps the most popular model of spoken word recognition is the **cohort model** (Marslen-Wilson and Tyler, 1980; Marslen-Wilson, 1987; Marslen-Wilson, 1990). According to this model, presentation of a spoken word initiates a set or "cohort" of words that have similar beginnings, e.g. all words beginning with "e". As more information comes on stream the cohort is reduced, e.g. "ele" → "electricity, elementary, elephant...", until sufficient information is available for only one candidate to be plausible, e.g. "eleph" can only become "elephant". An important feature of this model was that it allowed "bottom-up" information to interact with "top-down" information in order for recognition to occur. Thus, if the context of speech was the African savannah the word "elephant" might be identified prior to the point at which the "bottom-up" phonemic information defined it unambiguously within the cohort (see Fig. 10.8).

To explore the role of **context** in spoken word identification, an experiment was conducted in which participants listened to real sentences, meaningless but grammatically correct sentences, or random sequences of words. Their task was to identify particular target words (the words chosen were long words because this gave more scope for measuring identification time differences). If information about word identity requires full analysis then target detections should take the same time regardless of what type of spoken sentence they are embedded in. However, the results showed that targets were identified considerably faster in real sentences, thus suggesting that less

FIG. 10.8.
The cohort model of
word recognition.

"he said he was ready to	r	e	c	o	n	c	i
	raise	reach	recover	reconnect	reconnect	reconsider	reconcile
	rate	reason	reconnect	reconsider	reconsider	reconcile	
	rebel	reassess	reconsider	reconcile	reconcile		**identification**
	recall	repeat	recap	reconstruct	reconstruct	**cohort 6**	
	receive	reconnect	reconcile	reconstrue	reconstrue		
	rely	reconsider	reconstruct	recombine			
	rescue	recap	reconstrue	recompose	**cohort 5**		
	rest	reconcile	record	recompare			
	return	reconstruct	recombine	......			
	rid	reconstrue	recompose				
	ride	recover	recompare	**cohort 4**			
	ring	record	recline				
	riot	recombine	......				
	rise	recompose					
	risk	recompare	**cohort 3**				
	roast	recline					
	rob	refill					
	row	require					
	rub	reserve					
	ruin	......					
	rule						
	run	**cohort 2**					
	rush						
	......						
	cohort 1						

information is required when a sensible context is provided (e.g. Bronkhorst et al., 1993).

The cohort model also explained other findings, such as the evidence showing that early parts of a word are more important in identification than latter parts—the argument being that incorrect phonemes occurring later in a word might not be processed because a prior decision about the word had already been made. A modification also allowed for influence of word frequency on word identification and the fact that words with more similar sounding "neighbours" are identified faster (Marslen-Wilson, 1990). More recent work has also indicated that the cohort model needs to incorporate the fact that various semantic features become available at different rates during the process of lexical access (Moss et al., 1997).

However, the model does not easily explain the finding that words formed poorly because of imprecise information about the initial phoneme (see above) can nonetheless be identified by context. Another problem concerns the **late recognition effect** in which recognition of a spoken word appears to occur as a result of contextual cues occurring later in the spoken sequence. This was shown in an experiment by Bard et al. (1988) in which participants listened to utterances which increased in length one word at a time, e.g. "meet", "meet me", "meet me at", etc. The utterances were somewhat degraded and the participants' task was to write down what they heard each time. The crucial finding was that words from earlier parts of the utterances were often identified after more of the utterance had been heard, thus indicating that cues provided after a word had been heard could help in its identification. A revised version of the cohort model has been proposed to deal with these kinds of findings. However, in achieving this, the model loses its earlier advantage of making strong predictions (Marslen-Wilson, 1987).

The TRACE model

The **TRACE model** (McClelland & Elman, 1986) is a connectionist-based attempt to explain spoken word recognition (see Chapter 1 for a brief account of connectionist models). Like the cohort theory, it envisages that several sources of information can be brought to bear on word identification. The model comprises three kinds of nodes: one set for production features (i.e. manner and place of articulation); a second set representing phonemes; and a final set of nodes representing words. The nodes are organised on three levels: feature nodes are connected to phoneme nodes which, in turn, are connected to word nodes. Connections between these different levels are bi-directional and are excitatory, i.e. information travelling from a node at one level serves to activate the node at the next level. Within the same level, the activity of one node will inhibit other nodes at the same level. Nodes can vary in their level activation and how strongly they are connected to other nodes. Word recognition is a product of the excitatory and inhibitory activity caused by a given word. Within this model, bottom-up processing represents the pattern of excitation moving upwards from the feature nodes and top-down processing is the downward excitation arising from both the word and phoneme nodes (see Fig. 10.9).

To understand this model, consider how the word "door" might be recognised. The initial consonant "d" will first be analysed at the feature level and this will activate nodes representing "voiced" and "stop". As this occurs, inhibition of other features will occur (e.g. "unvoiced"). Information will then spread up the system and result in activation of

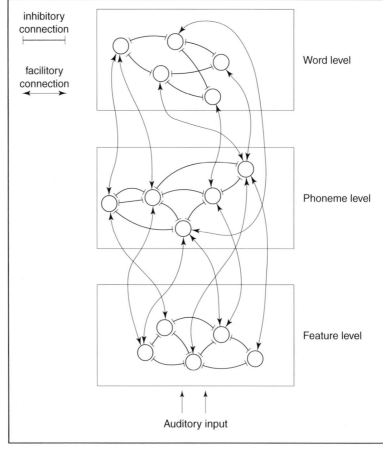

FIG. 10.9.
McClelland and Elman's (1986) model of speech perception. The three levels represent features, phonemes and words. Connections between the three levels are excitatory, whereas connections within a level are inhibitory.

the stop consonants but because the information is most consistent with "d" this will be recognised and the other stop consonants inhibited. Then "d" will feed up the system, resulting in a cohort of words beginning with "d" becoming active and simultaneous inhibition of words beginning with different initial phonemes. While this is happening, "o" goes through the same series of analyses which results in the word cohort becoming restricted to words beginning with "do". With the arrival of the second "o" the cohort becomes further constrained and information starts to feed down the system that the word is likely to be "door".

The TRACE model thus envisages an interaction between top-down and bottom-up information in spoken word recognition. A crucial question, however, is whether top-down information actually affects what you hear—a genuine influence on perception—or your readiness to respond and that you have heard something—a **response bias** effect. To test this out, an experiment was set up in which participants were asked to identify which member of a pair of words occurred following a context word (Elman and McClelland, 1988). The experiment exploited co-articulation effects of the type we discussed earlier. In one case a stimulus sequence was created which at one end was clearly the word "dear" which then transformed gradually into the word "gear". Each of these stimuli was preceded by either "Spanish" or "ridiculous". The results showed that for words in which the initial phoneme was midway between "d" and "g" participants were more likely to report hearing "dear" when preceded by "Spanish" and "gear" when preceded by "ridiculous". The next step was to show that this co-articulation effect was actually determined by higher level word information feeding down the system. To do this, the experiment was repeated with the context words altered so that the final constant sound was similar for each pair of context words (e.g. SpaniX; ridiculouX). The same patterns of bias were obtained, thus indicating that information had been fed down the system about what the last syllable might be and this had influenced what subjects heard.

While the above results support a top-down influence on perceiving people, there is also evidence involving changes in response bias. Samuel (1981) asked participants to listen to sentences in which meaningless noise was presented at some point. The task was to detect a particular phoneme and two conditions were compared, one in which the noise overlaid the critical phoneme and one where the critical phoneme was deleted, leaving just noise in its place. In addition, the experiment also varied whether the word carrying the critical phoneme occurred in a predictable sentence context or an unpredictable one. Context improved phoneme detection but crucially, participants were just as likely to decide that the phoneme was present in the noise-only condition compared with the noise-plus-phoneme. If top-down influences were affecting the actual perception of phonemes then the latter should have produced more detections. The fact that it did not suggests that context was serving to change participants' response bias.

It should be pointed out that the TRACE model has not met with universal acceptance. Norris (1994) has raised a number of objections to the model, including the view that the model over-emphasises the role of top-down information in spoken word recognition. Thus he criticises both the data supporting certain context-driven effects and describes an alternative model in which large scale word recognition is achieved without top-down influences.

Overview

- True language is the ability to communicate concepts via a symbolic signalling system such as speech or writing.
- Various characteristics of the speech signal are used to differentiate vowels and consonants.
- Perception of vowels is particularly influenced by the information derived from the associated consonants.
- Perception of stop consonants is influenced by voice onset time which provides a reliable basis for distinguishing voiced versus unvoiced stops.
- The perception of stop consonants is categorical; the speech system is able to tolerate distortions of a stop consonant until a point is reached where another consonant suddenly starts to be perceived.
- The motor theory of speech perception proposes that information about articulation is used, the identification of phonemes. Evidence such as the good speech perception of inarticulate infants argues against the theory.
- The fuzzy logic model stresses that multiple sources of information, including facial features, influence speech perception.
- There is considerable evidence that top-down effects can influence speech recognition and this has influenced models of spoken word recognition.
- The cohort model proposes that speech is processed in a linear fashion and that as analysis of a word proceeds the number of candidate words is modified. Contextual cues can also influence the formation of the cohort.

- A modified version of cohort theory has been put forward to handle effects such as late recognition.
- The TRACE model operates in a similar way to the cohort model in that spoken word recognition is a product of top-down and bottom-up influences on recognition.
- While context may simply act to bias what people think they hear, there is evidence that context can actually affect what people perceive.

Suggested further reading

Whitney, P. (1998). *The psychology of language*. Boston, MA: Houghton Mifflin.

Chapter 5 provides a more detailed account of material covered in this chapter.

Massaro, D.W. (1998). *Perceiving talking faces: From speech perception to a behavioural principle.* Cambridge, MA: MIT Press.

A recent book by the originator of the fuzzy logic model of speech perception. Contains an interactive CD Rom.

Yeni-Komshian, G.H. (1998). Speech perception. In J. Berko Gleason & N. Bernstein Ratner (Eds.), *Psycholinguistics*. Fort Worth: Harcourt Brace.

A good alternative to Whitney.

Revision questions

1 When is a language really a language and is this ability unique to humans?
2 How do spectrograms reveal to us the difference between vowels and consonants?
3 How does manner and place of articulation affect speech?
4 What are the factors determining the perception of vowels?
5 Explain the evidence showing that voice onset time is crucial to consonant perception.
6 What is categorical perception?
7 Explain and evaluate the motor theory of speech perception.
8 How does the Fuzzy Logic Model deal with speech perception?
9 What evidence is there that context affects speech perception?
10 Describe the nature of the cohort model of word recognition—how has the original model had to be modified?

11 Describe the TRACE model; what evidence is used to support the idea that word recognition involves an interaction between top-down and bottom-up processes?

Language: Word recognition and reading

11

A newspaper once carried the headline "Lead Boat Sinks in Solo Race". I remember staring at this strange sentence and finally concluding that it was no great surprise. Any boat made from lead would obviously sink. It was only a subsequent reading of the sentence that enabled me to make sense: "lead" refers to being in front, not to the metal. "Lead" is one of a small class of words in English that is a **heterophone**; one letter pattern, two or more sounds. This contrasts with the high frequency of **homophones** in our language; words with the same sound but different spellings (e.g. "sale", "sail"). The reason that the above headline causes problems is because "lead" is presented without any preceding context and, as a result, we opt for the commonest meaning (a metal) on our initial encounter. The fact that we are rarely aware of the potential ambiguity of words tells us that our word recognition system is very efficient in that it only allows through the meaning relevant to what we are reading or listening. A good example is the word "game" we considered in Chapter 8. Our ability to resolve ambiguity effortlessly under most circumstances is one of the many aspects of word recognition we will be considering in this chapter. However, our starting point will be where we first encounter words—the eye.

Eye movements

All reading begins with us looking at words and moving our eyes along the sentence. Subjectively, this appears to be a continuous process but it is not. Reading a line of words involves a series of successive **fixations** going principally from left to right, although around 12% of fixations involve going from right to left—these are known as **regressions**. Fixations typically last between 200msec and 250msec. The movement from one fixation to the next is known as a **saccade**. These take between 10 and 20msec to occur and range between 7 and 9 letters or spaces in length (Rayner, 1998). Saccade length is measured in this way because the size of saccades does not vary with viewing distance; thus whether reading a book or a sentence on a large roadside poster, the saccade length will be the same (see Fig. 11.1).

Although saccades take only a short time to occur, they take much longer to plan with the average value being about 175msec. This means that processes determining where the next saccade should go are occurring during most of the fixation period. Thus, comprehension and planning operate in parallel. There are two other important features of a saccade. First, they are ballistic movements in that once launched towards a particular point they cannot be modified—in the same way that when we throw a piece of paper toward the rubbish bin we cannot redirect it mid flight. Second, we are effectively blind during a saccade—a phenomenon known as **saccadic suppression**. Thus, if a light flashes while we are moving our eyes we will not notice it.

A crucial issue in reading research is to determine how fixations are controlled. To understand this we first need to introduce the concept of the **effective visual field** or **perceptual span**. For our present purpose the perceptual span can be defined as the visual area of text from which we can extract information during a fixation. The retina contains a small central area known as the **fovea** which has a visual angle of about 2 degrees. Outside is the larger **parafovea** which extends 5 degrees either

FIG. 11.1. Diagram showing a typical progression of fixations and variations in saccade length. The dots indicate the place of fixation, the first number below the dot indicates its position in the sequence (note, for example, that fixations 12 and 13 are regressions; note also the "overshoot" phenomenon, fixation 20, in which the first fixation on a new line often falls too far into a sentence and a regression is required). The second number below the dot indicates the duration of each fixation in msec.

Roadside joggers endure sweat, pain and angry drivers in the name of

•	•	•	•	•	•	•	•
1	2	3	4	5	6	7	8
286	221	246	277	256	233	216	188

fitness. A healthy body may seem reward enough for most people. However,

•	•	•	•	•	•	•	•	• •	•
9	10	11	12	13	14	15	16	17 18	19
301	177	196	175	244	302	112	177	266 188	199

for all those who question the payoff, some recent research on physical

•	•	•	• •	•	•	•
21	20	22	23 24	25	26	27

activity and creativity has provided some surprising good news. Regular

• •	• •	•	•	•	•	• •
29 28	30 31	32	33	34	35	36 37
201 66	201 188	203	220	217	288	212 75

An excerpt from a passage of text with fixation sequence and fixation durations included. The dots below the words indicate the fixation locations, the first number below a dot indicates its ordinal number in the sequence, and the second number below a dot is the duration of the fixation (in milliseconds).

A saccadic eye movement: the next saccade is planned during processing of the current fixation via covert attention.

side of fixation. Beyond this is the area known as the **periphery**. The fovea has the greatest visual acuity and the entire foveal region contributes to a fixation along with a small portion of the parafoveal area. Another feature of perceptual span is that it is asymmetric; more information about text is extracted from the right of fixation than from the left, i.e. more information is extracted from the right parafoveal region

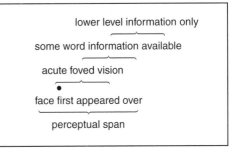

lower level information only

some word information available

acute foved vision

•

face first appeared over

perceptual span

FIG. 11.2.
Asymmetry of the
visual field.

than the left. This makes sense in that it is much more relevant to have information about what text is coming up than about text which has already been read (see Fig. 11.2). This asymmetry is not predetermined but varies according to the writing system being used—the extreme case being Hebrew in which the asymmetry is reversed—and variations in the difficulty of what is being read (Pollatsek et al., 1981).

It is important to note that the size of the perceptual span varies according to the type of information being extracted. The largest span, known as the total perceptual span, is the area in which any information relevant to reading can be extracted and this has been estimated to be

14–15 spaces to the right and 3–4 spaces to the left. Next there is the **letter-identification span** which is the area of fixation within which information about letters can be obtained. The smallest span is the **word identification span** and this is the area of fixation capable of word identification (Rayner, 1998).

What then, controls the length of a saccade? As we mentioned earlier, saccades are ballistic so they must be aimed at something picked up in the rightward portion of the total perceptual span. Many experiments have explored this issue and there seems to be a general agreement that a number of textual features influence where the next fixation falls in a sequence of text. Overall, the less informative a textual feature is, the less likely it is to be fixated upon. Thus, fixations rarely fall on spaces and punctuation marks or on small words, particularly "the". Longer words are more likely to be fixated upon and the longer the word, the further into the word the fixation occurs.

There is good agreement that basic features of the text play the major role in determining eye movements (what we can term "bottom-up" influences) but is there evidence that "top-down" influences also control where we look next in a sentence? There has been far less work on this but some evidence does indicate that contextual information can affect eye movement. In one experiment participants fixated on a cue word such as "reptile" and were told to pronounce an adjacent word in parafoveal vision. At this point, the word in the parafovea was actually a nonword that then transformed into a real word as participants made their saccadic movement. In one condition, the nonword changed into a semantically real word with the same general shape or **word envelope**, e.g. "snckrs" became "snakes", while on other trials a related but visually dissimilar word, e.g. "lizard", or a completely unrelated word "limits" appeared. Compared with various control conditions, visually similar word envelope information facilitated word recognition but this effect was most evident when context predicted the word.

Further evidence for top-down processing involved a study in which participants saw sentences such as:

> "Since the wedding was today, the baker rushed the wedding _____ to the reception."

The blank was filled in various ways, including the highly predictable "cake", the less predictable "pies" and the highly unlikely word "bomb". Words with similar word envelopes were also inserted, e.g. "cahc" and "picz". Of principal interest was the finding that participants were more likely to skip highly predictable words and also their similar nonword. This finding suggests that the mechanisms controlling saccadic movements can take semantic information into account when planning a saccade and the finding of a semantic effect with nonwords suggests that top-down influences are compensating for inadequate information in the text itself (Rayner et al., 1986).

While there seems general agreement on what factors influence eye movements, there is much debate on the exact mechanism involved. The two principal accounts are Morrison's (1984) **oculomotor theory** and O'Regan's (1992) **strategy–tactics model**. We can mention these only briefly here. The former theory links eye movements to word identification—once a word is recognised a rightward movement is initiated. In addition, it is assumed that the paravoveal region is already analysing the next word to the right. If this is completed before the word in foveal vision is recognised then "skipping" can occur, resulting in the word to the right not being fixated at all. This model explains why skipping might occur, e.g. non fixation of predictable words, but it does not readily handle regressive eye movement in which the reader moves back along the line to refixate (for a recent update on this type of model see Reichle et al., 1998 below).

The strategy–tactics model acknowledges that readers can adopt different strategies when reading. For example, the British prime minister, Harold Macmillan, read documents quickly by reading only the middle three or four words in a line of text. More common is **skip reading** in which parts or even whole sentences are not read because the reader is merely trying to get the gist of what is written. While tactics can be applied at a high level they can also be deployed at much lower levels. Central to this idea is that a word can have an **optimal viewing position**—i.e. a point of fixation which allows maximal information about the word to be obtained—and that adjustments within words can be used to achieve this. While the concept of an optimal viewing position seems viable, the measurement of this concept during the reading of connected prose has remained problematic (Rayner, 1998).

More recently Reichle et al. (1998) have put forward the E–Z reader model of eye movement control (non-Americans may have difficulty seeing the joke here; remember that Americans pronounce Z as "zee"). The model was driven by the need to explain several essential facts about how fixation times are determined. First, word type affects the probability of fixation. **Content** or **"open class" words** represent nouns, verbs and adjectives. This class of words is infinitely expandable as new words are added to the language (e.g. "netsurfing", "CD Rom"). In contrast **function** or **"closed class" words** represent the small group of articles, prepositions, pronouns, and conjunctions. This group includes many of the commonest words in the language (e.g. "the", "this, "they", "and") and it is not expandable—no function word can be replaced by another. Studies of eye movements show that content words are fixated around 80% of the time whereas function words are fixated only about 20% of the time.

Not surprisingly, low frequency words (i.e. words that do not crop up that frequently in the language, e.g. "accordion", "grommet") are fixated for longer than high frequency words—a reflection that the process of lexical access takes longer for low frequency words. As we have seen context also exerts an influence on fixation; if a word is predicted by context it is fixated for less time or may even be skipped. There is also a spillover effect in which a high frequency word will be fixated for less time if it is preceded by a low frequency word. In one study, participants' eye movements were compared in the following two types of sentence:

"The concerned *steward* calmed the child."
"The concerned *student* calmed the child."

These two sentences differ only in the frequency of the word preceding "calmed": "steward" is low frequency; "student" is high frequency. However, it was found that fixation times for the word immediately following were between 30 and 90 msec longer when the preceding word was low frequency (Rayner and Duffy, 1986).

Reichle et al.'s model is a development of that proposed by Morrison (see above) which assumes that the next eye movement is planned before the processing involved in the current fixation is finished. Thus, information from the inner right parafoveal region is being processed in parallel with later stages of the processing directly associated with fixation. Reichle's paper is quite complex and various versions of the model are put forward. However, the essential point is to understand the basis by which the general idea of the model attempts to account for the various aspects of fixation outlined above.

In terms of the model, the currently fixated word is given a familiarity check; this is a multi-component process in which the likely frequency of the word is assessed through the processing of various features. These include length (length is negatively correlated with word frequency), recency of encounter, and the extent to which a word contains familiar patterns of letters. Once frequency checking is complete, a signal indicates that the next saccade should start to be programmed. At the same time, **lexical access** is also engaged in order to achieve the meaning of the currently fixated word. Once this is complete, a second signal initiates covert (non-conscious) attention to the next word on the right (i.e. that in immediate parafoveal vision). The model is sensitive to word frequency effects with higher frequency words undergoing faster familiarity checks and, in particular, faster lexical access. In addition the speed of familiarity checks and lexical access can also be influenced by the predictability of the fixated word.

The model therefore handles the fact that high frequency words are fixated for less time because both the familiarity check and lexical access processes are frequency sensitive. The spillover effect is explained on the grounds that the longer the lexical access time, the shorter is the time available for covert attention to the rightward word before the next saccade is initiated. Thus, returning to our example, "calmed" receives less covert attention preceded by "steward" because lexical access is slower for this word than "student". In the case of high frequency words being skipped, it is assumed that the processing made available by covert parafoveal processing is often sufficient to allow lexical access and thus preclude the need for fixation.

Transsaccadic memory

Reading thus involves a series of fixations from which the meaning of text is extracted. However, there is a problem in that the information derived from a single fixation is usually an insufficient unit of information on which to base comprehension. Accordingly, this means that comprehension must be based on the combination of information from a series of fixations, a function that is attributed to **transsaccadic memory** (Intraub, 1997).

Experiments have shown that the information held over from one fixation to the next is not purely perceptual but some abstraction of the information. In one study, eye movements were monitored while participants read sentences in which the words appeared in alternating case (e.g. ThE mAn WaS eAtInG tHe ApPlE). Reading performance was assessed in conditions where the pattern of alternation did not change across saccades and also where it was directly reversed. No differences were found, suggesting the low level characteristics of the text were not retained across saccades (McConkie and Zola, 1979). A similar finding was recently reported by McConkie and Currie (1996); shifting a scene vertically or contracting its size up to 20% did not disrupt the pattern of saccadic movement.

The apparent abstract nature of transsaccadic memory is assumed to stem from the fact that percepts themselves are not uniformly detailed

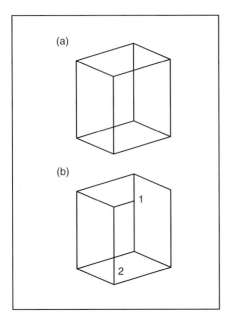

and that only part of a scene is fully analysed (Hochberg, 1978). A demonstration of this idea is shown in Fig. 11.3. The first involves the well known **Necker Cube** (Fig. 11.3a) which readily reverses perspective as you look at it. Fig. 11.3b is a redrawn Necker Cube which has been disambiguated. If you stare at point 1 the figure is unambiguous but if you look at point 2 it starts to reverse again—thus indicating that information about the whole array is not being fully processed. Hochberg has suggested that these variations in attention explain why people are generally poor at noticing minor continuity errors in films. This was confirmed by Simons (1996). He showed participants a video (example frames are shown in Fig. 11.4) in which a small change was made off-scene (switching the cola bottle for a box). Participants consistently failed to notice this switch.

FIG. 11.3 (above). (a) Standard Necker Cube. (b) Modified Necker Cube (see text for further instructions).

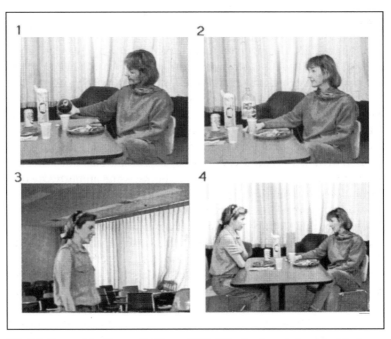

FIG. 11.4. Frames of the video used by Simons (1996). Notice the change in Frame 4 relative to Frame 2.

Word recognition

All theories of word recognition assume that we possess a **mental lexicon**—a form of dictionary-like structure in which there is a representation of each word we know including its visual characteristics, pronunciation, and meaning. Thus psychologists concerned with word recognition often refer to a word's **lexical entry** when discussing its internal representation and the process of word recognition is often known as lexical access.

One of the most influential models of word recognition was Morton's (1969) **logogen model.** In this model, each word is represented by a logogen that contains information about what a given word looks like. When a word is presented, each logogen is compared in parallel with input and the one with the most overlap "fires" and allows the meaning of that word to become available via semantic memory. The logogen model is a **threshold model** in that the degree of activation needed for

Searching for a word in the mental lexicon, where each word we know has information stored about it, as a lexical entry...

... the process of getting information out of the mental dictionary, which makes the word available to the person, is called lexical access.

a logogen to fire can vary depending on the top-down information available. Thus, if a text is about football, all words related to that topic will have a lowered threshold and be identified more quickly because less featural overlap will be needed for identification. In addition to these transient threshold changes, logogens can also vary in their absolute thresholds. This allows for the fact that more frequently encountered words are identified faster than less frequent ones.

The idea of variable thresholds was needed to explain a class of phenomena known as **semantic priming effects**. In a typical experiment, participants would be shown letter strings and asked to decide as quickly as possible whether or not each string was a word. It was shown that the speed of the participant's **lexical decision** was faster when a target string, e.g. "dog" was preceded by a semantically related word, e.g. "cat" (Meyer and Schvaneveldt, 1971). This result was predicted by the logogen model on the grounds that logogens were interconnected via the semantic system so that activation of "cat" could lead to a lowering of the threshold for "dog".

Although priming effects are demonstrated artificially they undoubtedly infiltrate our everyday speech. A good example is the unintentional pun. Take this extract from *The Times* concerning the recruitment of French bus drivers to work in London:

> "One of the biggest problems is coming to terms with driving on the left...The French drivers are given an extra week's training to help familiarise themselves with British traffic laws and a week long *crash* course in English."
>
> (*The Times,* June 7 1999, p. 3).

The word "crash" has almost certainly arisen in the piece because of its association with the context of "driving" and perhaps the writer's concern that the French bus drivers might have lapses and start driving on the wrong side of the road.

While the logogen model remained influential for a considerable time, it has encountered some difficulties. One of these concerns the **word superiority effect** (Reicher, 1969). This phenomenon is demonstrated in a task where participants are briefly presented with a string of letters that is either a real three-letter word or an equivalent nonword. Following a central mask, participants see a single letter and have to decide whether that letter was in the preceding letter string. Participants perform better when the letter is embedded in a real word. There is also a **nonword superiority effect** in which isolated letters are more easily identified when presented in pronounceable nonwords (e.g. MUSP) than random strings of letters (Carr et al., 1978).

Interactive activation

The problem with the logogen model was that, although it allowed for top-down information to influence word identification, it did not allow for this type of influence lower down the system, a property that is essential to explain word and nonword superiority effects. This is because the logogen model was a **serial processing model** in which featural analysis was presumed to precede lexical access. The **interactive activation** model (McClelland and Rumelhart, 1981) was put forward with the express aim of accounting for superiority effects and is similar in principle to the TRACE model of spoken word recognition we considered in the last chapter.

According to the interactive activation model, words are represented at three levels within a network: features, letters, and words. The connections between these levels can be both excitatory and inhibitory and within a level they are inhibitory. To give an example, consider the presentation of a D as the first letter of DOOR. This would activate all letters containing a downward stroke while other letters would be inhibited. At the letter level, D would be identified as the first letter. This would serve to inhibit other letters and also cause activation at the word level in that all words beginning with D would become more active and those beginning with other letters would be inhibited. The patterns of activation would change with the presentation of O and with presentation of the second O, information would start feeding down the system so as to expect the letter R. As a result, less featural analysis would be needed for its identification.

The interactive activation model explains the word superiority effect by proposing that activation of word information results in the letters in that word and their features being activated and competing letters suppressed. As a result, the constituent letters are easier to identify than when in a nonword because this does not activate anything at the word level. The nonword superiority effect occurs because it is assumed that pronounceable nonwords achieve some subthreshold activation at the word level (e.g. MUSP would partially activate MUST) and that this information feeds down so as to cause some excitation and inhibition at the letter and featural level.

The interaction activation model has been developed to include higher levels of word processing, including meaning. However, it has not as yet been developed to extend beyond the identification of four-letter words presented in isolation.

From print to sound

Virtually all the words we know we can pronounce. It has therefore been proposed that for each lexical entry we have a precise **phonemic code** which specifies the sounds that constitute that word's pronunciation. Thus confronted with the word BRICK we access its representation and produce the phonemic code associated with it. However, if you were travelling in an unusual part of the country and you come across the name "NEMBICK" you would still be able to pronounce it even though you have no lexical entry for that word. To explain this it has been suggested that we have, through experience of a language, acquired a set of **grapheme to phoneme correspondence rules** (GPCR's), that enable us to take any segment of letters and pronounce it. Thus for NEMBICK we would divide it into two syllables, NEM and BICK and use rules to assemble phonology for each (Coltheart et al., 1993).

At this point you may ask why we need word-specific phonemic codes when we have GPCR's. Could we not simply use rules to pronounce everything, word or nonword? For English this is not possible, because the language contains a high degree of irregularity in grapheme to phoneme correspondence. To illustrate this consider the following extract:

"Dearest creature in creation
Studying English pronunciation,
I will teach you in my verse
Sounds like corpse, corps, horse, and worse.
I will keep you, Susy, busy,
Make your head with heat go dizzy;"

This poem shows how variable English GPCR's can be. Note, for example, the four different pronunciations associated with 'ea', variations in the sound of 'ou' and so on. In fact there is not a single grapheme or pair of graphemes in the English Language that has a unique pronunciation, every one of them has at least two different ways of being pronounced. Thus in English it is judged that around 20% of words do not have a regular pronunciation.

The presence of so much GPC irregularity in English has led logically to the view that we must store away lexically specific phonemic descriptions of words that we know and, in combination with our ability to pronounce unknown words, has led to the idea that pronunciation can proceed by either of two routes, a **lexical route** and a **GPC** route (see Fig. 11.5). There is a problem, however, if we are presented with a word, e.g. PINT; how do we know which route to use? PINT is of course irregular so the lexical route should be used, but since the word has yet to be identified, what stops the word also being dealt with by the GPC rules?

One answer is to conceive of these two routes as a **race model**—one in which the two competing sources of information "race" one another to provide an output. Alternatively codes from both routes might be derived and discrepancies resolved in favour of the lexical information that must be right. Evidence favouring the race model comes from speeded pronunciation tasks in which subjects must pronounce words as quickly as possible. When irregular words are presented in these experiments subjects take longer to start pronouncing irregular words and frequently produce regularisation errors (e.g. "broad" pronounced "brode") which are quickly corrected; here it seems that the GPC route has "won" the race and produced the wrong pronunciation .

While most people accept the two route model there is an alternative view that all pronunciation, word and nonword, arises by **analogy** (Glushko, 1979). According to this theory, presentation of a letter string

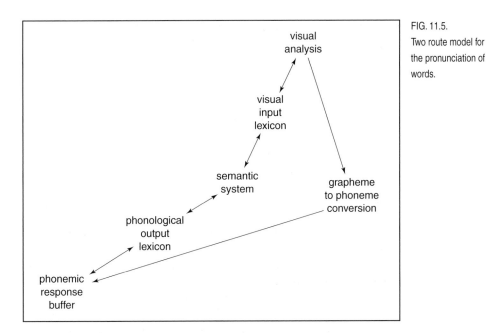

FIG. 11.5.
Two route model for
the pronunciation of
words.

results in the activation of a "neighbourhood"; this can be defined as a group of lexical entries all sharing the same visual characteristics of the presented string. Within this theory neighbourhoods can be consistent in that all the words in that neighbourhood share the same pronunciation, or they can be inconsistent in that one or more neighbours has a different pronunciation. When a letter string with a consistent neighbourhood is presented, e.g. BRICK, DRICK, pronunciation is straightforward, because all the neighbours indicate the same pronunciation. However, when the neighbourhood is inconsistent, e.g. PINT, HINT, SINT, pronunciation is slowed because a discrepancy has to be resolved.

The analogy theory makes a prediction that is not made by the two route theory, in that it suggests that regular words that have irregular neighbours, e.g. HINT, should be harder to pronounce than regular words with consistent neighbours. Glushko appeared to show just that, but subsequent work has shown that this effect only occurs if the irregular word precedes the regular word (e.g. PINT → HINT). This so-called consistency effect thus appears to be a rather specific priming effect, rather than a general reflection of how pronunciation is achieved (Parkin, 1986).

We can also find evidence against analogy theory from brain damaged adults. Damage to the left hemisphere frequently produces disturbances of reading known collectively as **acquired dyslexias**. Two of the commonest forms of this are **surface dyslexia** and **phonological dyslexia**. In the former the person appears to be reading using GPCR's alone and thus produces large numbers of regularisation errors (see Table 11.1) but normal performance on regular words and nonwords. In contrast the phonological dyslexic reads regular and irregular words well, but cannot read nonwords—thus suggesting that only the lexical route is available for pronunciation (Parkin, 1996). If all pronunciation is based on a common analogy process it is difficult to see how these dissociations could arise.

Phonology and word identification

When we read, we "hear" the sounds of the words in our heads. Existence of this "inner speech" has led some to assume that deriving the sounds of words is part of the process of word identification—in other words, information about sound as well as visual information is used in the process of lexical access. There are a number of logical reasons why this is not likely to be correct. First, there are far fewer phonemic combinations than letter combinations in English. For this reason, our language is littered with **homophones**, words that sound the same but are spelled differently, e.g. "sail", "sale"; "hole", "whole", etc. Emphasising sound would therefore tend to add confusion rather than clarity in word identification. There is also the problem of irregularity in pronunciation which we have just considered. This would make it difficult to derive the correct phonological code for about 20% of words (more about this problem in the next chapter). Finally, there is the sheer speed at which we read—approximately 300 words per minute—and the fact that individual word identification appears to be complete within 50msecs. These facts seem inconsistent with the idea that a phonological code is used in identification (Parkin, 1996).

TABLE 11.1

Pronunciation errors by someone with surface dyslexia. Mispronunciations are shown in phonetic script. Examples: beret → "berrit", deny → "denny", tomb → "tom", and pear → "peer".

pretty	/ prɛti /	were	/ wɪə /
beret	/ bɛrɛt /	tomb	/ tɒm /
regime	/ rɛgaɪm /	deaf	/ dif /
pint	/ pɪnt /	colonel	/ cɒlonel /
sweat	/ swit /	bear	/ bɪə /
vase	/ vez /	bowl	/ boual /
deny	/ dɛni /	pear	/ pɪə /
thyme	/ θaɪmi /	steak	/ stik /

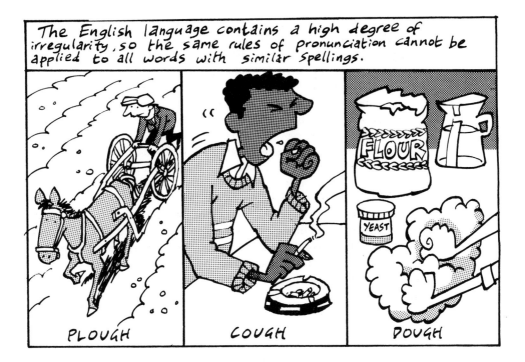

The English language contains a high degree of irregularity, so the same rules of pronunciation cannot be applied to all words with similar spellings.

PLOUGH

COUGH

DOUGH

Despite the above there have been claims that phonological information is used in lexical access. The principal basis has been the demonstration that people' ability to make lexical decisions takes longer when the words are irregular. On the face of it, this would seem to indicate some phonemic mediation in word recognition but there are problems. First, identification times in lexical decision times are much slower than those in normal reading so any effects of phonology may be occurring because a specific strategy is being used or because phonology may be influencing decision processes occurring after the word has basically been identified. Another problem is that many irregular words also have unusual letter combinations, e.g. "yacht", "khaki" and, when this is controlled for in the generation of irregular word sets, the irregularity effect in lexical decision disappears (Parkin et al., 1986).

Word recognition and ambiguity

One of the enduring problems in language research has been to explain how our word recognition system handles the frequent occurrence of ambiguous words, known as **homographs**, in our language (Simpson,

1994). Essentially, there are three differing explanations of how we deal with ambiguity.

- **Context-dependent**: Here the meaning attributed to a homograph is determined by the context of the sentence within which it occurs. In the case of "the dog's *bark* scared the children" only the meaning *bark* as related to a sound would be activated (e.g. Glucksberg et al., 1986).
- **Dominant meaning**: Homographs can be roughly divided into two types, balanced and unbalanced. A balanced homograph is one in which the various meanings are equally frequent, e.g. *mass, lean, fair*, and unbalanced homographs are ones where one meaning is far more dominant, e.g. *fence, plain, treat*. According to this theory, the dominant meaning of the homograph is accessed first, with other meaning being examined subsequently if the sentence context does not fit that meaning. As *bark* is an unbalanced homograph favouring the sound of a dog, only that meaning would be activated in the example sentence (Hogaboam and Perfetti, 1975).
- **Automatic activation**: In Chapter 3 we saw that the meaning of a word can be activated automatically but that this pattern of

Homographs are ambiguous words that are spelt the same but can be interpreted in different ways, such as "bark" in the sentence "the dog's bark scared the children".

activation is short lived. This type of theory has been applied in ambiguity research and led to the proposal that all meanings of a homograph are activated initially and that the context provided by the sentence then selects the relevant meaning for further processing. Thus in our example, *bark* would activate information concerning the surface of a tree trunk but this would be rapidly discarded as irrelevant to the context (Swinney, 1979).

Evidence for the automatic activation of meaning

In a key experiment, Swinney (1979) asked people to listen to short passages such as:

> "Rumour had it that, for years, the government building had been plagued with problems. The man was not surprised when he found several *bugs* in the corner of his room."

> "Rumour had it that, for years, the government building had been plagued with problems. The man was not surprised when he found several spiders, roaches, and other *bugs* in the corner of his room."

The difference between the first and second passages is that the former offers no context within which to interpret the homograph *bug* whereas the second passage biases us toward *bug* as an insect. In addition to listening, participants were also told that a string of letters would appear occasionally on a screen and that they should decide as quickly as possible whether or not it was a word. These strings either appeared immediately after the homograph or several words later. The relevant aspect of the experiment concerned the extent to which presentation of a homograph primed its various meanings. In relation to our example, this involved comparing the amount of priming for ANT vs. SPY. Also of interest was the extent to which a biasing context affected the results.

The experiment showed that immediately after presentation both meanings of a homograph were active, i.e. there was priming for both ANT and SPY, but when priming was tested later on only the contextually relevant meaning resulted in priming, i.e. ANT. This result held whether or not the meaning biased by the sentence context reflected the dominant or non-dominant meaning.

Automatic activation of meaning is not universal

Although additional studies confirmed Swinney's findings, other research has led to a different view of ambiguity in word recognition.

In a series of experiments, Tabossi (1988) has shown that if the preceding context of a sentence is sufficiently biased towards a particular meaning then only associations of that meaning are activated. Thus, using a task similar to Swinney, a sentence such as "The violent hurricane did not damage the ships which were in the *port*, one of the best equipped along the coast", only the meaning of port in relation to a safe haven appeared to be activated. A series of experiments by Simpson and Kreuger (1991) yielded similar results. Their participants viewed three types of sentence, each terminating in a homograph:

"This really is not a good *spring*" (ambiguous)
"This has been a cold and rainy *spring*" (biased dominant)
"This is a broken and rusty old *spring*" (biased non-dominant)

The results showed that biased sentences only primed recognition of words related to that meaning. Thus "...cold and rainy *spring*" only primed "summer" and "...rusty old *spring*" only primed "coil". When there was no bias both meanings appeared to be activated but the dominant meaning was more strongly available. Finally, using eye

movement recordings, Rayner et al. (1983) showed that only the dominant meaning of a homograph will be activated if the preceding context biases toward that meaning (see also Rayner and Frazier, 1989).

The results from studies are therefore mixed and provide some support for all three theories of ambiguity. Thus it seems that meanings can become available automatically but that sentence context, combined with the meaning dominance pattern of a particular homograph, can also influence what meaning is made available. It should also be noted that the above experiments have concentrated on the pattern of meaning activation caused by the homograph itself. However, it has been noted that the sentence context itself can make additional contributions to the meaning activated by a homograph (Tabossi, 1991). Consider the sentence "The boy dropped the *plant*". If asked to say which words are associated with *plant*, participants reliably produce "leaves" but also "spill" even though the latter would not be generated as a response to *plant* when presented in isolation. It was subsequently shown that priming occurred for both the obvious associate, "leaves" and the inferred information "spill", thus indicating that sentence context constrains the activation of meaning at an inferential level (Paul et al., 1992).

Overview

- Eye movements are ballistic and their length is principally determined by the physical features of text.
- The effective visual field is asymmetric, offering more information to the right than to the left.
- The effective visual field varies in the quality of information about text which it can extract.
- There is some evidence that higher level information can influence the pattern of eye movements but physical aspects of text gathered from the parafoveal region appear to be the dominant source of information guiding eye movements.
- Recent models of eye movements stress that the next saccade is planned during processing of the current fixation via a mechanism of covert attention.
- Reading comprises the combined output of a series of fixations which are stored in some form of short-term visual memory.
- Our internalised knowledge of words is referred to as the mental lexicon and the process of word identification is referred to as lexical access.

- The logogen model has been superseded by the interactive activation model which proposes that top-down and bottom-up information interact at all levels to facilitate word recognition.
- The dual route model of pronunciation proposes that a word's sound can be derived either via a lexical route or by means of the GPCR route.
- The dual route model is supported by the existence of surface and phonological dyslexia. These deficits are hard to explain in terms of an analogy model of pronunciation.
- It is unlikely that phonological information plays any role in the process of lexical access.
- There is evidence supporting the idea that ambiguous words automatically activate all their meanings and other evidence that the meaning accessed is constrained by the context of the sentence within which the word appears and the relative frequencies of a homograph's different meanings.

Suggested further reading

Balota, D.A. (1994). Visual recognition: The journey from features to meaning. In M.A. Gernsbacher (Ed.), *Handbook of psycholinguistics.* San Diego, CA: Academic Press.

A good, although detailed, overview of theories of visual word recognition.

Harley, T.H. (1997). *The psychology of language.* Hove, UK: Psychology Press.

Chapter 3 of this book provides a good basic account of issues surrounding visual word recognition.

Rayner, K. (1998). Eye movements in reading and information processing: 20 years of research. *Psychological Bulletin, 124,* 372–422.

This is a very detailed review of all aspects of eye movement research.

Simpson, G.B. (1994). Context and the processing of ambiguous words. In M.A. Gernsbacher (Ed.), *Handbook of psycholinguistics.* San Diego, CA: Academic Press.

Chapter provides a detailed overview of experiments concerned with how lexical ambiguity is resolved.

Revision questions

1 Describe the basic characteristics of eye movements—why are they considered "ballistic"?

2 How do the characteristics of our perceptual span relate to the control of eye movements?

3 What evidence is there for top-down influences in the control of eye movements?

4 What is meant by "strategy tactics" in relation to eye movements and reading?

5 What is the E–Z model of reading and how does it explain various phenomena in eye movement control?

6 What is transsaccadic memory, why do we need it, and what sort of information does it contain?

7 What were the basic features of the logogen model and what findings challenged it?

8 What were interactive activation models of word recognition and how did they improve on the logogen model?

9 Why is it unlikely that phonological codes play any role in the process of lexical access?

10 How does the word recognition system deal with ambiguity?

Language: 12
Comprehension

"Can you pass the wine?"
"Sure."

Tim leaned back, he had enjoyed the dinner and he knew that she had too.

"You have expensive tastes."
"Not me, my sister. Works in the City. I can only afford plonk."

The above passage should be perfectly interpretable to you but take a moment to reflect on what you extract from the text compared with what is actually in front of you. First, you will know that the response "sure" was not simply confirming that Tim is capable of passing the wine. The construction "Can you pass the wine" is a **speech act** in which we accept that questions can sometimes be used to make requests. In this sense you are therefore aware of the **pragmatics** of English rather than its literal usage. You are also aware of an **elliptical form** in that you know that "she had too" refers to having dinner. Additionally, you assume that the reference to expensive tastes refers to the wine, that the wine was given to Tim by his sister, that she is wealthy because she works in the City, and that Tim is far less well off than his sister.

The above passage illustrates the extent to which **inference** is crucial in our understanding of language and we will be considering this later in the chapter. However, language also has its own basic structure or **grammar**, and an initial question is the extent to which our grammatical knowledge can affect how we use and comprehend language.

Competence and performance

The discrepancy between what people know about a language and how they use it has been emphasised by the linguist Noam Chomsky in his distinction between **competence** and **performance** (Chomsky, 1965).

Competence can be defined as the rules that describe a person's use of language and these are laid down in grammars. A grammar describes the acceptable and unacceptable sequences of words within a language. This process of ordering is known as **syntax**. Thus the sentence "I am going to the cinema" is syntactically correct whereas "To the cinema I am going" is unacceptable. In contrast, performance relates to how people actually use a language.

A central feature of work on sentence comprehension has been to explore how closely related competence and performance actually are. Thus an essential question has been whether the characteristics of a grammar provide an insight into how language is actually dealt with in the brain.

Phrase structure grammar

Phrase structure grammar (PSG) is a logical mechanism that can be used to break down sentences into their constituent elements, a process known as **parsing**. Consider the sentence:

(1) "The man kisses the woman."

This is a **simple active affirmative sentence** (SAAS). It is simple because it has only one clause, it is *active* because the subject of the sentence ("the man") is performing the action ('kissing"), and affirmative because it makes a positive statement. This sentence can be parsed using PSG (Fig 12.1):

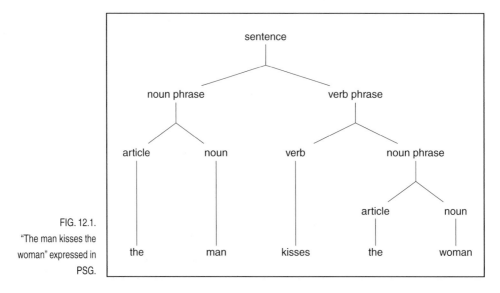

FIG. 12.1. "The man kisses the woman" expressed in PSG.

An alternative form of sentence is the **passive** in which the object precedes the subject:

(2) "The woman was kissed by the man."

This produces the parsing tree illustrated in Fig. 12.2:

Sentences can be made more complex by combining two or more sentences, e.g.

(3) "The man is kissing the woman; they are probably married."

In this case, each sentence is called a **clause**.

Transformational grammar

Chomsky proposed a set of additional rules, known as **transformational rules**, which when added to PSG could provide a linguistically based mechanism for generating an infinite variety of sentences; for this reason, Chomsky's grammar is referred to as a **generative grammar**. According to the idea, production of a sentence begins with a SAAS which can then be grammatically transformed via various rules into different grammatical forms. Within this theory, the SAAS is referred to as the **deep structure** and the sentence as the **surface structure**. Thus the SAAS "The man kissed the woman" could be modified by a passive transformation or turned into a question using an interrogative transformation. Another important feature of Chomsky's linguistic ideas was the assumed independence between syntactic operations and meaning. To illustrate this

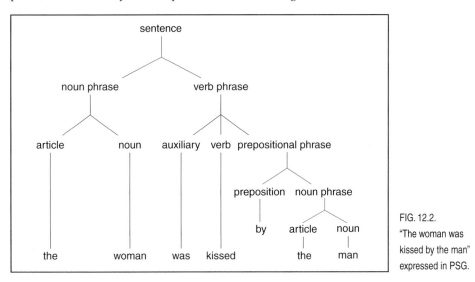

FIG. 12.2.
"The woman was kissed by the man" expressed in PSG.

point, Chomsky noted that the meaningless sentence "Colourless green dreams sleep furiously" is nonetheless very easy to parse.

Although Chomsky was somewhat ambivalent as to whether his transformational grammar was a psychological theory, i.e. a theory of performance, psychologists seized on his ideas as a source of experimental hypotheses. In particular it was reasoned that the more transformationally complex a sentence was the more difficult it would be to comprehend or remember. Initially, a number of findings were consistent with this idea. Passive sentences, for example, were comprehended more slowly than active sentences. However, additional research showed that the concept of transformational rules was not an adequate basis for explaining sentence comprehension. In addition, other research questioned Chomsky's assumption that syntactic analysis and meaning were independent of one another. It was found, for example, that the slower identification of passive sentences did not occur when the subject and object of the sentence were not interchangeable at a meaningful level, e.g.

(4) "The flowers were watered by the girl."

In contrast an interchangeable passive:

(5) "The boy was hit by the girl."

did take longer to identify than its SAAS equivalent (Slobin, 1966).

Parsing and ambiguity

While Chomsky's transformational rules failed to develop as a psychological theory, there is general agreement that comprehension does involve some form of parsing. Because our normal processes of sentence comprehension operate so quickly, it has not proved easy to examine parsing in normal situations. As a result, psychologists have resorted to using ambiguous sentences as a means of exploring how the grammatical structure is analysed. The advantage of ambiguous sentences is that people take much longer to deal with them and this offers the psychologist more scope for measurement (Mitchell, 1994). As an example, consider the sentence:

(6) "She bit into the doughnut with relish."

In this sentence the phrase "with relish" cannot be assigned unambiguously—it could refer to the state of the doughnut or the enjoyment of the subject. By examining how people go about resolving these kind of difficulties it has been hoped that some light will be shed on how normal parsing occurs.

PARSING AND AMBIGUITY: "She bit into the doughnut with relish".

"She bit into the doughnut, with relish"

"She bit into, the doughnut with relish"

A number of parsing theories have been put forward. The first of these is the **garden-path theory** which states that the comprehension process favours one syntactic structure initially and only considers alternatives if this first attempt at parsing is unsuccessful (Frazier, 1987; Frazier and Rayner, 1982). According to this theory, the form of grammatical analysis chosen first is the simplest. "Simplicity" is defined according to two rules: **minimal attachment**, which involves selecting the parsing arrangement with the fewest branches; and **late closure**, which involves assuming that new words are part of the phrase or clause currently being "wrapped up".

Although there is considerable support for the idea that people prefer to parse sentences in the simplest way there have been a number of objections to this approach. First, the greater frequency of structural ambiguity in normal English as opposed to carefully crafted prose means that the comprehension process would too often be slowed down by always preferring the simplest grammatical structure. This has led some to argue that parsing initially involves setting up all possibilities, not just the simplest. Another objection is the assumed independence between syntactic analysis and meaning which we criticised earlier in relation to Chomsky's generative grammar. One can also raise concerns about the concept of late closure. Support for this idea came from an experiment in which participants saw sentences such as:

(7) "Since Jay always jogs a mile seems like a short distance."
(8) "Since Jay always jogs a mile this seems like a short distance to him."

Applying the principle of late closure leads us into trouble with the first sentence because "a mile" is erroneously used to wrap up the first clause when in fact it is the beginning of the second clause.

Problems with late closure have been demonstrated using so-called on-line measures of comprehension. An on-line measure is one that is gathered at the time a person is actually reading or listening to text. Most commonly this involves measuring reading times for individual words, phrases, or sentences, or by examining the pattern of eye movements a person makes when dealing with a particular sentence. On-line measures contrast with off-line measures which assess what people have comprehended some time after the text has been presented. A typical off-line measure would be to ask people what they remembered about a piece of text.

Returning to the issue of late closure, studies showed that sentences such as (7) caused longer reading times than (8) in which late closure gives the correct reading. A problem, however, is that the theory is being supported on the basis of showing that people have problems with a sentence which is highly unlikely to occur in real life without either a punctuation mark or a pause to indicate that there is a phrase boundary after "jogs". In addition, there is recent evidence that the preference for late closure can be overridden if it is inconsistent with preceding context (Altmann et al., 1998).

A second approach is known as the **lexical frame theory**, that proposes that specific information derived from words, particularly verbs, can guide the choice of structure. Thus an intransitive verb such as "sneeze" cannot have an object (e.g. "The woman sneezed"), the transitive verb "smash" has a subject and an object (e.g. "The man smashed the egg") and the transitive "give" can involve a subject, a direct object and an indirect object (e.g. "The woman gave the man a watch"). Unfortunately, evidence suggests that, if anything, lexical information about the status of a verb gets in the way of correct parsing. In one study (Mitchell, 1989), participants read sentences of two types:

(9) "After the private had fainted the sergeant * decided to end the military drill."
(10) "After the private had saluted the sergeant * decided to end the military drill."

The results showed that reading times were longer at point * in (9) than in (10). If parsing were able to take account of the fact that "fainted" is an intransitive verb then this should have made it easier not harder for people to realise that a new clause had started.

Other theories have suggested that meaning influences parsing at higher levels. In the **content-guided theory** it is argued that the general meaning of the sentence can guide the particular form parsing adopted (Taraban and McClelland, 1988). Thus people find it easier to read a sentence such as:

(11) "The reporter exposed corruption in the government."

compared to

(12) "The reporter exposed corruption in the article."

even though, according to minimal attachment theory, the latter has a simpler grammatical structure. To explain this result, it was argued that the ending of the first sentence was more in line with people's meaningful expectations than the latter.

Additional theories have proposed that parsing strategies are directly influenced by our experience (so-called **exposure based strategies**). In a sentence such as:

(13) "The spy shot the daughter of the colonel who was standing on the balcony."

the relative clause "who was standing on the balcony" can be attached to either the earlier noun phrase "the daughter" or the later noun phrase "the colonel." Studies of English show that English speakers tend, in these situations, to attach the relative clause to the second noun phrase. The conclusion that this is determined by experience comes from data showing that in Spanish there is a bias to attaching to the first noun phrase. However, when Spanish children read a large number of stories in which sense depends on opting for second noun phrase attachment they then develop a preference for second noun phrase attachment (Mitchell et al., 1992).

Sentence comprehension—a summary

There is strong evidence that people make use of grammatical structure when comprehending sentences. This is revealed particularly when people deal with ambiguous sentences which lead them to construct initial parsings of sentences that are incorrect or problematic. However, it is not an easy task to explain what factors people use to derive these grammatical structures. The garden-path theory assumes that the simplest analysis is initially preferred, but there have been a number of arguments against this view; in particular the idea that meaning does not influence parsing has come under considerable attack. Attempts to explain how meaning influences parsing take many forms. Constraints imposed by the nature of verbs (e.g. transitive, intransitive) do not seem apparent but there is evidence for other aspects of meaning influencing parsing. In addition, there is some suggestion that experience of a language may initiate biases in how particular types of sentence are parsed.

Syntax, clauses, and memory

While debate continues about how detailed aspects of syntax are derived there is little doubt that the clause is significant in comprehension. In one experiment (Caplan, 1972), participants listened to prose and were asked periodically whether a particular word was in the sentence they had just heard. The sentences were arranged so that the target word was the same number of words away from the end of the second clause. The only difference was that for one sentence type (14), the target word was in the first clause and in the other sentence (15), it was in the second clause:

(14) "Now that artists are working fewer hours/*oil* prints are rare."
(15) "Now that artists are working in *oil*/ prints are rare."

It was found that reaction time was faster when the target word appeared in the second clause thus suggesting that the sentences were being processed on a clause-by-clause basis. This work was supported by other work using the technique of "clickology". In these experiments, participants listened to sentences during which a clicking sound was randomly added. When asked when this occurred participants reliably placed it at clause boundaries.

Further experiments have shown that the availability of information in a preceding clause is not determined by some passive forgetting process but is influenced by the demands of the clause currently being dealt with. Jarvella (1971) compared the recall of preceding clauses which were either structurally independent or dependent on a following clause:

(16) *"The document also blamed him for having failed to disprove the charges.* Taylor was later fired by the President."
[structurally independent]

(17) "The tone of the document was threatening. Having failed to disprove the charges, *Taylor was later fired by the President.*" [structurally dependent]

In (17) clause 2, in italics, is linked to the final clause whereas this is not so in (16). It was found that the structurally dependent condition resulted in better verbatim recall of clause 2, thus suggesting that the forgetting of syntax depends on its relevance to ongoing comprehension.

The above studies suggest that syntax is forgotten fairly rapidly and this was shown convincingly in an experiment by Sachs (1967). Her participants listened to passages which contained a key sentence, e.g. "He sent a letter to Galileo, the great Italian scientist." The participants were given a probe recognition test immediately after the sentence, 80, or 160 syllables later. The test required participants to say whether the sentence they were looking at was one they had just heard. With an immediate test, participants were very accurate but with a delay they failed to detect probe sentences that had been switched to the passive although they did correctly reject sentences that changed the meaning of the original sentence. This suggests that syntax is discarded very rapidly under normal conditions and that people retain the **gist** of what they hear.

Inference

As we saw at the outset of this chapter, there is a great deal more to comprehension than can be derived directly from the text—much of what we derive from a text is produced by the process of inference. Typically, psychologists distinguish between two types of inference: **bridging inferences** and **elaborative inferences**. A bridging inference is one that is needed to maintain coherence of text, whereas an elaborative inference is optional adding information that is not necessary for basic understanding (Singer, 1994).

Perhaps the commonest form of bridging inference involves the resolution of **anaphora**; this comes from the Greek "carrying back" and describes a word that refers back to a preceding word. Anaphora can take a number of forms, the most common of which involves pronouns (he, she, etc.). In the majority of instances the referent of a pronoun is easy to resolve. Thus in the following sentence the referent of "she" can be easily identified:

(18) "Bill wanted to lend Susan some money. *She* was hard up and really needed it."

Sentences involving pronouns are not always so easy to resolve. In the sentence:

(19) "Mike spoke to Peter and then *he* spoke to Dave."

it is not clear whether Mike or Peter is the antecedent. There has been a lot of work on how people resolve this kind of ambiguity. One influential idea is that during comprehension of connected prose a limited number of potential referents are available at any point in time. Thus in (18) both names are available as referents but the constraints of the pronoun lead to "Susan" being selected. When the set of referents remains ambiguous, as it does in (19), clearly other processes must be involved. In spoken text this ambiguity can be overcome by the use of stress—thus with appropriate intonation it is possible to indicate that "he" in (19) refers to Peter. In written text it is more difficult, although evidence shows that we tend to go for the subject of the sentence (so-called **first mention effect,** i.e. Mike).

While the mechanisms determining the referent of a pronoun are flexible, they are constrained in one important way—anaphors cannot be used to refer to only a component of the meaning. Thus in the sentence:

(20) "The unemployed are traditionally apathetic and Murphy does not deny *it* exists, but he sees the danger of harping on about the fact."

"it" is meant to refer to "unemployment" but the sentence does not work because the process of resolution is unable to infer that "unemployment" can be derived from "The unemployed". Given this fact it is surprising how common the appearance of so-called **anaphoric islands** is in written text (Oakhill and Garnham, 1992).

Bridging inferences extend beyond establishing the referents of pronouns. Haviland and Clark (1974) created materials of the following kind:

(21) "Mary unpacked some picnic supplies."
(22) "Mary unpacked some beer."
(23) "The beer was warm."

It was found that the time taken to comprehend (23) was longer when preceded by (21) than by (22). This was attributed to the additional time needed to form a bridging inference that the picnic supplies must have included beer.

How much inference do we actually make?

So far we have seen that the characteristics of text require us to make a certain number of bridging inferences in order to maintain a cohesive representation of the text. A more difficult question is to what extent we might make additional elaborative inferences. Proponents of the **constructivist position** argue that a full range of inferences is drawn while we are reading a text. In a classic study (Bransford et al., 1972), participants heard sentences such as:

(24) "Three turtles rested on a floating log, and a fish swam beneath them."

Later, they were given a recognition test asking them to identify sentences that had been in the text. One of these was:

(25) "Three turtles rested on a floating log, and the fish swam beneath it."

Participants were extremely confident that they had seen this sentence and this led to the conclusion that an inference, i.e. that the fish swam under the log, had been drawn during comprehension.

A problem with the above study is that it relies on an off-line measure, memory, and it does not necessarily follow that the inference was drawn at the time of reading—subjects could have worked out the inference at the time of recall. This proposal was tested by Singer (1979) in an experiment where participants first saw sentences such as:

(26a) "The boy cleared the snow with a shovel."
(26b) "The boy cleared the snow from the stairs."

and were then given a recognition test in which the following sentence occurred:

(27)   "The shovel was heavy."

In line with earlier work it was found that the inference sentences (27 following 26b) were readily accepted as true but that the on-line decision times for these sentences were longer than in the no inference condition (27 following 26a). Singer reasoned that if the inference had been drawn during initial comprehension there should be no reaction time difference between the two types of sentence. The derivation of inferences at the time of memory testing is underlined in a further study (Corbett & Dosher, 1978) in which the cue "scissors" was used to cue memory for various types of sentence:

(28)   "The athlete cut out an article with scissors for his friend."
(29)   "The athlete cut out an article for his friend."
(30)   "The athlete cut out an article with a razor blade for his friend."

"Scissors" was an equally effective cue for recalling all three sentences. Since there is no reason to suppose that the "razor blade" version of the sentence (30) could in any way cause readers to infer "scissors" during comprehension it was concluded that the cue was serving to elicit inferences at recall rather than indicate what was comprehended at the time.

These problems highlighted the need to use on-line measures as the basis for discovering what inferences people make as they are reading text. In one experiment using such measures (O'Brien et al., 1988), participants saw short paragraphs such as:

(31)   "All the mugger wanted was to steal the woman's money. But when she screamed, he (assaulted/stabbed*) her with his (weapon/ knife*) in an attempt to quiet her. He looked to see if anyone had seen him. He threw the knife into the bushes, took her money, and ran away."

(*Only one of each pair presented at any time).

The critical aspect of this experiment was how long participants fixated on the word "knife" in the last sentence as a function of what preceded. When participants saw a version of the paragraph in which "stabbed" preceded "weapon", they spent similar amounts of time reading "knife" as they did when "stabbed" preceded "knife". This suggests that an elaborative inference (weapon → knife) was made at the time of initial reading. However, this effect was not an automatic one because when "weapon" was preceded by the less specific "assaulted", participants did dwell longer on "knife", indicating that the inference had not been drawn. Elaborative inferences thus seem influenced by the degree of context available.

An additional form of inference is the **causal antecedent inference** in which it is proposed that people use what they have already comprehended about a text to predict what might be coming next. Duffy (1986) asked participants to read the two following types of paragraphs:

(32) "John was eating his first meal ever in the dining car of a train. The waiter brought him a large bowl of bean soup. John tasted the hot soup carefully. *Suddenly the train screeched to a stop."*

(33) "John was eating his first meal ever in the dining car of a train. The waiter brought him a large bowl of bean soup. John tasted the hot soup carefully. *The train began to slow down entering a station."*

Following each of these paragraphs, participants were asked to judge whether or not a final sentence was related to the preceding text. For the related condition the sentence was of the type:

(34) "The hot soup spilled on John's lap."

and the unrelated was:

(35) "That night the whole forest burned down."

Reading times for (34) were found to be much faster following (32) compared with (33). This was explained on the grounds that the last sentence of (32) strongly predicted (34) whereas paragraph (33) did not. At a theoretical level it was proposed that comprehension involves a focusing process in which sentences that appear to need explicit consequences are highlighted and used to generate predictions.

How much inference is actually made "on-line"?

The above studies indicate that certain inferences appear to be made on-line but it is a matter of some debate as to how many inferences are made. At one level is the **extreme constructionist** view which would hold that all possible inferences are drawn at the time of reading. The **minimalist hypothesis** asserts that only relatively few inferences are made; principally those needed to make the current text coherent (e.g. anaphoric reference) and inferences or provided by general background knowledge (McKoon and Ratcliff, 1992). The minimalist position has been criticised by a number of researchers, perhaps most notably in the recent account of text comprehension and inference provided by Graesser et al. (1994).

Their approach to text comprehension follows the idea that readers form a **situation model** or **mental model** of what a text is about (Johnson-Laird, 1983; Van Dijk and Kintsch, 1983). A situation model can be defined as a "mental representation of the people, setting, actions, and events that are mentioned in explicit clauses or that are filled in inferentially by world knowledge" (Graesser et al., 1994, p.371). This type of representation is contrasted with any view supposing that comprehension involves solely a representation of the text itself. The idea of a situation model is difficult to dispute in absolute terms; if we could not derive a text-independent representation of a text it would be impossible for us to realise that a television news story corresponds with a newspaper article we have read.

The key issue with regard to situation models has not been whether situations are created from text, but the extent to which inferences used to build these situations occur during comprehension. Graesser et al.'s approach is based on the concept of **effort after meaning** originally emphasised by Bartlett (see Chapter 7). According to this idea, the reader has a **goal** when addressing a text and aims to achieve a representation of the text which is coherent at both the **local** and **global** level—this distinction is often referred to as **microstructure** vs. **macrostructure**. Finally, the reader is continually attempting to explain why actions, events and states are mentioned in the text. Graesser et al. argue that there are 13 different forms of inference that can contribute to a situation model. They illustrate their argument in relation to a parable by the humourist Ambrose Bierce:

How Leisure Came

A Man to Whom Time was Money, and who was bolting his breakfast in order to catch a train, had leaned his newspaper against the sugar bowl and was reading as he ate. In his haste and abstraction he stuck a pickle fork into his right eye, and on removing the fork the eye came with it. In buying spectacles the needless outlay for the right lens soon reduced him to poverty, and the Man to Whom Time was Money had to sustain life by fishing from the end of the wharf.

Table 12.1 shows the different classes of inference identified by Graesser et al. They then went on to discuss experimental evidence concerning which of these inferences are constructed on-line. The evidence they discuss is extensive and we can consider it only briefly here. Their conclusion was that the inference classes 1–6 are constructed on-line whereas the others may be constructed later on. An illustration of how they came to this conclusion is provided by Graesser et al. Participants read a story in which a variety of different inferences could be drawn; in the given instance this involved inference classes 4, 10, 3, 7, and 11. Readers comprehended the stories clause by clause and, by the use of specific questions presented after each clause, the researchers were able to establish which inferences had been constructed on-line. This was backed by the use of a priming manipulation in which participants made lexical decisions following each clause. Lexical decisions were primed only for words related to certain types of inference.

The distinction between those inferences that are generated on-line and those that are not was related back to the general assumptions about the reader's effort after meaning. Thus a superordinate goal is inferred on-line because it provides information about the participant's motivation, something that is crucial to understanding the point of a story (in the above example the fact that the man was in a hurry to get to work). In contrast, an inference based on instantiation, i.e. that "breakfast" could have been "bacon and eggs" is not relevant to the point of the story.

While this theory provides a useful framework for understanding the extent to which people make inferences while they are reading, it should be recognised that forms of inference made may vary depending on what the reader is trying to make out of the text. Thus although "bacon and eggs" is not inferred from "breakfast" in the example story it might well be if the story read "the breakfast was greasy". Graesser et al.'s ranking should therefore be thought of as flexible with those inferences nearer the top more likely to be inferred on-line.

Overview

- In studying language it is important to distinguish between the rules that describe a person's language (competence) and how people actually use a language (performance).
- A central issue has been whether grammars are psychological models of language use.
- Phrase structure grammar is the basis used to parse sentences.
- Transformational grammar is a grammatical basis for generating sentences. Unfortunately, it failed as a psychological model. A particular problem was the separation of grammatical rules (syntax) from meaning (semantics).

TABLE 12.1

Inferences relevant to "How Leisure Came"

Type of inference	Brief description	Text that elicits inference	Inferences
Class 1: Referential	A word or phrase is referentially tied to a previous element or constituent in the text (explicit or inferred).	"...on removing the fork the eye came with it"	Fork is the referent for it.
Class 2: Case structure role assignment	An explicit noun phrase is assigned to a particular case structure role, e.g., agent, recipient, object, location, time.	"the man leaned his newspaper against the sugar bowl"	Against the sugarbowl is assigned to a location role.
Class 3: Causal antecedent	The inference is on a causal chain (bridge) between the current explicit action, event, or state and the previous passage context.	"In his haste and abstraction he stuck a pickle fork into his right eye..."	The man was careless and mis-aimed his fork.
Class 4: Superordinate goal	The inference is a goal that motivates an agent's intentional action.	"A Man to Whom Time was Money, and who was bolting his breakfast in order to catch a train..."	The man wanted to get to work and earn money.
Class 5: Thematic	This is a main point or moral of the text.	The entire passage	Haste makes waste.
Class 6: Character emotional reaction	The inference is an emotion experienced by a character, caused by or in response to an event or action.	"...the needless outlay reduced him to poverty"	The man became sad.
Class 7: Causal consequence	The inference is on a forecasted causal chain, including physical events and new plans of agents. These inferences do not include the character emotions in class 6.	"...on removing the fork the eye came with it"	The man became blind in his right eye.

TABLE 12.1 (continued)
Inferences relevant to "How Leisure Came"

Type of inference	Brief description	Text that elicits inference	Inferences
Class 8: Instantiation of noun category	The inference is a subcategory or a particular exemplar that instantiates an explicit noun or an implicit case role that is required by the verb.	"...breakfast..."	Bacon and eggs.
Class 9: Instrument	The inference is an object, part of the body, or resource used when an agent executes an intentional action.	"...the Man to Whom Time was Money had to sustain life by fishing from the end of a wharf"	The man used a rod and reel (to fish).
Class 10: Subordinate goal-action	The inference is a goal, plan, or action that specifies how an agent's action is achieved.	"...who was bolting his breakfast"	The man grasped his fork and moved it toward his mouth.
Class 11: State	The inference is an ongoing state from the time frame of the text that is not causally related to the story plot. The states include an agent's traits, knowledge, and beliefs; the properties of objects and concepts; and the spatial location of entities.	"...the Man to Whom Time was Money had to sustain life by fishing from the end of a wharf"	Fishermen are poor, the city has a wharf.
Class 12: Emotion of reader	The inference is the emotion that the reader experiences when reading a text.	"...on removing the fork the eye came with it"	The reader is disgusted.
Class 13: Author's intent	The inference is the author's attitude or motive in writing.	The entire passage	Bierce wants to lambast workaholics.

- There is good evidence from how people deal with ambiguous sentences that some form of grammatical parsing is involved in comprehension.
- The garden-path theory proposes that the simplest parsing of a sentence is favoured initially as determined by the principles of minimal attachment and late-closure.
- There is no evidence that lexical content influences parsing but some evidence that the higher level content does. Parsing may also be influenced by linguistic tradition.
- There is substantial evidence that the clause is an important construct in the psychological processes dealing with comprehension.
- Syntactic form is quickly forgotten although the extent of this depends on the relationship between successive clauses.
- Inference plays a vital role in comprehension.
- A bridging inference is one that is vital for comprehension to proceed and is most commonly encountered in the resolution of anaphora.
- An elaborative inference is one that embellishes the meaning of the text. Some elaborative inferences appear to be made at the time of reading whereas others are made only when the reader is prompted through questioning.

Suggested further reading

Altmann, G.T.M. (1998). Ambiguity in sentence processing. *Trends in Cognitive Sciences, 2*, 146–152.

Provides a review of how ambiguity in sentences is handled by various accounts.

Berko Gleason, J., & Bernstein Ratner, N. (1998). *Psycholinguistics* (2nd ed.). Fort Worth: Harcourt Brace.

Chapter 5 provides an introductory account of sentence comprehension.

Mitchell, D.C. (1994). Sentence parsing. In M.A. Gernsbacher (Ed.), *Handbook of psycholinguistics*. San Diego, CA: Academic Press.

This article provides a thorough review of different theories of sentence parsing.

Whitney, P. (1998). *The psychology of language*. Boston: Houghton Mifflin.

Chapter 7 also provides a more introductory account of sentence comprehension.

Revision questions

1 What is meant by the distinction between competence and performance?
2 What is the idea behind transformational grammar and why did it fail?
3 Outline the garden-path theory and the evidence that both supports and refutes it.
4 What is lexical frame theory and does it provide a satisfactory account of any aspect of sentence parsing?
5 What are content-guided and exposure-based accounts of parsing?
6 What evidence implicates the clause as a functional unit in sentence comprehension?
7 What is anaphora and how do theories of comprehension explain how we deal with it?
8 How constructivist is text comprehension?
9 What is meant by the microstructure vs. macrostructure level of a text?

Language: Speaking and thinking 13

In 1964 Susan Ervin-Tripp (Ervin-Tripp, 1964) conducted an intriguing study on Japanese women who had married American soldiers after World War II. It involved a sentence completion task in which the women responded to open-ended questions. The interesting manipulation was that the women answered each question twice; once in English and once in Japanese. Here are some examples:

"When my wishes conflict with my family…
    J: It is a time of great unhappiness"
    A: I do what I want"

"I will probably become a…
    J: housewife"
    A: teacher"

"Real friends should…
    J: help each other"
    A: be very frank"

The fascinating aspect of these replies is that they are very different in content depending on which language is being spoken. The Japanese (J) responses reflect one cultural tradition and the American (A) responses another. The above study is not easy to interpret and the results may have arisen for a number of reasons, such as social conformity, but one possibility is that it illustrates how the language we speak can determine thought. We will return to this intriguing question later but, for now, we are concerned with more basic mechanisms of speech production.

Speech production

The study of how we produce speech is unusual in that it is based largely on analysing the types of errors that people make during normal

discourse. This may at first seem surprising but the nature of speech errors is remarkably systematic and this has enabled psychologists to use these data as a very reliable source of evidence. Speech errors are perhaps best known from the existence of **spoonerisms**. This name derives from the Reverend William Spooner, an academic who was renowned for producing utterances such as "you have hissed my mystery lesson". Here the phonemes of two words appear to have got mixed up, but errors exist at other levels as well. My ageing aunt for example, on hearing that a record was not playing properly, suggested that we should "emmanuel it", thus producing an incorrect word that was a blend of the intended word and another related word ("eject" and "manual"). On other occasions she simply substituted the wrong word, thus a budgerigar losing its feathers was said to be "melting". In addition we have the so-called "Freudian slips" in which the speaker's intended utterance is distorted to provide, apparently, evidence of hidden sexual intention (e.g. "Everyone likes the *breast* in *bed*" when this should be "Everyone likes the *best* in *bread*"). These examples indicate that speech errors can occur at different levels and it is this systematic variation that has provided the basis for modelling speech production.

A model of speech production

Figure 13.1 describes a model of speech production outlined by Bock and Levelt (1994). Although there are similar alternatives, such as that proposed by Dell et al. (1993), this model seems to be the most widely accepted as a framework for speech production. The top **message level** is the speaker's intended meaning that feeds down into a **functional processing level** which has two components: **lexical selection** and **functional assignment**. Lexical selection involves choosing the correct words for an intended utterance and functional assignment involves the assignment of grammatical roles to the chosen words. Next comes the **positional level** that involves two components: **constituent assembly** and **inflection**. The first component ensures that the words are in the correct syntactic order and the second ensures that words have the correct endings; thus if a verb is to be produced in the past tense the inflection process will ensure that the suffix *-ed* is added appropriately. Finally, there is the **phonological level** at which the sounds of the words are assembled and produced.

The model is illustrated using the sentence "She was handing him some broccoli". At the message level the intent is clear in describing an ongoing event involving a female subject in the act of giving an object (broccoli) to a recipient (a male). At a functional level, production of this utterance requires the selection of appropriate **lemmas**—these can be defined as representations containing information about a word's class (e.g. noun, verb). For the "broccoli" sentence it is necessary to select lemmas representing male and female pronouns, "broccoli", and the verb "to hand".

Lemmas need to be distinguished from **lexemes**; the latter comprise information about how a particular word sounds. The most striking demonstration of the distinction between lemma and lexeme levels is the **tip of the tongue state**. In one study, participants were given definitions relating to unfamiliar words (e.g. "sampan") and asked to try and produce the word. In many cases, participants had partial information available including number of syllables and where the stress was (i.e. lemma information) but no word form knowledge (lexeme information). See Brown and McNeill (1966) for the original observations and Brown (1991) for a recent review of the phenomenon.

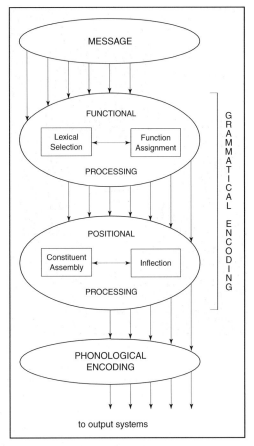

FIG. 13.1.
The model of speech perception proposed by Bock and Levelt.

A number of errors can arise at the lexical selection level resulting in the selection of the wrong lemma. In a **substitution error**, the person produces a word related to the one they intended, e.g. "car" instead of "truck". Substitutions can also occur in less obvious ways, such as "environmental contamination". This arises when a speaker catches sight of a word that is similar sounding to the one they are attempting to utter and this is produced instead. Harley (1984) gives an example of someone meaning to say "I got into my *car*" but saying "I got into my

Clark" as a result of seeing a shop sign. Incorrect lemma selection may also occur due to semantic priming, e.g. "The branch fell on the tree" where the intended word "roof" is replaced by a strong associate of "branch".

Blend errors arise when two words are put together to form a different word which may or may not exist. Typically, as with the example I gave of my aunt, they involve a phonological blending of two words that are associated in meaning, e.g. "The competition is a little *stougher*" is a blend of "stiffer" and "tougher". The fact that blends are formed from near synonyms suggests that their origin lies somewhere close to the message level. It has therefore been a puzzle that this problem in selecting the correct lemma does not show itself until the phonology of the word is assembled. Some blends are, however, formed at the lexeme level. The British politician John Prescott, well known for his speech errors, once stated that he was going to a "a watery meeting"—he had intended to say "a meeting about water metering" but in an attempt to speak quickly certain parts of the lexeme level were dropped, resulting in a bizarre phrase.

Functional assignment involves attaching the correct grammatical role to each of the activated lemmas. Thus, returning to our "broccoli" sentence, "she" is labelled the subject, "was handing" is the verb, and "him" and "broccoli" become the indirect and direct objects respectively. Problems in functional assignment can be revealed from **exchange errors** in which nouns with different roles are switched, e.g. "Seymour sliced the *knife* with a *salami*". There are many ideas about how functional assignment occurs but perhaps the most influential is the idea that verb properties strongly influence grammatical assignment. Earlier we noted that verbs have different properties depending on whether they are transitive or intransitive. In our example, "was handing" is transitive and can have both a direct and an indirect object. This provides a valuable cue concerning grammatical assignment made to other activated lexemes.

At the next level, the constituent assembly process specifies an order for the utterance that contains information about the grammatical status of each word in the utterance. It is usual to consider these in terms of PSG trees (see Chapter 12). There is evidence that information concerning the grammatical status of a particular word slot is specified independently of the word that arrives in that slot. This idea is supported by exchange errors in which words are formed in the right grammatical way for their incorrect position, e.g. having intended to say "*They* must be too tight for you", the speaker produced "You must be too tight for *them*".

The inflection level involves the specification of any information that needs to be added to words to indicate features such as tense and plural. In the "broccoli" sentence the verb "hand" needs the suffix "*ing*" to comply with the tense involved. There is evidence that inflection information is also specified independently of activated lemma. This is illustrated by a phenomenon known as **stranding** in which the correct inflections remain in place but the root morphemes are wrongly specified: e.g. "You *ordered* up *ending* some fish dish" instead of "You *ended* up *ordering* some fish dish".

The final stage of the model involves the assembly of phonology and it is at this level that spoonerisms occur. Investigations show that the character of spoonerisms is very consistent. Vowels always swap with vowels and consonants with consonants—this suggests that the specification of a phoneme string is somewhat abstract. In addition, virtually all spoonerisms occur within a clause, thus reinforcing the view that the clause represents a processing unit in language.

Inner speech

When we read, we "hear" the words we are reading; this is known as **inner speech** or, sometimes, **subvocalisation**. It has long been a matter of interest as to what role inner speech plays in the reading process. At one extreme is the old behaviourist view that inner speech is an epiphenomenon—a reflection of the end result of thought that has no functional role in cognition. However, even before the behaviourists, there were other psychologists who argued that inner speech played an important part in reading. Thus Huey (1908) wrote:

> "The carrying range of inner speech is considerably larger than vision… The initial subvocalisation seems to help hold the word in consciousness until enough others are given to combine with it in touching off the unitary utterance of a sentence which they form…It is of the greatest service to the reader or listener that at each moment a considerable amount

of what is being read should hang suspended in the primary memory of inner speech"

Hardyck and Petrinovich (1970) carried out an interesting study involving students reading essays judged as either "easy" or "hard" in content. All the participants were wired up to apparatus that measured both throat muscle and forearm muscle activity. One group of participants (normal group) simply read with the inconvenience of being attached to the apparatus. A second (feedback) group were told not to subvocalise and if they did a buzzer sounded. A third (control) group read while maintaining their forearms in a particular level of flexion. Subsequently, the participants answered questions on the essays and the results are shown in Fig. 13.2. They indicate no difference between the three experimental conditions when reading essay passages, but participants forced to suppress vocalisation remembered considerably less about the hard passages.

The Hardyck and Petrinovich result has been related to the working memory model which we discussed in Chapter 7. To recap, working memory comprises a central executive along with two slave systems; a visuo-spatial scratch pad and a phonological store. It is considered that the Hardyck and Petrinovich result arises because participants in the feedback condition are prevented from generating an articulatory code and that their reading is impaired subsequently because the phonological store cannot be employed as effectively. A more direct link between the working memory model and articulatory suppression is

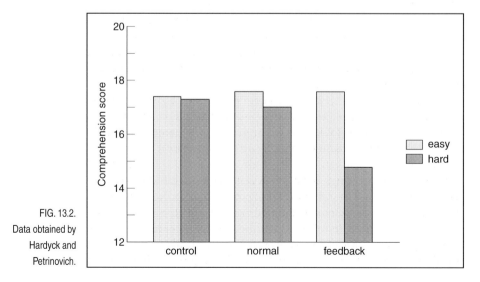

FIG. 13.2. Data obtained by Hardyck and Petrinovich.

provided by Slowiaczek and Clifton (1980). Participants were presented with a passage which they either listened to or read. Within each group, half undertook articulatory suppression (meaningless repetition of "the") and half were silent. The participants were then given a series of statements about the passage and asked to verify them. Statements varied as to whether or not they were simply a paraphrase of something in the text or required the integration of concepts across the passage. The results showed that there were no differences between reading and listening with paraphrase questions. However, with more complex questions there was clear impairment for participants who read while carrying out articulatory suppression.

Both of these studies suggest that the articulatory loop might be particularly useful when dealing with more complex material, perhaps because it provides a useful memory system for retaining word order—a specific device for reading insurance policies! In addition, it might also be a means of holding the **intonation contour**; those aspects of phonology that enable different meanings of the same basic sentence to be understood, e.g. using stress to disambiguate a syntactically ambiguous sentence. A problem, however, is that both tasks assess reading comprehension by means of a memory measure. As a result, the observed effects may be the result of the effects of articulatory suppression on reading or on memory storage subsequent to reading.

This difficulty can be got around by taking on-line measures of reading ability under both suppression and control conditions. Kleiman (1975) found that those participants repeating aloud digits as a secondary task did not differ from controls in their ability to detect a category instance in a sentence. However, when the same secondary task was imposed on participants judging whether sentences such as "Pizzas have been eating Jerry" were anomalous or not, control subjects performed significantly better.

Baddeley and Lewis (1981) examined how articulatory suppression interfered with participants' abilities to detect anomalous words in text. These sentences were quite complex (e.g. *She doesn't mind going to the dentist to have fillings, but doesn't like the pain[rent] when he gives her the injection at the beginning*). Anomaly detection was less accurate if participants engaged in articulatory suppression but this did not affect their ability to classify meaningful sentences correctly. In a second study, Baddeley and Lewis examined how articulatory suppression affected participants' detection of word-order errors in real text. Here performance was compared with both a silent control condition and a condition in which they had to tap their fingers in time with a metronome. Only the articulatory suppression condition produced an increase error rate.

Language and thought: The Sapir–Whorf hypothesis

The idea that language determines the way we think and perceive the world was popularised by Benjamin Whorf (Whorf, 1956) who had studied under an anthropologist called Edward Sapir (Sapir, 1949). According to Whorf (1956):

> "We dissect nature along lines laid down by our native languages. The categories and types that we isolate from the world of phenomena we do not find there because they stare every observer in the face; on the contrary, the world is presented in a kaleidoscopic flux of impressions which has to be organised by our minds—and this means largely by the linguistic systems in our minds."

One observation that impressed Whorf involved a comparison of Navajo-speaking children and English-speaking children. Whorf noticed that the Navajo language tended to concentrate more on the form of objects than English did. Observations such as these led to the formulation of the Sapir–Whorf or, more commonly, **Whorf hypothesis**, that language determines perception and thought.

Evidence for a strong version of the Whorf hypothesis

In its strong form, the Whorf hypothesis states that the language we have available directly determines the way we perceive and think about the world. This issue has been most extensively developed within the area of colour perception and memory. Languages vary greatly in the way they provide verbal labels for colours. At one extreme, for example, is Italian which has four different words relating to what we would call "blue" in English. At the other end of the spectrum, the Dani tribe of Papua New Guinea has only two colour words: "black" and "white".

All colours have variants but we show widespread agreement about which particular shade of a colour is typical—these are known as **focal colours**. In one experiment, people from the Dani were compared with English people on their ability to remember colours that varied in how close they were to their focal colour. Both groups recognised focal colours better than non-focal colours and, in a subsequent experiment, both groups also learned associations to focal colours more readily (Heider, 1972; Heider and Oliver, 1972).

These findings appear to provide strong evidence against the Whorfian hypothesis because, if language determined perception, one should have expected the Dani, with their minimal colour vocabulary, to perform much worse than English speakers. There has been criticism of these experiments on the grounds that the focal colours are simply more perceptually distinct and thus easier to remember. However, Lucy and Schweder (1979) pointed out that the focal colours used by Heider were more saturated (stronger) than the non-focal colours. They repeated Heider's experiment using focal and non-focal colours matched for saturation and found that the availability of colour names did determine recognition.

There is evidence that language affects how we hear. In Chapter 10 we considered the phenomenon of categorical perception which, to recap, is the demonstration that we perceive a sharp distinction between two sounds even though they are varying along a continuum which makes them more or less distinguishable. Thus when English speakers listen to a continuum of sounds from /l/ to /r/ there is a sudden change from hearing one phoneme to the other. This effect is not found in Japanese people because they do not distinguish between /l/ and /r/. As Hunt and Agnoli (1991) point out, this is an overlooked example of a direct effect of language on perception—although it is occurring at a much lower level than the types of influence envisaged by Whorf himself.

Evidence for a weak version of the Whorf hypothesis

An alternative and less controversial idea is that the language we have available can influence cognitive processes to some extent. An example of this involved an experiment in which participants were shown three colour chips and then asked to pick out each colour from an array of similarly coloured chips. One group was asked to provide a verbal description during memorising and another asked to "visualise" each colour. The latter group performed twice as well on recognition, indicating that the inadequacy of verbal labels can interfere with visually-based memory (Schooler and Engstlerschooler, 1990).

Kay and Kempton (1984) presented people with three colour chips. Two of which, A and B, were obviously green and blue respectively, whereas the third, C, varied between the two colours. The task was to say whether the participants thought that chip C was green or blue. English subjects showed a form of "categorical perception" in that as the intermediary chip varied in hue on the green–blue continuum they suddenly switched their naming from one colour to the other. In contrast, participants who spoke Tarahumara (a Mexican–Indian language), in which there are no words distinguishing green and blue, did not show this "categorical" effect. However, these effects did not indicate differences in how the colours were actually perceived by the two groups because when the English group was allowed an additional "blue and green" category, it performed the same as the Mexican group.

There have been additional attempts to show how language can affect other forms of cognition. There have been claims, for example, that some languages are better than others for representing certain types of argument but other research refutes this (Au, 1983; Bloom, 1981). Languages differ in the way numbers are represented (e.g. "twenty-four" in English), "four and twenty" in Dutch, but this does not have an influence on the way people carry out numerical calculations (Brysbaert et al., 1998). Within the social realm, however, there is some possible influence. Hoffman et al. (1986) exploited the fact that languages have economic labels which can, for example, neatly characterise a particular type of person (e.g. *slob*, *nerd*). These labels do, however, vary. In Chinese, for example, the phrase "shi gu" translates as "worldly experienced, socially skilled, devoted to family and

Economic labels can neatly characterise a particular type of person.

somewhat reserved" and has no corresponding economic label in English. In the study it was shown that the ability to remember particular character types was strongly influenced by whether the language had an economic label for that type of person.

Before leaving this topic we should note that there is another sense in which weak version of the Whorfian Hypothesis is undoubtedly correct. This relates to the inter-relations between words in different languages. In a previous chapter we noted the extent of ambiguity in English. Putting some figures on this, it is estimated that English words have an average of between five and six different meanings. This compares with an average of about three meanings per word in Italian. It is therefore reasonable to argue that the thoughts arising from these languages may differ, particularly when ambiguity is involved; for example, "bank" has a different range of meanings compared with the Italian "banco".

Overview

- The study of speech production is based principally on the study of speech errors.
- Models of speech perception envisage a series of levels. The message level is what the subject intends to say. The functional level involves word selection and grammatical role assignment. The first component of the positional level ensures that the words are in the correct syntactic order and the second ensures that words have the correct endings (e.g. a plural, past tense). Finally there is the **phonological level**, at which the sounds of the words are assembled and produced.
- Knowledge about a word's properties is termed the lemma and its phonological form is known as a lexeme.
- Substitution errors reveal the existence of the lexical selection level. Blends also indicate lexical selection. Exchange errors reflect the functional assignment process including the separate nature of inflection assignment. Spoonerisms indicate that assembly of phonology involves constituent phonemes.
- Inner speech is the speaking we hear in our heads when we read.
- Inner speech is thought to reflect use of the phonological loop as a means of aiding comprehension.
- Use of the phonological loop is more apparent in dealing with more complex text.
- The Whorf hypothesis, in its strong form, states that language governs the way we perceive and think about the world.

- There is no great evidence for a strong version of the Whorf hypothesis.
- The weak version of the Whorf hypothesis states that the language we have available influences the way we talk and remember the world. There is evidence for this idea.

Suggested further reading

Bock, K., & Levelt, W. (1994). Language production: Grammatical encoding. In M.A. Gernsbacher, (Ed.), *Handbook of psycholinguistics*. London: Academic Press.

This chapter provides a detailed overview of models speech perception, in particular evidence for the model discussed in this chapter.

Brysbaert, M., Fias,W., & Noel, M.P. (1998). The Whorfian hypothesis and numerical cognition: Is 'twenty-four' processed in the same way as 'four-and-twenty'? *Cognition, 66*(1), 51–77.

The introduction to this article provides a good account of evidence for and against the Whorf hypothesis.

Fromkin, V.A., & Bernstein Ratner, N. (1998). From concept to expression. In J. Berko Gleason and N. Bernstein Ratner (Eds.), *Psycholinguistics*. Fort Worth: Harcourt Brace.

Covers different models of speech production and goes into considerable detail about the role of speech errors in generating theories.

Levelt, W.J.M. (1999). Models of word production. *Trends in Cognitive Sciences, 3*, 223–232.

Provides a recent overview of speech production models including connectionist modelling accounts.

Whitney, P. (1998). *The psychology of language*. Boston: Houghton Mifflin.

Chapter 9 provides an overview of issues discussed here plus other factors affecting speech production.

Revision questions

1 What are the different levels proposed in Bock and Levelt's model of speech production?
2 What is the difference between a lemma and a lexeme?
3 What is the tip of the tongue state and why is it of interest?

4 How do different forms of speech error support the Bock and Levelt model of speech production?
5 What role might inner speech play in silent reading?
6 Evaluate evidence for the strong view of the Whorf hypothesis.
7 Evaluate evidence for the weak view of the Whorf hypothesis.

Reasoning 14

There was only one catch and that was Catch-22, which specified that a concern for one's own safety in the face of dangers that were real and immediate was the process of a rational mind. Orr was crazy and could be grounded. All he had to do was ask; and as soon as he did, he would no longer be crazy and would have to fly more missions. Orr would be crazy to fly more missions and sane if he didn't, but if he was sane he had to fly them. If he flew them he was crazy and didn't have to; but if he didn't want to he was sane and had to. Yossarian was moved very deeply by the absolute simplicity of this clause of Catch-22 and let out a respectful whistle.

Joseph Heller, *Catch 22*

Fortunately none of us has to cope with the above reasoning problem in our own lives but reasoning is an essential part of human mental life. For example, many of you will be players of the National Lottery and some of you will have various strategies such as selecting certain numbers every time. Others might follow curious advice such as "the number 39 has not come up for a year so it must come up soon". Some players may be more "strategic" in their choice of numbers in that they select numbers higher than 31. This is sensible because many people use their birth date as one of the numbers they select. This means that, on average, the payout for a winning combination will be less when lower numbers are involved because of the "birth date bias" in number choice. It is also possible to increase your chances of being the sole winner of the jackpot by selecting high numbers that are consecutive, e.g. 43, 44, 45, 46, 47, 48, 49. It is unlikely, however, that any of you would do this because you believe, wrongly, that a consecutive sequence could not arise by chance. In fact, the above sequence is just as likely as any other sequence because the selection of one number does not influence what other numbers appear. In this chapter we will see that many important insights about human reasoning arise from observing the reasoning errors that people make.

Induction versus deduction

An essential distinction in reasoning is that between **inductive** and **deductive reasoning**. In inductive reasoning we attempt to derive more general conclusions from available facts, e.g. "Jim seems a nice man, I expect he enjoys his job". In deductive reasoning we derive a specific fact from a general set of facts, e.g. "Hay fever causes people misery in the summer. Alan has hay fever, therefore he is miserable in the summer". While people can understand the process of deduction, it is abundantly clear that they do not do this reliably in the real world. In the lottery example above, deductive reasoning would lead us to conclude that the consecutive number sequence is as likely as any other. The fact that people do not accept this suggests that they are making their judgement on some other basis. It may be that people rely on their memory for winning sequences and recall that a consecutive sequence has never been drawn. However, millions of other non-consecutive sequences have never been drawn either and the inference that consecutive sequences are special is false.

Availability heuristics

While some situations do present all the available facts and thus allow deductive reasoning, many others do not, and the human being must

INDUCTIVE REASONING : "Jim seems a nice man. I expect he enjoys his job".

DEDUCTIVE REASONING : "Hay fever causes people misery in the summer. Alan has hay fever, therefore he is miserable in the summer".

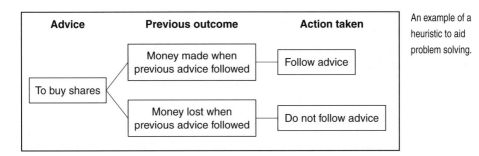

An example of a heuristic to aid problem solving.

rely on induction to guide decisions. One obvious source of information about what decision to make is to reflect on what has happened before. Consider a friend, Chris, who advises you that shares in a particular company are likely to rise sharply in price. This is one of a number of recommendations Chris has made in the past. In deciding whether to accept his advice you may recall the frequency with which his recommendations have previously been successful and, by weighing the positive and negative instances, come to a decision. You will note that this form of reasoning does not involve any particular analysis of the current recommendation; acceptance or rejection is determined solely by the balance of good and bad previous outcomes. The above form of reasoning is based on a **heuristic**—this is a problem-solving strategy that uses "a rule of thumb" to avoid lengthy decision-making processes. A heuristic is considered a good one if it results in the correct decision most of the time. Heuristics based on comparing remembered frequencies are called **availability heuristics** (Tversky and Kahneman, 1974); in many instances they can provide accurate answers but they can also be misleading for a number of reasons. Most obviously, availability heuristics can be constrained by knowledge. Asked, for example, if there are more species of bird than beetle, many people would incorrectly opt for birds simply because they know more different types of birds.

The availability heuristic can also be distorted by the prominence given to events. A recent UK survey showed that the majority of elderly people feared going out at night because they might get attacked. In fact, their actual risk of assault is very low compared with, for example, young males. Bias arises because any vicious attack on an elderly person attracts publicity whereas those involving youths very often do not. The same type of distortion doubtless contributes to fear of flying. Despite acceptance that it is more hazardous driving to an airport than going on a flight, many people believe the reverse to be true. This is because road deaths, although far more frequent, occur in small and often unreported instances whereas most air crashes receive substantial media coverage.

Recently the availability heuristic has been invoked in studies of marketing. It has always been assumed that an individual's willingness to make a purchase is influenced by the extent of choice available—the so-called "assortment effect". However, a recent study by Broniarczyk et al. (1998) indicated that reduction of lower preference items, thus reducing availability, had no effect on purchasing behaviour providing shelves remained full. Unfortunately, the availability heuristic does not always operate in situations where one might expect it to. Greenleigh et al. (1997) examined the perception of personal risk in students who lived in weather disaster areas and those who did not. While a number of factors did influence their recollective experience of weather disasters, the assumed measure of availability, accounted for only a small amount of their risk assessment.

Anchoring

Given the above facts about flying versus driving, you might think that we could use our reasoning to overcome inaccurate estimates of risk. However, humans exhibit a phenomenon known as **anchoring** in which an initial estimate, no matter how inaccurate, can serve to guide subsequent responses. Anchoring was demonstrated in an experiment where participants were briefly presented with either of two multiplication problems:

(A) $8 \times 7 \times 6 \times 5 \times 4 \times 3 \times 2 \times 1$
(B) $1 \times 2 \times 3 \times 4 \times 5 \times 6 \times 7 \times 8$

As there was not enough time to calculate the answer, participants were asked to estimate it. The average estimates were 2250 for problem A 512 for B, (the correct answer is 40,320). It seems therefore that larger initial numbers anchored the participants to a greater estimate than low numbers. In the same way, excessive media coverage of a certain type of event might anchor people towards substantial overestimates of occurrence.

Representativeness

"Steve is very shy and withdrawn, invariably helpful, but with little interest in people, or in the world of reality. A meek and tidy soul, he has a need for order and a passion for detail." On the basis of this description, do you think Steve is a farmer, librarian, doctor, pilot, or salesman? Most of us, I suspect, would consider it most likely that Steve is a librarian because the description conforms to our prototypical idea of librarians. Judgements derived in this way are said to be based on a **representativeness heuristic** in which a sample (i.e. Steve) is compared with the general characteristics of the various possible populations from which he might come.

People are also quite willing to treat even single instances as representative. One example is the frequent case in which a person with an unhealthy habit (e.g. smoking) justifies it on the grounds that their uncle "smoked 50 a day and lived until 90", notwithstanding the millions who have suffered premature death as a result of smoking. One could, however, argue that the person in this case is aware of the non-representativeness but chooses to ignore it for personal reasons. However, experimental studies have shown that people will still assume that single instances are representative of a group even when they are explicitly told that the given instance is atypical.

Use of the representativeness heuristic can cause other problems. In one study (Kahneman and Tversky, 1980), participants were introduced to imaginary populations of individuals who were either engineers or lawyers. The populations were uneven in that they were either 70% engineers to 30% lawyers or the reverse. In the baseline condition, participants were simply asked what the probability was of picking either an engineer or lawyer at random from the sample. In both populations subjects correctly calculated the probabilities as 0.7 and 0.3. The experiment was then repeated but this time the individual sampled was given a neutral character description:

> "Dick is a 30 year old man. He is married with no children. A man of high ability and motivation, he promises to be quite successful in his field. He is well liked by his colleagues."

Participants were asked whether the individual sampled was more likely to be a lawyer or an engineer. The description of Dick has no bearing on this decision so the participants' responses should be guided by the known ratio of engineers to lawyers, i.e. in a 70–30% population Dick is more likely to be an engineer. Instead, participants consistently, and wrongly, rated the probability of either profession at around .5 thus indicating that they were attempting to use a representative heuristic rather than their knowledge about the population.

Another difficulty relates to what might be termed **local representativeness**. We have already touched on the problems people have in understanding randomness and this is exemplified in the so-called **gambler's fallacy**. If we toss a coin six times we can generate a range of possible sequences including HHHHHH and TTTTTT. Furthermore, if tossed a further six times it is just as likely that the pattern could be HHHHHH or TTTTTT again. This is because each coin toss is independent of the previous one. However people, particularly gamblers, have trouble understanding this and expect that heads and tails will alternate fairly frequently (Kahneman and Tversky, 1972). This arises because people mistakenly believe that the sample they are observing, in this case a short sequence of coin tosses, is typical of coin tossing overall where, of course, the probability of heads or tails is .5 (see Peterson and Ulehla, 1965 for a particularly good example of gambler's fallacy in operation).

People fail to appreciate that a small sample is not a sufficient basis for predicting an outcome. People are also insensitive to the importance of sample size in other ways. In an experiment (Kahneman and Tversky, 1972), participants studied the following passage:

"A certain town is served by two hospitals. In the larger hospital about 45 babies are born each day and in the smaller

hospital about 15 babies are born each day. As you know, about 50% of babies are boys. However, the exact percentage varies from day to day. Sometimes it may be higher, sometimes it may be lower.

For a period of one year, each hospital recorded the days on which more than 60% of the babies born were boys. Which hospital do you think recorded more such days?"

(A) The larger hospital
(B) The smaller hospital
(C) Both hospitals the same

Try this for yourself. If you decide that the answer is C you are in agreement with most of the students who did this experiment, but you are also wrong. The answer is B, for the following reason. All samples show variability but, as samples get larger, the extent of the variability declines because the sample becomes more and more representative of the population it is drawn from. It therefore follows that hospital B, because it has smaller samples, is more likely to have percentages of boys that diverge significantly from the population norm of around 50%.

Correlation

The ability to notice that two things regularly co-occur, correlation, can be very useful when we are attempting to solve problems. A good example is criminal investigation where an efficient detective might notice that a group of crimes shares some common characteristic that suggests that they were committed by the same person. Scientists also frequently look for correlation when they are attempting to understand a phenomenon. Predicting earthquakes well in advance from particular seismic patterns is a good example of using correlation scientifically.

Given the value of correlation it is therefore a pity that humans in general seem very poor at detecting the relationship between events in the world. Indeed it has been suggested that, for example, our poor ability to appreciate correlation can lead to the negative stereotyping of minority ethnic groups. By concentrating on the few instances of an ethnic minority person behaving poorly it seems all too easy to assume that this behaviour is a characteristic of the whole group.

In order to understand correlation we need to make use of a **2 x 2 contingency table** (see Fig. 14.1). Our illustration concerns the often cited, but wholly incorrect, belief that madness is more likely when there

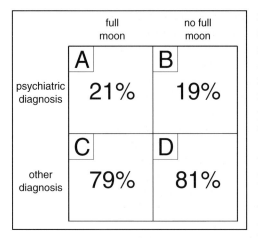

	full moon	no full moon
psychiatric diagnosis	**A** 21%	**B** 19%
other diagnosis	**C** 79%	**D** 81%

FIG. 14.1.
2 X 2 contingency table regarding the association between the presence or absence of a full moon and the percentage of the population of a city being admitted per day for psychiatric care. Studies of how people detect the presence of correlation indicate a strong over-reliance in the figure appearing in Cell A.

is a full moon. Our table has two variables: full moon/no full moon; and extent of reported madness—above average/below average. This results in four cells: (A) full moon/psychiatric diagnosis; (B) full moon/other diagnosis; (C) no full moon/ psychiatric diagnosis; (D) no full moon/ other diagnosis.

Early studies of people's attempts to understand correlation suggested that people based their conclusions only on the amount of information in cell A, i.e. only those instances when the expected correlation occurred, the so-called cell A heuristic. One study illustrating the cell A heuristic is by Smedslund (1963) who asked nurses to decide whether the presence of a symptom determined the presence of a disease. The data presented indicated that patients with the symptom had just over a 50% chance of having the disease yet the nurses rated the association between the symptom and disease at 85%. With regard to lunacy and the moon, therefore, people's erroneous belief in this idea arises because they only recollect examples of lunacy being associated with madness. Other studies have suggested slightly more sophistication in that covariance estimates can be based on the difference between A and B (Arkes and Harkness, 1983).

There appears to be a wide range of factors that contribute to people's poor ability to detect co-variation accurately. Predominance of the cell A heuristic is undoubtedly very influential but other factors are also important. People do give far too much weight to low frequencies of occurrence and this may be exaggerated by pre-existing beliefs. Memory load is also important. Requiring participants to keep a running estimate of correlation may be more effective than asking them just to make a final decision. When participants have to base their judgements on remembering a large number of instances they tend to opt for the cell A heuristic. However, removal of the memory load allows them to use a more accurate sum of diagonals strategy in which the sums A+D and B+C are computed. If A+D is greater, participants conclude that correlation is present (Arkes and Harkness, 1983).

Illusory correlation

Given how poor people can be at detecting correlation it is perhaps unsurprising that they can sometimes detect illusory correlations. In one study (Chapman and Chapman, 1971), people were presented with fictional profiles of mentally ill patients alongside their equally fictional performance on the draw-a-figure test. The latter is a test in which it is claimed that personality characteristics can be inferred from the way a human figure is drawn. The fictional descriptions and drawings were randomly paired and participants asked whether they could detect any relationships. The participants reliably reported that narrow eyes were associated with suspicious patients even though, objectively, no such relationship existed. It has been suggested that the participants made use of an availability heuristic—the idea that suspiciousness can be detected in someone's eyes—as a basis for deriving a correlation. This result is quite worrying in that tests such as draw-a-figure and the Rorschach inkblot test, a test which is also associated with illusory correlation, continue to be used in clinical practice.

Phobias appear linked to illusory correlation, i.e. the over-estimation of an association between a stimulus and unpleasant outcome. This was shown experimentally in a study by Pauli and Weidemann (1998) who randomly paired electric shocks or nothing with pictures of aeroplanes or different types of mushroom. Although the probability of shock for the two types of picture was 50%, those people with a fear of flying over-estimated the probability of shock being associated with pictures of aeroplanes compared with non-phobic participants. Similar differences between the groups were not found when different types of neutral picture were used, thus indicating that the over-estimation was specific to the phobic stimulus.

Deduction

As we saw earlier, deduction involves deriving a conclusion when all the facts needed for the conclusion are available. Research in this area has been dominated by examining how people deal with **syllogisms**. A syllogism involves two statements, usually called premises, followed by a conclusion which the person has to judge as logically valid or not. For example:

(1) All of the artists are beekeepers
    All of the beekeepers are chemists
    Are all of the artists chemists?

The above conclusion is valid. Now try this following.

(2) All of the artists are beekeepers

Some of the beekeepers are chemists
Are some of the artists chemists?

This conclusion is not valid because, although some of the artists could be chemists, it is also possible that none of the beekeepers who are chemists are also artists.

Experiments have shown that people quite readily draw invalid conclusions from syllogisms. In one study, 81% of participants shown

syllogisms such as (2) above, wrongly accepted the invalid conclusion and error rates even higher have been recorded in other studies (Gilhooly, 1995; Johnson-Laird and Byrne, 1991). A number of factors contribute to people's poor performance on syllogisms. One of these is **belief bias** in which participants accept or reject a conclusion more on the basis of what they believe to be true in general, as opposed to a conclusion warranted by the syllogism itself (Oakhill and Garnham, 1993). For example, with the premises:

The fictional character Sherlock Holmes is known for his skills of logical deduction, working with his partner Watson to solve the most complex of mysteries.

(3) All Frenchmen are wine drinkers
    Some of the wine drinkers are gourmets

participants were highly likely to accept the false conclusion that:

(4) Some of the Frenchmen are gourmets.

Another source of error in syllogistic reasoning involves the **atmosphere effect** in which participants' conclusions can be influenced by the terms used (Chapman and Chapman, 1959; Woodworth and Sells, 1935). Thus if a premise begins with "All", participants show a greater inclination to accept conclusions beginning with "All" as opposed to "some" or "none", whereas negative premises appear to favour the acceptance of negative conclusions. Explanations of the atmosphere effect are not clear (see Gilhooly, 1995 for a discussion) but it provides an additional example of how people fail to act logically. Another example of faulty logic in syllogistic reasoning is the **conversion error** in which people draw the invalid conclusion that, if "All A are B" then "All B are A". There are a number of explanations of conversion errors including the idea that they reflect contamination from natural language habits in that we frequently hear reversible statements in real life (Cahan and Artman,

1997). Another factor affecting conversion errors is **content**. Thus, the following would not be acceptable (Newstead, 1990):

> All dogs are animals
> All animals are dogs

but the following equally invalid conclusion meets with considerable acceptance because it seems likely for common sense reasons:

> All ticket holders may enter the exhibition
> All the people who are allowed to enter the exhibition are ticket holders

Conditional reasoning is somewhat similar to syllogistic reasoning. However, conditionals take the form "If P then Q" meaning that if P is true then Q is also true. Studies of conditional reasoning show that people make errors for similar reasons to those underlying syllogism errors (Johnson-Laird and Byrne, 1991). In particular, natural language usage appears to interfere with our ability to deal with conditionals. In logical terms, if P is true then Q is true does not allow the additional conclusion that Q is only true when P is true. Thus we might say "You cannot have your sweet until you have finished your main course". You would interpret this to mean that once you have eaten your main course you would be allowed to have your sweet. However, in making this conclusion you are actually making a logical error because you are making the false assumption that finishing your dinner is the only condition preventing you having your sweet when, in fact, there could be other reasons as well. This error is described in terms of converting a conditional into a **biconditional**, i.e. "If P *and only if P* then Q".

Hypothesis testing

A hypothesis can be defined as a "starting point for investigation" or a "supposition about the world". Hypotheses can be derived in various ways. Induction is one obvious means by which people create hypotheses but they may occur in other ways including what we might term "intuitive leaps" or "insight". Within science it has been argued that scientists make use of the **hypothetico–deductive method** when carrying out experiments. Briefly, their hypothesis serves as a set of premises from which a set of predictions can be logically derived. The experiment is then conducted to establish whether the predictions are confirmed. Popper (1959), the originator of this idea, emphasised that a valid hypothesis must be falsifiable, i.e. it must be possible to conduct an experiment that could prove the hypothesis to be incorrect. Thus although we may suppose that "X causes Y" we must be able to envisage a set of conditions that would arise if "X did not cause Y".

Popper argued that science would progress more effectively if it concentrated its efforts on falsification rather than confirmation of hypotheses. Unfortunately, scientists rarely act like this, except when considering other scientists' work, and instead show a **confirmation bias** in which they continue to seek positive evidence for their hypothesis as opposed to negative. A startling example of this was the recent series of events surrounding the massive use of baby monitors, particularly in the USA, to assess the breathing of children thought to be susceptible to cot death. The hypothesis derived from the view that babies at risk of cot death show increased amounts of apnoea (breathing difficulty). Evidence for the hypothesis came from a series of five successive children in the same family who experienced apnoea-type breathing problems and then died. This discovery made the scientist very famous and he continued to seek confirmation of his hypothesis through an extensive research programme. However, as the evidence for his theory failed to develop it was discovered that the five children upon which he had based his hypothesis had actually been murdered by their mother. If he had sought to falsify his hypothesis by examining other aspects of the children's case histories it is unlikely that his theory would ever have got off the ground.

Everyday hypothesis testing

Hypothesis testing in normal people has been investigated extensively using a number of seemingly simple tasks. The most well known is the **selection task** (Wason, 1960) in which the participant is presented with four cards:

E   K   4   7

and told a rule that may or may not be true in relation to the cards,

"If a card has a vowel on one side, it has an even number on the other side".

The participant is asked which cards must be turned over to decide if the rule is true. Most people doing this task select the "E" card alone, or "E" and "4" or "E" and "4" and "7". The correct answer is "E" and "7". The errors have been explained by suggesting that, despite the instructions, participants seek to confirm the hypothesis by checking that not only does "E" have an even number on the back but also that "4" is backed by a vowel. Showing that both of these are true does not rule out the possibility that an uneven number could also be paired with a vowel (falsification of the rule) this can only be shown by turning over "7".

Rule: If there is a vowel on one side, the card has an even number on the other side.

An alternative account of errors in the selection task is the **pragmatic reasoning hypothesis** (Cheng and Holyoak, 1985). This idea proposes that we have various schemata that we can employ when attempting to solve particular types of problem. One example is the **permission schema** which states the general point that "a particular action can only occur if permission is granted". In one experiment, similar in format to the basic selection task, two groups were presented with four cards:

ENTERING	TRANSIT	CHOLERA TYPHOID HEPATITIS	TYPHOID HEPATITIS

Both groups were given the same basic instructions:

> "You are an immigration officer…Among the documents you have to check is a form which on one side states whether the person is entering the country or is in transit and on the other side lists names of tropical diseases. You have to make sure that *If the form says entering on one side, then the other side includes cholera among the list of diseases*."

However, one group received similar instructions with additions designed to evoke use of a permission schema. Thus they were told that the disease names represented inoculations that the passenger had received and, directly following the conditional rule (shown in italics), told that "this ensures that entering passengers are protected against the disease".

The "cholera" problem has exactly the same abstract structure as the basic selection task so, if it is solved in purely logical ways (i.e. If P then Q) there should be no effect of the additional information. The results, however, showed that performance was substantially better when the extra rationale involving inoculation was given. On this basis, Cheng and Holyoak suggested that the additional information had led participants to employ a permission schema that helped them form a solution. To back up this claim, it was also shown that participants can be effective in their ability to solve conditional problems phrased in abstract terms, "If one is to take Action A, then one must first satisfy

Precondition P", provided they are also given information designed to evoke a permission schema.

While the above results indicate that participants perform the selection task better when encouraged to invoke permission schemas, there is now evidence that the selection task enhanced by permission schemas may be conceptually different for people compared with Wason's original task. In a recent study, for example, Griggs and Cox (1993) found that factors influencing participants' success on permission schema versions of the selection task had no influence on how participants performed the standard task.

Mental models

Another influential theory about how people solve problems such as syllogisms and conditionals is known as the **mental models** theory (Johnson-Laird, 1980). Mental models can be illustrated most easily using another form of deduction task: the **three-term series problem**. A typical example is one where participants have to order according to height:

> Bob is taller than Mike
> Mike is taller than Dave

The deduction one make from this is that Bob is taller than Dave. Mental models theory is based on the idea that people construct an internal representation of the premises and from this they are then able to deduce additional information. At a slightly more complex level, consider the following statement:

> The ball is on the right of the jug
> The cup is on the left of the jug
> The pen is in front of the cup
> The saucer is in front of the ball

If you create a mental representation of this set of premises you will be able to make additional deductions such as the "the pen is to the left of the saucer" (to understand this idea, try drawing a layout).

In the above case the mental model is coherent in that it fully specifies the arrangement of the depicted objects. However, consider this case:

> The ball is on the right of the jug

The cup is on the left of the ball
The pen is in front of the cup
The saucer is in front of the jug

This description is indeterminate in that there are two possible layouts so the statement, "The pen is to the left of the saucer" cannot be verified because the pen could also be to the right of the saucer.

The idea of mental models, therefore, is that the premises can be used to derive one or more internal representations and any given statement can be verified by checking whether it is consistent with all the possible models generated by a particular set of premises. If a statement does not concur with one or more of the models then it is considered invalid. If we return to the syllogism:

All of the artists are beekeepers
Some of the beekeepers are chemists

we could construct a mental model both for the explicit premises, e.g. imagining a row of artists, each of whom is associated with their own beehive, and a row of beekeepers, complete with hive, each of whom is holding a test tube to denote being a chemist. We can also **flesh out** the implicit aspect of the syllogism, "some of the beekeepers are not chemists" by envisaging a row of beekeepers who are not chemists, e.g. those with beehives but not test tubes. If we take the invalid conclusion "All of the artists are chemists", we can envisage what that would look like in our model—every artist would have both a beehive and a test tube. As we would not be forced to construct a model in which this is the case, we can decide that the conclusion is invalid.

Mental models theory has been extensively developed to cover a variety of reasoning tasks. As a theoretical approach, it is contrasted with **rule-based theories of reasoning** (e.g. Braine, 1978). These propose that people employ the rules of logic when attempting to solve syllogisms and other related tasks. The debate concerning the value of these two approaches and the extent to which they differ is complex and we are unable to go into it here. However, the crucial findings relate to predictions about how certain factors make problems easier or more difficult to solve. According to mental models theory, the solution of a problem is determined by the number of mental models created by a given set of premises; the greater the number of models the more difficult the problem. In contrast, rule-based accounts predict that it is the number of logical operations needed that determines solution difficulty. Support for the mental models theory has come from studies showing that the number of models associated with a set of premises still influences performance when the number of logical rules required is held constant (for a full appreciation of this debate, see Johnson-Laird, 1997; Rips, 1994; 1997).

Overview

- Studies of reasoning have frequently revealed that people are not logical about the decisions they make.
- Deduction involves coming to a conclusion when all the available facts are known. Induction involves a conclusion derived from only partial information.
- Heuristics are rules of thumb that enable a decision to be made on the basis of limited information.
- The availability heuristic bases a decision on an analysis of past outcomes. Use of this heuristic can be distorted by the prominence given to certain types of outcome.
- Anchoring is a form of distortion in which exposure to a level of magnitude results in subsequent unrelated estimates being biased in the same direction.
- The representativeness heuristic involves basing a decision on what is thought typical of a particular category.
- People's ability to appreciate correlation is poor because they attend too much to positive instances of the assumed correlation (the cell A heuristic). People are also quite able to detect illusory correlations.
- Deduction has been studied largely through the study of syllogisms.
- A number of factors influence people's errors on syllogisms. These include belief bias (accepting a wrong conclusion because it seems reasonable); the atmosphere effect (which phrasing influences a decision); and conversion errors in which "All A are B" is thought to allow "All B are A".
- The hypothetico–deductive method is widely used in science but too often scientists opt for confirmatory evidence rather than falsification.
- In everyday reasoning problems such as the selection task, people make errors that suggest a confirmation bias.
- Solving everyday problems can be made easier if people are able to relate a problem to a general situation such as "giving permission".
- Mental models theory proposes that people construct a representation of the problem they are trying to solve. This contrasts with rule-based accounts which propose that people just use logical rules.

Suggested further reading

Baron, J. (1994). *Thinking and deciding* (2nd ed.). Cambridge: Cambridge University Press.

Chapter 4 of this book covers many of the issues of this chapter in more detail.

Garnham, A., & Oakhill, J.V. (1994). *Thinking and reasoning*. Oxford: Blackwells.

This book provides detailed coverage of reasoning studies.

Revision questions

1 What is the difference between inductive and deductive reasoning?
2 What is meant by the term heuristic?
3 Using examples, what is meant by an availability heuristic?
4 What is the gambler's fallacy?
5 Why are people so poor at understanding variance and correlation?
6 What underlies illusory correlation?
7 What is a syllogism, and what factors contribute to the very high error rate we see on these types of problem?
8 What is the hypothetico–deductive method and why does it not serve science as well as it might do?
9 Why do people make so many errors on the Wason selection task?
10 What are mental models and how might they be used in reasoning?

Problem solving 15

In 1927 the Gestalt psychologist Wolfgang Kohler conducted a classic experiment in animal problem solving (Kohler, 1927). Chimpanzees were placed in a caged area outside of which was a banana. Nearby were some sticks and Kohler was interested to know whether the chimps would make use of the sticks as a rake to haul the banana into the cage. The chimps were able to use the sticks effectively in other situations: as a pole to climb up to get fruit, and as a club to knock fruit down from a tree. Even more impressively, the chimps learnt to use a pile of boxes as a ladder to retrieve fruit. They also showed remarkable generalisation. Thus when the boxes were removed they would find other objects to climb up on. In one case, a chimp known as "Sultan" led Kohler himself under the hanging banana and used the unsuspecting researcher as a ladder.

This kind of problem solving was seen as highly problematic for the behaviourists and other psychologists who based their ideas about problem solving on **trial and error** (e.g. Schmidt and Boshuizen, 1993; Thorndike, 1955). Kohler argued that the problem solving by chimps did not have the incremental quality of trial and error learning. Rather, the chimps appeared to move from having no solution to an effective solution with no intervening steps. Also, the fact that the animals could use the same problem-solving strategy in different situations argued against the idea that it had been learned on a trial and error basis.

Kohler described the chimps problem solving as a form of **insight**—a sudden ability to see the solution to a problem without any intervening steps; sometimes known as the "ah-ha" experience. Insight was also demonstrated in a range of human studies. Maier (1931) introduced participants to a room in which two pieces of string were hanging from the ceiling. In addition, there were various other objects in the room such as poles and pliers. The participant's task was to tie the two strings together. As they were too far apart to brought together, another solution was needed. Many participants had the insight to use the pliers as a weight and turn one string into a pendulum. This string could then be set swinging and caught while holding the other string, thus enabling them to be tied together. Additionally, Maier showed that participants having difficulty with the problem could suddenly discover the solution if he just set one of the strings swinging.

Duncker (1945) introduced the term **functional fixedness** to describe a certain form of difficulty that people experience when solving problems. In one study, participants were given a candle, a box of nails and matches, along with several other objects, and asked to put the candle on the wall while ensuring that the wax did not drip on to the table below. Numerous ineffective solutions were produced with only a few people coming up with the correct one: take all the nails out of the box, nail the box to the wall, and put the candle in the box. Duncker argued that failure on this problem arose because people were "fixed" on the idea of the box as a container for nails and therefore could not envisage its alternate use.

The Gestalt psychologists' contribution to problem solving very much mirrored their achievements in the area of visual perception (see Chapter 2). They demonstrated a number of interesting phenomena but the explanatory constructs derived from the phenomena were rather vague. Their greatest contribution, perhaps, the demonstration of insight, provided little information about what insight actually was in terms of a mental process.

States, goals, and operators

A problem can be defined as any situation in which a person has a goal but does not know how that goal is to be reached (Duncker, 1945). Modern psychologists typically have thought of problems in terms of three components: **a starting state**; **a goal state**; and a **set of operators** that transform the starting state into a goal state (Newell and Simon, 1972). There may also be **path constraints** that limit the possible solutions. These could range from the mundane, such as the physical properties of things involved, right through to considerations about ethics, i.e. whether "an end would justify a means".

The relation between states, goals and operators can be illustrated by a **state action tree**. This can be defined as a representation of all possible states that could intervene between the starting state and the goal. An example of a state action tree is given by the "Hobbits and Orcs" Problem (formerly known as the Missionaries and Cannibals Problem):

> "Transport three hobbits and three orcs across a river using a boat that can only carry two people, and needs at least one person to get it across the river. There must never be more orcs than hobbits on either bank because the hobbits will get eaten by the orcs."

The state action tree for the Hobbits and Orcs Problem is potentially enormous. Initially there are five intermediary states possible but this grows enormously as additional moves are considered. Collectively, all the possible states considered when attempting a solution are known as the **problem space**.

One naive idea about problem solving is that we might create a problem space that contains all the possible actions we could take and then search it systematically to find the correct answer. The difficulty with this idea is that, as we have seen, even relatively simple problems, such as the Hobbits and Orcs, have enormous potential problem spaces, even if path constraints such as the out-numbering rule are applied. In addition, there is a short-term memory problem in that people are not capable of holding more than two or three possible moves in their mind. This indicates that our problem space most likely involves the evaluation of one or two moves at a time rather than one in which a large series of options is examined.

HHH/OOO	➝	H/O
HHH/OO	⬅	O
HHH	➝	OOO
HHH/O	⬅	OO
H/O	➝	HH/OO
HH/OO	⬅	H/O
OO	➝	HHH/O
OOO	⬅	HHH
O	➝	HHH/OO
H/O	⬅	HH/OO
	➝	HHH/OOO

FIG. 15.1. The shortest solution to the Hobbits and Orcs Problem. This diagram also enables you to see the enormous number of moves (right and wrong) that could be possible—the problem space; and that at various stages the solution appears to temporarily move away from the goal (e.g. move 2; move 4).

Problem-solving heuristics

If people cannot search their problem space to determine that a particular move will lead to a series of other moves which will eventually achieve the goal, how do they evaluate that any given move is correct? The crudest strategy would be that of trial and error but this would result in human problem solving being a lumbering process. Instead, it has been argued that people solve problems by employing **heuristics** which, as we saw in the last chapter, are a "rule of thumb" device which makes use of a manageable amount of information in order to come to the correct solution on most occasions. One heuristic is the so-called **hill climbing strategy** in which participants always choose the course of action that gets them closest to their goal. A strategy of this kind is of limited value. For example, it fails to find the minimum move solution to the Hobbits and Orcs problem (see Fig. 15.1). It is sometimes necessary to move away from the stated goal (i.e. ferry Hobbits or Orcs back to the start) to move away from the desired goal. There is evidence that the need to make "backward moves" is a particular source of trouble for people when they attempt problems such as the Hobbits and Orcs.

An alternative is the **means–ends analysis** in which knowledge is applied about the way a problem should be solved. A particular version of this is **problem reduction** in which a big problem is broken down into a set of sub-problems, each of which is more easy to deal with. Newell and Simon (1972, p.416) gave the following example of problem reduction:

> "I want to take my son to nursery school. What's the difference between what I have and what I want? One of distance. What changes distance? My automobile. My automobile won't work. What is needed to make it work? A new battery. What has new batteries? An auto repair shop. I want the repair shop to put in a new battery; but the shop doesn't know I need one. What is the difficulty? One of communication. What allows communication? A telephone."

FIG. 15.2.
The Tower of Hanoi problem.

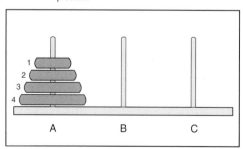

Thus the main goal is reached via a succession of subgoals.

A clear example of subgoals helping problem solving can be found in the **Tower of Hanoi**. The task, shown in Fig. 15.2, is to move all of the discs from peg A to peg C. There are two rules: you can move only one disc at a time and you can never put a bigger disc on top of a smaller one. This task can be made much easier by breaking it up into subgoals providing you choose the right ones!

The problem can be simplified if you start by moving disc 4 to peg C. This involves a sequence of actions as follows:

$$1 \rightarrow B; 2 \rightarrow C; 1 \rightarrow C; 3 \rightarrow B; 1 \rightarrow A; 2 \rightarrow B; 1 \rightarrow B; 4 \rightarrow C.$$

Having got disc 4 to C the same process can be repeated, but this time it now involves only three discs, then two discs, then one disc. Because this task can be reduced to subgoals, similar problems involving far more discs are, in principle, no more difficult to solve (Baron, 1994). Interestingly, Baron reports that, during the 1930s, some priests were working on a 64-disc version of the problem which, when solved, would result in the end of the world. One can assume that they never discovered the use of subgoals!

Problem solving using analogy

Understanding the structure of the atom has been one of the great scientific discoveries of the 20th century. In his work on atomic structure, Rutherford was greatly aided by the use of **analogy**. In this particular case, Rutherford's understanding of how sub-atomic particles were related to each other involved drawing an analogy between the parts of an atom and the solar system—thus the nucleus was seen as the sun and the revolving electrons were conceived of as planets.

Analogies play an important role in scientific discovery and, as you have seen repeatedly in this book, psychology has had to rely heavily on analogy to tackle a range of theoretical problems. Use of analogy—usually referred to as **analogical mapping** or **analogical transfer**—is also of great importance to human problem solving more generally because it gives us immense flexibility when trying to seek the answer to a problem.

Consider the following problem:

"Suppose you are a doctor faced with a patient who has a malignant tumour in his stomach. It is impossible to operate on the patient, but unless the tumour is destroyed the patient will die. There is a kind of ray that can be used to destroy the tumour. If the rays reach the tumour all at once at a sufficient high intensity, the tumour will be destroyed. Unfortunately, at this intensity the healthy tissue that the rays pass through on the way to the tumour will also be destroyed. At lower intensities the rays are harmless to healthy tissue, but they will not affect the tumour either. What type of procedure might be used to destroy the tumour with the rays, and at the same time avoid destroying the healthy tissue?" (Duncker, 1945)

Think about this problem for a while and if you cannot think of a sensible answer read on.

> "A fortress was located in the centre of the country. Many roads radiated out from the fortress. A general wanted to capture the fortress with his army. The general wanted to prevent mines on the road from destroying his troops and neighbouring villages. As a result, the entire army could not attack the fortress along one road. However, the entire army was needed to capture the fortress. So an attack by one small group would not succeed. The general therefore divided his army into several small groups. He positioned the small groups at the heads of different roads. The small groups simultaneously converged on the fortress. In this way the army captured the fortress."

Now return to the "tumour problem". Hopefully you will now realise that the answer is that the tumour can be destroyed by dividing the ray into several separate low intensity rays entering the body from different locations but converging on the tumour, thus providing the high intensity needed for the tumour destruction.

If you were helped by the "fortress" story it was because the problem depicted there is an analogy of the tumour problem and, by seeing the resemblance, you were able to reach a solution. However, research using this task showed that people were poor at realising the analogy was there unless explicitly told that this was the case, or given a general statement of the analogical similarity: "if you need a large force to accomplish some purpose, but are prevented from applying such a force directly, many smaller forces applied from different directions may work just as well" (Gick and Holyoak, 1980; 1983).

However, other studies have suggested that people can make spontaneous analogies more frequently. Holyoak and Koh (1987) made use of a textbook discussion of the tumour problem to familiarise a group of students with the "convergence solution". Several days later, the same students were presented with an analogue of the tumour problem involving a light bulb that could only be repaired using low intensity laser beams. It was found that the students previously exposed to the tumour problem solved the light bulb problem far better than those who were not familiar with the tumour problem.

How, though, does analogical mapping occur? Holyoak and Koh suggest that there are two plausible ways in which the target problem makes contact with an appropriate **analogue source**. First, the target and source domains may share **surface similarities** (e.g. involve the same sorts of objects), or they may have **structural similarities** (e.g. although involving dissimilar objects the elements of the target and source both operate according to some higher order principle, i.e. operating on the basis of convergence). Holyoak and Koh propose that effective use of analogy depends on recognising a structural similarity between target and source and that reliance on surface similarity would lead to the selection of many, superficially similar, but irrelevant sources of analogy. They went on to confirm this by showing that analogical transfer was more likely to occur with a structurally informative source analogue that had low surface similarity to the target compared with a structurally uninformative source analogue with strong surface similarity.

Games and expertise

The experiments we have considered so far have deliberately employed problem-solving tasks with which people are unfamiliar. This means that they are knowledge-lean in that people can bring little existing knowledge towards the solution. However, many problems we encounter are knowledge-rich and involve us using our pre-existing knowledge to come to a solution. Psychologists interested in this type of problem solving have been particularly interested in chess for a number of reasons. First, it is a game that many people play at different levels, ranging from grand master to novice. This has made it an ideal basis for studying expertise. In addition, chess is amenable to analysis in terms of a problem space: there is a start, a goal (checkmate), and operators that allow the transition from one state to another (moves). Also chess has attracted the attention of computer programmers who produce chess-playing software. It has proved interesting to compare the way humans play chess and the strategies used by a computer program.

The potential problem space of chess is truly gigantic. After just three moves by each player there are over 9 million possible moves that could be made. Chess-playing computer programs operate by searching the vast problem space created by chess and examining each possible move in turn. Recent developments in computing science has produced chess programs that can examine possible moves at over 10 billion moves a second. The first research on chess playing was carried out by DeGroot (1965; 1966) who compared the skills of grand masters and experts by asking them to think aloud. Using this **think-aloud protocol method**, he demonstrated that human players consider only a few moves and are not in any sense operating like the chess programs (see also Charness, 1981). Intuitively you might think that given their vast computational advantage, chess-playing computers should easily outperform humans, but this is not so. Even a modest chess player is able to beat a program that might be considering millions of possible moves at each turn—though the *very best* computer programes play at grand master level.

So, how do humans, particularly experts, play chess? A clue lies in the fact that expert chess players appear to have a remarkable memory, not only for their own previous games, but for others that they have studied. This led to the idea that experts store away knowledge about particular positions and then match these with new situations that they encounter. Thus their decision to move in a particular way rests largely on detecting the similarity between a current board position and one encountered previously.

Karpov   Kasparov

A competition between two Russian world champion chess players, Anatoly Karpov and Garry Kasparov.

The idea that experts rely on previous instances to guide their moves has been supported by a series of memory experiments. DeGroot briefly presented grand masters and tournament players with board positions either drawn from real games or where the pieces had been arranged randomly on the board. The participants' task was to reconstruct each game. The grand masters performed much better for real games, but no difference was found when random board positions were used. This result was interpreted as showing that grand masters could use their extensive knowledge of different positions to impose an organisation on a real game, but this was not possible with random positions and thus the grand masters had no advantage over the tournament players.

DeGroot's original findings have been replicated and extended by Chase and Simon (1973a,b). An important element of this work has been to show that expert chess players, as opposed to novices, needed less time to memorise chess positions and, in addition, were able to remember information about more pieces. Chase and Simon's account of chess expertise is known as chunking. In the course of skill acquisition, chess players store chunks in memory that correspond to arrangements of pieces which recur frequently in games. Experiments indicated that more expert players formed chunks averaging 2.5 pieces compared with smaller chunks in novices. At any one time, a player can only hold around seven chunks in STS. It is estimated that an expert would needs to acquire at least 50,000 chunks, thus explaining why it takes around 10 years to become an expert.

The chunking model has been developed to explain a number of features of chess playing but our specific concern is the fact that it can explain why chess grand masters remember real board positions better than novices but show no such advantage with random positions; real positions are presumed to map on to stored chunks which provide a much better basis for remembering.

More recent work has indicated that the chunking theory needs to be modified and extended if it is to account fully for the nature of chess playing, particularly by experts. In its original form, the chunking model is constrained by the capacity of STS, i.e. the player can only deal with around seven possible chunks at a time. However, it has been demonstrated that grand masters can deal with far more pieces than would be predicted if chunks were the sole basis for remembering positions. In addition, superior players can outperform novices when asked to devise the best move from a randomly determined position of pieces—this would not be possible if the advantage of experts rested solely on the number of chunks available.

It is now proposed that, along with basic chunks (now known as **clusters**), there are also **templates** and **retrieval structures**. Templates represent larger arrangements of pieces, e.g. a particular type of opening gambit or endgame, and also contain "slots" into which more specific move information from a particular chunk could be placed. Retrieval structures serve to unite sets of templates and can be organised in various ways. Thus it was shown that one grand master could improve his ability to remember the positions on different chess boards by classifying the pattern of moves as characteristic of a particular grand master, e.g. Fischer or Kasparov (Gobet, 1998; Gobet and Simon, 1996).

Other forms of expertise

Although studies of chess have dominated research on expertise, other areas have been investigated. It has been shown in many other domains, ranging from bridge to basketball, that experts are more sensitive than novices to meaningfulness when asked to remember game positions (Ericsson and Lehmann, 1996). The solving of physics problems has also been investigated extensively (Larkin et al., 1980) and important differences between novices and experts have been found. In one study, novices and experts were asked to sort problems into groups based on similarity. Novices centred their sorting on superficial similarities, e.g. placing all the problems involving the angle of an inclined plane together, whereas experts grouped problems according to the particular principles involved (Chi et al., 1981). These studies also showed that experts took longer to start forming a solution and that they tended to work forward in a problem—from principle to solution. In contrast, novices tended to work backwards—starting with the goal and trying to find a principle to fit (Larkin, 1983). However, a subsequent study of physics has suggested that experts and novices both work forwards but that experts produce a more elaborate plan before starting (Priest and Lindsay, 1992). A similar distinction appears to separate expert and novice computer programmers.

Medical expertise has been investigated examining doctors' think-aloud protocols while making a diagnosis. This method has led to the view that, as doctors become more expert, they rely less on basic biomedical information (knowledge about how pathological processes affect basic bodily mechanisms) and more on clinical information (the kinds of complaints that could be associated with particular patterns of symptoms) (Boshuizen and Schmidt, 1992; Patel et al., 1993; Patel et al., 1996). Studies of medical expertise have also unearthed an interesting phenomenon known as the **intermediate effect** (Schmidt and Boshuizen, 1993). In a typical experiment, doctors with different levels of expertise study half a page of information about a patient (e.g. basic presentation, blood results etc.). The text is removed and the participants asked to recall as much of the text as possible. Typically those with intermediary levels of expertise remember most information. This is thought to arise because the experts, with their greater knowledge, are able to create a better **situation model** (see Chapter 11). It has been suggested that the better situation models of experts allow them to filter out information that is irrelevant to a diagnosis. Thus, having sufficient information that the patient has illness X there is no need to remember detail only relevant to the alternative diagnosis Y. In contrast the intermediate has less ability to develop a situation model and thus retains more information than is needed for accurate diagnosis. However, it should be noted that more recent attempts to replicate the intermediate effect in medical diagnosis have failed (van de Wiel et al., 1998).

Medical expertise can also affect perceptual processes as well as problem-solving strategy. Myles-Worsely et al. (1988) examined the ability of radiologists with different levels of experience on three types of recognition memory test: faces; X-rays showing an abnormality; and normal X-rays. The results, shown in Fig. 15.3, showed that recognition of abnormal X-rays increased with expertise. This was not due to better memory overall because the groups did not differ on the face memory control task. However, the performance on recognising previously-seen normal X-rays decreased with expertise—presumably because experts took less notice of unimportant details on these X-rays which could aid their subsequent recognition.

Creativity

Creativity is the ability to do something that is both novel and successful. Not surprisingly, there has been a lot of interest in how creativity comes about. One obvious approach has been to study creative people in detail and see if they differ in some obvious way. One idea has been that creative people rely more on unconscious thought processes than normal people. An apparently famous example of this is the chemist Kekule who

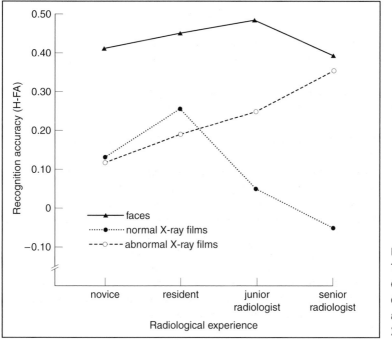

FIG. 15.3.
The performance of experts and novices on remembering faces and remembering X-rays.

had a dream about snakes chasing their tails. It is claimed that from this dream Kekule discovered that the benzene molecule involves a ring of six carbon atoms. Hardy (1979) believed that the evidence for unconscious thought in mathematical creativity was undeniable and that the "flashes of illumination" experienced by mathematicians were often preceded by periods of ineffective activity. Poets such as Coleridge and Poe also claimed that much of their inspiration was unconscious.

On the basis of biographical evidence, Wallas (1926) proposed that there were four stages to creative thought: **preparation**, **incubation**, **illumination**, and **verification**. Preparation reflects the often long-term consideration of a problem without coming to an answer; incubation is the time spent not thinking about the problem; illumination is the sudden gaining of partial or complete insight into the solution following incubation; and verification is proving that the answer is correct. Wallas was particularly influenced by the biographies of two scientists, Helmholtz and Poincaré, who both believed that they had made important discoveries following a period of incubation.

A number of studies have looked for evidence of incubation during human problem solving. Typically these have involved comparing two groups who have equal amounts of time to solve a problem but where, in one case, the time is split by introducing an irrelevant alternative activity half way through. On balance, these studies have not found effects of incubation (e.g. Witelson et al., 1999) and, even where this has occurred, it may not be because the incubation period has facilitated problem solving. It might be, for example, that an interval enables participants to make a fresh start—when solving problems, people often show a resistance to abandoning one line of reasoning even though it is giving no indication that it will work; being forced to do something else for a short time may make it easier to break from this (Baron, 1994).

What then, about the creative scientists and poets? Is incubation only associated with genius? While there is some evidence that this is so other explanations are also possible. Kekule's "snake" may be an example of what has been termed **suggestion from below**; the snake was not representative of some complex unconscious thought process, it was a random event that just happened to provide Kekule with the insight he was seeking. In addition, creative individuals did not do controlled experiments on themselves so it is impossible to say whether they would have reached a solution more slowly if they had not thought about something else, or whether they really did incubate a problem.

Another aspect of Wallas's theory is the "moment of illumination". This is illustrated by Poincaré in his account of discovering a particular mathematical rule: "At the moment when I put my foot on the step, the idea came to me... I did not verify the idea... I went on with my conversation already commenced, but I felt a perfect certainty" (Poincaré, 1952, p. 53).

This quote suggests that creative insight is in some way special in that the solution has some index of truth associated with it. Unfortunately, studies of problem solving fail to support this. Spitzka (1907) gave participants insight problems and asked them to rate how "warm" they were to achieving a solution. As solution time progressed, the participants reported being "warmer" but, at the point of solution subjects who were wrong felt just the same as those who were right.

The nature of creative individuals

An alternative approach to creativity is to try and find objective differences between creative and less creative people (see Sternberg and Lubart, 1999 for a review and synthesis of the many differing ideas about what determines creativity). Studies have shown a number of differences: creative people are more able to see the real problem presented by a situation; they are more willing to delay a decision and thus tolerate uncertainty; they have a desire for originality and a dislike of social conformity; they are more self-critical; they work extremely hard; and tend to have an extensive knowledge of the area they work in (Baron, 1994; Weisberg, 1999).

There have been attempts to devise tests to measure creativity in the general population. Guilford (1956) drew a distinction between **convergent** and **divergent thinking**. Divergent thinking, sometimes called **lateral thinking**, is the ability to think in a novel way about a typical situation. Guilford captured this idea in his **Unusual Uses Test** in which people are required to think up novel uses for everyday objects such as a brick and a pencil. While people vary considerably on this test it has not been possible to link these differences to more general variations in creative ability.

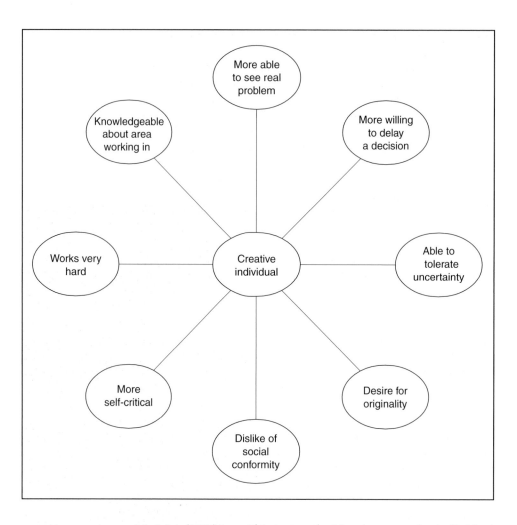

Mednick (1962) based his test on the idea that a creative individual is one who sees links between things that others do not. He devised the **Remote Associations Test** in which participants are shown three words and asked to provide a fourth word that goes with all three:

> snow, down, out—fall
> ache, sweet, burn—heart

More creative people are thought to be better able to think of the remote association linking the words together. Performance on this test was found to have some relation with creativity in architects and a creativity test devised by Torrance (1988) has also shown some relations with creative achievement.

There has long been a view that the brains of geniuses might be different to those of normal people (e.g. Spitzka, 1907). Lenin's brain, for example, was preserved for just that reason. Early analyses focused on the crude idea that geniuses might simply have bigger brains but this has been disproved by showing up to 100% differences in the brain weight of different geniuses. However, more recent work has begun to identify certain physiological and neuroanatomical differences between the brains of geniuses and normal people (Martindale, 1999). Most recently, examination of Albert Einstein's brain showed that a region of his right parietal lobe linked to imagery and mathematics was 15% larger than average and that a normally present sulcus (groove), which prevents interconnection between adjacent brain regions was missing—an arrangement that could well allow unusual and creative patterns of thought not possible in a normal individual (Witelson et al., 1999). This finding is also consistent with other recent evidence that the right hemisphere has a special association with creativity (Fiore and Schooler, 1998).

EINSTEIN'S BRAIN

Einstein's brain
Normal brain

Sylvian fissure

Parietal operculum formed by sylvian fissure meeting postcentral sulcus (absent in Einstein's brain)

Parietal lobe

Postcentral sulcus

Einstein's parietal lobe is 15% larger than normal and shows unusual symmetry between hemispheres in this region

$Eb = 1n + 15\%$

A recent examination of Einstein's brain showed that his right parietal lobe, which is linked to imagery and mathematics, was 15% larger than average.

If there are neuroanatomical and physiological differences between geniuses and normal people then, apart from developing extensive knowledge of a particular area, there is really not much else one can do to become a genius. Martindale (1999) looked at a number of composers and found that the number of popular pieces of work they produced rose steadily for the first 10 years of their writing career and then levelled off. Similar findings emerge for painters and scientists and suggest, like chess expertise, that about 10 years is needed before a person's full degree of creativity is apparent.

The last word on creativity should thus be left to Baron (1994, p.126).

"The best piece of advice we can give to people who want to be poets is this: Read a lot of poetry, try to write poems and see how it goes. If you are an immediate success that is a good sign. If you are not it may be too soon to tell. Eventually, if success still eludes you, it would seem reasonable to try something else. "

Overview

- The Gestalt psychologists carried out a number of interesting problem-solving tasks, particularly ones that demonstrated insight. However, they did not have much of a theory to explain what was going on.
- Modern accounts of problem solving conceive of it as a starting state and a goal and a set of operators that create intervening states between the start and the goal.
- The number of states examined in the solution of a problem is known as the problem space.
- Because problems can be difficult, heuristics are often employed. These include trial and error, hill climbing, means–end analysis— particularly reducing a problem to subgoals, and working backwards.
- Analogies are often used in problem solving although very often people must be prompted to use them.
- Expertise has been studied in a number of domains but particularly chess.
- Chess experts do not operate like chess-playing computers because humans can look only a few moves ahead .
- It is thought that chess experts are able to recognise particular board positions as instances that provoke a particular strategy.
- The idea that chess experts remember board positions is backed up by their superior memory for real as opposed to random arrangements of chess pieces.
- Initially it was thought that expertise was based on memory for a large number of relatively small board positions. However, more elaborate structures in addition to this are now proposed.
- Experts are distinguished by their greater ability to understand the principles reflected in problems.
- Studies of medical expertise suggest that experienced doctors are more able to derive a situation model of a patient's symptoms and are thus less reliant on remembering detail—hence less expert doctors remember more details about a patient.
- It has been suggested that creativity is, in part, mediated by an unconscious mediation process but there is no strong evidence to support this.

- Measuring creativity is difficult but some tests, such as the remote associations test, do have some success.
- Creative individuals do show differences from normal people but there is little to suggest that they have something "special".

Suggested further reading

Baron, J. (1994). *Thinking and deciding* (2nd ed.). Cambridge: Cambridge University Press.

Provides a good overview of factors underlying both problem solving and creativity.

Garnham, A., & Oakhill, J.V. (1994). *Thinking and reasoning*. Oxford: Blackwells.

A good alternative to Baron.

Sternberg, R.J. (1999). *Handbook of creativity*. New York: Cambridge University Press.

This book covers a wide range of issues concerning creativity.

Revision questions

1 Why do people often fail to show insight in problem-solving tasks?
2 Describe the various heuristics that people use in problem solving.
3 What determines the use of analogy in problem solving?
4 In what ways do expert chess players differ from computers that play chess?
5 How do novices and experts differ in their approach to problems (excluding chess)?
6 Does creative thought involve incubation?
7 What possible differences are there between creative and non-creative individuals?

Glossary

2½D sketch: a viewer-centred representation of the visible parts of an image in terms of their distance and surface orientation which follows on from the Primal Sketch in David Marr's theory of early spatial vision.

2 x 2 contingency table: a table showing a cross classification of people or objects according to two logically independent classifications, each with two possible levels (e.g. male or female, heart disease or no heart disease).

acetylcholine: a neurotransmitter which has been shown to play an important role in memory function.

active storage: in memory research, the proposal that information is held temporarily in an active form (in short-term stores) before it can be modified for storage in long-term memory.

active vs passive sentences: in an active sentence the subject of the sentence is typically the person carrying out the action and the object is the person or thing acted upon (e.g. "John made a shoe"); in a passive sentence the thing acted upon becomes the subject and the actor is relegated to a "by" phrase (e.g. "The shoe was made by John").

ad hoc categories: categories that humans do not normally encounter and therefore have to be created just on the basis of information supplied to them.

affordance: an inherent and invariant property of an object which is directly signaled to an observer without the latter needing to perform any processing on the visual input; therefore, a chair will afford sitting on and a banana will afford eating.

after image: the visual sensation left after a (high-contrast) stimulus has been taken away; it persists for a few seconds and stays on that part of the retina where the stimulus initially fell, the result being that the image can seem to move with the eye.

Alternate Uses Test: a test used, mainly in neuropsychological research, which requires a subject to name as many different uses of an everyday object; this will involve the subject needing to use divergent, i.e. novel, thinking.

Alzheimer's Disease: a degenerative disease in the elderly which has, as one hallmark, increasingly failing memory followed by disorientation and then difficulty in finding words when speaking.

ambiguous sentence: a sentence which can have more than one meaning, e.g. "visiting aunts can be a nuisance" can either refer to the difficulty of going to visit one's aunts or it can refer to the annoyance caused when such relatives come to visit.

Ames Room: a distorted model of a room made so that, when viewed from the correct position, the size and distance of objects in the room are mis-perceived.

amnesia: a general term for the loss of memory; it can be permanent or temporary and can have a variety of causes.

amnesic syndrome: a specific term for a core set of symptoms shown by all people who have lost their memory due to some sort of brain damage .

amplitude: the intensity of a stimulus; in hearing research, it is the loudness of a sound.

analogical mapping or analogical transfer: the use of analogy when attempting to solve a problem.

analogue representation: a representation that is related to the original object such that any dimension in the object has a corresponding dimension in the analogue; e.g. in an analogue watch, the position of the hands on the watch-face is supposed to represent the current hour of the day.

analogue source: when using analogy in problem-solving, the system that the target to-be-solved problem is being compared to.

analogy: the use of a similar situation when attempting to either explain something or solving a problem, e.g. comparing the movement of the planets around a star to conceptualise the movement of electrons around the nucleus of an atom.

analogy (in pronunciation): the use of a similar-looking word to determine the pronunciation of a non-familiar word, e.g. accessing the pronunciations of BENT and RENT to attempt to say the word FENT.

analogy and metaphor (in cognitive psychology): the use of certain constructs (e.g. the workings of a computer) in an attempt to explain how another construct (e.g. processing within the brain) works; the analogy is not supposed to be the *same* but is suggested as a possible representation.

anaphora: the process by which one word or phrase (an anaphor) takes its meaning from another part of a text; the most typical anaphors are pronouns such as "he", "she', "it", and "they".

anaphoric islands: a pronoun cannot properly refer to part of the meaning of a word (e.g. "them" cannot mean Max's parents in "Max is an orphan and he deeply misses them"); in describing this phenomenon, the word (e.g. "parents") is referred to as an anaphoric island.

anchoring: the phenomenon of using and staying close to an initial estimate of the solution to a problem even if it is inaccurate.

anterograde amnesia: the inability to learn new information which is a classic hallmark of amnesia.

anthropomorphism: the attribution of human-like features (e.g. emotions) to animals.

articulatory loop: a speech-based portion of Working Memory which has limited capacity.

articulatory suppression: a secondary task used in short-term memory research whereby a subject continually repeats a meaningless string which itself does not need to be remembered.

artificial grammars: rules governing legal and illegal combinations of individual stimuli; these rules are created by the researcher and are used to test whether participants can learn the underlying rules either consciously or unconsciously.

associative interference theory: if a person has to learn to associate a set of A items with a set of B items (A-B learning), performance on a test in which the person is given the A items and has to retrieve the corresponding B items will be impaired if the person also has had to learn an A-C pairing.

associative priming: the quicker identification of a word (e.g. WHITE) if it is preceded by a related word (e.g. BLACK).

asymptote: the middle part of a serial position curve which shows poorer recall of "middle" items relative to both the earliest and most recent ones.

atmosphere effect: in solving syllogisms the tendency to select a conclusion that share properties (e.g. being negative) with one or more of the premises.

atomistic: the view that memory involves specific representations of information which is invariant, i.e. it is the same irrespective of how and when the information is activated.

attenuator model: a model of attention in which all stimuli, including unattended information receive some meaningful analysis; the majority of the processing power, however, is devoted to the attended material.

attribute theory: any theory of representation which suggests that a concept (e.g. cat) is represented as a list of attributes (e.g. has fur, four legs, meows) which can allow one to categorise any object that is encoutered; extreme versions such as the defining-attribute theory postulate that every concept has a definitive set of criteria all of which must be fulfilled for judging membership.

automatic activation of meaning: in the reading of ambiguous words (e.g. bank), the suggestion that all alternative meanings (i.e. referring to both waterways and financial institutions) are accessed as soon as the word is encountered.

automaticity: the suggestion that some mental processes do not require any attention input for successful completion.

availability heuristics: heuristics that make use of information that readily comes to mind from memory.

behaviourism: the study of psychology using observable behaviour as the source of information rather than mental processes (e.g. as in introspection or cognitive psychology).

belief bias: drawing a conclusion, particularly in a logical reasoning problem, that is consistent with what one knows about the world rather than basing the conclusion on logical principles.

biconditional: a statement of the form "A if and only if B", which is equivalent to "if A then B" and "if B then A".

binocular cue to depth: in vision, a cue which needs information from the two eyes to be combined to compute a sense of depth.

biological process: a general term for functions (e.g. memory) that are known to be mediated by physical biochemical processes in the brain.

blend error: a mistake in speech production where two words are put together forming a third word which may or may not exist.

blob: a blob-like primitive image feature represented in Marr's Primal Sketch.

bottom-up vs top-down processing alternatively data-driven vs conceptually driven processes: a distinction between processing which simply keeps processing raw information through successive stages without the influence of or need for any prior knowledge (bottom-up/data-driven) and processing where stored knowledge is used to influence how new raw data is perceived (top-down/conceptually driven).

bridging inferences inferences needed to link information in two (usually adjacent) parts of a text; if the inference is not made the text will not make sense.

brightness masking or peripheral masking: in visual memory research, the disruption of iconic memory of a stimulus by following its presentation immediately with a flash of bright light.

buffer store: a hypothetical storage site where information is held temporarily before it is passed onto subsequent stages of processing.

categorical perception: occurs when listeners can discriminate sounds no better than they can label them; for most stimulus dimensions (e.g. frequency) we can hear that two sounds are different much more easily than we can give them different labels when they are presented separately.

categorisation: the process by which the common features of a category (e.g. birds) are learned as a result of successive encounters with different exemplars (e.g. robin, sparrow, turkey) of that category.

category similarity effect: the ability to note the similarity (e.g. in terms of membership to the same biological category) between two items; this can make rejecting statements involving the items more difficult (e.g. it takes longer to say that "a dolphin is a fish" is false than it does to say the same of "a chair is a fish").

causal antecedent inference: an inference about the cause of an event described in a text, which can be contrasted with a *causal consequence inference* which is an inference about the effect of an event described in a text.

central executive: the part of Baddeley & Hitch's Working Memory model which controls the other aspects of the system and which can make conscious decisions.

central processing unit: the most important part of a computer which manipulates information provided to it.

central processor: the part of a memory or attentional system that corresponds to the central processing unit of a computer.

channel capacity: the limit of information that can be held or transmitted by a processing system.

characteristic features: features shared by most members within a category (e.g. most birds can fly).

cholingeric blockade: an experimental technique in memory research which involves administration of a drug that impedes the action of acetylcholine; this allows the researcher to see what role this neurotransmitter plays in memory functioning.

chromatic adaptation: a short-term loss in sensitivity to light having a particular colour following prolonged exposure to light of that colour.

chunking: a method of remembering information by organising it into easier-to-remember groups, e.g. remembering a taxi company's phone number such as 204060 is easier to remember as the three numbers 20, 40 and 60 than as theindividual six numbers.

circularity in ESP: the problem within the encoding specificity principle whereby if a cue is successful in aiding memory recall, then it is inferred that that cue overlaps with the memory trace that was set down during learning but the only way of deciding whether or not it was encoded is to see how good it is at aiding recall.

circularity problem in LOP: the temptation to treat orienting tasks that lead to good retrieval as *ipso facto* deep orienting tasks; those orienting tasks that can be assigned a relative depth *before* a memory experiment has been performed with them (e.g. rating the pleasantness of a word is clearly deeper than noting how many times the letter "e" occurs) do not suffer from the circularity problem.

classical conditioning: the process of teaching an animal or human to associate a previously neutral stimulus with a particular response.

clause: a phrase that includes a finite verb and that describes an action, event, state or process.

closure picture: a type of stimulus often used in memory research which involves sketchy degraded visual information but with enough effort, it is possible to put the information together (i.e. close it) to gain an intact representation.

clusters: a synonym for chunks in problem-solving.

co-articulation: a term describing the fact that a consonant cannot be articulated without the vocal tract also assuming the position for a particular vowel, e.g. the position of the lips and tongue when saying "see" versus "Sue" are quite different; as a consequence of co-articulation, the sound of consonants varies widely with their vowel context.

co-ordinality assumption: the assumption that a participant actually processes a stimulus in the way suggested / demanded by an orienting task.

cocktail party problem: the ability to follow one conversation only while a number of other conversations may be going on at the same time.

codes: a representation of something else, e.g. a letter string to represent a spoken sound.

coding: a method of representing one type of information (e.g. a sound) in another form (e.g. as a string of letters).

cognitive architecture: the hypothesized stucture of mental processes outlining how particular functions are carried out.

cognitive economy: the principle of using up only as many cognitive resources as necessary without needless repetition of information; therefore, for example, since all mammals suckle their young, this piece of information does not need to be stored with the definition of each individual mammal but is instead stored with the superordinate definition of mammals.

cognitive map: an internal mental representation of external space.

cognitive mediation: the use of conscious thought processes (e.g. when trying to learn definitions of words in a new language) which over time will need less conscious input and will become relatively automatic.

cognitive neuroscience: any research which attempts to investigate cognitive function by assessing brain function; this can range from studying brain-damaged patients' performance on tasks to studying intact individuals using a variety of methodologies.

cohort model: in speech recognition research, a model which suggests that upon hearing the intial portions of a word, all words within one's mental lexicon that begin with that sequence will be activated; however, as additional segments of the word are processed, words from the newly-activated group (the cohort) that do not share these segments will now be ignored until finally the spoken sequence matches only one word.

collinearity: a property of image features that all lie along a single line in the image.

colour constancy: the ability to see an object have the same colour despite apparent changes that might be caused by how it is illuminated, e.g. whether it is in direct sunlight or in shadow.

competence vs performance: the distinction between a person's (implicit) knowledge of their language and their use of that language in everyday situations.

compliance (in hypnosis): a person deliberately and knowingly responding according to their understanding of hypnosis in order to fool others that they are genuinely hypnotized; it is to be contrasted with the case in which response to hypnotic suggestions is accompanied by the sincere experience that the response was involuntary.

computational modelling: a form of research which involves attempting to simulate human behaviour using computer programmes; if the model created using the computer performs similarly to humans, it is assumed that the structure of the model may mimic the way the human system works.

computer analogy: using the workings of a computer as a way of thinking how the human brain may work.

concavity: bulging inwards as if "caving in".

concrete vs abstract words: a distinction between words referring to physical nouns (e.g. cat, foot) and those referring to concepts without a physical form (e.g. love, peace).

conditional reasoning: a type of deductive reasoning in which one or more of the premises has the form "if A then B".

conditioned reflex: the association of a neutral stimulus with a primary stimulus producing a particular behaviour, e.g. the sound of a bell making a trained dog salivate in anticipation of food.

confirmation bias: in testing hypotheses, the tendency to look for evidence that conforms with a hypothesis, rather than evidence that disconfirms it.

consolidation: a term used for the hypothetical physical modification of specific brain areas in the period after experiencing a stimulus/event; this change then fixes the event into long-term memory.

constancy: the non-changing view of a visual scene despite the apparent changes in the way we see it which can be caused by our movement, changes in visual contrast or different perspectives of the scene.

constant ratio rule: a theory to explain recency as being due to a ratio of the time interval between two adjacent items in a list and the time delay between presentation of the last item and the recall period.

constituent assembly: the process of ensuring that words that have been chosen for an utterance are in the correct syntactical order.

constructivist position: the theory that comprehension requires the combination of information explicit in a text and background knowledge via a process of inference.

content or "open class" words: the class of words in a language that can always be added to (i.e. is expandable) as new words are created; this includes all nouns, verbs and adjectives.

content-guided theory: a theory of parsing according to which meaning guides the choice of structure assigned to a sentence.

contention scheduling: a mechanism within Norman & Shallice's model of attenion which evaluates the relative importance of competing actions so that everyday routine behaviour can be adjusted if necessary.

context: the environment that learning occurs in; this can be features that are part of the stimulus itself or features outside the stimulus, e.g. the room in which testing occurs.

contrast: generally, the difference between two objects or situations; in vision, it is a measure of the difference in luminance between two adjacent areas.

control process: any form of processing (e.g. rehearsal) which occur in the short-term store which can maximize the chances of information being passed into the long-term store.

convergence: in vision, the coming together of the eyes when fixating on a moving object; in such situations, the feedback from the eyes is thought to act as a binocular cue to depth.

convergent and divergent (lateral) thinking: a distinction between seeing a problem only in one standard way and being able to see it in a novel non-typical way; sometimes it is divergent thinking that will result in the most effective solution.

conversion error: in solving syllogisms, illegitimately reversing the order of terms in a premise (e.g. taking "all B are A" to be true when told "all A are B").

convexity: bulging outwards towards the viewer or away from the main surfaces.

correspondence problem: the problem faced by image-processing systems that attempt to match two images of the same scene taken at different times and/or places—how to match up corresponding features in the two images (features that arise from the same object or part of an object in the world).

covert attention: a type of attention which a subject has no conscious knowledge of but which is seen in clearly in their behaviour.

creativity: the ability to do something that is novel and successful.

cued recall: memory research in which a subject is given some information to aid recall, e.g. the first two letters of the word that they need to remember.

decay vs interference: two forms of forgetting, one involving simple weakening of a memory trace over time (decay) and the other involving degradation of a trace as a result of confusion with information learned prior to or after the to-be-remembered item.

decision processes: a control process within the short-term store for making evaluative judgements, e.g. whether information retrieved from the long-term store is what is required.

declarative memory: memory for specific facts and events.

deep structure vs surface structure: some types of grammar (e.g. transformational grammar) distinguish between the underlying form of a sentence (deep structure) that reflects its meaning and its actual form (surface structure).

defining attributes: the features (e.g. feathers) that are common to all members of a particular category (e.g. birds).

demand characteristics: the knowledge that participants may have about the point of an experiment which can influence them to behave in a way which is consistent with those ideas.

depth effect: the finding that semantic processing of a stimulus results in better subsequent memory of that stimulus than other forms of processing.

depth perception: in vision, the ability to use two-dimensional information, e.g. a drawing, to infer three dimensions and therefore perceive depth.

dichotic listening: an experimental paradigm in which messages are relayed simultaneously to the two ears.

direct perception: a theory of vision which suggests that internal representations and processing are not required for visual recognition because the visual scene has all the information directly available for accurate comprehension to occur; this is a non-constructivist theory in which all that is required is the visual input as opposed to other theories which invoke top-down processing using stored knowledge and memory.

double dissociation: the finding in neuropsychological research where one patient can perform task A (e.g. lip-reading) but cannot perform another task B (e.g. analyzing emotional expression) whilst another patient can perform B but not A; this pattern would suggest that the two processes are separable.

dual coding hypothesis: the theory that all stimuli, regardless of how they are first presented to a person, are stored in memory in both verbal and visual forms.

dual process theory: an attentional theory which suggests that when a subject experiences a stimulus, both the representation of the stimulus and information that is associated with it, is activated.

dual task method: an experimental paradigm in which a participant carries out a secondary task at the same time as the main primary task.

dual task or divided attention method: an experimental paradigm which involves a subject having to perform two tasks at the same time with each task presumably making its own attentional demands.

dynamic memory theory: a theory of memory proposed by Schank which was more flexible than earlier schema-based theories which were rooted in the storage of typical events; the dynamic theory allows elaboration of the core elements of the old scripts such that non-canonical events can be both interpreted and remembered (e.g. a surprise birthday cake being delivered by the waiters in a restaurant).

early selection model: a model of attention that postulates that a decision regarding which information will be passed on for further processing is made at a very early stage before any elaborate processing.

echoic memory: very short-lived memory for sounds; a form of sensory memory.

economic label: in language, the idea that there are words that neatly characterise a whole concept without the use of a large number of words, e.g. nerd .

effective visual field or perceptual span: in reading research, the visual area of text during fixation which can have information extracted; text outside this area cannot yet be seen effectively until the eyes saccade to that point.

effort after meaning: because the message conveyed by a text is not completely explicit, it is necessary to devote cognitive effort to derive its meaning (e.g. by making inferences).

eidetic memory: the experience of seeing an image of as if the object was actually present.

elaboration effect: the finding that more involved processing of a word, e.g. judging whether or not it can fit into a particular sentence, results in better retention of a word.

elaborative inferences: inferences that elaborate on information in a text without, in the first instance, creating links with other parts of the text.

elliptical form: a linguistic expression from which a part, which can usually be recovered from context, has been missed out (e.g. a second "buy a car" is missing from "I want to buy a car and I will").

emergent property: a property possessed by a system due to the interaction between its parts, particularly when the system as a whole does something useful even though the parts appear to behave in a very simple or random fashion; for example, neurones passing activation amongst themselves produce properties like perception and memory storage.

encapsulated: the doctrine that modules in the cognitive system perform only one function for which they are specialized, e.g. the language module cannot perform memory functions.

encoding dimensions: different levels of representation of a concept, e.g. its sound versus its meaning.

encoding specificity principle (ESP): a theory of memory which states that the likelihood of recalling something is directly proportional to the overlap between features that were encoded when the stimulus was first encountered and features that are present now in the retrieval environment.

encoding variability hypothesis: the suggestion that as a result of the multiplicity of representations of words, two different encounters with the word can result in different memory traces being formed.

environment dependent memory: the finding in memory research that the likelihood of recall is increased if the subject is placed in the same environment (e.g. room) in which they initially experienced the information.

epiphenomena : outcomes of a process that do not give an insight into the workings of the process itself, e.g. a stereo system becoming hot after prolonged continuous usage tells us nothing about how it produces sound.

episodic vs semantic memory: memory for events (episodic) as opposed to memory for facts (semantic).

exchange error: an error in speech production in which two words which are both nouns but perform different roles are switched creating a sentence that does not make sense.

exemplar: an instance (e.g. robin) of a particular category (e.g. birds).

explicit memory or direct memory: memory for an event which involves conscious recollection of having experienced the event.

exposure based strategies: methods of parsing that use stored information about the relative frequencies of sentence structures a person has encountered in the past to assign a structure to the current sentence.

extra-experimental association: the effect of a stimulus *not* presented to the subject which could influence learning due to its association with one of the experimental stimuli, e.g. the word "chair" being a good retrieval cue to remember "table" even though "table" was never presented.

extreme constructionist vs minimalist: the extreme constructionist (or constructivist) view is that many inferences are made in the course of text comprehension; minimalism claims that inference making is severely restricted, perhaps to those inferences necessary for local coherence and those based on readily available knowledge.

extrinsic/non-interactive context or context alpha: features that are not part of a to-be-remembered item, e.g. the particular room in which one was presented the material.

eye movements: a measure taken in language research to study reading processes.

facilitation vs inhibition: in participants' performance whether extra-stimulus information (e.g. cues presented before or with the stimuli) either aids or interferes with responding.

false alarms: errors in recall where subjects think that they have seen a stimulus before when in fact it was never presented.

false memory syndrome: a term given to the recovery of memories by adults of memories (usually involving sexual or physical abuse) from childhood; this is a highly contentious topic with strong arguments for and against the accuracy of the memories .

familiarity check: during the reading process, a hypothetical multi-component procedure to ensure that the current word being fixated on is one that has probably been encountered before; following this check, a signal to the eyes will allow a saccade to move onto the next word .

familiarity vs recollection: the distinction between knowing that one has been exposed to a test stimulus before (familiarity) and actually being able to consciously recollect the previous exposure (recollection).

family resemblance: the similarity between exemplars of ill-defined categories, e.g. games, which cannot be defined by a specific set of defining features.

feature comparison models: in language, models of the semantic system which involve representing concepts as a list of all their features; in vision, theories of pattern or object recognition in which the pattern is broken down into parts (features) and recognition is achieved by matching those features with stored representations of the features of known patterns or objects.

figure/ground segregation: the differentiation of a visual scene into those objects that are nearby (figure) and those that are further away (the ground); this involves deciding which contours on a 2-dimensional retinal image belong to which object.

filter: a device (e.g. neuron, mathematical function) that selectively extracts certain information from an image (e.g. edges).

filter model: a cognitive model in which the input from to-be-unattended stimuli is blocked only allowing relevant information to pass through to subsequent stages of processing.

first derivative: that part of an intensity function which is the difference in intensity between each point and its neighbour in a specified direction.

first mention effect: an effect found particularly in certain types of experiment where the first mentioned person or thing in a sentence is more readily available in memory than other people or things mentioned in the same sentence.

fixation: in vision, the mechanism by which the direction of eye gaze is fixed temporarily so that light from the viewed object falls on the centre of the fovea.

focal colour: the most typical shade of a particular colour.

forgetting rate: the speed at which memory decays over time.

formant transitions: changes in a formant's frequency over time which occur when the vocal-tract changes shape, as when it moves from a consonant into a vowel; formant transitions are important cues to the perception of both consonants and vowels.

formant: a resonant frequency of the vocal tract; different shapes of the vocal tract (as for articulating different vowels) have different formant frequencies.

fovea: the most central part of the retina.

fragment completion task: an experimental technique in which participants are given some letters of a word (e.g. as in a crossword) and asked to complete the sequence with the first word that comes to mind.

fragmentary hypothesis: the suggestion that learning that a set of stimuli come from the same category could occur by remembering fragments of the training stimuli and regarding new test stimuli as coming from the same category if they contain the same fragments.

free recall: attempting to remember information without any information about the learning period being provided.

frequency: the rate at which something repeats itself; it is a basic feature of sound.

function or "closed class" words: a finite set of words comprising of articles (e.g. the), prepositions (e.g. this), pronouns (e.g. they) and conjunctions (e.g. and) which serve specific grammatical functions within a language.

functional double dissociation: the finding that it is possible to manipulate two different aspects of a human performance selectively which implies to the researcher that the processes underlying them are separable (see double dissociation).

functional assignment: the process of assigning correct grammatical roles to the words that have been chosen for a particular utterance.

functional fixedness: an inability to solve a problem because of being stuck in seeing the use of objects only from one typical perspective, e.g. thinking of a hammer only as a means to hit nails into a wall rather than also as a heavy weight .

functional magnetic resonance imaging (fMRI): an extension of magnetic resonance imaging (MRI) to look at which functions are carried out in which part of the brain.

functional neuroimaging: any form of brain-imaging which attempts to look at which part of the brain specific cognitive functions are carried out in.

functional processing level: in models of speech production, a stage in which the the roles of the various people and objects are assigned in a way that relates to the words that will be used to describe them and the relations between them.

Fuzzy Logic Model of Perception: a model of perception proposed by Massaro that matches input features against stored templates using fuzzy logic; fuzzy logic represents the degree of match of features as real numbers between 0 and 1, rather than the conventional discrete truth values of 0 or 1.

galvanic skin response: a physiological measure of the change in electrical conductivity of the skin; this can provide clues about non-conscious processes and has been employed notably in the design of lie detectors.

gambler's fallacy: the belief that because, say, red has come up more frequently than black in the last few spins of a roulette wheel, the next spin is more likely to be black than red.

garden-path theory: a theory of parsing that claims that when faced with an ambiguity in the way a sentence might be structured, people commit to one option, and hence are sometimes "lead down the garden path".

generalisation: the process of extrapolation in behaviour, i.e. even though a rat may not have seen a particular stimulus, due to exposure to similar stimuli before, its response to this can be predictable.

generation-recognition: a theory of memory which proposes that the subject (usually unconsciously) generates a list of what could *possibly* have happened and then goes through this list until the to-be-remembered item is recognised.

generative grammar : a grammar that is written in such a way that its rules can be used to produce sentences.

geons: a finite set of basic shapes proposed by Biederman in his Recognition by Components Model of vision; according to the model, a combination of these geons can be used to construct any visual scene.

Gestalt Psychology: a school of psychology founded early in the 20th century which emphasized that in perception, the whole is more than the sum of its constituent parts.

gist: the general meaning, without any specific details, of a body of information.

goal state: the final desired stage when solving a particular problem.

grammar: an abstract system of rules that governs a language, e.g. when talking about a particular cat, one would use the term "the cat" whereas when talking about any cat, one would use the term "a cat" or "cats".

grapheme to phoneme correspondence rules: pronunciation rules that are learned through experience which allow an individual to see an unfamiliar string of letters, e.g. ZAPDAR and still pronounce it by breaking it into two familiar-looking strings (ZAP and DAR) for which pronunciation can be guessed at by their similarity to known words.

habit vs event memory: a distinction between memory for overly-learned skills (e.g. language and how to tie one's shoelaces) and memory for distinct episodes.

haptic perception: perception of touch/tactile information.

heterophone: a letter string (e.g. lead) which can be pronounced in more than one way.

heuristics: in problem-solving, rules of thumb, e.g. always taking the left-hand turn in a maze when attempting to leave.

hierarchy: a system with distinct levels with many systems at lower levels feeding into fewer systems at higher levels.

hill climbing strategy: a method of trying to solve a problem by reducing the difference between the solution and the current position at each step.

hippocampal formation: a part of the temporal lobes which has been shown to play a crucial role in the laying down of new memories.

homograph : a word (e.g. bank) which has more than one meaning depending on context (e.g. river bank Vs bank account).

homophone: a sound that can represent two words which have different spellings (e.g. "mail" and "male").

hypothetico-deductive method: a method of scientific investigation, suggested as a norm by Karl Popper, in which one forms a hypothesis, deduces a consequence of the hypothesis, and tests the consequence in an empirical study.

iconic memory: that part of sensory memory that holds visual memory for a very short period of time.

illusory correlation: the phenomenon of seeing a relation that one believes to exist, but which does not actually exist in the data one is looking at.

image files: the stores that contain the visual information about an object or concept.

implicit learning: learning which does not involve conscious knowledge of the skill or rule that is being learned/acquired.

implicit memory or indirect memory: memory which does not involve conscious awareness of the previous learning episode.

incubation: when attempting to solve a problem, the time spent actually not thinking about a problem.

individual differences: discrepancies between different participants in a study; this may be just personal characteristics, e.g. intelligence, or it may be actual performance on the experimental task.

inductive vs deductive reasoning: inductive reasoning goes beyond the information given (e.g. from the observation of many white swans to the conclusion that all swans are white) whereas deductive reasoning brings out the certain consequences of what is already known.

infantile amnesia: the robust finding that few people can remember many events from the first few years life, typically up to age 6.

inference: the process of deriving additional information from what is explicitly stated; also used to refer to the piece of information that the process produces.

inflection: the particular ending of a word which can change its meaning, e.g. walk*ing* as opposed to walk*ed*.

information buffer: the part of a computer that holds information temporarily before it can be processed by the next stage of processing.

information processing system: a system which receives data as input, manipulates it internally and then produces an output.

information stores: the parts of a computer that keep permanent records of information provided to the system.

inhibition of return: the slowing down of eye movements to a location that had just previously been fixated.

innate language mechanism: the idea put forth by some linguists that children inherit a specific ability to learn a language .

inner speech or subvocalisation: the process of saying things to oneself without overt use of the vocal apparatus; i.e. speaking silently to oneself.

insight: the sudden ability to see the solution to a problem without going through any obvious intermediate steps in solving the problem.

instance theory: a theory put forward by Logan that we can become better at performing a task because we store memories of previous instances of dealing with situations encountered in the task; those memories contain the correct response to the situation so the correct response does not need to be worked out but instead just pops into our minds automatically.

intelligence: the ability to solve problems that require some form of thought; this does not necessarily have to be academic intelligence, e.g. one can have social intelligence.

intensity map: a representation of an image as an array or 'map' of numbers, in which each number represents the intensity at the corresponding location in the image.

interactive activation: a type of process, found for example, in models of word identification, in which detectors (e.g. for letters and words) become partially activated by evidence from the world and then interact to determine a final solution to the problem (e.g. "what word is this?").

intermediate effect: in problem-solving, the finding that experts can look at only part of the information regarding a problem (i.e. an intermediate amount) and can still remember more information than novices who see the same amount of information.

interposition: a monocular depth cue that arises when one's view of a far object is partially blocked by a nearer object.

intrinsic/interactive context or context beta: features that are an integral part of a target stimulus, e.g. the words that one associates with a particular word .

introspectionism: the study of mental processes using one's own self-study as opposed to observation of others' behaviours.

intrusions: recall of information that was not part of the original learning set but which may have come from another learning experience.

irregularity (in pronunciation): the fact that in some languages, (e.g. English), some words may not follow regular pronunciation rules, e.g. the string INT is not pronounced in PINT in the same way as it is regularly pronounced in the words MINT and LINT.

isomorphism: literally "same shape", an isomorphism exists when the structure of one system can be mapped one-to-one to the structure of another system; gestalt psychologists used this principal to suggest that a neurophysiological event has the same structure as the mental state it is trying to represent, e.g. a continuous dimension such as depth will be represented by continuous electrical activity.

lack of invariance problem: this describes the fact that the vowel and consonant phonemes of speech do not have a constant sound with underlying causes including: co-articulation, differences between speakers in head size and in dialect, and elisions arising in rapid speech.

language as symbolic representation: the idea that language is actually independent of what it represents and is therefore symbolic of that representation; the word "cat" merely represents the concept of "catness" but this could be just as easily presented by the symbol pronounced "zar" without it affecting the actual concept being represented.

language acquisition: the process of learning language during childhood (without specific tuition) .

late closure: a rule of parsing stating that, when the next word in a sentence can be part of the current phrase, it should be taken to be part of that phrase, and not an earlier one or a following one; part of the garden path theory of parsing.

late recognition effect: in speech processing, the finding that the recognition of a word can occur due to information that is provided later on in the spoken utterance; the effect of these contextual cues shows the meaning of words does not have to be extracted immediately upon hearing the word .

late selection: a model of attention in which a decision regarding which information will receive further processing is made after all stimuli has undergone meaningful processing.

lemmas: in language processing, the representations that contain information regarding a word's class, e.g. noun, verb, adjective, etc.

letter-identification span: the area of current fixation from which letter-information can be extracted.

Levels of Processing (LOP): a theory of memory that suggests that the likelihood of remembering a stimulus will be directly proportional to the depth of processing (e.g. structural versus semantic) that it received on presentation.

lexemes: in language processing, information about how a word sounds.

lexical access: in reading, the process of looking for a word in one's mental dictionary to find information concerning meaning.

lexical decision (task): a experimental paradigm in which participants are presented with letter strings (e.g. CAT or DAX) and asked to decide whether or not the string is a real word.

lexical entry: the representation of a word in one's mental lexicon.

lexical frame theory: a theory of parsing according to which information about the structures in which verbs occur guides the choice of structure assigned to a sentence.

lexical route vs GPC route: two different hypothetical routes to reading a word, one of which requires accessing the lexical entry for a word in one's lexicon whereas the other relies on using learned grapheme to phoneme correspondence rules to sound out the constituent elements to a word.

lexical selection: the process of selecting the correct words for a particular utterance.

limited capacity channel: an information-processing channel that can only hold a finite amount of data; if this is exceeded, the extra data may be lost.

linear perspective: a monocular depth cue arising from parallel lines viewed at an angle: they converge toward a vanishing point as they recede into the distance.

local representativeness: a heuristic according to which one assumes that the lcoal characteristics of something (e.g. a few coin tosses in a longer sequence) are representative of the whole.

local vs global levels in text representation (microstructure vs. macrostructure): representations of local structure (microstructure) encode relations between bits of information close together in the text whilst representations of global structure (macrostructure) encode relations between larger portions of the text.

logogen: the hypothetical representation of a word which can be activated by any encounter with that concept, e.g. its spoken form, its printed form or seeing an object .

logogen model: a model of reading proposed by Morton in which each word has a representation, a logogen, containing information about the physical appearance of a word.

long-term recency: the finding that recency effects (better recall of the most recent items in a list) can extend over long periods of time and can be for items that are no longer thought to be in short-term memory; this finding challenged the suggestion of recency being a result of the outpouring of information from short-term memory.

long-term store (LTS): the last stage of the multistore model where information can be held for an indefinite period of time, maybe even a whole lifetime.

magnetic resonance imaging (MRI): a form of brain-imaging which uses microscopic magnetic properties of brain tissue to look (only) at the structure of the brain.

manner of articulation: consonants that are produced with different types of constriction of the vocal tract, or with different voice-onset times, are said to have different manners of articulation; manner of articulation is independent of place of articulation—therefore, the sounds /s/, /z/, /t/, /d/ have different manners of articulation but similar places of articulation.

McGurk Effect: this is the name given to an illusion which illustrates the profound effect that seen articulatory movements have on the perception of speech in normal listeners who are not aware of any ability to lip-read, e.g. someone hearing the sound /ba/ while seeing someone's lip movements for /ga/, would report hearing /da/.

means-ends analysis: a problem-solving strategy which involves finding out the difference between the current state and the final goal state and then devising actions to reduce this difference as much as possible.

memory organisation packets (MOPs): generalised representations of particular action-sequences in Schank's Dynamic Theory of Memory; a MOP (e.g. going to see a film) is an organisational structure which allows groups of scenes (e.g. go to box office, pay for ticket, find a seat you like) to be combined such that some of the scenes (e.g. going to the box office) can be shared with other MOPs (e.g. going to the opera) but others cannot (e.g. at an opera, one usually has assigned seating and so you can't sit wherever you want).

memory span: the number of singly presented digits that a person can recall in the same order as their original presentation; this is a hallmark of short-term memory.

memory trace: the physical representation stored in the brain of an experienced event.

mental fluency: the term given to any range of tasks that requires a subject to show the ability to process information as quickly and efficiently as possible, e.g. name as many countries beginning with the letter A within a minute.

mental images: the subjective picture one has in mind when asked to imagine something.

mental lexicon: one's hypothetical internal dictionary which stores information about all the words that an individual has encountered thus far.

mental model: a mental representation of any idea, e.g. when told that Eric is bigger than Mike, one can set up a mental model of two people, one larger than the other to represent this proposition.

mental rotation: the spatial manipulation of an internal mental image, e.g. rotating the image of a chair seen from the front so that the back can now be seen.

mere exposure effect: the tendency for people to like stimuli simply because they have been exposed to them previously, e.g. the way people can come to like a pop song just because they have heard it a few times on the radio.

message level: the speaker's intended meaning when making an utterance.

minimal attachment: a rule of parsing stating that, when faced with a choice of two or more structures for part of a sentence, the simplest should be chosen; it is part of the garden path theory of parsing.

minimal core encoding: within Levels of Processing theory, the notion that any exposure to a stimulus will involve a minimal but finite degree of semantic processing; it is semantic processing above and beyond this minimal core amount that causes increases in retrieval of material processed according to semantic rather than shallow orienting tasks.

mnemonics: any of a range of memory aids which uses mental imagery in an attempt to improve one's memory.

models: suggestions about how certain cognitive functions (e.g. recognition of a familiar face) occurs by hypothesizing a coherent set of processes needed to undertake the task.

modularity: the viewpoint that the cognitive system is composed of individual systems for particular functions (e.g. language and memory) which together carry out another bigger function, e.g. communication.

monocular cue to depth: in vision, a cue to depth perception which can be derived simply from the input to one eye.

mood congruency: the similarity in mood states between the learning environment and the testing enviroment.

mood induction: an experimental manipulation in which the subject's emotional state is influenced by the experimenter, e.g. by giving them an impossible set of general knowledge questions to try to make the subject feel less intelligent and worthless.

morpheme: the smallest unit of language that has any meaning, e.g. "s" at the end of a word usually implies plurality.

motion parallax: a monocular cue to depth whereby the relative speed of moving objects past an observer is used to infer depth, e.g. when an aeroplane is landing, the airport buildings next to the runway seem to be moving past much quicker than the buildings outside the airport but since they are both stationary, this relative motion is a cue that the buildings outside are further away .

motor skills: skills used in physical actions, e.g. riding a bicycle or tieing one's shoelaces.

motor theory of speech perception: a theory of speech perception that claims to reduce the lack of invariance problem and to explain categorical perception by postulating that listeners perceive, when listening in a special speech mode, the motor commands that lead to speech rather than the sounds themselves.

Müller-Lyer Illusion: a geometrical illusion in which the apparent length of long horizontal lines is distorted by the presence of arrow-head shapes attached at the ends of the lines.

multistore model: an early model of human memory which suggested three separate serial stages and stores of processing.

nativism: the doctrine that human or animal abilities are inherited at birth as opposed to learned through experience.

nature-nurture debate: a longstanding debate concerned with whether human characteristics or behaviour are inherited (nature) or learned through experience (nurture).

Necker Cube: a line-drawing of a cube which can be viewed reversibly in one of two different ways; this shows the ability of the cognitive system to take the same

piece of information and arrive at a number of different interpretations.

negative priming: the worsening of performance on a task caused by presentation of related information prior to presentation of the target stimulus.

negative recency effect: items at the end of a list being remembered very well but then on later testing being recalled more poorly than earlier items from the list.

network theory: the theory that memory can be conceived of as a set of inter-connecting ideas (or "nodes") and activation passes between the nodes along the connecting links; once an idea exceeds a threshold amount of activation it enters consciousness and is retrieved.

neurological specificity: the suggestion that different cognitive functions are carried out in different separable regions of the brain.

neurotransmitters: specialized chemicals in the brain that effectively carry messages from one nerve to another.

nomotheism: an attempt to derive general laws of behaviour by studying individuals using the assumption that each individual is representative of the general population.

non-accidental properties: unusual properties of an image (e.g. collinearity) that are used in Biederman's RBC model to identify the parts of an object present in an image; they are 'non-accidental' because they are very unlikely to have arisen by chance alone).

nonword superiority effect: if a letter is embedded in a nonword that is pronounceable (e.g. ZARD), its identification is much better than if it is presented in a nonword that is not pronounceable (e.g. ZNRO).

normal science vs revolutionary science: the distinction between science that conforms to a particular paradigm and that which is "created" when enough anomalies in traditional approaches require a radical change in viewpoint.

normalisation: a process of transforming an image into a standard form, such as a standard size, position, or contrast.

object centred: a representation of an object and its parts in terms of the intrinsic structure of the object, and independent of viewpoint.

object constancy: the fact that objects are not seen as ever-changing even though our view of them might be changing because of our position relative to them, different lighting conditions, etc.

oculomotor theory: a theory of reading which states that a saccadic eye-movement is made to the next word as soon as the word being fixated on has been recognised.

on-line vs off-line measures: a distinction between measurements taken as something as it happens (on-line) and those taken after it has already happened (off-line).

on-line vs off-line measures of comprehension: on-line measures of comprehension are measures taken while a person is reading a text (typically reading times or other reaction times); off-line measures are taken after the text has been read (e.g. answering a question about it, or writing a continuation).

operant conditioning: the process of training a subject to emit an action (e.g. pressing a lever) in order to obtain a particular form of reward.

optic array: a term introduced by gibson to describe the pattern of light reaching a point in space (usually an observer's eye) from all directions.

optic flow: the fluctuating pattern of light in the optic array that results from relative motion between the observer and the environment.

optimal viewing position: the suggestion that for every word, there is a fixation point (along the word) which will allow the reader to obtain the most information about the word itself .

orienting tasks: instructions to participants in an experiment to pay attention to one particular dimension (e.g. category membership) of a presented stimulus.

orthography: the visual characteristics of letters making up a particular word.

paired associate learning (PA): learning of a link between two unrelated words such that later presentation of one of the words will make the subject produce the other.

paradigm shift: a radical change in the way a particular issue is viewed, e.g. changing from seeing human behaviour from a behaviourist standpoint to seeing it from a cognitive one.

parafovea -an area around the central fovea of the retina which extends 5 degrees either side of the point of current fixation.

parallel distributed processing (PDP) or connectionism: a way of modelling psychological processes based on the way the brain (rather than a normal personal computer) carries out computations; the model consists of a set of units (analagous to neurones) that can be active to some degree with activation being passed between units through connecting weights (similar to neural connections) and the strength of the weights being changeable according to fixed rules (this is how learning occurs).

parsing: the process of working out the structure of sentences.

partial report technique: an experimental technique in which, having been shown a visual display, a subject is asked to report back just a portion of it, e.g. all the items on the left-hand side.

passive (storage): the suggestion that in long-term memory, information is stored in a non-active way for very long periods of time.

path constraints: the restrictions when attempting to solve a problem, e.g. time or space allotted.

pattern masking or central masking: in visual memory research, the disruption of the to-be-remembered information by following it with an array comprising lines of similar thickness / pattern; the fact that the mask could be presented to the eye that didn't receive the initial stimulus shows that information on patterns is being processed after data from the two eyes has been brought together centrally in the brain.

pattern recognition: the act of comparing a currently viewed pattern with internal stored representations of patterns, for the purpose of recognising the viewed pattern as an instance of a stored pattern.

percept: the internal representation of information (gathered through one of the senses) of an external stimulus; this is processed further to allow indentification.

perception is reconstructive: the idea that what we end up experiencing of an external stimulus has been built up through a succession of stages using many inferential processes.

perceptual learning: learning which involves a perceptual stimulus, e.g. a face, which will enable one to recognise the same stimulus more quickly on a subsequent exposure.

periphery: the area beyond the parafovea on the retina; it is the external part of the visual field and is not being fixated upon.

permission schema: one of the schema postulated by the pragmatic reasoning hypothesis, which contains information such as "if you satisfy a condition, you may perform an action".

perseveration: a synonym for behavioural rigidity which refers to the inability of a subject to disengage from a task that they are carrying out, e.g. continuing to wash the dishes over and over again even though they are already clean.

phonemes: the individual component sounds of words which need to be coalesced to say the word whole.

phonemic code: the sound patterns, stored with the representation of a word in the lexicon, which consitute the whole word's pronunciation.

phonemic restoration effect: the phenomenon in hearing, whereby if the sound of a consonant is removed from a sentence and replaced by noise, listeners are unable to identify which consonant was replaced, hearing the speech as continuous behind the intruding noise.

phonological confusion effect: the finding that recall of a list of items will be reduced if the items have similar sounds (e.g. C, V and E) than if they do not (e.g. R, T and N).

phonological level: the level during making an utterance when the constituent sounds of words are assembled and then produced.

phonological loop: a refinement of the older articulatory loop first proposed by Baddeley & Hitch as part of their Working Memory model.

phonological store: the part of the phonological loop within the Working Memory model which stores speech-based information.

phonology: the sound of a particular word.

phrase structure grammar (PSG): a type of grammar that includes rules showing how phrases are constructed from smaller units (words and shorter phrases).

pitch: the subjective experience of the frequency of a sound; as the frequency of a sound increases, the pitch will sound more sharp.

place of articulation: for a consonant, this describes where the mouth is constricted in order to produce it, e.g. / p / and / b / are produced by constricting the vocal tract at the lips (bilabial) whereas / t / and / d / are produced at the teeth ridge (alveolar).

Ponzo Illusion: a geometrical illusion in which converging vertical lines surrounding shorter horizontal lines alter the apparent relative length of the horizontal lines.

positional level: in models of speech production, a stage in which the phonological forms of the words are selected and entered into a frame that specifies their positions in the sentence.

positive priming: the faster response to a target stimulus if it had just previously been ignored.

positive reinforcement: rewarding a behaviour such that the likelihood of that behaviour being emitted again increases.

positron emission tomography (PET): a form of brain-imaging which looks at which parts of the brain are most active when it is performing particular tasks.

Posner Matching Task: an experimental paradigm in which participants have to decide whether or not two letters are the same (e.g. CC) or different (e.g. CD); different manipulations (e.g. whether or not each letter is in upper or lower case) and different cues given before the presentation of stimuli can allow insights into attentional processes.

practice: repetition of a task which eventually results in improved performance.

pragmatic reasoning hypothesis: the claim that in reasoning about hypotheses we use schemata, for example, about permissions or about causation, that help us with particular problems, but not with similarly structured problems in a different domain.

pragmatics: the branch of linguistics that studies those aspects of the meaning of expressions that depend on the context in which they are used.

precategorical: the finding that in sensory memory, the information has not received any coding, e.g. into different letters or numbers, and therefore is in a very raw form.

preparation: the initial stage of problem-solving which involves reflecting on the situation without attempting any moves towards a solution.

primacy effect: the enchanced recall (relative to later items) of the earliest items in a list of stimuli.

Primal Sketch: part of David Marr's theory of early spatial vision, in which images are represented in terms of a small set of primitive features such as bars, edges, and blobs.

primary memory: memory of the most recent moments.

priming effect: the easier processing of a stimulus caused by the prior presentation of related information.

principal axis: in marr's theory of vision, the principal axis of an object provides the frame of reference to which all the object's parts are related; it usually corresponds to the object's axis of elongation or of symmetry.

probe digit task: a memory task in which a subject is presented with a continuous series of individual numbers and at some point is presented with one of the numbers (the probe digit) and asked to report the number that preceded it in the series.

problem reduction: in problem-solving, breaking down the task into a set of smaller more manageable sub-problems.

problem space: all the different permutations that are possible when attempting to solve a problem.

procedural memory: memory for actions, e.g. how to ride a bicycle.

process dissociation framework: an experimental paradigm in which the researcher tries to differentiate items that the subject consciously remembers and those that they merely have a sense of familiarity with.

processing domain: within the Levels of Processing framework, a discrete form of information processing (e.g. semantic) which contrasts with the earlier notions in which processing could occur anywhere along a continuum from very shallow (e.g. are any English letters involved in the stimulus) to very deep (e.g. how does this stimulus make me feel emotionally?) .

propositional files: stores that contain propositional or semantic (i.e. modality-independent) information about objects or concepts.

propositions: statements with declarative meaning which can either be true or false.

prototypes: the most characteristic exemplars of a category (e.g. robins are prototypical birds).

psychogenic or functional amnesia: memory loss with no known physical origin, caused usually by a highly emotionally traumatic event.

punishment: an event (e.g. mild electric shock) that discourages a subject from emitting the same response (e.g. bar pressing) again.

race model: a cognitive model in which there is more than one route to achieve an outcome resulting in a competition between the two routes to succeed most quickly.

random dot stereograms: a pair of random patterns of dots which when viewed such that one pattern falls only on the left eye and the other only on the right eye, a figure with depth can be seen.

reaction time: the time gap between a subject being presented a stimulus and their response to it.

recency effect: the finding that most recent items in a list of stimuli tend to be recalled more accurately than other items in the list.

Recognition by Components model (RBC): a model of object recognition based on structural descriptions, first proposed by Biederman.

recognition: a technique used in memory research in which the subject is given a list of possibilities and asked to choose the correct one, e.g. as in a multiple choice test.

reconstructive process: the concept within memory research that recall involves actively piecing together what the to-be-remembered event *could* have been rather than simply retrieving one particular representation of that event.

reduction mnemonic: a simple short-hand way of remembering information by reducing it to a shorter grouping such as an acronym.

referential links: connections within the cognitive system which allow related concepts to activate one another during processing.

regional cerebral blood flow: a measure of how much blood is flowing through a particular area of the brain while it is performing a specific task; the assumption is that highly active areas of the brain will need more oxygyen for processing which will require an increase in the amount of blood flowing in that area.

regressions: the movement of the eyes from right to left during reading which is contrary to the usual left-right direction of reading English.

rehearsal: a mechanism of repeating information in an attempt to remember it for longer.

reinforcement history: the prior pattern of reward and punishment which can together predict future behaviour.

remember (R) vs know (K): experimental terms to differentiate items that a subject can consciously recall having seen before and those that they just have a sense of familiarity with without being able to remember when they might have experienced them.

Remote Associations Test: a test in which subjects are shown three words, with their task being to provide a word that goes with all three of the target words.

repetition priming: the finding that participants tend to perform better on tasks involving stimuli that they had recently been exposed to, relative to new stimuli, irrespective of whether or not they consciously recall having seen the words before.

representativeness heuristic: a heuristic for judging class membership based on the similarity between something and a prototypical member of a class to which it might belong.

repression: a term from Freudian psychology that suggests that forgetting is caused because a subject has had an emotionally traumatic experience which makes them unconsciously block access to that information.

resonant frequencies: when an enclosed body of air (such as the vocal tract) is excited by sound, some frequencies are amplified more than others, the ones being amplified most being called the resonant frequencies; most people have noticed the effect of resonance when singing in a tiled bathroom: particular notes will be amplified at the resonant frequencies of the bathroom, thereby flattering the singer.

resource limitation models: models that explain the interference that occurs between two simultaneously performed tasks by assuming that the tasks both require the use of a common resource limited in supply; the resource may be conceived of as general purpose, needed for any task that is performed with concentration, or as a specific type, required for example, just for visual tasks.

retrieval strategies: mechanisms for accessing information that has been stored in the long-term store.

retrieval structures: particularly in chess playing, memory representations of a set of templates which might correspond to, for example, the style of play of a particular player.

retrograde amnesia: difficulty in remembering information that was acquired before a patient became ill or brain-damaged.

Ribot's Law: the relative difficulty in remembering very recent pre-injury memories as opposed to more distant pre-injury ones.

rule-based theories of reasoning: theories that claim than reasoning is performed using mental representations of logical rules, such as the rule of *modus ponens* (if A then B, A, therefore B).

saccade: in reading, the movement from one point of fixation to the next.

saccadic suppression: the effective blindess that one experiences when making a saccade; this is caused by the fact that the eyes are temporarily not being fixated on any point.

savings: the decrease in time or effort that a subject requires to relearn or recognise a previously presented stimulus.

savings method: an experimental technique in which participants are presented the same stimuli a number of times and the reduction in effort required to learn or identify the stimulus on each new presentation is measured as the "effort saved".

schema: an organized mental model of a complex set of information; this model will make it easier to structure information when setting it down for memory storage and will also facilitate its retrieval during recall.

scopolamine: a drug known to block the action of acetylcholine; used in research to investigate the role played by the latter in memory functioning.

script: part of schema theory involving the actions that are normally involved in a particular event (e.g. the various stages of having a meal at a restaurant).

secondary memory: memory of the past extending beyond the most recent moments.

segmentation: the ability of the human hearing and speech recognition systems to separate a continuous stream of speech into the individual words intended by the speaker.

selection task: a task invented by Peter Wason, in which subjects are shown one face each of four cards that have a letter on one side and a number on the other; subjects have to say which cards must be turned over to see if they all obey a rule such as "if there is a vowel on one side, there is an even number on the other side".

selective (amnesia): in amnesia research, the finding that the memory loss is for specific types of information rather than everything that the person ever knew.

selective attention: the process of attending to just one or a range of stimuli whilst excluding other stimuli.

selective filter: a mechanism which only allows certain information to pass onto subsequent stages; the rule for selection can be varied, e.g. depending on physical characteristics.

semantic priming effect: a priming effect caused when meaningfully-related information is presented prior to the presentation of the target stimulus.

semantics: the meaning evoked by a word.

sensory memory: the form of memory that holds primary perceptual memory for a very short period of time and which has a very limited capacity.

sensory registers: the first stage of the multistore model where information from the different sense organs (e.g. primary visual information) is held very briefly before being passed onto the next stage for processing.

sentence verification task: an experimental paradigm in which a participant has to judge whether the content of a sentence is true or not.

serial position curve: a graph showing the probability (or accuracy) of recall of individual items from a finite set of stimuli as a function of which position in the list they were initially presented.

serial processing model: any model of cognitive processing in which information needs to be processed in discrete stages where each stage passes its output to the following stage for further computation.

serial vs parallel processing: the distinction between systems where information from one stage is passed onto the next for further processing (serial) and one in which many processors work at the same time on separate aspects of information before passing it onto the next stage (parallel).

set of operators: the steps that one can use when attempting to solve a problem.

shadowing: part of an experimental paradigm in which the subject is required to repeat aloud a message heard in one of the two ears.

shape constancy- the ability to see the correct shape of an object despite current visual information from any angle varying, e.g. if looking at a wine bottle from above, one might see two concentric circles for the neck and the base of the bottle but this does not change our notion of the shape of the bottle itself.

short-term store (STS): the second stage of the multistore model where information can be held for a few seconds and depending on its importance, can be passed onto the third stage of the model.

situation model: a mental representation of part of the world (situation) used in language comprehension and problem-solving .

size constancy: the ability to see objects retain their size despite their visual images drastically changing size with distance, e.g. on a snowscape, if two similar cars are seen, one looking much bigger than the other, our knowledge that these cars are likely to be similar in size allows us to compute the relative distance from them rather than thinking that one car is much bigger than the other.

skip reading: a method of reading in which the reader misses either parts or even whole sentences since they are simply trying to get the gist of what is written.

spacing effect: the finding that having activities between a number of different presentations of a word will increase memory of that word more than if there were no activities between presentations.

span of apprehension: the amount of information that it is possible for a subject to take on at any one time before reaching overload.

spatial location: the physical position in space of a stimulus.

spatial medium: a hypothetical cognitive medium in which spatial thought, e.g. mental rotation can occur.

spectrogram: a graph that shows how much energy is present at particular frequencies over time; time is plotted on the abscissa (x-axis), frequency on the ordinate (y-axis) and the amount of energy at a particular time and frequency is represented by a grey-scale: the blacker the point, the more energy.

speech act: act performed by saying something, such as making a promise or marrying someone by saying "I do".

spillover effect: in reading, the phenomenon whereby if a low frequency word (e.g. zebra) precedes a high frequency word (e.g. ran), then the latter will be fixated for a shorter duration than if it is preceded by another high frequency word (e.g. cat).

split-span task: an experimental paradigm in which participants are presented digits to the two ears simultaneously and have to subsequently report back as many of the digits as possible.

spoonerisms: a speech error in which phonemes from two or more words are produced in the wrong sequence creating a new somewhat meaningful sentence.

starting state: the initial situation in a given problem that needs to be solved.

state action tree: a diagrammatic representation of all the possible states that one could go through while attempting to solve a problem.

state-dependent memory: a form of environment dependent memory in which the subject's physiological state (which can be altered with, for example, drugs) can influence whether or not they will remember information accurately.

stereopsis: a binocular cue to depth resulting from the fact that the two eyes are slightly displaced from one another and will therefore have different perspectives of objects, particularly those close by; this discrepancy is a cue to depth.

stimulus onset asynchrony (SOA): the time between the presentation of a prime and the stimulus that the subject needs to make a response to.

stochastically independent: two tasks are stochastically independent (over items) if knowing how well a person did for some material on one task allows no prediction of how well the perrson did on that material on the other task.

stopped consonant: a consonant that is produced when airflow through the mouth is stopped either by the use of the tongue (e.g. in /d/) or the closing of the lips (e.g. in /p/).

stranding: a speech error in which the correct inflection of a word remains but the root of the word is transposed to another word; this type of error suggests that inflection information is independent of the lemma that is activated for a word.

strategies: systematic plans used to solve a particular problem.

strategy-tactics model: a model of reading which proposes that individuals can have varying methods of reading depending on their own abilities and expertise.

Stroop Effect: the finding that the naming of the colour in which a word is written is slowed down if the word itself is the name of a different colour, e.g. saying that the word WHITE is written in black ink.

structural description: a description of an object in terms of its parts and the relations between those parts.

structural descriptions as propositions: abstract symbolic representations of structural descriptions in terms of a list or propositions, that could be expressed in words.

structural neuroimaging: any form of brain-imaging technique which is concerned with looking at the anatomical structures of the brain.

structural similarities : in analogical problem-solving, similarities between the underlying structure of the problem to be solved and the underlying structure of the problem being used as an analogy to find the solution.

sub-vocal rehearsal process: a mechanism within the phonological loop that allows recycling of speech-based material but without involvement of overt vocal processes.

subliminal perception: nonconscious processing of a stimulus which only reveals itself in subsequent behaviour by the subject; the subject is not aware of the prior exposure to the stimulus.

subliminal priming: priming which occurs when a person is exposed to a stimulus so briefly that they can sincerely claim they do not believe that they saw anything; nonetheless, their behaviour is influenced by the meaning of the stimulus.

subordinate: at a lower level.

substitution error: an mistake in speech production where one produces a word that is related to the target word, e.g. "sword" instead of "dagger".

superordinate: at a higher level.

Supervisory Activating System (SAS): a hypothetical structure in Norman & Shallice's model of attention which is activated whenever routine selection of behaviour is no longer appropriate, e.g. if the person finds themselves in an unfamiliar environment.

supraspan: in memory research, presenting the subject with a list of items that is longer than the supposed capacity of short-term memory (typically seven plus or minus two items).

surface dyslexia vs phonological dyslexia: two forms of reading problems (acquired through brain injury) which render the person able to use only the surface grapheme to phoneme correspondence rules (surface dyslexia) or only the lexical access route which has information about words that the person has already encountered and pronounced before (phonological dyslexia); the former have problems with irregularly spelt words while the latter have problems with nonwords which by definition have no lexical entry.

surface similarities: the superficial things that two objects or situations may have in common, e.g. their overall shape.

syllogism: a type of deductive reasoning problem with two premises relating three terms one of which is eliminated from the conclusion (e.g. all cats are mammals, all mammals are vertebrates, so all cats are vertebrates).

symbol: a code (e.g. a heiroglyphic) to represent something else (e.g. the concept of a cat).

syntax: a branch of linguistics dealing with how sentences are structured out of words and phrases.

tabula rasa: the standpoint that the human brain begins as a "clean slate" with no information on it which then learns through experience.

template theories: simple theories of pattern recognition in which the image is compared to a stored copy or template of the image.

templates : particularly in chess playing, memory representations of arrangements of pieces (e.g. an opening gambit) that can be used to decide what move to make.

temporal lobes: a major part of the brain situated to the sides roughly from the area of ones temples extending back towards the ears; this area is heavily implicated in memory processes.

test awareness criterion: a checking procedure used in implicit memory research which compares performance of those participants, who were, and those who were not, aware of the link between previous exposure to the stimuli and the learning test itself.

texture gradient: in vision, the change in retinal size and density of information from a visual scene which can act as a monocular cue to depth; for example, looking from the top of a building at a carpark, some cars will look much smaller than others but since generally cars tend to have roughly similar sizes, the ones that look very small are likely to be at a greater depth, i.e. further away.

thematic organisation units (TOPS): an organisational level within Schank's Dymanic Theory of Memory which allowed general thematic information to be available for understanding and remembering events; thus for example, as well as the MOPs that would be involved in the different situations of reading a book and seeing a piece of art, common themes (e.g. strength and power) would allow links to be made through the TOPs.

think-aloud protocol method: in problem-solving research, asking subjects to verbalise each stage of their attempt to find a solution; this protocol can be studied to look at problem-solving structures.

three-term series problem: a type of reasoning problem based on relations, such as "is longer than", in which three people or objects are related to each other, e.g. "A is more expensive than B, B is more expensive than C, so A is more expensive than C".

threshold model: any model in which a certain amount of activity, the threshold level, has to be reached to activate subsequent stages, e.g. as in word recognition in Morton's logogen model of reading.

tip of the tongue state: in speech, the inability to produce a particular word while having the feeling that one actually knows the word; often, the person has some knowledge of the word without being able to produce the word itself.

top-down inferences: the use of prior knowledge to interpret potentially ambiguous situations, e.g. using the fact that most humans are of similar height to infer that a person who looks very small is probably further away than one that looks larger.

total (amnesia): in memory research, the folklore idea of amnesia making a person lose memory for all information that they ever knew; this is seldom the case.

Tower of Hanoi: a popular task used in problem-solving research, based on an ancient Buddhist puzzle which involves the movement of an array of differently sized disks between a number of pegs using a number of constraints.

Trace Model: a connectionist model of speech recognition proposed by McClelland and Elman in 1986 that represents features, phonemes and words at different levels; it has excitatory connections between levels and inhibitory connections within levels.

trans-saccadic memory: in reading, the memory required for storing information from a number of successive fixations of a piece of text since the information from one individual fixation is seldom enough.

trans-situational identity assumption: the view that when activating one particular aspect of a word's meaning in a given situation, all other aspects of that word's representation are also activated and will be available in a subsequent situation and can therefore affect behaviour.

transfer appropriate processing: the notion that the processing operations optimally performed during the encoding of a stimulus are those that match the processing operations to be performed during retrieval; e.g. if the test is asking what word rhymes with "cat", the optimal training procedure is one that emphasizes attention to rhyme.

transformational grammar: a type of grammar in which, in addition to phrase structure rules, there are rules (called transformations) that convert one type of sentence into another (e.g. active into passive).

transformational rules in syntax rules for producing one type of sentence from another (e.g. a question from the corresponding statement: "Did John go to bed?" from "John went to bed").

trial and error: in problem-solving, attempting to reach a solution by attempting a solution, making mistakes, learning from the mistakes and then attempting a new solution maybe using feedback from the first attempt.

typicality effect: the finding that judgements to decisions involving very common exemplars of a category (e.g. a robin being a bird) are made more quickly than those involving less common exemplars (e.g. turkey).

utilisation behaviour: the phenomenon sometimes reported in patients with frontal lobe lesions wherby they will attempt to grasp at objects that have been placed near them without any instruction to do so.

verbal protocols: written reports of what a subject said or did when performing a task.

viewer centred: a representation of an image or object that is specific to the particular viewpoint of the observer .

visual neglect: a disorder caused by brain injury which leaves the patient unable to show an understanding of objects placed in parts of the visual field; it is a complex disorder which can affect the right side of space as well as the left side and in most cases tends to be only a temporary impairment.

visual search task: an experimental paradigm in which subjects are presented, either on a computer screen or on paper, with an array of stimuli which contains targets which need to be detected.

visuo-spatial scratch pad: a part of Baddeley & Hitch's Working Memory model which deals with short-term visual information, primarily using the spatial characteristics of the stimulus.

voice onset time (VOT): The time interval between the release of a stop consonant (e.g. the parting of the lips in /p/) and the start of voicing (the vibration of the vocal chords).

Whorf Hypothesis: a linguistic theory that suggests that the language that a person uses will affect their perception and the way they think.

whole report: in visual memory research, the situation in which following presentation of a stimulus, the subject is asked to report as much of the display as possible.

word envelope: the shape of a word, when written in lower case letters, defined in terms of whether each letter has an ascending stroke (e.g. b, d, f, etc.) a descending stroke (e.g. g, j, p, etc.) or neither.

word identification span: a subset of the letter-identification span (within visual fixation) from which word identification can occur.

word length effect: the finding in short-term memory research that more words of shorter spoken duration are remembered than words of longer duration.

word superiority effect: if a letter is embedded in a briefly-presented string of letters, its subsequent recognition will be much more accurate if the string was a real word as opposed to a non-word.

Working Memory: a model of short-term memory put forward initially by Baddeley & Hitch.

zero-crossing: a place in the output image of a filter where the filter's response changes from positive to negative, or vice-versa.

References

Abernethy, E.M. (1940). The effect of changed environmental conditions upon the results of college examinations. *Journal of Psychology, 10,* 293–301.

Allport, A. (Ed.) (1993). *Attention and control: Have we been asking the wrong questions? A critical review of twenty-five years.* (Vol. XIV). London: MIT Press.

Allport, D.A., Antonis, B., & Reynolds, P. (1972). On the division of attention: A disproof of the single channel hypothesis. *Quarterly Journal of Experimental Psychology, 24*(2), 225–235.

Allport, G.W. (1924). Eidetic imagery. *British Journal of Psychology, 15,* 99–120.

Altmann, G.T.M. (1998). Ambiguity in sentence processing. *Trends in Cognitive Sciences, 2,* 146–152.

Altmann, G.T.M., van Nice, K.Y., Garnham, A., & Henstra, J.-A. (1998). Late closure in context. *Journal of Memory and Language, 38,* 459–484.

Anderson, J.R., & Bower, G.H. (1972). *Human Associative Memory.* Washington, DC: Winston.

Anderson, R.C., & Pichert, J. (1978). Recall of previously unrecallable information following a shift in perspective. *Journal of Verbal Learning and Verbal Behavior, 17,* 1–12.

Arkes, H.R., & Harkness, A.R. (1983). Estimates of contingency between two dichotomous variables. *Journal of Experimental Psychology: General, 112,* 117–135.

Armstrong, A.C. (1894). The imagery of American students. *Psychological Review, 1,* 496–505.

Atkinson, R.C., & Shiffrin, R.M. (1968). Human memory: A proposed system and its control processes. In K.W. Spence (Ed.), *The psychology of learning and motivation: Advances in research and theory II* (pp. 89–195). New York: Academic Press.

Atkinson, R.C., & Shiffrin, R.M. (1971). The control of short-term memory. *Scientific American, 225*(2), 82–90.

Au, T.K.F. (1983). Chinese and English counterfactuals—the Sapir–Whorf hypothesis revisited. *Cognition, 15*(1–3), 155–187.

Baddeley, A.D. (1971). Language habits, acoustic confusability and immediate memory for redundant letter sequences. *Psychonomic Science, 22,* 120–121.

Baddeley, A.D. (1976). *Psychology of Memory.* London: Harper & Rowe.

Baddeley, A.D. (1978). The trouble with levels: A re-examination of Craik and Lockhart's framework. *Psychological Review, 85,* 139–152.

Baddeley, A.D. (1982). Domains of recollection. *Psychological Review, 89,* 708–729.

Baddeley, A.D. (1997). *Human Memory: Theory and Practice* (rev. ed.). Hove, UK: Psychology Press.

Baddeley, A.D. (1998). The central executive: A concept and some misconceptions. *Journal of the International Neuropsychological Society, 4,* 523–526.

Baddeley, A., Gathercole, S., & Papagno, C. (1998). The phonological loop as a language learning device. *Psychological Review, 105*(1), 158–173.

Baddeley, A.D., & Hitch, G. (1974). Working memory. In G.A. Bower (Ed.), *Recent advances in the psychology of learning and motivation*, (Vol. 8, pp. 647–667). New York: Academic Press.

Baddeley, A.D., & Hitch, G.J. (1977). Recency re-examined. In S. Dornic (Ed.), *Attention and performance VI*. Hillsdale NJ: Lawrence Erlbaum Associates Inc.

Baddeley, A.D., & Lewis, V. J. (1981). Inner active processes in reading: The inner voice, the inner ear and the inner eye. In A.M. Lesgold & C.A. Perfetti (Eds.), *Interactive processes in reading*. Hillsdale, NJ: Erlbaum.

Baddeley, A.D., Thomson, N., & Buchanan, M. (1975). Word length and the structure of short-term memory. *Journal of Verbal Learning and Verbal Behavior, 14*(6), 575–589.

Baddeley, A.D., & Warrington, E.K. (1970). Amnesia and the distinction between short-term and long-term memory. *Journal of Verbal Learning and Verbal Behavior, 9*, 176–189.

Baddeley, A.D., & Warrington, E.K. (1973). Memory coding and amnesia. *Neuropsychologia, 11*, 159–165.

Bahrick, H. (1970). Two-phase model for prompted recall. *Psychological Review, 77*, 215–222.

Balota, D.A. (1994). Visual recognition: The journey from features to meaning. In M. A. Gernsbacher (Ed.), *Handbook of Psycholinguistics*. San Diego, CA: Academic Press.

Bard, E.G., Shillcock, R. C., & Altmann, G. A. (1988). The recognition of words after their acoustic effects in spontaneous speech. *Perception and Psychophysics, 44*, 395–408.

Baron, J. (1994). *Thinking and deciding.* (2nd ed.). Cambridge: Cambridge University Press.

Barsalou, L. (1985). Ideals, central tendency, and frequency of instantiation. *Journal of Experimental Psychology: Learning, Memory and Cognition, 11*, 629–654.

Bartlett, F.C. (1932). *Remembering: A study in experimental and social psychology.* Cambridge: Cambridge University Press.

Bass, E., & Davis, L. (1988). *The courage to heal.* New York: Harper & Rowe.

Berko Gleason, J., & Bernstein Ratner, N. (1998). *Psycholinguistics.* (2nd ed.). Fort Worth: Harcourt Brace.

Berry, D.C., & Broadbent, D.E. (1984). On the relationship between task-performance and associated verbalizable knowledge. *Quarterly Journal Of Experimental Psychology Section A: Human Experimental Psychology, 36*(2), 209–231.

Berry, D.C., & Dienes, Z. (1993). *Implicit learning: Theoretical and empirical issues.* Hove, UK: Lawrence Erlbaum Associates Ltd.

Berry, D., & Dienes, Z. (1997). Implicit synthesis. *Psychonomic Bulletin and Review, XX*, 68–72.

Besner, D., Davies, J., & Daniels, S. (1981). Reading for meaning: The effects of concurrent articulation. *Quarterly Journal of Experimental Psychology, 33A*, 415–437.

Biederman, I. (1987). Recognition-by-components—a theory of human image understanding. *Psychological Review, 94*(2), 115–147.

Biederman, I. (1995). Visual object recognition. In S.M. Kosslyn & D. N. Osherson (Eds.), *Visual cognition: An invitation to cognitive science.* Cambridge, MA: MIT Press.

Bisiach, E., & Luzatti, C. (1978). Unilateral neglect of representational space. *Cortex, 14*, 129–133.

Blaney, P.H. (1986). Affect and memory: A review. *Psychological Bulletin, 99*, 229–246.

Block, R.I., & Wittenborn, J.R. (1985). Marijuana effects on associative processes. *Psychopharmacology, 85*, 426–430.

Bloom, A.H. (1981). *The linguistic shaping of thought: A study in the impact of language on thinking in China and the West.* Hillsdale, NJ: Lawrence Erlbaum Associates Inc.

Boakes, R.A., & Gaertner, I. (1977). Development of a simple form of communication. *Quarterly Journal of Experimental Psychology, 29*, 561–575.

Bock, K., & Levelt, W. (1994). Language production: Grammatical encoding. In M.A. Gernsbacher (Ed.), *Handbook of psycholinguistics*. London: Academic Press.

Boshuizen, H.P.A., & Schmidt, H.G. (1992). On the role of biomedical knowledge in clinical reasoning by experts, intermediates and novices. *Cognitive Science, 16*(2), 153–184.

Bower, G.H. (1970). Imagery as a relational organizer in associative learning. *Journal of Verbal Learning and Verbal Behavior, 9*(5), 529–533.

Bower, G.H. (1981). Mood and memory. *American Psychologist, 36*, 129–148.

Bower, G.H., Black, J.B., & Turner, T.J. (1979). Scripts in memory for text. *Cognitive Psychology, 11*, 177–220.

Bower, G. H., Gilligan, S. G., & Monteiro, K. P. (1981). Selectivity of learning caused by affective states. *Journal of Experimental Psychology: General, 110*, 451–473.

Bowers, J., & Schacter, D.L. (1993). Priming of novel information in amnesic patients: Issues and data. In P. Graf & M.E.J. Masson (Eds.), *Implicit memory: New directions in cognition, development and neuropsychology*. Hillsdale, NJ: Lawrence Erlbaum Associates Inc.

Braine, M.D. (1978). On the relation between the natural logic of reasoning and standard logic. *Psychological Review, 85*(1), 1–21.

Brakke, K.E., & Savage-Rumbaugh, S.E. (1996). The development of language skills in PAN: II Production. *Language and Communication, 16*, 361–380.

Bransford, J.D., Barclay, J.R., & Franks, J.J. (1972). Sentence memory: A constructive versus interpretative approach. *Cognitive Psychology, 3*(2), 193–209.

Broadbent, D.E. (1958). *Perception and communication*. Oxford: Pergamon.

Broniarczyk, S.M., Hoyer, W.D., & McAlister, L. (1998). Consumers' perceptions of the assortment effect offered in a grocery category: The impact of item reduction. *Journal of Marketing Research, 35*, 166–176.

Bronkhorst, A.W., Bosman, A.J., & Smoorenburg, G.E. (1993). A model of context effects in speech recognition. *Journal of the Acoustical Society of America, 93*, 499–509.

Brooks, L.R. (1968). Spatial and verbal components of the act of recall. *Canadian Journal of Psychology, 22*(5), 349–368.

Brown, A.S. (1991). A review of the tip-of-the-tongue experience. *Psychological Bulletin, 109*(2), 204–223.

Brown, R., & McNeill, D. (1966). The "tip of the tongue" phenomenon. *Journal of Verbal Learning and Verbal Behavior, 5*(4), 325–337.

Bruce, V., Green, P.R., & Georgeson, M. (1996). *Visual perception: Physiology, psychology, and ecology*. (3rd ed.). Hove, UK: Psychology Press.

Brysbaert, M., Fias, W., & Noel, M.P. (1998). The Whorfian hypothesis and numerical cognition: Is 'twenty-four' processed in the same way as 'four-and-twenty'? *Cognition, 66*(1), 51–77.

Burke, M., & Mathews, A. (1992). Autobiographical memory and clinical anxiety. *Cognition and Emotion, 6*, 23–36.

Butter, C.M., Kosslyn, S.M., Mijovic-Prelec, D., & Riffle, A. (1997). Field-specific deficits in visual imager following hemianopia due to unilateral occipital infarcts. *Brain, 12*, 217–228.

Butters, N. (1984). Alcoholic Korsakoff's Syndrome: An update. *Seminars in Neurology, 4*, 226–244.

Cahan, S., & Artman, L. (1997). Is everyday experience dysfunctional for the development of conditional reasoning? *Cognitive Development, 12*, 268–271.

Calev, A., Ben-Tzvi, E., Shapira, B., Drexler, H. et al. (1989). Distinct memory impairments following electroconvulsive therapy and imipramine. *Psychological Medicine, 19*, 111–119.

Canfield, J.V. (1995). The rudiments of language. *Language and Communication, 15*, 195–211.

Caplan, D. (1972). Clause boundaries and recognition latencies for words in sentences. *Perception and Psychophysics, 12,* 73–76.

Carlesimo, G. A., Marfia, G. A., Loasses, A., & Caltagirone, C. (1996). Recency effect in anterograde amnesia: Evidence for distinct memory stores underlying enhanced retrieval of terminal items in immediate and delayed recall paradigms. *Neuropsychologia,* 177–184.

Carr, T. H., Davidson, B. J., & Hawkins, H. L. (1978). Perceptual flexibility in word recognition: Strategies affecting orthographic computations but not lexical access. *Journal of Experimental Psychology: Human Perception and Performance, 4,* 674–690.

Ceci, S.J., & Bruck, M. (1995). *Jeopardy in the courtroom.* Washington, DC: American Psychological Society.

Chapman, L.J., & Chapman, J.P. (1959). Atmosphere effect re-examined. *Journal of Experimental Psychology, 58,* 220–226.

Chapman, L.J., & Chapman, J.P. (1971). Test results are what you think they are. *Psychology Today, 5*(6), 18–22.

Charlot, V., Tzourio, N., Mazoyer, B., & Denis, M. (1992). Different mental imagery abilities result in different regional cerebral blood flow activation patterns during cognitive tasks. *Neuropsychologia, 30,* 565–580.

Charness, N. (1981). Search in chess: Age and skill differences. *Journal Of Experimental Psychology: Human Perception and Performance, 7*(2), 467–476.

Chase, W.G., & Simon, H.A. (1973a). The mind's eye in chess. In W. G. Chase (Ed.), *Visual information processing.* London: Academic Press.

Chase, W.G., & Simon, H.A. (1973b). Perception in chess. *Cognitive Psychology, 4*(1), 55–81.

Cheng, P.W., & Holyoak, K.J. (1985). Pragmatic Reasoning Schemas. *Cognitive Psychology, 17*(4), 391–416.

Cherry, E.C. (1953). Some experiments on the recognition of speech, with one and with two ears. *Journal of the Acoustical Society of America, 25,* 975–979.

Chi, M.T.H., Feltovich, P.J., & Glaser, R. (1981). Categorization and representation of physics problems by experts and novices. *Cognitive Science, 5*(2), 121–152.

Chomsky, N. (1959). Review of Skinner's "Verbal Behavior". *Language, 35,* 26–58.

Chomsky, N. (1965). *Aspects of a theory of syntax.* Cambridge, MA: MIT Press.

Clark, D.M., & Teasdale, J.D. (1981). Diurnal variation in clinical depression and availability of positive and negative experiences. *Journal of Abnormal Psychology, 91,* 87–95.

Cleeremans, A., Destrebecqz, A., & Boyer, M. (1998). Implicit learning: News from the front. *Trends in Cognitive Sciences, 2,* 406–416.

Cohen, M.S., Kosslyn, S.M., Breiter, H.C., & DiGirolamo, G.J. (1996). Changes in cortical activity during mental rotation: A mapping study using functional MRI. *Brain, 119,* 89–100.

Collins, A.M., & Quillian, M.R. (1969). Retrieval time from semantic memory. *Journal of Verbal Learning and Verbal Behavior, 8*(2), 240–247.

Coltheart, M. (1999). Modularity and cognition. *Trends in Cognitive Sciences, 3,* 115–120.

Coltheart, M., Curtis, B., Atkins, P., & Haller, M. (1993). Models of reading aloud: Dual route and parallel distributed processing approaches. *Psychological Review, 100,* 589–608.

Coltheart, M., & Glick, M.J. (1974). Visual imagery: A case study. *Quarterly Journal of Experimental Psychology, 26,* 438–453.

Conrad, R. (1964). Acoustic confusions in immediate memory. *British Journal of Psychology, 55*(1), 75–84.

Conway, M.A. (1997). *Recovered memories and false memories.* Oxford: Oxford University Press.

Corbett, A.T., & Dosher, B.A. (1978). Instrument inferences in sentence encoding. *Journal of Verbal Learning and Verbal Behaviour, 17,* 479–491.

Corkin, S. (1984). Lasting consequences of bilateral medial temporal lobectomy.

Clinical course and experimental findings in HM. *Seminars in Neurology, 4,* 249–259.

Cowan, N. (1995). *Attention and memory: An integrated framework.* Oxford: Oxford University Press.

Cowan, N. (1998). Visual and auditory working memory capacity. *Trends in Cognitive Sciences, 2,* 77–87.

Craik, F.I.M. (1970). The fate of items in primary memory. *Journal of Verbal Learning and Verbal Behavior, 9,* 143–148.

Craik, F.I.M. (1977). Depth of processing in recall and recognition. In S. Dornic (Ed.), *Attention and Performance VI,* (pp. 679–698). London: Wiley.

Craik, F.I.M., & Lockhart, R.S. (1972). Levels of processing: A framework for memory research. *Journal of Verbal Learning and Verbal Behavior, 11*(6), 671–684.

Craik, F.I.M., & Tulving, E. (1975). Depth of processing and the retention of words in episodic memory. *Journal of Experimental Psychology: General, 104*(3), 268–294.

Crowder, R.G. (1976). *Principles of learning and memory.* Hillsdale, NJ, Lawrence Erlbaum Associates Inc.

Daneman, M., & Carpenter, PA. (1980). Individual differences in working memory and reading. *Journal of Verbal Learning and Verbal Behavior, 19,* 450–466.

Darwin, C.J., Turvey, M.T., & Crowder, R.C. (1972). An auditory analogue of the Sperling partial report procedure: Evidence for brief auditory storage. *Cognitive Psychology, 3*(2), 255–267.

Davies, G.M. (1993). Witnessing events. In G.M. Davies & R.H. Logie (Eds.), *Memory in everyday life.* Amsterdam: Elsevier.

DeGroot, A.D. (1965). *Thought and choice in chess.* The Hague: Mouton.

DeGroot, A.D. (1966). Preception and memory versus thought. In B.K. (Ed.), *Problem solving.* New York: Wiley.

Delk, J.L., & Fillenbaum, S. (1965). Differences in perceived colour as a function of characteristic colour. *American Journal of Psychology, 78,* 290–293.

Dell, G.S., Juliano, C., & Govindjee, A. (1993). Structure and content in language production—A theory of frame constraints in phonological speech errors. *Cognitive Science, 17*(2), 149–195.

Deutsch, J.A., & Deutsch, D. (1963). Attention: Some theoretical considerations. *Psychological Review, 70*(1), 51–61.

De Vreese, L.P. (1991). Two systems for colour naming defects: Verbal disconnection vs colour imagery disorder. *Neuropsychologia, 29,* 1–18.

Dienes, Z., Altmann, G.T.M., Kwan, L., & Goode, A. (1995). Unconscious knowledge in artificial grammar is applied strategically. *Journal of Experimental Psychology: Learning, Memory and Cognition, 21*(5), 1322–1338.

Dienes, Z., & Fahey, R. (1995a). Modality independence of implicitly learned grammatical knowledge. *Journal of Experimental Psychology: Learning, Memory and Cognition, 21,* 899–912.

Dienes, Z., & Fahey, R. (1995b). Role of specific instances in controlling a dynamic system. *Journal of Experimental Psychology: Learning, Memory and Cognition, 21,* 848–862.

Dienes, Z., & Fahey, R. (1998). The role of implicit memory in controlling a dynamic system. *Quarterly Journal of Experimental Psychology, 51A,* 593–614.

Donaldson, W. (1996). The role of decision processes in remembering and knowing. *Memory and Cognition,* 523–533.

Drachman, D.A., & Sahakian, B.J. (1979). Effects of cholinergic agents on human learning and memory. In R. Barbeau (Ed.), *Nutrition and the Brain,* (Vol. 5, pp. 351–366). New York: Raven Press.

Drummey, A.B., & Newcombe, N. (1995). Remembering versus knowing the past. *Journal of Experimental Child Psychology, 59,* 549–565.

Duffy, S.A. (1986). The role of expectations in sentence integration. *Journal of Experimental Psychology: Learning, Memory and Cognition, 12,* 208–219.

Dulsky, S.G. (1935). The effect of a change of background on recall and relearning. *Journal of Experimental Psychology, 18,* 725–740.

Duncker, K. (1945). On problem-solving. *Psychological Monographs*(5), 113.

Ebbinghaus, H. (1885). *Uber das Gedachtnis*. Leipzig: Dunker.

Eich, E., & Metcalfe, J. (1989). Mood dependent memory for internal versus external events. *Journal of Experimental Psychology-Learning Memory and Cognition, 15*(3), 443–455.

Eich, J.E. (1980). The cue-dependent nature of state-dependent retrieval. *Memory and Cognition, 8*(2), 157–173.

Eimas, P.D., & Corbit, J.D. (1973). Selective adaptation of linguistic feature detectors. *Cognitive Psychology, 4*, 99–109.

Elman, J., & McClelland, J. (1988). Cognitive penetration of the mechanisms of perception: Compensation for coarticulation of lexically restored phonemes. *Journal of Memory and Language, 27*, 143–165.

Ericsson, K.A., & Faivre, I.A. (1988). What's exceptional about exceptional abilities? In L.K. Obler & D. Fein (Eds.), *The exceptional brain: The neuropsychology of talent and special abilities* (pp. 436–473). New York: Guildford Press.

Ericsson, K.A., & Kintsch, W. (1995). Long-term working memory. *Psychological Review, 102*, 211–245.

Ericsson, K.A., & Lehmann, A.C. (1996). Expert and exceptional performance: Evidence of maximal adaptation to task constraints. *Annual Review Of Psychology, 47*, 273–305.

Ervin-Tripp, S. (1964). An analysis of the interaction of language, topic, and listener. *American Anthropologist, 66*, 86–102.

Estes, W. (1993). Concepts, categories, and psychological science. *Psychological Science, 4*, 143–153.

Evans, J.S.B.T. (1989). *Bias in human reasoning: Causes and consequences*. Hove, UK: Lawrence Erlbaum Associates Ltd.

Eysenck, M.W. (1978). Levels of processing: A critique. *British Journal of Psychology, 69*, 157–169.

Farah, M.J. (1988). Is visual imagery really visual—Overlooked evidence from neuropsychology. *Psychological Review, 95*(3), 307–317.

Farah, M.J., Soso, M.J., & Dashief, R.M. (1988). Visual angle of the mind's eye before and after unilateral occipital lobectomy. *Journal of Experimental Psychology: Human Perception and Performance, 18*, 241–246.

Finke, R.A.S., & Pinker, S. (1983). Directional scanning of remembered visual patterns. *Journal of Experimental Psychology: Learning, Memory and Cognition, 8*, 142–147.

Fiore, S.M., & Schooler, J.W. (1998). Right hemisphere contribution to creative problem solving. Converging evidence for divergent thinking. In M. Beeman and C. Chiarello (Eds.), *Right hemisphere language comprehension: Perspectives from neuroscience.*. Mahwah, NJ: Lawrence Erlbaum Associates Inc.

Fodor, J.A. (1983). *The modularity of mind: An essay on faculty psychology*. Cambridge, MA: MIT Press.

Franks, J.J., & Bransford, J.D. (1971). Abstraction of visual patterns. *Journal of Experimental Psychology, 90*, 65–74.

Frazier, L. (1987). Sentence processing: A tutorial review. In M. Coltheart (Ed.), *Attention and performance XII: The psychology of reading* (pp. 601–681). Hove, UK: Lawrence Erlbaum Associates Ltd.

Frazier, L., & Rayner, K. (1982). Making and correcting errors during sentence comprehension. Eye-movements in the analysis of structurally ambiguous sentences. *Cognitive Psychology, 14*(2), 178–210.

Freud, S. (1901). *The psychopathology of every-day life*. New York: W.W. Norton.

Fromkin, V.A., & Bernstein Ratner, N. (1998). From concept to expression. In J. Berko Gleason & N. Bernstein Ratner (Eds.), *Psycholinguistics*. Fort Worth: Harcourt Brace.

Gardiner, J.M., & Parkin, A.J. (1990). Attention and recollective experience in recognition memory. *Memory and Cognition, 18*, 579–583.

Garnes, S., & Bond, Z.S. (1976). The relationship between semantic expectation and acoustic information. In W. Dressler & O. Pfeiffer (Eds.), *Proceedings of the Third International Phonology Meeting*. Innsbruck: Phonologische Tagung.

Garven, S., Wood, J.M., Malpass, R.S., & Shaw, J.S. (1998). More than suggestion: The effect of interviewing techniques from the McMartin preschool case. *Journal of Applied Psychology, 83*, 347–359.

Gibson, J.J. (1950). *The ecological approach to visual perception*. Boston: Houghton Mifflin.

Gibson, J.J. (1994). The visual perception of objective motion and subjective movement. *Psychological Review, 101*, 318–323.

Gick, M.L., & Holyoak, K.J. (1980). Analogical problem solving. *Cognitive Psychology, 12*(3), 306–355.

Gick, M.L., & Holyoak, K.J. (1983). Schema induction and analogical transfer. *Cognitive Psychology, 15*(1), 1–38.

Gilhooly, K. (1995). *Thinking: Directed, undirected and creative* (2nd ed.). London: Academic Press.

Glanzer, M., & Cunitz, A.R. (1966). Two storage mechanisms in free recall. *Journal of Verbal Learning and Verbal Behavior, 5*, 351–360.

Glanzer, M., & Razel, M. (1974). The size of the unit in short-term storage. *Journal of Verbal Learning and Verbal Behavior, 13*, 114–131.

Glenberg, A.M., Bradley, M.M., Stevenson, J.A., Kraus, T.A., Tkachuk, M.J., Gretz, A.L., Fish, J.H., & Turpin, B.A.M. (1980). A two-process account of long-term serial position effects. *Journal of Experimental Psychology: Learning, Memory and Cognition, 6*, 355–369.

Glucksberg, S., & Cowan, G.N. (1970). Memory for nonattended auditory material. *Cognitive Psychology, 1*, 149–156.

Glucksberg, S., Kreuz, F.J., & Rho, S.H. (1986). Context can constrain lexical access: Implications for models of language comprehension. *Journal of Experimental Psychology: Learning, Memory and Cognition, 12*, 323–335.

Glushko, R.J. (1979). The organization and activation of orthographic knowledge in reading aloud. *Journal of Experimental Psychology: Human Perception and Performance, 5*, 674–691.

Gobet, F. (1998). Expert memory: a comparison of four theories. *Cognition, 66*(2), 115–152.

Gobet, F., & Simon, H.A. (1996). Templates in chess memory: A mechanism for recalling several boards. *Cognitive Psychology, 31*(1), 1–40.

Godden, D.R., & Baddeley, A.D. (1975). Context-dependent memory in two natural environments: On land and underwater. *British Journal of Psychology, 66*(3), 325–331.

Godden, D.R., & Baddeley, A. (1980). When does context influence recognition memory? *British Journal of Psychology, 71*(1), 99–104.

Goldenberg, G., Steiner, M., Podreka, I., & Deeke, L. (1992). Regional cerebral blood flow patterns related to the verification of low- and high-imagery words. *Neuropsychologia, 30*, 581–586.

Goldstein, E.B. (1989). *Sensation and perception*. (Vol. 3). California: Wadsworth Inc.

Goodwin, D.W. Poweel, B., Bremer, D., Hoine, H., & Stern, J. (1969). Alcohol and recall: State dependent effects. *Science, 163*, 1358–1360.

Graesser, A. C., Singer, M., & Trabasso, T. (1994). Constructing inferences during narrative text comprehension. *Psychological Review, 101*, 371–395.

Gray, J.A., & Wedderburn, A.A. (1960). Grouping strategies with simultaneous stimuli. *Quarterly Journal of Experimental Psychology, 12*, 180–184.

Greene, E., & Nelson, B. (1997). Evaluating Müller-Lyer effects using single fin–set configurations. *Perception and Psychophysics, 59*, 293–312.

Greenleigh, L., Dollinger, S.J., & Pitz, G. (1997). Adolescents' perceived risk and personal experience with natural disasters: An evaluation of cognitive heuristics. *Acta Psychologica, 91*, 27–38.

Greeno, J.G. (1994). Gibson's affordances. *Psychological Review, 101*(2), 336–342.

Gregory, R.L. (1998). *Eye and brain: The psychology of seeing.* Oxford: Oxford University Press.

Griggs, R.A., & Cox, J.R. (1993). Permission schemas and the selection task. *Quarterly Journal of Experimental Psychology Section A: Human Experimental Psychology, 46*(4), 637–651.

Guilford, J.P. (1956). The structure of the intellect. *Psychological Bulletin, 53*, 267–293.

Gummerman, K., & Gray, C.R. (1971). Recall of visually presented material: An unwanted case and a bibliography for eidetic imagery. *Psychonomic Monograph Supplements, 4* (Whole No. 58), 189–195.

Gummerman, K., Gray, C.R., & Wilson, J.M. (1972). An attempt to assess eidetic imagery objectively. *Psychonomic Science, 28*, 115–118.

Haber, R.N., & Haber, R.B. (1964). Eidetic imagery. I Frequency. *Perceptual and Motor Skills, 64*, 131–138.

Hardy, G.H. (1979). *The collected papers of G.H. Hardy.* (Vol. 7). Oxford: Clarendon Press.

Hardyck, C.D., & Petrinovich, L.F. (1970). Subvocal speech and comprehension level as a function of the difficulty level of reading material. *Journal of Verbal Learning and Verbal Behavior, 9*(6), 647–652.

Harley, T.A. (1984). A critique of top-down independent levels models of speech production: Evidence from non-plan-internal speech errors. *Cognitive Science, 8*(3), 191–219.

Harley, T.H. (1997). *The psychology of language.* Hove, UK: Psychology Press.

Haviland, S.E., & Clark, H.H. (1974). What's new? Acquiring new information as a process in comprehension. *Journal of Verbal Learning and Verbal Behavior, 13*, 512–521.

Heider, E.R. (1972). Universals in color naming and memory. *Journal of Experimental Psychology, 93*(1), 10–20.

Heider, E.R., & Oliver, D.C. (1972). The structure of the color space in naming and memory for two languages. *Cognitive Psychology, 3*(2), 337–354.

Hess, E.H. (1975). The role of pupil size in communication. *Scientific American, 233*, 110–119.

Hewitt, K. (1973). Context effects in memory: A review. *Cambridge Psychological Laboratory.*

Hintzman, D.L. (1991). Contingency analyses, hypotheses, and artefacts: Reply to Flexser and Gardiner. *Journal of Experimental Psychology: Learning, Memory and Cognition, 17*, 341–345.

Hintzman, D.L. (1992). Mathematical constraints on the Tulving–Wiseman law. *Psychological Review, 102*, 536–542.

Hintzman, D.L., & Hartry, A.L. (1990). Item effects in recognition and fragment completion: contingency relations vary for different subsets of words. *Journal of Experimental Psychology: Learning, Memory and Cognition, 17*, 341–345.

Hochberg, J. (1978). *Perception* (2nd ed.). New York: Prentice Hall.

Hoffman, C., Lau, I., & Johnson, D.R. (1986). The linguistic relativity of person recognition. *Journal of Personality and Social Psychology, 51*, 1097–1105.

Hogaboam, T.W., & Perfetti, C.A. (1975). Lexical ambiguity and sentence comprehension. *Journal of Verbal Learning and Verbal Behavior, 14*, 265–274.

Holender, D. (1986). Semantic activation without conscious identification in dichotic listening, parafoveal vision, and visual masking: A survey and appraisal. *Behavioural and Brain Sciences, 9*, 1–66.

Hollan, J.D. (1975). Features and semantic memory. *Psychological Review, 82*, 154–155.

Holyoak, K.J., & Koh, K. (1987). Surface and structural similarity in analogical transfer. *Memory & Cognition, 15*(4), 332–340.

Huey, A.B. (1908). *The psychology and pedagogy of reading.* New York: Macmillan.

Hunt, E., & Agnoli, F. (1991). The Whorfian hypothesis—a cognitive-psychology perspective. *Psychological Review, 98*(3), 377–389.

Intraub, H. (1997). The representation of visual scenes. *Trends in Cognitive Sciences, 1*, 217–222.

Jacoby, L.L. (1991). A process dissociation framework: Separating automatic from intentional uses of memory. *Journal of Memory and Language, 30*, 513–541.

Jacoby, L.L., Toth, J. P., & Yonelinas, A. P. (1993). Unconscious influences of memory: Attention, awareness and control. *Journal of Experimental Psychology: General, 122*, 139–154.

James, W. (1890). *The principles of psychology.* New York: Henry Holt.

Jarvella, J. J. (1971). Syntactic processing of connected speech. *Journal of Verbal Learning and Verbal Behavior, 10*, 409–416.

Johnson, M.K., & Raye, C. L. (1998). False memories and confabulation. *Trends in Cognitive Sciences, 2*, 137–145.

Johnson-Laird, P.N. (1980). Mental models in cognitive science. *Cognitive Science, 4*(1), 71–115.

Johnson-Laird, P.N. (1983). *Mental models.* Cambridge: Cambridge University Press.

Johnson-Laird, P.N. (1988). Freedom and constraint in creativity. In R.J. Sternberg (Ed.), *The nature of creativity.* Cambridge: Cambridge University Press.

Johnson-Laird, P.N. (1997). Rules and illusions: A critical study of Rips' Psychology of Proof. *Minds and Machines, 7*, 387–407.

Johnson-Laird, P.N., & Byrne, R.M.J. (1991). *Deduction.* Hove, UK: Lawrence Erlbaum Associates Ltd.

Johnston, W.A., Dark, V.J., & Jacoby, L.L. (1985). Perceptual fluency and recognition judgements. *Journal Of Experimental Psychology: Learning Memory and Cognition, 11*(1), 3–11.

Johnston, W.A., & Heinz, S.P. (1978). Flexibility and capacity demands of attention. *Journal of Experimental Psychology: General, 107*(4), 420–435.

Jolicoeur, P., & Kosslyn, S.M. (1985). Is time to scan visual images due to demand characteristics? *Memory and Cognition, 13*, 320–332.

Just, M.A., & Carpenter, P.A. (1992). A capacity theory of comprehension—Individual differences in working memory. *Psychological Review, 99*(1), 122–149.

Kahneman, D., & Tversky, A. (1972). Subjective probability: A judgement of representativeness. *Cognitive Psychology, 3*, 430–454.

Kahneman, D., & Tversky, A. (1980). On the psychology of prediction. *Psychological Review, 80*, 237–251.

Kay, P., & Kempton, W. (1984). What is the Sapir–Whorf hypothesis? *American Anthropologist, 86*, 65–79.

Kellog, R.T. (1995). *Cognitive psychology.* Thousand Oaks, CA: Sage.

Key, W.B. (1972). *Subliminal seduction.* New York: Signed Books.

Key, W.B. (1973). *Subliminal seduction: Ad media's manipulation of a not so innocent America.* Englewood Cliffs, NJ: Prentice-Hall Inc.

Kintsch, W. (1970). *Learning, memory and conceptual processes.* New York: Wiley.

Kintsch, W., & Van Dijk, T.A. (1978). Toward a model of text comprehension and production. *Psychological Review, 85*(5), 363–394.

Kleiman, G.M. (1975). Speech recoding in reading. *Journal of Verbal Learning and Verbal Behavior, 24*, 323–339.

Koffka, K. (1935). *Principles of Gestalt Psychology.* New York: Harcourt Brace.

Kohler, W. (1927). *The mentality of apes.* (2nd ed.). New York: Harcourt Brace.

Kosslyn, S.M. (1975). Information representation in visual images. *Cognitive Psychology, 7*(3), 341–370.

Kosslyn, S.M. (1978). Measuring the visual angle of the mind's eye. *Cognitive Psychology, 10*(3), 356–389.

Kosslyn, S.M. (1980). *Image and mind.* Cambridge, MA: Harvard University Press.

Kosslyn, S.M. (1983). *Ghosts in the mind's machine: Creating and using images in the brain.* New York: Norton.

Kosslyn, S.M. (1994). *Image and brain: The resolution of the imagery debate*. Cambridge, MA: MIT Press.

Kosslyn, S.M., Ball, T.M., & Reiser, B.J. (1978). Visual images preserve metric spatial information. *Journal of Experimental Psychology: Human Perception and Performance, 4*, 47–60.

Kuhl, P.K. (1986). Theoretical contributions of tests on animals to the special-mechanisms debate in speech. *Experimental Biology, 45*, 233–265.

Kuhn, T.S. (1970). *The structure of scientific revolutions*. Chicago: Chicago University Press.

Lachman, R., Lachman, J.L., & Butterfield, E.C. (1979). *Cognitive psychology and information processing*. Hillsdale, NJ: Lawrence Erlbaum Associates Inc.

Langs, R., Badalamenti, A.F., & Savage-Rumbaugh, S. (1996). Mathematically defined language structures in humans and chimpanzees. *Behavioral Science, 41*, 124–135.

Larkin, J., McDermott, J., Simon, D.P., & Simon, H.A. (1980). Expert and novice performance in solving physics problems. *Science, 208*(4450), 1335–1342.

Larkin, J.H. (1983). The role of problem representation in physics. In D. Gentner and L.A. Stevens (Eds.), *Mental models*. Hillsdale, NJ: Lawrence Erlbaum Associates Inc.

Lepley, W.M. (1934). Serial reactions considered as serial reactions. *Psychological Monographs, 46* (No. 205).

Levelt, W.J. M. (1999). Models of word production. *Trends in Cognitive Sciences, 3*, 223–232.

Levin, H.S., High, W.M., Meyers, C.A., von Laufen, A., Hayden, M.E., & Eisenberg, H. (1985). Impairment of remote memory after closed head injury. *Journal of Neurology, Neurosurgery and Psychiatry, 48*, 55–63.

Liberman, A.M., Cooper, F.S., Shankweiler, D.S., & Studdert-Kennedy, M. (1967). Perception of the speech code. *Psychological Review, 74*, 431–461.

Liberman, A.M., Harris, K.S., Hoffman, H.S., & Griffith, B.C. (1957). The discrimination of speech sounds within and across phoneme boundaries. *Journal of Experimental Psychology, 54*, 358–368.

Light, L.L., & Carter-Sobell, L. (1970). Effects of changed semantic context on recognition memory. *Journal of Verbal Learning and Verbal Behavior, 9*(1), 1–11.

Lloyd, G.G., & Lishman, W.A. (1975). Effect of depression on the speed of recall of pleasant and unpleasant experiences. *Psychological Medicine, 5*, 173–180.

Loftus, E.F. (1993). The reality of repressed memories. *American Psychologist, 48*(5), 518–537.

Loftus, E.F., & Ketcham, K. (1994). *The myth of repressed memory: False memories and allegations of sexual abuse*. New York: St. Martin's Press.

Loftus, E.F., & Loftus, G. (1980). On the permanence of stored information in the brain. *American Psychologist, 35*, 409–420.

Luck, S.J., & Vogel, E.K. (1997). The capacity of visual working memory for features and conjunctions. *Nature, 390*, 279–281.

Lucy, J.A., & Schweder, R.A. (1979). Whorf and his critics: Linguistic and non-linguistic influences on color memory. *American Anthropologist, 81*, 581–607.

Luria, A.R. (1968). *The mind of mnemonist*. Harmondsworth: Penguin.

Luria, A.R., & Solotaroff, L. (1987). *The mind of a mnemonist: A little book about a vast memory*. (Vol. xxv). Cambridge, MA: Harvard University Press.

MacKay, D.G. (1973). Aspects of the theory of comprehension, memory and attention. *Quarterly Journal of Experimental Psychology, 25*(1), 22–40.

MacKay, D.G., Stewart, R., & Burke, D. M. (1998). HM revisited: Implications for relations between language comprehension, memory, and the hippocampal system. *Journal of Cognitive Neuroscience, 10*, 377–394.

MacNeilage, P.F. (1972). Speech physiology. In J. H. Gilbert (Ed.), *Speech and cortical functioning*. New York: Academic Press.

Maier, N.R.F. (1931). Reasoning in humans. II. The solution of a problem and its appearance in consciousness. *Journal of Comparative Psychology, 12*, 181–194.

Mandler, G. (1980). Recognizing: The judgement of previous occurrence. *Psychological Review, 87*(3), 252–271.

Mandler, G., & Boeck, W. (1974). Retrieval processes in recognition. *Memory and Cognition, 2*, 613–615.

Marcel, A.J. (1983). Conscious and unconscious perception: An approach to the relation between phenomenal experience and perceptual processes. *Cognitive Psychology, 15*, 283–300.

Marr, D. (1982). *Vision: A computational investigation into the human representation and processing of visual information.* San Francisco, CA: W.H. Freeman.

Marr, D., & Hildreth, E. (1980). Theory of edge detection. *Proceedings of the Royal Society of London, B207*, 187–217.

Marr, D., & Nishihara, K. (1978). Representation and recognition of the spatial organisation of three-dimensional shapes. *Philosophical Transactions of the Royal Society (London), B200*, 269–294.

Marslen-Wilson, W.D. (1987). Functional parallelism in spoken word recognition. *Cognition, 25*, 71–102.

Marslen-Wilson, W.D., & Tyler, L.K. (1980). The temporal structure of spoken language understanding. *Cognition, 8*, 1–71.

Martindale, C. (1999). Biological bases of creativity. In R. J. Sternberg (Ed.), *Handbook of Creativity.* New York: Cambridge University Press.

Massaro, D.W. (1992). Broadening the domain of the fuzzy logical model of perception. In H.J.L. Pick , P. van den Broek & D.C. Knill (Eds.), *Cognition: Conceptual and methodological issues,* (pp. 51–84). Washington, DC: APA.

Massaro, D.W. (1998). *Perceiving talking faces: From speech perception to a behavioural principle.* Cambridge, MA: MIT Press.

McClelland, J.L., & Elman, J.L. (1986). The trace model of speech-perception. *Cognitive Psychology, 18*(1), 1–86.

McClelland, J.L., & Rumelhart, D.E. (1981). An interactive activation model of context effects in letter perception. 1. An account of basic findings. *Psychological Review, 88*(5), 375–407.

McConkie, G.W., & Currie, C.B. (1996). Visual stability across saccades while viewing complex pictures. *Journal of Experimental Psychology: Human Perception and Performance, 22*, 563–581.

McConkie, G.W., & Zola, D. (1979) Is visual information integrated across successive fixations in reading? *Perception and Psychophysics, 25*, 221–224.

McGurk, H., & MacDonald, J. (1976). Hearing lips and seeing voices. *Nature, 264*, 746–748.

McKoon, G., & Ratcliff, R. (1992). Inference during reading. *Psychological Review, 99*(3), 440–466.

Mednick, S.A. (1962). The associative basis of the creative process. *Psychological Review, 69*, 431–436.

Melton, A.W. (1970). The situation with respect to the spacing of repetitions. *Journal of Verbal Learning and Verbal Behavior, 9*, 596–606.

Metzler, C, & Parkin, A.J. (in press). Reversed negative priming following frontal lobe lesions. *Neuropsychologia.*

Meyer, D.E., & Schvaneveldt, R.W. (1971). Facilitation in recognising pairs of words: Evidence of a dependence between retrieval operations. *Journal of Experimental Psychology, 90*, 227–234.

Miles, C., & Daylen, J. (1998). State dependent memory produced by aerobic exercise. *Ergonomics, 41*, 20–28.

Milgram, S. (1963). Behavioural study of obedience. *Journal of Abnormal and Social Psychology, 67*, 371–378.

Mineka, S., & Nugent, K. (1995). Mood-congruent memory biases in anxiety and depression. In D. L. Schacter (Ed.), *Memory distortions: How minds, brains, and societies reconstruct the past,* (pp. 173–193). Cambridge, MA: Harvard University Press.

Mitchell, D.C. (1989). Verb guidance and lexical affects in ambiguity resolution.

Language and Cognitive Processes, 4, 123–154.

Mitchell, D.C. (1994). Sentence parsing. In M.A. Gernsbacher (Ed.), *Handbook of psycholinguistics*. San Diego, CA: Academic Press.

Mitchell, D.C., Cuetos, F., & Zagar, D. (1992). Reading in different languages: Is there a universal mechanism for parsing sentences? In D.A. Balota, G.B. F.D'Arcais, & K. Rayner (Eds.), *Comprehension processes in reading* (pp. 285–302). Hillsdale, NJ: Lawrence Erlbaum Associates Inc.

Moray, N., Bates, A., & Barnett, T. (1965). Experiments on the four-eared man. *Journal of Acoustical Society of America, 38*, 196–201.

Morris, C.D., Bransford, J.D., & Franks, J.J. (1977). Levels of processing versus transfer appropriate processing. *Journal of Verbal Learning and Verbal Behavior, 16*(5), 519–533.

Morrison, R.E. (1984). Manipulation of stimulus onset delay in reading: Evidence for parallel programming. *Journal of Experimental Psychology: Human Perception and Performance, 10*, 667–682.

Morton, J. (1969). Interaction of information in word recognition. *Psychological Review, 76*(2), 165–178.

Moss, H.E., McCormick, S.F., & Tyler, L.K. (1997). The time course of activation of semantic information during spoken word recognition. *Language and Cognitive Processes, 12*, 695–731.

Myles-Worsely, M., Johnson, W., & Simons, M.A. (1988). The influence of expertise on X-ray image processing. *Journal of Experimental Psychology: Learning, Memory and Cognition, 14*, 553–557.

Neely, J.H. (1977). Semantic priming and retrieval from lexical memory: Role of inhibitionless spreading activation and limited capacity attention. *Journal of Experimental Psychology: General, 106*, 226–254.

Nelson, H.E. (1976). A modified card sorting test sensitive to frontal lobe function. *Cortex, 12*, 313–324.

Nelson, T.O. (1977). Repetition and depth of processing. *Journal of Verbal Learning and Verbal Behaviour, 16*, 151–172.

Neumann, O., & Sanders, A.F. (1996). *Handbook of perception and action: Attention.* (Vol. 3). London: Academic Press.

Newell, A., & Simon, H.A. (1972). *Human problem solving.* Englewood Cliffs, NJ: Prentice Hall.

Newstead, S.E. (1990). Conversion in syllogistic reasoning. In K. Gilhooly, M. Keane, R. Logie, & G. Erdos (Eds.), *Lines of thinking: Reflections on the psychology of thinking,* (Vol. 1, pp. 73–84). Chichester: Wiley.

Nissen, M.J., & Bullemer, P. (1987). Attentional requirements of learning: Evidence from performance measures. *Cognitive Psychology, 19*, 1–32.

Norman, D.A., & Shallice, T. (1986). Attention to action: Willed and automatic control of behavior. In R.J. Davidson, G.E. Schwarz, & D.E. Shapiro (Eds.), *Consciousness and self-regulation* (Vol. 4). New York: Plenum Press.

Norris, D. (1994). Shortlist—A connectionist model of continuous speech recognition. *Cognition, 52*(3), 189–234.

O'Brien, E.J., Shank, D.M., Myers, J.L., & Rayner, K. (1988). Elaborative inferences during reading: Do they occur on-line? *Journal of Experimental Psychology: Learning, Memory and Cognition, 14*, 410–420.

O'Regan, J.K. (1992). Optimal viewing in words and the strategy-tactics model of eye movements in reading. In K. Rayner (Ed.), *Eye movements and visual cognition: Scene perception and reading* (pp. 333–354). New York: Springer Verlag.

Oakhill, J., & Garnham, A. (1992). Linguistic prescriptions and anaphoric reality. *Text, 12*, 161–182.

Oakhill, J.V., & Garnham, A. (1993). On theories of belief bias in syllogistic reasoning. *Cognition, 46*, 87–92.

Oakhill, J.V., & Garnham, A. (1994). *Thinking and reasoning.* Oxford: Blackwells.

Ofshe, R., & Watters, E. (1995). *Making monsters: False memories, psychotherapy, and sexual hysteria.* London: Deutsch.

Paivio, A. (1971). *Imagery and verbal processes.* New York: Holt, Rinehart & Winston (Reprinted by Lawrence Erlbaum Associates Inc. in 1979).

Paivio, A. (1986). *Mental representations: A dual coding approach.* Oxford: Oxford University Press.

Parkin, A.J. (1979). Specifying levels of processing. *Quarterly Journal of Experimental Psychology, 31*(2), 175–195.

Parkin, A.J. (1993). *Memory: Phenomena, experiment, and theory.* Hove, UK: Psychology Press.

Parkin, A.J. (1996). *Explorations in Cognitive Neuropsychology.* Hove, UK: Psychology Press.

Parkin, A.J. (1997a). The development of procedural and declarative memory. In N. Cowan (Ed.), *The development of memory in childhood.* Hove, UK: Psychology Press.

Parkin, A.J. (1997b). *Memory and amnesia: An introduction* (2nd ed.). Hove, UK: Psychology Press.

Parkin, A.J. (1998). The central executive does not exist. *Journal of the International Neuropsychological Society, 4,* 518–522.

Parkin, A.J. (2000). *Memory: A professional's guide.* Chichester: Wiley.

Parkin, A.J. (in prep). One hundred years of memory: Memory research in British universities 1900–1999. *British Journal of Psychology.*

Parkin, A.J. (in press). *Memory: Phenomena, experiment and theory.* (2nd ed.). Hove, UK: Psychology Press.

Parkin, A.J., Gardiner, J.M., & Rosser, R. (1995). Functional aspects of face recognition in face recognition. *Consciousness and Cognition, 4,* 387–398.

Parkin, A.J., & Leng, N.R.C. (1993). *Neuropsychology of the amnesic syndrome.* Hove, UK: Psychology Press.

Parkin, A.J., McMullen, M., & Graystone, D. (1986). Spelling-to-sound irregularity affects pronunciation latency but not lexical decision. *Psychological Research, 48,* 87–92.

Parkin, A.J., & Russo, R. (1993). On the origin of functional differences in recollective experience. *Memory, 1,* 231–237.

Parkin, A.J., & Streete, S. (1988). Implicit and explicit memory in young children and adults. *British Journal of Psychology, 79,* 362–369.

Parkin, A.J., & Walter, B.M. (1992). Recollective experience, ageing, and frontal lobe dysfunction. *Psychology and Ageing, 7,* 290–298.

Parkin, A.J., Ward, J., Squires, E.J., & Townshend, J. (in press). Perceptually-driven recognition memory: A new technique and some data on age differences. *Psychonomic Bulletin and Review.*

Pashler, H. (1998). *The psychology of attention.* Cambridge, MA: MIT Press.

Pashler, H., & Johnston, J.C.E. (1998). Attentional limitations in dual-task performance. In H. Pashler (Ed.), *Attention.* Hove, UK: Psychology Press.

Patel, V.L., Groen, G.J., & Arocha, J. (1993). Medical expertise as a function of task difficulty. *Memory and Cognition, 18,* 394–406.

Patel, V.L., Kaufman, D.R., & Magder, S.A. (1996). The acquisition of expertise in complex dynamic environments. In K.A. Ericsson (Ed.), *The road the excellence.* Mahwah, NJ: Lawrence Erlbaum Associated Inc.

Paul, S.T., Kellas, G., Martin, M., & Clark, M.B. (1992). Influence of contextual features on the activation of ambiguous word meanings. *Journal of Experimental Psychology: Learning Memory and Cognition, 18*(4), 703–717.

Pauli, P., & Weidemann, G. (1998). Co-variation in bias in flight phobics. *Journal of Anxiety Disorders, 12,* 555–565.

Penfield, W., & Roberts, L. (1959). *Speech and brain mechanisms.* Princeton, NJ: Princeton University Press.

Perfect, T., & Askew, C. (1994). Print adverts: Not remembered but memorable. *Applied Cognitive Psychology, 8,* 693–703.

Perrig, W.J., & Perrig, P. (1988). Mood and memory: Mood congruity effects in the absence of mood. *Memory and Cognition, 16*, 102–109.

Perruchet, P. (1994). Defining the knowledge units of a synthetic language: Comment on Vokey and Brooks, 1992. *Journal of Experimental Psychology: Learning, Memory and Cognition, 20*, 223–228.

Perruchet, P., & Gallego, J. (1997). A subjective unit formation account of implicit learning. In D. Berry (Ed.), *How implicit is implicit memory? Debates in psychology* (pp.124–161). New York: Oxford University Press.

Peterson, C.R., & Ulehla, Z.J. (1965). Sequential patterns and maximising. *Journal of Experimental Psychology, 69*, 1–4.

Pickett, J.M. (1980). *The sounds of speech communication.* Baltimore, MA: University Park Press.

Poincaré, H. (1952). Science and method. (F. Maitland, Trans.). New York: Dover.

Pollatsek, A., Bolozky, S., Well, A.D., & Rayner, K. (1981). Asymmetries in the perceptual span for Israeli readers. *Brain and Language, 14*(1), 174–180.

Popper, K. (1959). *The logic of scientific discovery.* New York: Basic Books.

Porrill, J., Frisby, J.P., Adams, W.J., & Buckley, D. (1999). Robust and optimal use of information in stereo vision. *Nature, 397*, 63–66.

Posner, M.I., & Snyder, C.R.R. (1975). Facilitation and inhibition in the processing of signals. In P.M.A. Rabbitt and S. Dornic (Eds.), *Attention and performance V*, (pp. 669–682). London: Academic Press.

Pratkanis, A.R. (1992). The cargo-cult science of subliminal persuasion. *Skeptical Inquirer, 16*, 260–272.

Pratkanis, A.R., Eskenazi, J., & Greenwald, A.G. (1994). What you expect is what you believe (but not necessarily what you get)—A test of the effectiveness of subliminal self-help audiotapes. *Basic and Applied Social Psychology, 15*(3), 251–276.

Priest, A.G., & Lindsay, R.H. (1992). New light on expert–novice differences in physics problem solving. *British Journal of Psychology, 83*, 389–405.

Prince, M. (1914). *The unconscious.* New York: Macmillan.

Pylyshyn, Z.W. (1973). What the mind's eye tells the mind's brain. *Psychological Bulletin, 80*, 1–24.

Pylyshyn, Z.W. (1981). The imagery debate—Analog media versus tacit knowledge. *Psychological Review, 88*(1), 16–45.

Rayner, K. (1998). Eye movements in reading and information processing: 20 years of research. *Psychological Bulletin, 124*, 372–422.

Rayner, K., Balota, D.A., & Pollatsek, A. (1986). Against parafoveal semantic preprocessing during eye fixations in reading. *Canadian Journal of Psychology, 40*, 473–483.

Rayner, K., Carlson, M., & Frazier, L. (1983). The interaction of syntax and semantics during sentence processing—Eye-movements in the analysis of semantically biased sentences. *Journal of Verbal Learning and Verbal Behavior, 22*(3), 358–374.

Rayner, K., & Duffy, S. A. (1986). Lexical complexity and fixation times in reading: Effects of word frequency, lexical complexity, and lexical ambiguity. *Memory and Cognition, 14*, 191–201.

Rayner, K., & Frazier, L. (1989). Selection mechanisms in reading lexically ambiguous words. *Journal of Experimental Psychology; Learning Memory and Cognition, 15*(5), 779–790.

Reber, A.S. (1989). Implicit learning and tacit knowledge. *Journal of Experimental Psychology-General, 118*(3), 219–235.

Reder, L.M., Anderson, J.R., & Bjork, R.A. (1974). A semantic interpretation of encoding specificity. *Journal of Experimental Psychology, 102*, 648–656.

Reicher, G.M. (1969). Perceptual recognition as a function of meaningfulness of stimulus material. *Journal of Experimental Psychology, 81*(2), 275–280.

Reichle, E.D., Pollatsek, A., Fisher, D.L., & Rayner, K. (1998). Toward a model of eye movement control in reading. *Psychological Review, 105*(1), 125–157.

Reisberg, D. (1983). General mental resources and perceptual judgements. *Journal of Experimental Psychology: Human Perception and Performance, 9*(6), 966–979.

Reiss, D., McCowan, B., & Marino, L. (1997). Communicative and other cognitive characteristics of bottlenose dolphins. *Trends in Cognitive Sciences, 1,* 140–145.

Richardson, J.T.E. (1999). *Imagery.* Hove, UK: Psychology Press.

Richman, C.L., & Mitchell, D.B. (1979). Mental travel: Some reservations. *Journal of Experimental Psychology: Human Perception and Cognition, 5,* 13–18.

Rips, L. (1975). Inductive judgements about natural categories. *Journal of Verbal Learning and Verbal Behavior, 14,* 665–681.

Rinck, M., Glowalla, U., & Schneider, K. (1992). Mood-congruent and mood incongruent learning. *Memory and Cognition, 20,* 29–39.

Rips, L.J. (1994). *The psychology of proof: Deductive reasoning in human thinking.* Cambridge, MA: MIT Press.

Rips, L.J. (1997). Goals for a theory of deduction. *Minds and Machines, 7,* 409–424.

Robinson, J.O. (1972). *The psychology of visual illusion.* London: Hutchinson.

Rosch, E., & Mervis, C.B. (1975). Family resemblances: Studies in the internal structure of categories. *Cognitive Psychology, 7,* 573–605.

Rosch, E., Simpson, C., & Miller, R.S. (1976). Structural basis of typicality effects. *Journal of Experimental Psychology: Human Perception and Performance, 2,* 491–502.

Rouw, R., Kosslyn, S.M., & Hamel, R.I. (1997). Detecting high-level and low-level properties in visual images and visual percepts. *Cognition, 63,* 209–226.

Rubin, E. (1958). Figure and ground. In D.C. Beardslee & M. Wertheimer (Eds.), *Readings in perception.* Princeton, NJ: Van Nostrand.

Rumelhart, D.E., & McClelland, J.L. (1986). *Parallel distributed processing.* (Vols. 1 and 2). Cambridge, MA: MIT Press.

Rundus, D. (1971). Analysis of rehearsal processes in free recall. *Journal of Experimental Psychology, 89,* 63–77.

Russo, R., Cullis, A.M., & Parkin, A.J. (1998). Consequences of violating the assumption of independence in the process dissociation procedure: A word fragment completion study. *Memory and Cognition, 26,* 617–632.

Ryle, G. (1949). *The concept of mind.* London: Hutchinson.

Sachs, J.S. (1967). Recognition memory for syntactic and semantic aspects of connected discourse. *Perception and Psychophysics, 2,* 437–442.

Samuel, A.G. (1981). Phonemic restoration— Insights from a new methodology. *Journal of experimental psychology: General, 110*(4), 474–494.

Sapir, E. (1949). In D. Mandelbaum (Ed.), *Selected writings of Edward Sapir.* Berkeley, CA: University of California Press.

Schacter, D.L. (1987). Implicit memory— History and current status. *Journal of experimental psychology: Learning, memory and cognition, 13*(3), 501–518.

Schacter, D.L. (1996). *Searching for memory.* New York: Basic Books.

Schacter, D.L. (1999). The seven sins of memory: Insights from psychology and cognitive science. *American Psychologist, 54,* 182–203.

Schank, R.C. (1982). *Dynamic memory.* Cambridge: Cambridge University Press.

Schank, R.C., & Abelson, R. (1977). *Scripts, plans, goals, and understanding.* Hillsdale, NJ: Lawrence Erlbaum Associates.

Schmidt, H.G., & Boshuizen, H.P.A. (1993). On the origin of intermediate effects in clinical case recall. *Memory and Cognition, 21,* 338–351.

Schneider, W., & Shiffrin, R.M. (1977). Controlled and automatic human information processings: 1. Detection, search, and attention. *Psychological Review, 84,* 1–66.

Schnorr, J.A., & Atkinson, R.C. (1971). Study position and item differences in the short- and long-term retention of paired associates learned by imagery. *Journal of*

Verbal Learning and Verbal Behavior, 9, 614–622.

Schooler, J.W., & Engstlerschooler, T.Y. (1990). Verbal overshadowing of visual memories—Some things are better left unsaid. *Cognitive Psychology, 22*(1), 36–71.

Selfridge, O.G. (1959). *Pandemonium: A paradigm for learning.* London: HMSO.

Shallice, T. (1988). *From neuropsychology to mental structure.* Cambridge: Cambridge University Press.

Shepard, R.N. (1978). The mental image. *American Psychologist, 33,* 125–137.

Shepard, R.N., & Metzler, J. (1971). Mental rotation of three-dimensional objects. *Science, 191,* 701–703.

Shiffrin, R.M., & Schneider, W. (1977). Controlled and automatic human information processing: II. Perceptual learning, automatic attending and a general theory. *Psychological Review, 84*(2), 127–190.

Shin, H., & Nosofsky, R. (1992). Similarity-scaling studies of dot pattern classification and recognition. *Journal of Experimental Psychology: General, 121,* 278–304.

Simons, D.J. (1996). In sight, out of mind: When object representations fail. *Psychological Science, 7,* 301–305.

Simpson, G.B. (1994). Context and the processing of ambiguous words. In M.A. Gernsbacher (Ed.), *Handbook of Psycholinguistics.* San Diego, CA: Academic Press.

Simpson, G.B., & Kreuger, M.A. (1991). Selective access of homograph meanings in sentence context. *Journal of Memory and Language, 30,* 627–643.

Singer, M. (1979). Processes of inference during sentence encoding. *Memory and Cognition, 7*(3), 192–200.

Singer, M. (1994). Discourse inference processes. In M. A. Gernsbacher (Ed.), *Handbook of psycholinguistics,* (pp. 479–515). San Diego, CA: Academic Press Inc.

Skinner, B.F. (1948). *Walden two.* New York: Macmillan.

Skinner, B.F. (1957). *Verbal behavior.* New York: Appleton.

Slobin, D.I. (1966). Grammatical transformations and sentence comprehension in childhood and adulthood. *Journal of Verbal Learning and Verbal Behavior, 5 ,* (219–227).

Slowiaczek, M.L., & Clifton, C. (1980). Subvocalisation and reading for meaning. *Journal of Verbal Learning and Verbal Behavior, 19,* 573–582.

Smedslund, J. (1963). The concept of correlation in adults. *Scandinavian Journal of Psychology, 4,* 165–173.

Smith, E.E., Balzanono, G.G., & Walker, J.H. (1978). Nominal, perceptual and semantic codes in picture recognition. In J. W. Cotton & R.L. Klatzky (Eds.), *Semantic factors in cognition.* Hillsdale, NJ: Lawrence Erlbaum Associates Inc.

Smith, S.M. (1986). Environmental context-dependent memory: Recognition memory using a short-term memory task for input. *Memory and Cognition, 14,* 347–354.

Smith, S.M., & Vela, E. (1992). Environmental context-dependent eyewitness recognition. *Applied Cognitive Psychology, 6,* 125–139.

Sperling, G. (1960). The information available in brief visual presentation. *Psychological Monographs, 74*(11, Whole No. 498), 29.

Spitzka, E.A. (1907). A study of six eminent scholars belonging to the American Anthroprometric Association. Together with a description of the skull of Professor E.D. Cope. *Transactions of the American Philosophical Society, 21,* 175–308.

Squire, L.R. (1987). *Memory and brain.* New York: Oxford University Press.

Sternberg, R.J. (1999). *Handbook of creativity.* New York: Cambridge University Press.

Sternberg, R.J., & Lubart, T.I. (1999). The concept of creativity: Prospects and paradigms. In R.J. Sternberg (Ed.), *Handbook of creativity.* New York: Cambridge University Press.

Stevenson, R. J. (1993). *Language, thought and representation.* Chichester: Wiley.

Strange, W. (1989a). Dynamic specification of vowels spoken in sentence context. *Journal of the Acoustical Society of America, 85*, 2135–2153.

Strange, W. (1989b). Evolving theories of vowel perception. *Journal of the Acoustical Society of America, 85*, 2081–2087.

Streete, R.F. (1931). *A Gestalt Completion Test.* New York: Teacher's College.

Stromeyer, C.F., & Psotka, J. (1970). The detailed texture of eidetic images. *Nature, 225*, 346–349.

Stroop, J.R. (1935). Studies of interference in serial verbal reactions. *Journal of Experimental Psychology, 18*, 643–662.

Sutherland, N.S. (1973). Object recognition. In E.C. Carterette & M.P. Friedman (Eds.), *Handbook of perception: Volume III. Biology of perceptual systems*. London: Academic Press.

Swinney, D.A. (1979). Lexical access during sentence comprehension: (Re)consideration of context effects. *Journal of Verbal Learning and Verbal Behavior, 18*, 645–659.

Tabossi, P. (1988). Accessing lexical ambiguity in different types of sentential context. *Journal of Memory and Language, 27*, 324–340.

Tabossi, P. (1991). Understanding words in context. In G.B. Simpson (Ed.), *Understanding word and sentence*. Amsterdam: North-Holland.

Tartter, V. (1986). *Language processes*. New York: Holt, Richard & Winston.

Taraban, R., & McClelland, J.L. (1988). Constituent attachment and thematic role assignment. *Journal of Memory and Language, 27*, 597–632.

Thorndike, E.L. (1955). *Animal intelligence: an experimental study of the associative processes in animals*. Providence, R.I.: The University Store, Brown University.

Tipper, S.P. (1985). The negative priming effect: Inhibitory priming by ignored objects. *Quarterly Journal of Experimental Psychology, 37A*, 571–590.

Torrance, E.P. (1988). The nature of creativity as manifest in creativity. In R.J. Sternberg (Ed.), *The nature of creativity: Contemporary psychological perspectives*, (pp. 43–75). Cambridge: Cambridge University Press.

Trappey, C. (1996). A meta-analysis of consumer choice and subliminal advertising. *Psychology & Marketing, 13*(5), 517–530.

Treisman, A.M. (1960). Contextual cues in selective listening. *Quarterly Journal of Experimental Psychology, 12*, 242–248.

Treisman, A.M., & Gelade, G. (1980). A feature integration theory of visual attention. *Cognitive Psychology, 12*, 97–136.

Treisman, A.M., & Riley, J G. (1969). Is selective attention selective perception or selective response? A further test. *Journal of Experimental Psychology, 79*(1, Pt. 1), 27–34.

Tulving, E. (1972). Episodic and semantic memory. In E. Tulving and W. Donaldson (Eds.), *Organization of memory*. New York: Academic Press.

Tulving, E. (1983). *Elements of episodic memory*. Oxford: Oxford University Press.

Tulving, E. (1989). Memory: Performance, knowledge, and experience. *European Journal of Cognitive Psychology, 1*(1), 3–26.

Tulving, E., Schacter, D.L., & Stark, H.A. (1982). Priming effects in word-fragment completion are independent of recognition memory. *Journal of Experimental Psychology: Learning, Memory and Cognition, 8*(4), 336–342.

Tulving, E., & Thomson, D.M. (1973). Encoding specificity and retrieval processes in episodic memory. *Psychological Review, 80*, 352–373.

Turvey, M.T. (1973). On peripheral and central processes in vision. *Psychological Review, 80*, 1–52.

Tversky, A., & Kahneman, D. (1974). Judgement under uncertainty: Heuristics and biases. Biases in judgements reveal some heuristics of thinking under uncertainty. *Science, 185*, 1124–1131.

Ullman, S. (1980). Against direct perception. *Behavioral and Brain Sciences, 3*, 373–415.

Vallar, G., & Shallice, T. (1997). *Neuropsychological impairments of short-term memory*. New York: Cambridge University Press.

van de Wiel, M.W.J., Schmidt, H.G., & Boshuizen, H.P.A. (1998). A failure to reproduce the intermediate effect in clinical case recall. *Academic Medicine, 73,* 894–900.

Van Dijk, T.A., & Kintsch, W. (1983). *Strategies of discourse comprehension.* New York: Academic Press.

Vokey, J. R., & Brooks, L. (1992). Salience of item knowledge in learning artificial grammars. *Journal of Experimental Psychology: Learning, Memory and Cognition, 18,* 328–344.

Wallas, G. (1926). *The art of thought.* London: Cape.

Warren, R.M., & Warren, R.P. (1970). Auditory illusions and confusions. *Scientific American, 223,* 30–36.

Warrington, E.K., & Shallice, T. (1970). The selective impairment of auditory verbal short-term memory. *Brain, 92,* 885–896.

Wason, P.C. (1960). On the failure to eliminate hypotheses in a conceptual task. *Quarterly Journal of Experimental Psychology, 12,* 129–140.

Watkins, M.J., & Gardiner, J.M. (1979). An appreciation of the generate–recognize theory of recall. *Journal of Verbal Learning and Verbal Behavior, 18,* 687–704.

Watson, J.B. (1924). *Behaviorism.* New York: J.B. Lippincott.

Waugh, N.C., & Norman, D.A. (1965). Primary memory. *Psychological Review, 72,* 89–104.

Wechsler, D. (1987). *Wechsler memory Scale–Revised.* New York: Psychological Corporation.

Weisberg, R.W. (1999). Creativity and knowledge: A challenge to theories. In R.J. Sternberg (Ed.), *Handbook of creativity.* New York: Cambridge University Press.

Welch, G.B., & Burnett, C.T. (1924). Is primacy a factor in association-formation? *American Journal of Psychology, 35,* 396–401.

Weldon, S.M. (1999). The memory chop shop. In J.K. Foster and M. Jelicic (Eds.), *Memory: Systems, process or function?* Oxford: Oxford University Press.

Whitney, P. (1998). *The psychology of language.* Boston: Houghton Mifflin.

Whorf, B.L. (1956). *Language, thought and reality: Selected writings of Benjamin Lee Whorf.* New York: Wiley.

Wickens, D.D. (1987). The dual meanings of context: Implications for research, theory, and applications. In D.S. Gorfein and R.R. Hoffman (Eds.), *Memory and learning: The Ebbinghaus Centennial Conference* (pp. 135–152). Hillsdale, NJ: Lawrence Erlbaum Associates Inc.

Wicklegren, W. A. (1968). Sparing of short-term memory in an amnesic patient: Implications for a strength theory of memory. *Neuropsychologia, 6,* 235–244.

Wilding, J., & Valentine, E. (1997). *Superior memory.* Hove, UK: Psychology Press.

Williams, J.M.G., & Broadbent, D.E. (1986). Autobiographical memory in suicide attempters. *Journal of Abnormal Psychology, 95,* 145–149.

Witelson, S.F., Kigar, D.L., & Harvey, T. (1999). The exceptional brain of Albert Einstein. *Lancet, 353,* 2149–2153.

Wittgenstein, L. (1953). *Philosophical investigations* (G.E.M. Anscombe). Oxford: Blackwells.

Woodworth, R.S., & Sells, S.B. (1935). An atmosphere effect in formal syllogistic reasoning. *Journal of Experimental Psychology, 18,* 451–460.

Yapko, M.D. (1994). Suggestibility and suppressed memories of abuse: A survey of psychotherapists' beliefs. *American Journal of Clinical Hypnosis, 36,* 375–380.

Yeni-Komshian, G.H. (1998). Speech perception. In J. Berko Gleason & N. Bernstein Ratner (Eds.), *Psycholinguistics.* Fort Worth: Harcourt Brace.

Young, A.W. (1998). *Face and mind.* Oxford: Oxford University Press.

Young, A.W., Newcombe, F., De Haan, E.H.F., Small, M., & Hay, D.C. (1993). Face perception after brain injury. *Brain, 116,* 941–959.

Author index

Subject index

Gestures, 189, 190
Gibson's direct perception theory, 47–49
Grammar, 99, 228–234
  artificial, 109–110
Grapheme to phoneme correspondence rules, 215–216

Hand signals, 190
Haptic perception, 28
Harrison, George, 97
Head, Henry, 134
Hearing and language, 255
Heller, Joseph, 261
Heterophones, 205
Heuristics, 262–264, 265, 281–283
Hill climbing strategy, 282
"Hobbits and Orcs" problem, 281
Homographs, 219–223
Homophones, 205, 218
How Leisure Came (Bierce), 240
Human body, cylindrical representation of, 39
Hypnosis, 153–154
Hypothesis testing, 271–274
Hypothetico–deductive method, 271–272

Iconic memory, 85–87
Identity priming, 75
Illumination and problem solving, 290, 291
Image files, 175
Imagery, 1–2, 169–185
  brain activity during, 181
  computational model of, 175–178
  criticisms of, 178–180
  dual coding hypothesis, 173
  eidetic, 131, 169–171
  image properties, 173–175

neuropsychological evidence for, 181–183
  as perception, 180–181
Implicit learning, 109–111
Implicit memory, 104, 105–109
Incubation, 290–291
Individual differences, 17
Infantile amnesia, 107
Inference, 227, 235–241, 242–243
  bridging, 235–236
  causal antecedent, 239
  elaborative, 235, 237–239
Information buffers, 13
Information processing, 10, 11–12, 14–16
Information stores, 13
Inhibition of return, 75
Innate abilities, 17
Inner speech, 251–254
Insight, 279–280
Instance theory, 110
Intensity maps, 30
Interactive activation model, 214–215
Interference, 84, 139–140
Intermediate effect, 288
Intonation contour, 253
Introspectionism, 1–2
Intrusion errors, 15–16
Isomorphism, 7

Judas Priest, 62

Kekule (chemist), 289–290
Knowledge, 157–168, 171, 179

Language, 8, 187–189
  competence, 227–228
  comprehension, 227–245
  economic labels, 256–257
  and hearing, 255
  innate abilities, 17
  over-regularisation, 9
  performance, 227, 228
  and thought, 254–257

see also Reading; Speech headings; Word headings
Late closure, 231, 232
Late recognition effect, 199
Lateral thinking, 291
Law of Pragnanz, 6
Learning
  implicit, 109–111
  perceptual, 99
  procedural, 99
Lemmas, 249
Letter identification span, 208
Levels of processing, 115–121
Lexemes, 249
Lexical access, 210–211, 213
Lexical decision task, 69, 98
Lexical entry, 213
Lexical frame theory, 232–233
Lexical selection, 248
Linear perspective, 34
Linguistic hedging, 160
"Little Albert", 3
Localisationalism, 24
Logogen model, 173, 213, 214
Long-term memory, 83, 97–112
Lottery numbers, 261

Magnetic resonance imaging, 23
Marijuana, 148
Marr's theory, 29–36
McGurk effect, 196
Means–end analysis, 281
Medical expertise, 288–289
Memory
  chunking in, 88–89
  and context, 140–142, 147
  drug-induced effects, 93, 148
  environment dependent, 147–149
  and mood, 149–152
  multistore model, 83

positive, 76
repetition, 105
semantic, 62, 213–214
Proactive interference, 139
Probe digit task, 80
Problem reduction, 282
Problem solving, 279–295
by analogy, 283–285
by experts, 285–289
functional fixedness, 280
heuristics, 281–283
insight, 279–280
stages of, 290–291
trial and error, 279
Problem space, 281
Problems, 280–281
Procedural learning, 99
Procedural memory, 98–100
Process dissociation
procedure, 145–146
Pronunciation, 215–218
Propositional files, 175–176
Propositions, 37–38, 171
Prosopagnosia, 22
Prototype theory, 160–162,
163
Punishment, 7

Random dot stereograms,
170
Rat-man figure, 64
Reaction time, 15
Reading
eye movements during,
205–211
inner speech, 251–254
letter identification span,
208
and memory, 126
perceptual span, 206–208
skip reading, 209
word recognition, 205,
213–223
Reasoning, 261–277
conditional, 271
deductive, 262, 269–271
inductive, 262
rule-based, 275

Recall, 15–16, 81–82, 134
Recency effect, 81, 88–91,
93–95
negative, 82
Recognition by Components
Model, 40–42
Recognition memory, 134,
135–138, 142–147
Recollection, 143
Recovered memory, 133,
152–154
Rehearsal, 83
sub-vocal, 125
Reinforcement, 7
Reinforcement history, 8
Remember/know tasks,
144–145
Remembering, 133–138
Remote Associations Test,
292–293
Repetition priming, 105
Representiveness, 264–267
Repression, 152
Resonant frequencies, 191
Resource models of
attention, 63–65
Response bias, 201–202
Retrieval structures, 287
Retroactive interference, 139
Reversible figures, 32, 64
Ribot's law, 101
Rubin's vase, 32
Rules of thumb, see
Heuristics

"S", memory man, 131
Saccades, 205–206, 208–209
suppression during, 206
transsaccadic memory,
211–212
Sapir–Whorf hypothesis,
254–257
Savings, 106–107, 132
Scenes, 166
Schema, 134, 164–165
Science, 9, 271–272, 288
Scopolamine, 93
Scripts, 165–167

Selection task, 272–274
Semantic memory, 98, 104
Semantic priming, 62,
213–214
Semantics, 114
Sensory memory, 84–87
Sentence comprehension,
227–245
Sentence parsing, 228,
230–234
Sentence verification,
157–158
Serial position curve, 81
Sexual abuse, 153–154
Shape constancy, 46–47
Short-term memory, 83,
88–89
Situation models, 240, 288
Size constancy, 43
Skip reading, 209
Sounds, 189–192
Spacing effect, 114
Spatial medium, 175
Spectrograms, 189–191
Speech
articulation, 191–192
sound analysis, 189–191
word pronunciation,
215–218
Speech, inner, 251–254
Speech, visual, 196
Speech acts, 227
Speech errors, 16, 247–248,
249–250, 251
Speech perception, 192–196
Speech production, 190–192,
247–251
Speech recognition, 196–202
Split-span task, 55–56
Spoonerisms, 16, 248
State action tree, 281
State-dependent memory,
148–149
Stereopsis, 35
Stimulus onset asynchrony,
69
Stranding, 251

Illustration credits

Chapter 1
Page 3: Science Photo Library. Page 8: TRIP. Page 9: Copyright © Bob Watkins/Photofusion. Page 17: TRIP. Page 23 (top): Science Photo Library. Page 23 (bottom): Science Photo Library.

Chapter 2
Page 29: Bipinchandra J. Mistry. Page 47 (bottom): Popperfoto.

Chapter 3
Page 53: Copyright © Steve Eason/Photofusion. Page 60: Figure 3.4 is reproduced from Key, W.B. (1972). *Subliminal seduction*. New York: Signed Books. Page 61: Figure 3.5 is reproduced with permission from Hess, E.H. (1975). The role of pupil size in communication. *Scientific American, 233,* 110-119. Page 64: Figure 3.7 is reproduced from Reisberg, D. (1983). General mental resources and perceptual judgements. *Journal of Experimental Psychology: Human Perception and Performance, 9(6),* 966-979.

Chapter 4
Page 93: Copyright © Sam Tanner/Photofusion.

Chapter 5
Page 97: Popperfoto. Page 98: Reuters/Popperfoto. Page 99 (bottom): Popperfoto. Page 102 (top row, left): Popperfoto. Page 102 (top row, middle): Popperfoto. Page 102 (top row, right): Popperfoto. Page 102 (bottom row, left): Popperfoto. Page 102 (bottom row, right): Copyright © Steve Eason/Photofusion. Page 106: Figure 5.4 is from Parkin, A.J. & Streete, S. (1988). Implicit and explicit memory in young children and adults. *British Journal of Psychology, 79,* 362-369. Reproduced with permission from the British Psychological Society, © The British Psychological Society. Page 108: Copyright © Falmer, supplied by Vin Mag Archive Limited.

Chapter 6
Page 113: Science Photo Library. Page 122 (bottom): Copyright © Crispin Hughes/Photofusion. Page 125: Copyright © Emily Barney/Photofusion.

Chapter 7
Page 150: Picture of Migram's shock experiment is from the film *Obedience*, copyright © 1965 by Stanley Milgram and distributed by Penn State Media Sales. Permission granted by Alexandra Milgram. Page 153 (left): Reuters/Popperfoto. Page 153 (right): Reuters/Popperfoto.

Chapter 8

Page 157: Copyright © MGM, supplied by Vin Mag Archive Limited. Page 161 (left): TRIP. Page 161 (right): TRIP. Page 166 (top): Copyright © United Artists, supplied by Vin Mag Archive Limited.

Chapter 9

Page 170 (top): Figure 9.1 is reproduced with permission from Gummerman, K. & Gray, C.R. (1971). Recall of visually presented material: An unwanted case and a bibliography for eidetic imagery. *Psychonomic Monograph Supplements, 4* (Whole No. 58), 189-195. Reprinted by permission of Psychonomic Society, Inc. Page 170 (bottom): Reuters/Popperfoto. Page 175: Figure 9.3 is reprinted with permission from Shepard, R.N. & Metzler, J. (1971). Mental rotation of three-dimensional objects. *Science, 191,* 701-703. Copyright © 1971 American Association for the Advancement of Science. Page 177: Figure 9.4 is reproduced with permission from Kosslyn, S.M. (1983). *Ghosts in the mind's machine: Creating and using images in the brain.* New York: WW Norton & Co, Inc. Permission granted by the author.

Chapter 10

Page 188: TRIP. Page 191 (top): Figure 10.2 is reproduced with permission from Tartter, V. (1986). *Language processes.* New York: Holt, Reinhart & Winston.
Page 191 (bottom): Figure 10.3 is reproduced from Pickett, J.M. (1980). The sounds of speech communication. Baltimore, MA: University Park Press. Page 197: Figure 10.7 is reproduced with permission from Massaro, D.W. (1998). *Perceiving talking faces: From Speech Perception to a behavioural principle.* Cambridge, MA: MIT Press.

Chapter 11

Page 212: Figure 11.4 is reproduced with permission from Simons, D.J. (1996). In sight, out of mind: When object representations fail. *Psychological Science, 7,* 301-305.

Chapter 14

Page 270: Copyright © HTV, supplied by Vin Mag Archive Limited.

Chapter 15

Page 286: Reuters/Popperfoto.
Page 293 Drawing of Einstein is reproduced with permission from *The Times,* London, June 18 1999. Copyright © Times Newspapers Limited, 29 July 1999.